FOSSILIZED CUSTOMS

By Lew White

CD 5760 / CE 2000

CONTENTS

Searching for Truth? In the hands of men who have sought to preserve their position and control, the Truth has become incomprehensible and garbled. The <u>calendar</u> used by the world perpetuates customs which are built upon Pagan foundations. Russ Hoban wrote: "Language is an archaeological vehicle ... The language we speak is a whole palimpsest of human effort and history." I would add that the calendar is also an archaeological vehicle ~ and most of the civilized world is riding this abomination of desolation. Learning the Truth, you will be set free from what has enslaved you.

ISBN 0-9584353-6-7

BOOK ORDERING:

DIRECT FROM PUBLISHER
1 book: $5.00, **5** books: $15.00, **10** books: $25.00
(Non-domestic add 30%) All S&H included.
Become a distributor of this book
Also the US source for *The Scriptures*, (a translation restoring the Name to the text—hardcover, $33); and the book *Come Out Of Her My People*, by Chris Koster ($12.95). See back page.
Author's ordering address:
Strawberry Islands Publishers
2303 Watterson Trail PMB 26
LOUISVILLE, KY 40299 USA
Web Site: www.fossilizedcustoms.com

OTHER ITEMS YOU CAN ORDER FROM AUTHOR:
STRAWBERRY ISLANDS CYBERSPACE HEALTHCAFE
~ SAMBUCOL (LOZENGES): $11.00
~ FLOR-ESSENCE (ESSIAC TEA — DRY, 3QTS): $25.00
~ NATURE'S PLUS MULTI-VITAMINS (90 TABLETS): $25.00
WHEN IN LOUISVILLE, VISIT STRAWBERRY ISLANDS!
2303 WATTERSON TRAIL, LOUISVILLE, KY 40299

What is this book about?

This book is intended to address the unanswered questions that lurk in the back of many people's minds. It exposes the lies, and reveals the truth. The origins of popular customs have been a life-long study of mine, and revealing them to others in a way that makes sense is my main goal with this effort. To most, the information presented here will be new and shocking. Please realize that anything in this study can be easily verified, and I encourage you to do some research on your own ~ in this way, you will have **facts** that you can believe, rather than just mysterious traditions. Try to be objective, and not "filter" the facts through what you've chosen to believe, or a denominational bias. No one alive is responsible for having woven together the Pagan designs we are embedded in, and even those who did it I do not judge.

As with any audience, there are those who will read this that are my superior in knowledge. But, the plan of our Creator is so simple, that being wise in certain specialized disciplines may be of little use. A small child can understand the secret that is locked in the Scriptures, but when the meaning is distorted, comprehension suffers. There are dozens of excuses for maintaining the status quo, but once the truth is available to the average person, hiding behind lies invented by men long-dead is useless. The distortions of the Truth came about because Paganism became **mixed** into it, and the "**bride**" (wife of the Creator) was attacked, along with the **Covenant** (a marriage covenant). Religion is not about money, or killing people who are different. The Inquisition burned and tortured millions of people to death. In this book, you'll find learn their true motives.

ISBN 0-9584353-6-7

WRITTEN FROM A MESSIANIC PERSPECTIVE

A Restoration of Our Israelite Roots
Engrafting into Israel
"Even the stork in the sky knows her appointed times. And a turtledove, and a swallow, and a thrush observe the time of their coming ~ but My people do not know the ordinance of YHWH."
- Jeremiah (Yerme Yahu) 8:7. (The people had stopped observing the appointed times, and had begun to observe the festivals of the Gentiles ~ read chapters 7—10 of Yerme Yahu).

"Seek YHWH, all you humble of the land, you who do what He commands. Seek righteousness, seek humility; perhaps you will be sheltered on the day of YHWH's anger."
Zephaniah (Zefan Yah) 2:3.
A REFERENCE TO THE NEW COVENANT:
"I will give you a new heart and put a new spirit in you; I will remove from you your heart of stone and give you a heart of flesh. And I will put My Spirit in you, and move you to follow My decrees and be careful to keep My Laws." - Ezek. 36:26,27.

HYPOTHESIS: Due to compromise, syncretism, ignorance, confusion, and the intentional deceit of humanity by fallen ethereal beings, mythological Pagan designs were assimilated into the lives of most every person on Earth. Unwittingly, humanity has embraced ancient Babylonian customs rooted in *sun worship.*

The customs were *re-invented* so as to have different meanings, yet behind them remain the cunning ruses of an ancient spatial being, who seeks to be worshipped by means of trickery, perpetrated upon everyone alive. There is *so much* Paganism active in cultures today, there can be no doubt that it was deceitfully placed into our traditions, then through fraud and disguise, obscured with new meanings. This camouflaged Paganism pollutes and rots the spiritual condition of all mankind, yet a little flock has always held on to the true faith delivered to those set apart. Here in the last days, the final message is now going out to the ends of the Earth. This book is written from the perspective that there is a Creator, as well as a spiritual enemy loose on Earth; and that the Scriptures of the Hebrew prophets are all true.

Hopefully, this book will lift some of humanity out of the dense fog of history, and awaken people who are dreaming, as they walk into a new dawn of living — with an eternal perspective. Love, the most powerful force in the universe, will save your life.

Fossilized Customs
THE PAGAN SOURCES OF
POPULAR CUSTOMS
2ND EDITION
ARE YOU READY TO GO TO THE NEXT LEVEL?

"He who answers before listening ~ that is his folly and is his shame." Prov. 18:13. In this book, you will discover the true origins of many cherished customs. They come from Babylonian sun worship, cleverly "inculturated" into Christianity over many centuries of darkness. **NIMROD TREE :** Wreaths, branches, boughs, and trees had been used by Pagans as emblems of Nimrod, used to <u>decorate</u> during the winter solstice, thought of as the "<u>re-birth</u>" of the sun. In their mythology, Nimrod had died and become the sun, worshipped as Baal (the LORD), Marduk, Mithras, Ahura Mazda, Gott, Aton, and Dagon.

SMELL SOMETHING FUNNY, HONEY?

SNIFF!

PAGAN CUSTOMS BECAME DISGUISED LONG AGO, AS CHRISTIANITY DEVELOPED AMONG ANCIENT SUN-WORSHIPPING PEOPLES. THE PAGANS WERE ABSORBED, <u>ALONG WITH THEIR RELIGIOUS MANNERISMS.</u> A BLEND OF THE TRUTH MIXED WITH ABOMINATIONS OCCURRED. PAGAN CELEBRATIONS WERE 'ADOPTED' TO REPLACE THE SCRIPTURAL OBSERVANCES. WITH EYES WIDE SHUT, BILLIONS ENTRUST THEIR ETERNITY TO MEN WHO EXPLOIT THEM, MASQUERADING AS MESSENGERS OF LIGHT.

YOU WANTED THE TRUTH, SO HERE IT IS. THIS IS NOT FICTION. YOU'LL *WISH* THIS WAS ONLY A BOOK.

Dedicated to Rabbi O W Y ⴵ Ⴀ ha Mashiach of Nazareth, our High Priest, Sovereign Ruler, and Image of the Invisible Elohim. Also to the goal of helping as many as possible be enabled to understand the message of the Kingdom, so they will be spared the awesome destruction ahead. "Repent, for the Reign of 'Heaven' draws near!"

PREPARE YOURSELF . . . . .

THE FIRST THING that will go through your mind when you see the **fire** consume people around you will be something like, *"why didn't I do more to reach them with the Truth, so this may not have happened to them?"* (See 2Pet.3:7, Zech. 14, Mt. 3:12).

This is what YHWH **Shabuoth** says: *"In those days, ten men from all languages and nations will take firm hold of one Yahudi by the hem of his robe and say, 'Let us go with you, because we have heard that Elohim is with you.'"* Zec. 8:23	*"Brothers, children of Abraham, and you Elohim-fearing Gentiles, it is to us that this message of salvation has been sent."* Acts 13:26 (The word "GOD" was used by translators in place of the Hebrew word "Elohim", meaning mighty one.) In this book, you will discover what other changes were made.

PROLOGUE

AT first glance, the title and what it suggests might enrage the average person. By reading a little, you will begin to understand the Truth ~ that what we see in the traditions practiced by Christianity were originally pagan designs. We will show how they admit this is so. We will look at the Scriptures to see if this is valid behavior. If you have ever prayed for Truth, or if you are diligently seeking it, you may find this very helpful. We inherited the habits we have from people of long ago, so no one alive is responsible.

"Most people, sometime in their lives, stumble across truth. Most jump up, brush themselves off, and hurry on about their business as if nothing had happened."
— Sir Winston Churchill.

To better understand things, this book will restore names and other words to the more accurate 'sound' of their originals. Letters, in any language, are symbols for sounds. Over the centuries, *translating* the Scriptures from Hebrew into Greek, then Latin, German, and English, led to some loss of meaning. This partly explains why people have difficulty understanding what the Scriptures are saying.

The idea of **translating** is to find the best word in your language that expresses the meaning of the original word. We say "hello", while a Hawaiian uses "aloha" for both "hello" and "good-bye". Similarly, "shalom" is used to say "peace", and is used as a greeting, or to signal departing. Many times an original Hebrew word is *transliterated* ~ which means the **sounds** of the original word are carried over using the letters of the new language. This is commonly done when there is no word in the new language that expresses the same idea. Hebrew is the inspired language.

This is also the way we correctly "sound-off" or pronounce the names of people. Israel's former PM, **Benjamin NatanYahu**, has a Hebrew name that was properly *transliterated* in the English language. In his own ears, he can hear his name perfectly pronounced by people of any language! His name also has a meaning, but it would be improper to "translate" his name, or anyone's, just because someone of another language uses it. Your name retains the same sound out of the mouth of people of any language. If you make a friend with someone from Taiwan, they will do their best to pronounce your name as closely as they can to accurately address you as you are accustomed to hearing it. Distortions of people's names have occurred, and we will attempt to restore them to their closest originals in this book. "Noah" was really "Noach", having a "K" sound at the end of it. His son's name, "Shem", means "name". Noach may have named him this as a reminder of the Name of the Creator, which you will discover in this book. The word "Semites" is derived from Shem's descendants, the people who bear the Creator's Name, as referred to at Daniel 9:19. The "SH" sound was lost because Greek has no such sound; so, the more correct word is "Shemites". We inherited little errors here and there. Wouldn't it be great to be able to hear how the Mashiach's Name really sounded? If you can accept it, we will attempt to explain how that can be done.

TRUTH and LIES Let's imagine you are 1000 feet in the air, standing on the high steel framework of a new skyscraper under construction. You are supported by each of the steel girders below you, and the massive concrete foundation resting on the bedrock of the Earth. Your primary interest at this point is your safety. The girders below must each be riveted well to one another; because if even ONE is just jammed in with no rivets, the whole structure could fall at any moment! Any girder with no rivets is like a lie, because you put your trust in it as if it were the truth. The only way to know if each girder is "true" is to closely examine each one. To appear to be a part of the structure is not enough in itself, because you place your trust in every girder below you believing they are "true". So, this book will shake and inspect some frameworks. If you are on a framework made up of 100% truth, then you are safe. If this book can show you the "girders" that have no rivets, exposing the deceptions as the lies they really are, then you would be wise to re-evaluate remaining where you are. *"For with much wisdom comes much sorrow; the more knowledge, the more grief"* Eccl. 1:18. This effort is to inform you and make you wise, and when you become aware, you will mourn. It would be senseless to defend a building which you knew had girders with no rivets, and it would be extremely hazardous to remain there. In fact, you would warn anyone who even went near it. Why? Because of LOVE. Your concern for others can be even greater than self-preservation. Lies are poison, but Truth is like fire; it tests the purity of metals.

In the writings of Daniel 2, a metal image of a man is used to illustrate the kingdoms of the Earth *over time*. The purity of the metals and their successive devaluation over time is significant. First, the 'head' (beginning) of gold represents the first "kingdom" on Earth, Babylon. It's man-made, ruled by men. Following is the chest and arms of silver, belly of bronze, legs of iron, and feet composed of a **mixture** of iron and clay. The 'clay' is sometimes thought of as people 'ruling' themselves, as we see today in a democracy. Well, that may well be ~ but also remember that the whole image from head to toe is man's attempt to rule himself. **All** of these kingdoms will perish, and man will not rule himself; the whole point is that our Creator is coming to restore the Earth. It is not our task to "fix" man's kingdom, or fight it, change it, argue about its economics, lack of moral leadership, or any of that. Conquering, overpowering, killing, dividing, controlling ~ these are not things we do, but they are the things which men ruling themselves do. Lies have become "mixed" into civil government as well as moral government (Church, pulpit), yet trusted in as truth. So, we are "called-out" of the kingdoms of men altogether. If we remain ignorant, we will be found participating in a paradigm (model, process) of traditions that date all the way back to Babylon, the head or beginning. A Rabbi from Nazareth came to deliver the message of the Kingdom: *"Repent! For the Reign* (Kingdom) *of YHWH* (Heaven) *draws near".* "Repent" means *turn back, turn around, or return.* The Rabbi was saying *"shub"* in His Hebrew tongue, not the Latin word *repent.* Today, we say *"what is your religion?"* "Re-ligion" is also Latin; *re*– means "go back", start again, return. "Ligare" is the second part, meaning "bind"; related to the word "ligament", which "binds" our bones together. So, it would appear that even the Latin word "re-ligion" carries the idea that something became unfastened! It was man and his Creator. By tradition, lies have become mixed with truth, and we will uncover, expose, or reveal to you some of the things we inherited from Babylon. They have become "fossilized" in our customs. You may not be able to comprehend everything well because there will be great emotional trauma resulting from what you are about to learn. Just hold on to the knowledge that what we will expose for the lies they are can be completely abandoned ~ and the Truth will suffer no harm at all. It is important to remain humble, continuing to learn. You can recognize a tree by its fruit. The fruit you should bear (show) is love, joy, peace, patience, kindness, goodness, faithfulness, gentleness, and self-control. This is the character of our Creator, and His children that walk in His teachings ~ His Commandments of love. They go against no law.

The real reason you have this information is because you have been called-out of the man-made kingdoms. What this book contains is not original, but is based on Scripture and many others' research work. Truth should be more than just entertaining facts. Ample evidence that the Writings are the Truth has been given by the fact that the Mashiach rose from the dead. He is the first "re-born" from the dead, and will never see death. He is the "first fruits" of a great harvest to come. If He spoke of Adam, Noach, and Mosheh (Moses), Daniel, and the creation of the Universe, then it happened the way the Writings explain it. ("Scripture" comes from the Latin word, *scriptum* meaning *hand-writing*.).

ETYMOLOGY

Etymology is the study of word origins. The word itself comes from the 2 Greek words, *etumo*(truth, true) + *logos*(word). So, it means "true-word". Being a student of etymology, I am an etymologist. In a way, I seek for the origins of words all the way back to the confusion of tongues at Babel. If the whole world was originally of one language, what was it? Since the Creator had a conversation with Adam and many others before the Flood, all His children spoke His language, rather than Him adapting to theirs. The Creator has been with us all through history, and all the prophets spoke and wrote in His language. Etymology can be used like an archaeological tool. The Hebrew word *"emet"* means *truth,* and later became the Greek word *"etumo"*. *Emet* is the root of another Hebrew word, *"emunah"* which means faithfulness, steadfastness, and fidelity. Emunah is most commonly translated to the English word *"faith"*. **"The tsedek** (righteous) **shall live by his emunah"** Hab. 2:4.

THIS BOOK'S PURPOSE is to expose the origins of everyday customs and rituals that have become camouflaged in new meanings. Common activities performed today have passed down through time from archaic Pagan cultures. Pagan rituals which have been dressed-up in "new clothing" will be exposed, so your view of the world will have clarity. All this came about because mythological Paganism, superstition, belief in majik, and ignorance were *tolerated* over the past 19+ centuries ~ in order for our political and religious ancestors to maintain control with a minimum of effort. The model for all mankind to live by will be shown to have been abandoned and outlawed. Our modern traditions could have easily been based on what is true, but instead pagan syncretisms were used to fuse together error and truth. This overwhelmed our ancestors, so we have inherited profaned patterns. Secret brotherhoods have passed much of this knowledge down through the centuries, never allowing the common people to learn about it, because it would cause disruption and loss of control. These "illuminated" men would often speak to one another in *Latin* (Italic, meaning *hidden*), to keep their secrets safe, and because Latin is a dead language, meanings of words don't change. You will see that the Earth is ruled by man-made domains focused in 3 main areas: *Ecclesiastical, Political,* and *Merchantile*. Presently, these are under the control of a fallen spatial being called Satan, and his many masquerading "angels of light". There is so much pagan design in Christianity that it leaves no doubt that what has been perpetrated on us is of cunning design; but it is still possible to see through it and escape. <u>The book is written in obedience to Ephesians 5:6-11.</u>

"Satan himself masquerades as a messenger of light . . . His servants also masquerade as servants of righteousness . . ." **2 COR. 11:14,15**

<u>**ANTI-LAW TEACHERS**</u> vs. dying to sin . . . . . The Mashiach could have *"fixed their wagon"* when He was being beaten to a bloody mess, but He didn't raise a finger. The political machine is used to "exterminate" whatever threatens the authority of the religious establishment.

Reading the Writings by "laity" was banned in 1229 CE, because it would be readily seen that the "system" was off-course. (CE means *Christian Era,* or *Common Era*).

"The understanding of this <u>message</u> will bring sheer terror" ~ so wrote a prophet called "Isaiah" (really *Yesha Yahu*) at 28:19. The message: **"Repent! For the Reign of ⁨ayaz⁩ draws near!"** While the Torah of the Creator was taught, the vineyard (mankind) was green (growing) and fruitful (peaceful) because the *living waters* provided life to the soil. The Torah, or Commanded Teachings, produce peace. By removing the living waters, the vineyard becomes "dry", withers, and the dead branches will be burned up. A "key" of knowledge has been withheld from the people: the Personal Name of the Creator! When the Bridegroom returns, those unwise "virgins" who think they will have a place in the household of YHWH, will be turned away; having had *insufficient* **light** to find their way. The "apostles" knew their way, and you can too. It's narrow, straight, and very easy to follow the path, because it's written down in the best-selling textbook in the history of the world: Scripture! Men have struggled to corrupt it, ignore it, and trick people out of obeying what it says. The first woman was told by the father of lies, *"You shall certainly not die"* (for ignoring YHWH's law). The liar is now leading millions to "just believe", and disobey the Torah ~ it's not even for you! And, it's working like a dream. WWJD? (What Would J-sus Do) ~ well, the Rabbi would definitely still obey the Torah; after all, He is the law-giver! (The term "rabbi" means *my teacher,* and is **transliterated** 17 times in the Messianic Writings. It was used in fact many *more* times, because whenever you see the word "teacher" or "master", the original word was most likely *rabbi*). If you don't understand, then you are confused. Learning from <u>drunken</u> (men in a stupor who don't understand) <u>merchants</u> (men who fleece the sheep), the message of the Reign of YHWH sounds like *"do and do, rule on rule, a little here, a little there"*. The message is "sealed" to them, because they have not received a love for the Truth (they have not received a <u>love</u> for the Torah, Wisdom). **"For you this whole vision is nothing but words sealed in a scroll"** Is. 29:11. *"These people come near to Me with their mouth and honor me with their lips, but their hearts are far from me. Their worship of me IS MADE UP ONLY OF RULES TAUGHT BY MEN"* 29:13. Now, lets find out which parts are "man-made" and not a part of the Eternal Kingdom. *"You will not see Me again, until you say, 'baruch haba bashem ⁨ayaz⁩'"* Mt. 23:39 / Ps. 118:26. Nazarenes are saying it again!

Doctrines of Demons

THE OBJECTIVE of the enemy of your soul is to keep you from the truth, and waste your time so you'll die without it. He must distract you, or lead you to think other "smarter" or "educated" men have it all figured, and all you have to do is get dunked, go to a Sun-day assembly, and pay, pay, pay. Arise, shine, for your light has come! The bookstores are filled with books that explain away our confusion. There are even books now that seek to prove that the Author of the Writings is in fact Who they claim it is, using special computer analysis. Names, phrases, etc., are found to be embedded in "harmonics", where words are built into a secret code, like in cryptography. This proves that the Torah is Supernatural. Soon, you will know more than your preacher about what Scripture teaches.

HOW THEY INVENTED YOUR WORLD:

CAMOUFLAGED PAGANISM "Doctrine" means *teaching.* It's a Latin word, related to "document" (written instruction) and "doctor", meaning "teacher". We have all been trained or *programmed* from birth with various traditions, rituals, and customs; all paganism is targeted at children. How we keep track of *time* is a world-wide type of programming. Here we will look into how we came to be trained to think of and organize time ~ in our *days, months,* and *years.*

One of the first things we do when we awake each day is check the **time**. Originally, the **hours** of daylight were measured using a **sundial**, and the shadow of the sun marked off 12 "hours" until it set. The marked hours on the dial pass more quickly in the winter months, and slower in the summer months. The variance in the length of an hour is less important than knowing where you are in time relative to the whole day, so this system worked fine. There was no "daylight-saving-time" trick to deal with! However crazy the sundial seems to us, the gaining and losing of an hour is at least as weird. There were always 12 hours in every "daytime". "Noon", Latin *nones* (9), was the 9th hour from sunrise, or 3 p.m. in the ancient world.

Each day of the week was originally referred to by a **number**. The 7th day also had a name: *Shabbat,* meaning *rest.* Yes, even Adam and Chuwah, the first man and woman, observed the 7-day week. (There is no one named "Eve" in the Hebrew; this name was embraced to appease pagans because one of the names for their *Earth Mother* was "Eve". The name *Chuwah* is derived from the Hebrew word *chai,* meaning "life" ~ thus her name means *mother of the living.* The ending *–ah* renders it feminine, similar to the ending in *Sarah. Sar* means prince, or ruler; *Sarah* means *princess*). If you check your "calendar", you will notice the days of the week have been given **names**. The names were taken from among pagan peoples who honored their deities by calling the days by the names of their idols.

SUN-DAY (day #1)
From Latin, *dies Solis,* the *Day-of-the-Sun.* Since Babylon was established, Pagans have worshipped the **Sun**. Here's a few of the names they've used:

CONSTANTINE I

Baal, Shamash, Moloch, Ahura-Mazda, Dagon, Sol, Marduk, Mithras, Krishna, Amon-Ra, Aton, Woden (Odin), Zeus, Deus, and the Druid / Teutonic "God". You may recall that the Pharaoh and the Caesar (Khazar/Czar) were worshipped as the sun. This began with the first king, **Nimrod,** discussed later. This pattern of worshipping the sun, moon, planets, and stars permeated the Babylonians, Persians, Chaldeans, Egyptians, Greeks, Romans, Celts, Mayans, Aztecs, and Indians. The governments were the religion. If they were "good" Pagans, at death they would be transported to the skies (Heaven) to live with their deities. This was called *Nirvana, Shambala,* or *Elysian Fields.* The Roman Consul/Emperor **Constantine I** gave us the term *Sun-Day,* which he also called *Sol Invictus Mithras* (the day of the unconquerable sun, Mithras). In 321 CE he decreed under the penalty of death that all artisans, merchants, and people of his Empire cease work on the Venerable Day of the Sun, to honor Mithras. This was a Universal Edict, and is still enforced in our western culture with our "blue laws". (Interestingly, the government phone numbers are printed on blue pages in our US phone books). It was a weekly ritual of sun-worshippers to assemble at dawn on this day to greet the sun at its rising. A great pillar, or sun-ray *obelisk* was the solar religion's primitive high place, condemned by Scripture as a "pillar of jealousy" ~ secretly interpreted as a male fertility symbol. Various tower designs such as steeples, pagodas, turrets, ziggarats, minarets, spires, obelisks, and pyramids have served Pagans well. The Temple did not have a high place, nor do synagogues! These high places would receive the first hallowed rays of dawn. At this point, bells were rung by hand, as in a shaker-grid, and large ones were struck with oak logs swung horizontally. Gongs struck with hammers were especially fun for the Oriental Pagan, but they also used the familiar bell shape too. In the book, _The Conquest of Peru_, Prescott is an eye-witness to blatant sun-worship:

"The Inca would assemble at dawn eagerly. They watched the coming of the deity, and no sooner did his first yellow rays strike the turrets, than a shout of gratulation broke forth from the assembled multitude, the wild tunes from barbaric instruments swelled louder and louder as his bright orb shone in full splendor on his votaries."

The Romans considered anyone who did not worship the sun to be an atheist and a traitor, since Caesar was the sun enthroned in a man. Religion, politics, and sports were all different facets of the same thing. Sun-Day will be discussed later too.

MON-DAY (day #2)

MONA

The _Day-of-the-Moon_.
To the Romans, _lunae dies_.

The 𝕺𝕷𝕯 𝕰𝖓𝖌𝖑𝖎𝖘𝖍 term was _monan daeg_, as translated from Latin, where _mona_ means _moon_. _Mona Lisa_ means "moon lily". We get our word _month_ (_moonth_) from _mona_, the 29.5 day orbital cycle, but this 2nd weekday is named what it is because it has been dubbed the moon's day! The moon was identified with Artemis (Diana), but in some cults the sun and moon were the 'eyes of heaven'. Artemis is depicted with the crescent moon beneath her feet as if riding in a boat ~ exactly as you will see Miryam (Mary) in Roman Catholic illustrations. The Astral King, the sun, and his sister the moon, were the dominant figures that shaped the astro-biological mind. The futility of honoring Pagan deities resulted because their foolish hearts were darkened, because they did not honor or give thanks to the Creator, though His invisible attributes are clearly seen.

TUES-DAY (day #3)

TEUTATES

Tyr's Day: "day of Tiu".
Teutonic Druid-Celtic idol.

Unable to help themselves, the population of the Angles and Saxons were kept under control by various Druid priest cults. Like any other Pagan religion, the population lived in fear and ignorance, while the **parasite** fed off of them and kept them brain-washed. The Druids still worship the sun at Stonehenge every Summer Solstice.

Tyr, or Tiu, was the Norse deity of **war,** considered the son of Odin (Woden). The French call this day _Mardi_ (Mar's Day), after Mars, the Roman's deity of war! _Mardi Gras_ is the French name meaning "fat Tuesday", still bearing the name of the Roman deity. This festival falls the day before _Ash Wednesday_, the beginning of _Lent_, both to be discussed later.

WEDNES-DAY (day #4)

Well, _DUH_ ~ as expected by now, it's another Pagan idol's name! An elder in Iceland couldn't stand it anymore, and changed the days back to numbers for that island several hundred years ago. By saying it's "Wednesday"(Woden, Odin), we are declaring it to be _Woden's Day_. Considered highly skilled in magic (majik), this Celtic deity was, to the Teutonic Pagan, the husband of Freya, or _Frigga_. The Romans honored _Mercury_ on this day, calling it _Mercurii dies_ (Mercury's Day).

This mid-week evening was highly regarded as a night of majik ~ the Druids met to hold hands in a **circle**, chant, enchant, cast spells, and do it while surrounding a **burning cross**, the symbol of Woden (Odin). Some believe the Celtic crux is a Pagan majik symbol, the _Trifolium clover leaf_ representing _Woden, Frigga, and Thor_. Other Druid trinities included _Esus, Teutates, & Taranus_. Anglo-Saxon xenophobia (_fear of foreigners_) and Druid customs are seen today in the modern _Ku Klux Klan_. They still call their leaders _wizards_ and use the Celtic term "clan", a traditional social unit in Scot Land. The word comes from the Greek _kuklos,_ meaning "**circle**". A very secretive society, it rose up mainly in the South US after the civil war, to reassert "white supremacy" by terroristic methods. The Druids were _very_ nationalistic, so it was difficult for Rome to conquer them. The only way "Christianity" could win them over was to _absorb_ their culture. This is called _inculturation_.

"Syncretisms" — the attempt to reconcile or combine differing beliefs in philosophy or religion by uniting them — mixes of two or more behaviors together, re-inventing the meaning "on the surface". Is this the real reason some Christians meet together on this night? Catholics have always had a "novena" session on this night. What is this idea we call _syn_-cretism?

"Syn" means _together,_ and the Dictionary defines

"Cretin" (kret'n) as "*a fool; and idiot.* [French *cretin,* idiot, from Swiss French, *crestin,* CHRISTIAN". Sorry, look it up yourself. We will have a look at the word "Christian" as a translation of *Mashian* (a follower of any generic "messiah"/mashiach) a bit later. For now, let it be enough to say that the sect which was established by the true *Mashiach* was called *Nazarenes.* But most hang their hat on one text, or never question a translator's choices. Well, did you know that the word "Christian / Christians" is only used a total of 3 times in all of Scripture, and it is only in the Greek translation? Woden's emblem was the Celtic Crux, a cross with the **circle** (the sun). No wonder we see so many pictures of crosses with the sun nimbus behind it, and sunsets in Christian art — not to mention the "halos" of yellow around the heads of "Jesus" and the "saints". This will be shown to be a world-wide Pagan influence; Buddha, Krishna, Ahura-Mazda, and Jupiter are only a few!

THURS-DAY (day #5)

The Celtic *Thor's Day;* the deity of thunder and son of Woden and Freya. The same as *Taranus,* Thor was associated with thunder; the Dutch *donder,* or Germanic *donner* (one of Santa's reindeer!). The Romans honored *Jupiter* on this day, which was originally **IU-PITAR,** meaning *Jovis-father.* "Jove" corresponds to *Zeus.* The altar of Zeus, used at every Olympic game, is lit by a torch. The altar is shaped like a "T". Thor's emblem was the hammer, secretly interpreted as the letter "T", harkening back to *Tammuz* (Babylonian *Duzu*), the son of Nimrod and Semiramis.

FRI-DAY (day #6)

𝕺𝖑𝖉 𝕰𝖓𝖌𝖑𝖎𝖘𝖍 *Frigedaeg,* this was Frey Day or Frigga Day. Frigga was the wife of Woden. The fertility concept associated with this day is very ancient. The Greeks honored *Aphrodite* on this day, and the Romans venerated *Venus* (Astarte). This day was the Egyptian's day of **Isis,** depicted with the symbol of the fish on her head. The fish symbol pre-dates the Egyptians, coming from the Phoenician/Philistine cult of Dagon (Jdg. 16:23, 1Sa. 5:2). "Dag" is Hebrew for *fish,* and the Latin is *Pisces.* It was chosen by Pagans because a female fish lays hundreds, sometimes thousands, of eggs ~ a symbol of fertility. The Romans believed *Venus* (Astarte) came from the sky in a huge egg (not a saucer). We'll go into more detail when we study the Great Mother, Queen of Heaven. Frigga's emblem was also the FISH, hence it is seen today that Roman Catholics inculturated this into avoiding red meat on this day, replacing it with fish: the "fish fry" (even the word "fry" is describing a young fish). The Great Mother

(Magna Mater) was universally represented by the fish emblem. The Greek word **ichthys** (ikhthus) spelled iota (Ι), chi (X), theta (Θ), upsilon (Y), sigma (Σ) — spells "ICHTHYS" ("fish"). ΙΧΘΥΣ doesn't mean "Christ", but *fish.* With considerable craft, the fish has become a Christian symbol, due to a Greek anagram, Ιησους – Χριστος – θεου – Υιος – Σωτηρ (Iesous Christos Theou Huios Soter). Not to worry, it's only a man-made tradition—too bad it just spells "fish". The real "sign" of the Mashiach isn't a crux or a fish, but a "lampstand" (menorah) Rev. 1&2. The Hebrew "menorah" has 7 lamps, and represents His body, the 7 assemblies, through which flows the "living water" (lamp oil, the laws which give light to the world). At Rev. 2:5 he said He would remove their **menorah** if they didn't repent (stop breaking Commandments). Have you noticed any menorahs in any Christian homes or meeting houses? Soon, you'll learn why — He never threatened to remove any *fish.*

SATUR-DAY (day #7)

This was the Greco-Roman *Day of Saturn.* *Saturn* was the Romans' deity of agriculture, corresponding to the Greeks' deity *Cronus.* This day was dedicated to *Saturnus,* as was the big party at the end of the Roman year at the Solstice, *Saturnalia.* Satur Day was also called *Sater Day,* and is unmistakenly linked to other Greco-Roman mythology. The *SATYR,* a goat-legged half man with horns and pointed ears, was believed to be a drunken, lecherous demon with an abnormal sexual appetite. The 7th day and the festival of "Satyrnalia" was modeled perfectly after the satyr profile; mischievousness, drunkenness, and orgiastic revelry. As you consider the wild week-ends enjoyed today by dating couples and party animals with their "mojo' drives, it's clear nothing has changed.

Here's a big foundational girder with no rivets, installed by Constantine in the Roman year 321 CE. This 7th day, the commemoration of Creation in which we honor the Creator *AS* the Creator is a

"Temple in time" from sunset "Frey Day" to sunset "Satyr Day" ~ changed to his "Sun Day" under penalty of death, by only the authority of a man! All theologians and scholars admit there is no Scriptural basis for this change, but it was done by the authority of "the Church". This day which was set-apart at Creation to be a day of complete rest from work has been "superseded" by traditions that served to unite Pagans with the Nazarene sect. Constantine's historian, *Eusebius*, records the Emperor's edict: *"All things what so ever that is was duty to do on the Sabbath, these WE have transferred to the Lord's Day"*. He also recorded Constantine's infuriated words, *"The cursed wretches who killed our Lord . . .* (the Italian Romans executed Him, Constantine's people!) *. . . We will have NOTHING in common with the hostile rabble of the Yahudim* ("Jews")". Remember, the Romans executed our Nazarene Rabbi for *sedition*, or the claim that He was a king ~ Caesar ruled as a religious king. Sabbath is the "sign" of the Everlasting Covenant, indicating who we worship.

A WORD ABOUT TIME ~ Y6K is coming!

Since Creation, just under 6000 years have been completed. Given the distances in *light years* that we can see into the heavens (outer space), many have fixed the age of the universe at almost 20 billion years. To look at Adam 5 minutes after he was created, they might estimate him to be 20 years old too. The trees with fruit on them were brought into being fully developed. The animals, created the day after the plants, needed the oxygen from the plants, that's possibly why the animals came second. Relativity has been at work also since the beginning. When YHWH created the quasars and galaxies of stars, He **brought** their light to shine upon the Earth ~ that's what it says. That's why it's called *super*-natural. He created space-time. You just have to keep in mind just how *awesome* the true Creator is, instead of trying to figure out the whole scheme without factoring Him in.

The **real** moons and years are based on the signs and seasons, and measured in packages of years called *Jubilees* (Yob-hel), numbering 50 years each. However, the reprobate Pagan mind interpreted the sun, moon, stars, and changing seasons based on **SEX**. That's what is at the root of all Paganism! Plant and animal sex is a created thing, but the fallen state of man caused him to worship it, and established Pagan religion based on its processes, as we will see. All of history was recorded by the "winners" — usually the tyrants. So, it is only natural that their process of measuring time be what we use today. The original pattern of Roman **time-keeping** established by the authority of Julius Caesar in 46 BCE is still with us (There were only **10 months** in a Roman year). Our Roman 'moonths' totally disregard the real new moons. The proclaiming of the new month settled into when Caesar **announced** it, and this act was called Caesar's *calends*, Latin for *proclaim*. Originally, the first Roman month was March. After you have read this a number of times, you may begin to see this Pagan process of keeping **time** is a kind of **MARK** on us.

ROMAN TIME: THE MONTHS

MARCH (1st month): Named for the war deity Mars. When the weather began to show signs of warming, the Roman armies would 'march' out to war. Marching is what armies have done ever since, to conquer in the power of the deity "Mars".

APRIL (2nd month): The month of Venus, also called *Aprilis*, from Etruscan *Apru*, from Greek *Aphro*, a short form of *Aphrodite*, the Greek fertility deity. This was the primary month of the Great Mother Earth, known by many names. The Earth Mother was "fertilized" or impregnated on a Sun-Day after the Vernal (Venus) Equinox (when the length of days and nights are equal). This Sun-Day was called "Easter". Prior to this, the Pagan priests imposed a "fast" from sexual relations. We get the term **LENT** from the Germanic word *lengten*, which refers to the *lengthening* of the days as winter turns to spring. The first day of this fast, the mark of Tammuz was placed on the foreheads of the worshippers, the ancient "TAU" (see back cover palaeo-Hebrew). The 40th day prior to "Easter" was always a "Woden's Day", giving us the term *Ash Wednesday*. Nine months **after** the Earth Mother was impregnated at "Easter" (a gestation period), the SUN was "re-born" at the winter solstice, December 25th, further explained under "December".

MAY (3rd month): This month was named after the Italic fertility deity **MAIA**.

JUNE (4th month): This was the month dedicated to **JUNO**, an important Roman female deity, the wife and sister of Jupiter, identified with the Greeks' Hera. "Father's Day" was always in this month, and on a Sun-Day, because the sun was the Pagans' father. He was in his strength at the summer solstice, so you will notice this is still practiced.

JULY (5th month): This month was dedicated to Julius Caesar, the first emperor. He was honored as a deity, son of the sun.

AUGUST (6th month): This word is Latin meaning venerable, magnificent, awesome. Gaius Octavius took the name "Augustus Caesar" after becoming Emperor, and had his name used for this month. He did this to honor himself, as Julius had done before.

SEPTEMBER (7th month): This is the Latin word for the number "7" ~ "*septem*". Now things will begin to make sense a little, but hang on!

OCTOBER (8th month): This is the Latin word *october*, "eighth month", from *octo*, meaning "eight".
NOVEMBER (9 month): This month was *Novembris*, from the Latin word *novem*, meaning "nine".
DECEMBER (10th month): Latin *Decembris*, from the number *decem*, ten. We get the word *decimal* from the Latin also.

All these months are shifted by two now, as you know. Even though we are saying "December", the Latin for "10", we number it the 12th moon. Rather than correcting this, we just keep it up. Not only that, but the whole beginning point is based on the "rebirth" of the sun! According to the Writings (Scripture), we are to begin our counting of the moons in the Spring ~ watching for the "green ears" of barley to appear, then watching for the next new moon. The Creator has spoken, but man's kingdoms ignore Him! Speaking to the converts at Galatia, Paul mentions *"You are observing special days and months and seasons and years!"* Gal. 4:10. The Galatians were once Pagan, enslaved in the weak, miserable principles, turning back to that which was based in what was their heathen, Babylonian mythology (you must read this in context, because your footnotes will lead you to think Paul was speaking about Sabbaths, and the way the Creator established our "watch" in the skies). He said, *"Let there be lights in the expanse of the sky to separate the day from the night, and let them serve as signs to mark seasons and days and years . . ."* Gen. 1:14. It is written, *"This month is to be for you the first month, the first month of your year"* Ex. 12:2. He had to tell them, because they had been captive as slaves for over 400 years, and were now "called-out".

JANUARY & FEBRUARY With only 10 months in the Roman year, the seasons were appearing later and later every year! Julius Caesar began hearing many complaints, so he appointed an Alexandrian astrologer named **Sosigenes** to devise the needed corrections. Sosigenes added the 2 months of *January* and *February* to the year 46 BCE, and it was called the *year of confusion*. He even set up the cycle of *leap years*, which added a day to the month of February every 4 years. January is named for a domestic deity, **Janus**, who was the ruler of "beginnings", and protected doorways, gates, and arches. You will recall processions through great "arches" when ancient kings would march their armies in triumphant display? February was named for the female idol **Februa**. The authority to proclaim new moons, and change the system, resided with the Caesar; his seat of power ruled, and he was the *priest of Janus*. The Roman title, *Pontifex Maximus* is Etruscan, bestowed on Caesar as the Pagan head of the Pontifical College of Priests of Janus: the **Cardinals**. "Cardinal" is Latin (*cardo*) meaning *hinge*. They assisted the priest of Janus in opening "the door" to the Elysian Fields, the Pagan "Heaven".

"Pontifex Maximus" means *highest priest* in Etruscan, so Caesar was the gateway to the after-life for a Roman Pagan. Julius Caesar's calendar is called the *Julian Calendar*. We now have the *Gregorian Calendar* because the title "Pontifex Maximus" was inherited by the Roman Catholic popes. The authority of Caesar was transferred to this bishop, the Roman Catholic pope! He also kept his "cardinals". This "Bishop of Rome" also uses Caesar's title, *"papa"* (pope), a Mithraic title. In 1582, "pope" Gregory implemented a 10-day adjustment to the calendar designed by Sosigenes, by *wiping out 10 days for that year*. This was obeyed by the "papal states", but the rest of the western world remained on the former timetable. It was not until the time of Benjamin Franklin that the rest of society came into line with Rome. Up to then, landowners thought they would lose 10 days' rents, but Franklin convinced them they would actually be receiving their rents 10 days *sooner* by obliging the pope; and so now we have the *Gregorian Calendar*. This same pope authorized what is known as *Gregorian Chant*. These "chants" stem directly from Pagan monks' hymns, originally called *Orphic Hymns*, or the *Hymns of Orpheus*. He simply "sanctified " the Pagan hymns.

NIMROD YEARS

The Pagan priests were astrologers who closely monitored the positions of the sun, moon, 5 of the planets, and constellations of stars. These were the physical deities they worshipped, and they modeled time over their year based on **sex**. They knew the path of the sun "crossed" the celestial equator at the Vernal and Autumnal Equinoxes, producing equal days and nights at those events. So, who's "Nimrod"? He was the first king on the Earth, the grandson of Ham (see Gen. 10). His secular name is suspected to be Sargon I, and he built Babylon and Nineveh. It was possibly Nimrod who built the *Tower of Babel*, a ziggurat made of bricks; the ruins exist still. Nimrod was a tyrant, and that is what his name means! He was a *"mighty hunter before YHWH"*. The word "before" means "against" in the Hebrew if you check a concordance. Nimrod turned the people against the truth, and began the worship of the sky luminaries. Children were sacrificed in exchange for prosperity. He wore a headpiece with a "horn" in front as ruler, a symbol of power and authority. In fact, all crowns that are modeled with "horns" are based on this design. The marauding heathens of Ghengis Khan and the Vikings of the Norse wore horned hats and helmets in their wars. Nimrod's idolatry and ruthlessness caused his uncle, Shem, to destroy him, cutting his body into parts and distributing them around the kingdom. It is said Nimrod took his mother, **Semiramis** as a wife. At his death, his wife/mother consoled the people of Sumer by saying she carried Nimrod's child, and named him Tammuz. Nimrod, she explained, had gone into the heavens and was now the sun! So, the sun was the "father", and the Earth was now the "mother". Semiramis was, in effect, a deity representing the Earth. "Ish" is Hebrew for "man", and she was worshipped as "Ishtar". Babylonian pillars—obelisks—represented the generative powers of the male, and were simultaneously images of the phallus, Nimrod, and a sun-ray! Fertility rituals such as "May Pole" dances are still seen today. "Ishtar" is the same word we have today in "Easter", which superseded Passover. It's Nimrod's mother, also known around the world as Asherah, Astoreth, Ishtar, Eostre, Astarte, Maia, Gaia, Diana, Ninurta, Nana, Ceres, Ostara, Austron, Isis / Nut (the sky), Aphrodite, Venus, Indrani, Devaki, Tanit, Cybele, Artemis, **Athena** (pictured), and many others. The Canaanites called their shrines to the Earth Mother "Asherim".

EASTER

This word has been adopted from Pagans as an attempt to "inculturate" by syncretism a behavior that is absolutely an abomination. If you recognise "Halloween" for what it is, then this will be

ISHTAR & LILIES

no different after you learn the truth. Easter was already one of the two biggest celebrations observed by Pagans, long before Christianity came along. It is my belief that when this is exposed, it will fulfill the prophecies of Revelation 18. Go read it

now. Babylon is still with us, but it is going to fall. Easter was celebrated by the Assyrians, the Phoenicians, and the Philistines (Goliath no doubt had an Easter basket). You should look up "Easter" in a Webster's Dictionary, and do further research in other sources! This festival involved the *"Rites of Spring"* near the Equinox of Venus, when Pagans believed the Earth Mother was **impregnated by the sun**. They engaged in ritual sex acts, and used symbols of fertility like eggs, rabbits, and "hot cross buns". The Babylonian symbol for the "female" was, and is, <u>a circle with a crux beneath</u>.

The round cakes were baked for the "Queen of Heaven" (Regina Coeli), and "Great Mother" (Magna Mater), with the <u>**"cross"** symbol indicating the female</u>. The cross also indicated the Equinox, when the Earth's orbit "**crossed**" the celestial equator. Hold on now, because everything will be just fine. This must sound so wild you may think I'm a heretic; but by the end of this you will be very glad to have acquired the truth. This book will only shatter myths, not the "rock" of truth.

To ensure a prosperous growing season, Pagans rolled eggs decorated with bright colors of Spring on their fields, hoping to imbue fertility. These eggs were then hidden from "evil spirits" in rabbits' nests, another symbol of fertility. "Easter" is the *name* of the Babylonian "Mother of Harlots", Rev. 17, and her image stands as the sungoddess "Lady Liberty" in New York Harbor. This Colossus statue even has the "tower" headpiece, as seen worn

by Artemis. The 7 horns or sunrays should be a strong indication for her true identity. Her emblem is the flower of the lily, seen illustrated with her on this page. An American society, the *Easter Seals Society,* uses the *fleur-de-lis* (French, *flower of the lily*) as their logo, and they have no religious affiliations whatsoever. Most "churches" decorate with the lilies on "Easter morning". Instead of inheriting the truth, they inherited Babylon! If we only study history as people, places, and dates without comprehending "why" things occurred as they did, then everything is unorganized. It's a junkpile. When you assemble it correctly, it all fits together perfectly, clarifying the path we walk on. "Satan" disguises "himself" — "he" is quite often "female". We know "he" was behind Nimrod, as Moloch, Baal, Mithras, and so on; but "he" is also Ishtar. Sun-Day is "his" diversion; it's a lie. I refer to "Easter Sun-Day" as **"Beaster Sun-Day"**. We don't have to wait for a "beast", it's here right now. The patterns and appointments found in the Writings are the ones that are snubbed, excused, and ignored you will notice.

FLEUR-DE-LIS

But you say, *"The word 'Easter' is in my King James Version"*. Translations are not "inspired", and errors exist by the tens of thousands in many translations! The word in the Greek that underlies the word "Easter" in the KJV is **pascha**, and it means *Passover*, from the Hebrew word "Pesach". All scholars admit that this is an error in translation, and it only appears ONCE, at Acts 12:4. Luke, who wrote almost 40% of the Mashian writings (NT), didn't put it there as "Easter". The KJV is the **only one** with this error, since translators corrected it in all others! There was a previous English translation made by the Catholic priest John Wycliffe during the 14th century. He lived from 1320-1384, and his bones were burned in effigy for this unauthorized English work. He never used the word "Church", but the word "congregation" for the word *ecclesia*. Before the KJV, no one had ever used the word "Church", and soon you'll learn why.

Pagan religions through time paralleled each other, carrying the Sun, Earth Mother, and child model from Babylon to Media Persia, Phoenicia, Egypt, Greece, Rome, and Celts. The Medes cooked the mythology into "Zoroastrianism", producing the magician priests called "Magi". T ey worshipped Ahura, Haoma, and Ohrmazd as their trinity. (We'll survey them all under "Trinities" later). The Greeks' "Zeus" was their sun deity, whose mother was "Lydia", shown here riding a swan. Notice her headpiece; very much like "Lady Liberty". Take another look at "Athena" and "Ishtar" on the previous page; those heads are indications that we are seeing the same person.

The Britannica Encyclopedia (1934) states:
"EASTER (es'ter). Ostara, or Eastre, was the goddess of Spring in the religion of the ancient Angles and Saxons. Every April a festival was celebrated in her honor. With the beginnings of Christianity, the old gods were put aside. From then on the festival was celebrated in honor of the resurrection of Christ, but was still known as Easter after the old goddess." (emphasis mine).

In contrast, the Creator says:
"Break down their altars, smash their sacred stones and burn their Asherah (Easter) **poles in the fire; cut down the idols of their gods and WIPE OUT THEIR NAMES from those places. YOU MUST NOT WORSHIP ꮓꓬꭤꮓ YOUR ELOHIM IN THEIR WAY."** Dt. 12. OK, that's pretty clear. But what

happened? The hypothesis of this book states on the outset that as the Pagans were absorbed into Chrisianity, it was the policy to accept everything they were accustomed to celebrating also. Let's hear it directly from the Catholic organization itself; the Catholic Cardinal John Henry Newman's book, **_The Essay on the Development of Christian Doctrine_**, published in 1878, states in chapter 8:

*"The rulers of the Church from early times were prepared, should the occasion arise, to adopt, to imitate, or to sanctify the existing rites and customs of the population, as well as the philosophy of the educated class. The use of temples and those dedicated to particular saints, and ornamented on occasion with **branches** of trees (wreaths), incense, lamps, candles, votive offerings on recovering from illnesses, holy water, holy days and seasons (the entire Church calendar), use of calendars, processions, blessings on the fields, sacerdotal vestments, the ring in marriage, chants, the Kyrie Eleison — **are all of Pagan origin, and sanctified by adoption into the Church.**"* There you have it. But, you may ask, *"If Easter was a Pagan festival celebrating the impregnation of 'Mother Earth', how did it get mixed up with Christianity?"* Christianity's "Pagan Connection" started with one man more than any other. In 325 CE, the Roman Emperor **Constantine I** convened what is now called the **Nicene Council**, gathering 220 elders (bishops) together, in order to unify basic doctrines (teachings), and establish common practices. This "universalizing" produced the **Roman Catholic Church** (RCC). The Latin word "Catholic" means *universal*. There was no "Catholic" on planet Earth prior to this Council. The only Council mentioned in the Writings conducted by the first Nazarenes is mentioned at Acts 15, the purpose of which was to determine how to accommodate **Gentile converts** who were turning to the true Creator. The only topic: circumcision ~ and since immersion in the Name and receiving the Spirit into your heart is our "circumcision", it was decided that physical circumcision was not necessary (this is a very important beginning text to be understood by all Gentiles!).

Constantine's Council sought to institute new tolerances for Pagan patterns, and outlaw the patterns that the Savior lived by and taught ~ he had already proclaimed "Sun-Day" as a day of rest dedicated to the

14

sun (321 CE), and now it came time to "sycretise" more Paganism. By not "repenting" and turning away from elementary foolishness, it was simpler to just "absorb" the behavior. Political and religious **CONTROL** is a *slippery* thing; so by keeping the Pagan rituals in place, control was maintained with a minimum of effort! "Truth" was twisted by the "spin doctors" so the opposite of truth became our custom. Rather than make 99% of the people conform to a totally new behavior, it was easier to just exterminate the 1%, and put a Scriptural "spin" on the Pagan customs. This is what overwhelmed all our ancestors, <u>being taught these things as young children</u>. Paganism has always been highly skilled at wrapping dissimilar things together, making things appear one way on the surface, and making the loosely understood things shrouded in what they call the "mysteries of the faith".

In order to blend practices into universal (Catholic) behavior, the real Shabbat (Sabbath) was outlawed, along with Passover and other annual "Jewish" observances. This was a prophecy revealed to Daniel. In the prophecy, four "beasts" or kingdoms would arise, which are clearly (1) Babylon, (2) Media-Persia, (3) Greece, and (4) Rome. At Daniel 7:25, the 4th beast is clearly described:

*"**The fourth beast is a fourth kingdom that will appear on Earth** (Rome). **It will be different from all the other kingdoms and will devour the whole Earth, trampling it down and crushing it. The ten horns are ten kings who will come from this kingdom** (Caesars/Khasars/Kaisers/Czars ~ Julius Caesar up to Constantine). **After them another king will arise, different from the earlier ones** (Constantine "fused" the sun worshippers with the Nazarene writings, and was not of the family name "Caesar"); **he will subdue three kings. He will speak against the Most High, and oppress His saints** (qodeshim, those set-apart, especially the Hebrew people), **and try to <u>change the set times and the law</u>"**. Scripture is a pattern for our living in peace, guiding us with its "LAW". The *changing* of the "set times" (or seasonal appointments decreed*

at Deut. 16 and Lev. 23) were wiped-out and replaced with Pagan observances, imposed by Constantine.

Instead of PEACE, we have inherited WAR.

The coveting (desiring) of power, land, and wealth is ravaging the whole Earth, and this picture illustrates one of the tiny victims of war. The fruit of the Spirit (when the Torah is lived by) produces love, peace, patience, kindness, goodness, faithfulness, gentleness, and self-control. Aggression produces poverty and death. At Constantine's **Nicene Council**, he put such fear in some of the visiting elders, that encyclopedias state that many <u>ran for their lives</u> when they heard the things being discussed! The <u>*Edict of Milan*</u> had already outlawed synagogues, but Constantine's Council boldly outlawed the **Torah**, fulfilling the prophecy of Daniel 7:25. Everything that we know went wrong long ago, and it became a powerful institutionalized "beast", just as the Writings called it. If there were just a few little traces that were Pagan, that would be error; but let's investigate further, so we can decide whether or not the steel framework on which we stand has any rivets in *any* of its girders.

There is not ONE encyclopedic article that does not bring Constantine's (pictured here) so-called "c o n v e r s i o n" to "Christianity" into question. Yet, a couple of billion people today are following

his edicts. He founded Catholicism, and there is no dispute about that. The 95 issues that Martin Luder (called "Luther") nailed to the door put the Reformation into full blown splendor, beginning with "<u>indulgences</u>" being **sold** to shorten one's stay in "Purgatory". The seeds of this "Reformation" began with John

Wycliffe's unauthorized translation of the Messianic Writings (NT) into English. This is not intended to make Catholicism into a "whipping boy", but let's just stop and think for a moment. Does the Creator's religion, or the one that everyone believes was founded by our Good Shepherd have any popes? No? How about "monks"? Or nuns? Well, Pagans have all of these things, and always have. The "Dalai Lama" means "highest monk". Has someone "monked around" with a few things? Nuns were Pagan temple prostitutes; or virgins who kept watch over the "sacred fires". In Zoroastrian ritual, men did this. They wore black, being called "dark ones"

because their robes became soiled too easily with the soot and ashes of keeping the "sacred fires" going. These fires were used to sacrifice human lives. Monks also wear red ceremonial robes, symbolic of the fire of the sun. Israel had <u>no one dressed in black or red</u> ~ the priests wore white linen. Try to picture Rabbi O W Y ョ Ⅎ wearing black! There were no shaven-headed monks, because such "trimming" was specifically forbidden by the Creator at Lev. 19, most likely **because** the Pagans did it. It doesn't take a rocket scientist to figure it out, but people wear black today to funerals because the pagans often burned their dead on raised platforms. The smoke and ashes soiled their garments, so ashes became a symbol of mourning. You see corpse burning occasionally in movies. The new *Star Wars* movie ends with a scene where they burn one of their fallen comrades, and Luke Skywalker burned his dead father in a previous episode. The dead were burned because Pagans believed that burying them would "defile" the Earth. Fire, water, winds, and the Earth were sacred to the Pagans. Cremation is very popular still. "Holy water" is an echo of the Pagan belief that water is sacred. Since the Roman "papa", monks, nuns, wearing black, shaving heads into "tonsure" cuts, burning the dead, playing with "holy" water, "Sun-Day", and Easter are not in the Writings, then it's pretty obvious we don't need them. However, if they originated in Pagan worship, then what creature can you think of who masquerades as a messenger of "righteousness" caused mankind to embrace them?

The definition of "science" is interesting, when you consider what we're exposing here:
"Sci-ence (si'ens): n. 1. Learning or study concerned with demonstratable truths."
Science is the *"search for truth"*, based on the Latin *scire*, *"to know"*. To ignore "the truth" and continue to follow lies would be unthinkable; but even if people never find out the truth, they still participate in *"pseudo-science"* (false knowledge, untruth) if they stay in error. Pretty much the lower floors supporting Christianity as practiced today have been taken away. But, now we are going to pause, and deal with the **REAL** Name of the Creator. This is foundational material in a better building. It is not guile, so you will not be "beguiled". Don't overlook His Name!
"The art of being wise is the art of knowing what to overlook" ~ William James. (Bad advice).
"The first to present his case seems right, till another comes forward and questions him." Prov. 18:17 (Good advice).
HAS YOUR PREACHER EXPLAINED AWAY THE TRUE NAME FOR YOU YET? MOST DO.

"The Name of ョ Y ョ Ⅎ is a strong tower; the righteous run to it and are safe." Prov. 18:10

Covenant Name:
The Sinai Autograph
The truth is right beneath a false façade. Once again, *to maintain control*, and keep everyone from having to change anything, we have inherited the long-standing custom of only using "generic" terms and devices to refer to the true Creator. Non-specific, general terms were employed to conceal the personal names of Pagan deities, and only the "initiated" would know them. Secret societies still have special hand signs and passwords, and they control their membership with strict hierarchical designs. Examples are the Rosicrucians, Masons, Illuminati, Knights Templars, etc.,. The expressions we are "familiar" with, like "GOD", "LORD", "Almighty", "Eternal" or even the "Creator" as I've been using up to now in this book have all been used in the past to refer to Pagan deities; NONE of them, except one, was ever a name. Everyone who defends the use of these expressions uses the excuse that we are speaking "English", and these terms we are familiar with are "translations". No, these words are not even originally English. The term "GOD" was never used to refer to the true Creator, until Christianity went into the Norse areas in the 6th century CE. The original Hebrew term which underlies the word "GOD" in our English translation is either **EL, ELOI, ELOAH,** or **ELOHIM**. This word *means* "mighty one", strength, or awesome one. This is describing a Being of tremendous power. The Pagans' deities never became angry, or pleased, because they simply aren't there. Even these Hebrew terms are only expressions for "what" the true Creator *is*, but not used as His personal Name. But He has one, and **ONLY ONE**. <u>Adjectives</u> attached to His Name cause people to think He has more than one, but really there is just one; and you can prove it from a good dictionary or encyclopedia. Look up **YAHWEH**. It is only an <u>attempt</u> to "sound" the Name using English letters, and *originally* comes from **four palaeo-Hebrew letters;**

ョ Y ョ Ⅎ
"PALEO" or *palaeo* means "ancient". The letters are written from right-to-left in this original script. It is called "Hebrew", derived from one of Shem's descendants, whose name was **EBER** (Gen. 10). A few generations later, **ABRAM** was born, the son of

Terah, one of Eber's descendants. When Abram's nephew **LOT** was carried off by invading armies, the text says *"one who had escaped came and informed Abram the Hebrew"* (Gen. 14:13). Hebrew is called the *Lashon Qodesh*, or set-apart tongue.

IS THE NAME OF THE CREATOR LOST?

Encyclopedias state that the proper personal Name of the Most High began to be suppressed by the true worshippers, the children of Israel, because of their dispersion among Pagans. For their failure to honor the Law to let the land rest, and release debts every 7 years, ㄣYㄣZ allowed them to be carried off to Babylon for 70 years, beginning in 586 BCE. Daniel's lifetime encompassed this "Babylonian Captivity". The Babylonians knew they were called "Yahudim", bearing the Name of "YAH", their Elohim. To ridicule them, these Pagans began to call them *Yahoo's*. Hearing the Name blasphemed (treated commonly) on the lips of Pagans was so offensive, the Name was avoided completely. Over time, it became an offense worthy of death by stoning for pronouncing the Name aloud, except by a Kohen (priest). This is why Shaul (Paul) was sent out to arrest the early Nazarenes, because this "Key of Knowledge" was being used by them openly. At Acts 9:21, Luke records that Paul was converted, and teaching in the synagogues of Damascus. There they began saying, *"Is this not he who in Jerusalem destroyed those who called on this Name . . . ?"* Then it goes on to describe how they plotted to stone Paul; but he slipped away. Indeed Paul was stoned for the Name, but didn't expire that way.

Stephen's death (Acts 7) came because he uttered the Name, causing the Sanhedrin to cover their ears, and stone him to death. This is also why the other sects, the Pharisees and Sadducees, picked up stones to try to kill the Savior. Carefully reading 3 Jn. 1:7, Jn. 5:43, 17:6, 17:26, and Acts 4:7, 4:12 & 4:17, will give insight to the problem of using the Name. The followers' immersion into the Name and the "placing of hands on them" certainly involved using the Name. The "priestly blessing" involved placing hands on the head, and saying:

"ㄣYㄣZ bless you and keep you;

ㄣYㄣZ make His Face shine upon you and show favor to you;

ㄣYㄣZ lift up His countenance upon you, and give you peace.

So, they will put My Name on the Israelites, and I will bless them." Numbers 6:22-27.
This is the way He wrote it at Sinai, with His own finger: ㄣYㄣZ. The 4 letters are called the *Tetragram*, or **Tetragrammaton**, the Greek word meaning *"four letters"*. The Hebrew letters individually you'll find on the back cover: YOD, HAY, WAW, HAY. Some of the *transliterations* for these four letters have been J e H o' V a H, J a H, J a H'- V e H, Y a H' W e H, IAOUE, Y a H u' W a H, Y a H o' W a H, Y a H u' W a H, Y a H u' eH, Y a H u' aH, I A U E, Y a H V e, and others. (hovah means ruin).
First, we must eliminate blatant errors. Even a rather shallow encyclopedia will explain the error of "Jehovah". The Tetragram YHWH is changed to JHVH, and the vowels of another word, *adonai*, are stuffed into the spaces. This happened because Christian translators' ignorance of Hebrew failed to alert them that the "vowel points" placed beneath the Name were to "cue" the reader NOT *to pronounce it, but say "Adonai" instead.* (The man who gave us the hybrid word "Jehovah" was Petrus Galatinus). **You can easily find that the letter "J" didn't even exist on the planet until about 1520 CE.** The letter is less than 500 years old! " J " came from the letter YOD in Hebrew, and was brought into the Greek with the letter "IOTA", or our letter " I " since they had no " Y ". Gradually, customs developed that put a tail on the letter I when it began a sentence, or was used as the first letter of a proper name. There is no " J " or " V " in Hebrew. The V has a W sound in European languages. The letter WAW in Hebrew is commonly the sound of *"OO"* as you hear in hallelu-Yah. It has the same sound in NatanYahu. Even our " W " is named *double—U* (UU), giving us the symbol of the European double V, " W ". The importance of doing our best to be accurate concerning the Name of YHWH cannot be overstated. You may have already become convinced of one special way of writing it, but remember He only wrote it as ㄣYㄣZ. Later, after the Babylonian Captivity, it became ה ו ה י . The first translation into Greek by the Sanhedrin during the 2nd century BCE is called *The Septuagint,* and in its original, the Name was always preserved in its original palaeo-Hebrew, ㄣYㄣZ. I prefer to call Him YAHUEH or YAHU'AH (ya-HOO'-ah), but I will write it as ㄣYㄣZ. Clement of Alexandria wrote that it can be transliterated in Greek as **IAOUE**, but the original is better!

Because the Name was not to be blasphemed by improper use, it became the custom to NEVER use it. They could not **destroy** it in any way, and that's why they buried the worn-out scrolls in jars at the Dead Sea. Yet, they DID destroy it by not speaking it, and this also violates the 3rd Commandment.

Who Is "The LORD"?

You may already be familiar with some of the "Hebrew" forms like *Y'shua* and *Yeshua*. Footnotes say it means *"the LORD is our salvation"*. If your translation has a preface, it may explain that the translators *"adopted the device"* of using the capital letters *"LORD"* in place of the Name of ⴰYⴰⵣ because it has become the "tradition". I'd like you to look up **BAAL** in a good dictionary; you will discover it means "LORD". To appease Pagans, and not use the proper Name, the generic term "LORD" was adopted. Pagans often veiled the proper names of their deities. The Romans worshipped "SOL" by the names "Deus" (a variant of Zeus), and "Domini" (Latin for "LORD"). "D" and "Z" were interchanged sounds, often heard as a "DZ" sound. The Pagan prophet Zarathustra (Zoroastrianism) called the sun *Ahura Mazda*. "Ahura" means "LORD" in Old Persian, and "Mazda" means "wise" — so it means *Wise Lord*. They were referring to *Mithras*. In the time of Daniel, the ruler of Babylon, *Darius*,

AHURA MAZDA

worshipped Ahura Mazda. **"Ormazd"** is the contraction. Pictured here wielding the power of the sun as a fire weapon, the bird could be a Nazi logo or even the original model for the US Presidential Seal. The anthromorphic symbol used was an eagle, but they worshipped FIRE in fire temples. Fire was sacred, associated with the sun. The torch held by the Statue of Liberty, and the Olympic Games torch relate directly to this. Pagans used eagles on gold balls to illustrate the sun being carried across the sky. The priests of Ahura Mazda were *Magians* (magi, magicians; Greek "magus"). Simon Magus (Acts 8) was a magician, and for attempting to "buy" the abilities he witnessed in the Nazarenes, we now have the word "simony". In India, the sun is called "LORD KRISHNA". We have inherited the term "LORD" from these Magians, carried through other religions like *Manichaeanism*. Augustine, one of the "Church fathers", was previously a Manichaean; a sun-worshipper.

THE NAME ABOVE ALL NAMES

If you study the Writings of the *Brit Chadasha* (New Covenant), you will notice that the Mashiach is called **RABBI** and **RABBONI** (*my teacher*) by the people who addressed Him. (*There is only ONE Rabbi, and we are not to be called such* ~ Mt. 23:8). His Name was given to Yosef (called "Joseph") by the messenger Gabriel because He would **save** His people from their sins. The Hebrew term for "save" is SHUA, while the Greek term is SOTER, and the Latin is SALVARE. So, why do we see the word **Jesus** written in our English translations? "Jesus" isn't a Hebrew name, and has no meaning in Hebrew. It isn't a "translation" either, because it is supposed to mean ⴰYⴰⵣ *is our salvation*. He came in His Father's Name, YAH. You hear the Name of the Father when you say *hallelu Yah* (praise you Yah). You should be hearing the Father's Name in Mashiach's Name also. Encyclopedias agree that the Mashiach has the same name as "Joshua". At Acts 7 and Hebrews 4, where both the names "Jesus" and "Joshua" are written in Greek, the letters in the Greek are the same for both names : **IESOUS** (Ιησους). The Hebrew Name "Joshua" is really Yah+shua. Mosheh changed Hoshua's name to Yahushua. It is seen written in the interlinears as יהושע in "modern" Hebrew, which Mosheh himself couldn't read. It was originally written in palaeo-Hebrew as: OWYⴰⵣ. This later changed letter shapes during the Babylonian Captivity to the "modern" Hebrew.

Our traditions were shaped by people attempting to smooth-over differences. By avoiding the real Name, and using "devices" and generic terms, no one would be offended; but we violate the 3rd Commandment! (You will not find even one instance in the Writings where anyone referred to ⴰYⴰⵣ as "HaShem", The Name). The monks couldn't "monk" with all the Torah Scrolls held by the Yahudim, but they could "monk" with the Greek. For 2 centuries, the Nazarenes held a copy of the memoir of Mattit Yahu (Matthew's real name), penned in the original Hebrew. A copy of it was discovered in the *Dead Sea Scrolls*. I wonder if that was what the document was that made the pope faint when he saw it several decades back. As a transliteration of the above palaeo-Hebrew Name, people have used Y'shua, Yeshua, Yasua, Yehoshua, Yahushua, and Yahusha. I prefer ya-HOO-shua, but I will print it as it was originally written, OWYⴰⵣ. For one thing, Mosheh could read it!

Daniel could read it too, as well as King Dawid (remember, no "V"). Why am I so "hung-up" on the "old" Hebrew? It's the inspired script. Remember at Daniel 5, there was a feast for 1000 nobles in Babylon, and King Belshazzar took out the Temple utensils his father had plundered from

18

the Yahudim ? Emerging from thin air near the lampstand (the menorah?) where Belshazzar was sitting, a **HAND** wrote these words in the plaster of the wall:

ןיסרפ לקת אנמ אנמ

It was NOT written in modern Hebrew. During the Babylonian Captivity, the Hebrew letters became altered, and only the older educated Hebrews would recall the original letters shapes. הוהי chose to write in His own "hand", uncorrupted by human whims and designs. When no one could be found to even read the letters themselves, Belshazzar's mother recommended that Daniel (by now an elderly man) be summoned. He could read it. The words transliterated were *mene mene tekel uparsin* (measure, measure, weighed, divided). That night Belshazzar was killed, and his kingdom was taken over by Cyrus the Mede. The kingdom of the "head of gold" had just passed into the chest and arms of silver! The original script is part of what is being restored in the world today; and with it, the rock of truth in the real Name. Peter quoted the prophet Yah el (Joel) when he said *"And everyone who calls on the Name of הוהי will be saved"* Acts 2:21. The inspired script is our foundation, and I simply stopped making excuses that it can be ignored. It will change everything. Acts 4:12 states *"there is no other name under heaven* (the skies) *given among men by which we must be saved"*. The Name is the hidden treasure! At Yesha Yahu (Isaiah) 33:6, this is clear: *"The fear* (respect) *of הוהי is the key to this treasure".*

Mashiach's Name Altered?

So, what does the name "JESUS" mean? The beginning part in Greek, Iη (IE), is the sound "Yeh" which is a "hail" . It's not "Yah", because it was changed! Now, we're left with the "SUS" part. It may be significant, so I should tell you that the word we sometimes see in the Latin, "YESU" (yeh' zoo) has been traced to a Hebrew word meaning "a curse be upon". According to the *Dictionary of Christian Lore and Legend* by J. C. J. Metford, page 126:

"It is known that the Greek name endings of sus, seus, and sous (which are phonetic pronunciatations for Zeus) were attached by the Greeks to names and geographical areas as a means to give honor to their supreme deity, Zeus. Examples are Parnassus, a sacred mountain in Greece; *the Greek deity of wine and son of Zeus, Dionysus; the Greek hero of the Trojan War was Odysseus, and the Greek deity of healing was Ieusus (which is a variant spelling of Iesous or the Latin Iesus / Jesus). They also changed the names of the prophets EliYahu (whose name means 'my mighty one is Yah') and Elyesha (whose name means 'my mighty one saves'), to 'Elias' and 'Eliseus' (which means 'my mighty one is Zeus'). This was done so often that it later was the basis for their rules of written grammar which followed the common or vernacular spoken language."*

There are plenty of other Greek words that end with 'sus'; like the city of *Tarsus* (meaning *'sweat of Zeus'*), and *Pegasus*. How can we explain the Spanish "Hey-Zeus"? Even the name 'Yosef" was corrupted to 'Joseph', then Guiseppe; but they didn't tack the name 'Zeus' on it. As a syncretism, the Greeks *had* to hear 'Zeus' in the Mashiach's name! If you stop 50 people walking out of a "Church service" and ask them what the name of the Creator of the Universe is, you will usually hear them respond with GOD, The LORD, or *"JESUS"*. The fact is, the word "Jesus" has no meaning in Hebrew, and the closest Hebrew word to the Greek "sus" is *soos, meaning HORSE*. The adversary (ha satan) has stolen much more as you will learn later on in this book. Let's look at our English word, "GOD". It's not a name, because the Writings say there are "many gods". Also, you should know that there is no difference if the letters are capitalized or not, because there are no different-sized letters at all in Hebrew. "Small" letters began with the Greek alef-bet (yes, we even get our word *alpha-bet* from the first two Hebrew letters, but use the later Greek letter names!).

This is what the *Encyclopedia Americana* (1945 Edition) says under the topic "GOD":

*"**GOD** (god) Common Teutonic word for personal object of religious worship, formerly applicable to super-human beings of heathen myth; on conversion of Teutonic races to Christianity, term was applied to Supreme Being."*

This just about knocked me out the first time I read it. Most of my research was done without anyone telling me these little details, I just looked it up. I could hardly stand it. Righteous anger consumed me. Further research revealed that these Teutonic 'Druids' called the sun Gud, Gudh, Goth, or 'GOTT'. In Sweden, Finland, and other nearby lands, they still call the sun "GOTT" in everyday speech. Another related term is *GOTH*, used in *Visigoths* (western goths) and *Ostragoths* (eastern goths—see the term 'Ostra'? It refers to the "east" where the sun rises, and is a variant of Easter or

Ishtar / Astarte). Woden was pictured in some books riding his 8-legged steed in *GOTLAND*. Gotland is the equivilent to Mount Olympus, where Zeus lived in their mythology. So, we've inherited the custom of calling ayaz "GOTT", and His Son Owyaz "YEH-ZEUS". The Rabbi's Name is ravaged, and we call the Father by a Pagan name originally used for the proper name of their sun-deity. And just for fun, they have us calling Him "LORD" which means "BAAL" in Hebrew! What next? Everyone who calls upon the name of GOTT or BAAL will not be saved. You have to prove all things. Rabbi Owyaz revealed His Father's Name to his *talmidim* (students, disciples). A "disciple" is a *student of a discipline.* "John" was originally *Yahuchanon* (gift of Yah), corrupted to *Jonathon*, then *Johann,* and finally just "John". At Yahuchanon 17:6, Rabbi says: *"I have revealed* (uncovered) *Your Name to those whom You gave me out of the world."*

After *Hebel* (Abel) was killed by *Qayin* (Cain), and Seth was born to Adam and Chuwah, Gen. 4:26 says: *"At that time, men began to call on the Name of* ayaz *".*

One Shabbat, Rabbi Owyaz healed a man (see Yahuchanon 5), and the ruling Yahudim sought to kill Him for breaking Shabbat, and calling ayaz His Father. At 5:43, He says, *"I have come in my Father's Name . . ."* Not only in His Father's "authority", but literally in His Name: Yah. As He was entering Yerushaliyim (12:13) He was greeted by throngs of followers shouting *"Hushanu"* the Syraic Aramaic Hebrew word "save us" (Ps. 118:25). They also cried out the Hebrew words from Psalm 118:26, *"Baruch haba baShem* ayaz *"* meaning *"Blessed is he who comes in the Name of* ayaz*".* This vocalization of the Name of ayaz caused some of the Pharisees in the crowd to yell out *"Rabbi, rebuke your talmidim!"* (Luke 19:39). Rabbi Oywaz was spreading the Name of the Father all around — revealing the true Name of the Father to all the world! Ha Satan had stolen it away, and it was being restored! Since ha Satan is still in the world, he rules over mankind religiously to deceive, and has once again destroyed the use of the true Name. "Ha Shatan" is the original sound of the Hebrew words "the adversary". When Owyaz told Cephas (Peter) *"get behind me shatan"* He was simply calling Cephas His *adversary* in accomplishing His mission! Cephas wasn't "possessed". Nazarenes are now re-appearing on the Earth to proclaim the Name of ayaz, just before Rabbi Owyaz returns, with the message of the kingdom of ayaz:

"Repent—for the Kingdom of ayaz *draws near."* Matt. 4:17. Mark 1:15 records these very words of Mashiach's as the "Gospel"; *"The King-*

dom of ayaz *draws near. Repent and believe the good news!".* When the true message or "Gospel" is proclaimed anywhere in the world, an important "sign of authenticity" will accompany it: the woman who came to Owyaz with an alabaster jar of very expensive perfume will also be told, in memory of her! (see Mt. 26:7-13). This must be one of those "real" messages, because I just made mention of her. As I illustrated earlier, Shaul (Paul) was sent out at first by the Sanhedrin to arrest the early Nazarenes for openly using the Name, citing how Stephen was stoned as Shaul held the outer cloaks of the killers (he admitted this at Acts 22:19,20). At Acts 4, Cephas and Yahuchanon had been arrested by the Sanhedrin. The elders of Israel were so steeped in the tradition of not saying the Name aloud, they conferred among themselves saying *"But to stop this thing from spreading any further among the people*(the Name)*, we must warn these men to speak no longer to anyone in this Name."* Acts 4:17. The Name Owyaz contains the Name of ayaz. Acts 4:8 begins their examination. Brought before the elders, Cephas and Yahuchanon are asked *" By what power or by what name did you do this?".* This was to entrap them into saying the Name aloud, as they had Stephen. Cephas said it was by the Name of Owyaz ha Mashiach of Nazareth that a man had been healed of being crippled at beyond the age of 40. When they were released, they returned to the other Nazarenes, addressing ayaz by Name at verse 24, after which the Earth shook. His Name is power, authority over disease, daemons, and a strong tower of refuge!

A CONSPIRACY TO CONCEAL?

We've surveyed only a few examples of how the real Name became veiled or concealed. If it is not known, how can we "call" (Hebrew qara) on it and so be delivered as Yah el and Cephas said we must? ayaz says *"My people will know My Name".* The prophet Yerme Yahu (Jeremiah ~ note the ending -iah in many prophets names?) declared at 23:27:

"They think the dreams they tell one another (made-up words, substitutions) *will make My people forget My Name, just as their fathers forgot My Name through BAAL* (LORD)*".* Lying teachers of the people were misleading them, and their teachings were just being "dreamed-up". That's what "spin-doctors" do. This was during the time the Name was first being avoided, and they

were substituting the term "Adonai" (Heb. *MY LORD*). The Babylonians were worshipping the sun with the name "Baal", meaning "LORD", and were concealing the deity's real name from even their people. It was **DAGAN**, which later was **DAGON** to the Philistines and Phoenicians. You can read about the half-fish, half-man image that kept falling down when the Philistines put the Ark of ᴐYᴐ乙 in the temple of Dagon in 1 Sam. Chaps. 4 & 5. The Ark itself was called by the Name of ᴐYᴐ乙 (2 Sam. 6:1,2). The English word "LORD" isn't even a name of any kind. It comes from the Celtic term *hlafweard*, meaning *keeper of the loaf*. "Monking" with the texts have led to not only doctrinal *"slants"*, but also mutilations and maskings of original words. Some have even said, *"If the King James version was good enough for the Apostles, then it's good enough for me!"* This version contains one of the best opportunities to see what was added, because the words the translators *added* are printed in *italics* ~ but what was changed and omitted they didn't tell us. It was authorized by the Queen, not King James (1611). Translations are **not inspired** as the original prophets were who wrote the words of ᴐYᴐ乙 in Hebrew. Scholars admit that *"of the 5000 Greek manuscripts which contain all or part of the New Testament, every one of these handwritten copies differs from every other one."* These scholars confess that *"There is not one sentence in the NT in which the manuscript tradition is wholly uniform"*; this is due to *"variants put in them deliberately"*, and *"careless handling of the text"*, or *"many created for theological or dogmatic reasons"*. The Greek text itself was being *"constantly interpreted and re-interpreted by each succeeding generation"*. In constrast, the consistency of the Hebrew *"Old Testament"* text which was copied with a reverent fear by the scribes remains without discrepancy in its many copies. They would not change even one LETTER! Since the discovery of the Dead Sea Scrolls, the myth that the "NT" was inspired in the Greek language has been exploding.

DEAD SEA SCROLLS

In 1947, a young bedoin shepherd boy was in the northwestern area of the Dead Sea, chasing after one of his clever animals. The animal scrambled into a cave hole. The boy couldn't easily get to him, so he threw some rocks in to spook him out. The boy heard a loud crashing sound, like a large jar breaking!

He entered the cave, now called "cave 1", and discovered many jars with lids containing old scrolls. He took one to an antiquities dealer in town, and it turned out to be an ancient scroll written in Hebrew! Of course he sold it, and the dealer wanted to know where he found it. The rest is modern history. What you will usually not hear is WHY the scrolls were there. As scrolls of "Scripture" were used in the Temple or synagogues, they would <u>wear out</u> eventually, and were carefully copied by scribes. They would not discard or destroy the worn out copy profanely, but bury it respectfully. WHY? Because these worn scrolls contained the personal Name of ᴐYᴐ乙 <u>written on them</u>! Every scroll was placed in a jar with a lid, and buried. Now the scrolls are either in the Rockefeller Museum, or the Scroll of the Book, both in Yerushaliyim. Every one of them has the Name on them. Since it is used 6,823 times, ~ more than any other word, you would think the "scholars" would bring it the recognition it deserves! But, you will often find these men are "sectarian", or even unbelievers that happen to be familiar with ancient languages. Just look up the word "LORD" in any concordance. The scrolls that <u>did not</u> contain the Name are absent, such as the scroll we call "Esther". (The scroll of "Esther" has the Name in "acrostic" <u>4 times</u>, but it is concealed from Pagan eyes). The scrolls of Enoch, Baruch, Jubilees (Yob-hel), and all the others we call "Old Testament" are present. The Scroll of the Book building is designed like a huge jar lid, like the kind the scrolls were found in. This is a good place to bring up another oddity. What do the Scrolls call themselves? We use the traditional term "Scriptures", which is a Latin-rooted word, from *scriptum* meaning *hand-writing*. The most common term heard is "**Bible**".

BIBLE

The word "Bible" is not found anywhere in the text of the Writings themselves! This is a traditional term given to the inspired words by mankind. The term has been used for so long, people have come to accept it readily.

OWYᴐ乙 never used the word "Bible", nor did any Nazarene after Him. No prophet uttered the word. And, it's not a translation for what the Writings call themselves either. At Luke 24:44 you will be given insight into what our Prophet of prophets called the Writings themselves. The term was (as He said it): *Torah* (Law), *Nebi'im* (prophets), and *Kethubim* (writings, beginning with Psalms). This is shortened to the one-word TaNaKh, an acronym. We use the words "scuba" and "laser" as acronyms (**S**elf **C**ontained **U**nderwater **B**reathing **A**pparatus). A "scroll" is the Hebrew word "megillah". The Bereans examined the "scrolls", which we now call "books". In fact, the Greek word "biblia" means the same idea. But, you know that "books" are just that; books. Of course everyone knows what "scrolls" the Bereans were examining. They weren't consulting the Egyptian Book of the Dead, or an operating guide to some computer hardware. Shaul, imprisoned (2 Tim. 4:13), requests his cloak for warmth, and his scrolls, especially the "parchments". Hey, that looks like they were using a different term than we do today ~ but where am I going with this? First, let's reflect on an important but overlooked item. We attempt to worship the same Awesome, Mighty, Jealous, and Everlasting ﾑＹﾑﾋ that Mosheh did, Who states *"I ﾑＹﾑﾋ do not change"* Mal. 3:6. This is what He says at Ex. 23:13:

"Be careful to do everything I have said to you. Do not invoke the names of other elohim; DO NOT LET THEM BE HEARD ON YOUR LIPS."
(See also Ps. 16:4). Today, we assume we can ignore a little thing like that, and call the days of the week by Roman and Norse deities, even calling the planets by ancient idols' names. If we love Him, we will do whatever pleases Him. He watches us, to see if there is any who understand. He is big enough to hold the universe together, and knows where every hair is on your head. He knows if you care, too. He knows your dreams, and your thoughts. No other created being can know what He knows.

The Origin of the Word "Bible"
This word was originally Phoenician, then passed into Greek, then Latin. It means "books" in Greek, and is only on the cover and commentary text of what we call our "Bibles". It became the name of a Phoenician port city that exported papyrus; so, scrolls, or what we would call "books" came to be called by the name of this port, a city called *BYBLOS*. Don't let the "Y" fool you! There is no "Y" in Greek. This port was about 50 miles north of Sidon, and you'll see it on your maps in your "Bible". The reason the city was named "BYBLOS" is because the Phoenicians worshipped a fertility deity named BYBLIA, and her temple was there ! ! ! See the "etymology" now? Calling the words of ﾑＹﾑﾋ by the name of "BYBLOS" / Bible is yet another trick foiled upon us by men long dead. And you can bet it was on purpose. Who would be cunning enough to pull this off? A spatial being bent against us getting at the Truth, ha Shatan. Diablos is blamed again; but those in ignorance are not held accountable, except for what they know. Designs have been made to entrap everyone in a dragnet of false worship, having no basis in The TaNaKh, or Brit Chadasha. Shaul wept for what he knew would happen, and Yahuchanon wrote the Revelation of ＯＷＹﾑﾋ which clearly illustrated to him how Babylon would

fill the Earth, and collapse on the "Day of ﾑＹﾑﾋ". He searches for any who understand. Without wisdom, His **Torah**, it cannot be understood.
"

In the past, He let all nations go their own way, yet He did not leave Himself without Testimony . . . " Acts 14:16,17.
"

In the past, Elohim overlooked such ignorance, but now He commands all people everywhere to repent. For He has set a day when He will judge the world with justice by the man whom He has appointed. He has given proof of this to all men by raising Him from the dead." Acts 17:30,31.
"

And this message of the Kingdom shall be preached in the whole world, as a Testimony to the nations, and then the end will come." Mt. 24:14.

WHAT IS "WORSHIP"?
The word "worship" is two words, *worth-ship*. It simply means the outward showing of respect and esteem to a higher authority. The key elements necessary are fear and humility, and ultimately **LOVE**. Fear is not used in the sense of terror, but rather respect for another's awesome power and authority. The Hebrew concept basically has always been termed **obeisance**, or the status of a servant who obeys his master. The word "obey" comes from the Hebrew word OBED, or servant; the prophet "Obadiah" means *servant of Yah*. The generosity and Fatherhood of ﾑＹﾑﾋ demands His creatures to return praise and recognition. He has feelings; wrath, humor, compassion, and desires a relationship with each of us. How would you feel if your pet ignored you, and even bit your hand whenever you came into its "space"? But He considers us His children! Rabbi ＯＷＹﾑﾋ even calls us "brothers" (and sisters). The Writings of the TaNaKh and Brit Chadasah show His love for us by providing the rules for living in peace, and it is the perfect "book" of law. It is a "light" for us to "walk" in, and without it we stumble in "darkness". He has literally created us to be a part of His **family**. Worship is something we perform, and is seen as obedience. In the hands of men, this "worship" has become perverted, and we serve another entity, deceived by diversion tactics. Worship is not something we do only one day each week, but everyday; by adopting the pattern of living we see in the 10 Commandments. These are the living waters, and the "food" which ＯＷＹﾑﾋ desired Cephas

22

(Peter) to "feed" His sheep. Today, the sheep are being "fleeced", and are feeding the predators, or wolves, who parasitically plunder them and lead them away from obeying ΑΥΑZ. The parable about the "hirelings" who work in the vineyard while the Owner is away illustrate that they want the "business" to be their own (Mt. 21:33-45). This whole planet is the vineyard. ΑΥΑZ "dwells" in His Temple, His people, who make up the "living stones". OWYΑZ threw the merchants out of the physical Temple, who had turned it into a den of thieves. Instead of being a place of worship and learning, it had become defiled because tradition had turned it into a business.

LEGALISM or ILLEGALISM?

Obeying specific "Commandments" with the thinking that this somehow **"earns"** salvation, or a place in the coming Kingdom, has been called "legalism". This grew out of the Reformation, when the teaching of the Protestant sects based their doctrine of salvation on the work of OWYΑZ and His atoning death. We **are** "saved" by "grace", and grace alone. Yahuchanon 3:16-21 needs to be studied carefully; one should not stop reading at verse 16:

"For ΑΥΑZ so loved the world that He gave His one and only Son, that whoever believes in Him shall not perish but have eternal life. For ΑΥΑZ did not send His Son into the world to condemn the world, but to save the world through Him. Who ever believes in Him is not condemned, but whoever does not believe stands condemned already because he has not believed in the Name of ΑΥΑZ's one and only Son. This is the verdict: Light has come into the world, but men loved darkness instead of Light because their deeds were evil. Everyone who does evil hates the Light, and will not come into the Light for fear that his deeds will be exposed. But whoever lives by the Truth comes into the Light, so that it may be seen plainly that what he has done has been done in ΑΥΑZ." Obedience is evidence of salvation. What is "Light", and "Truth"? Proverbs 6:23 defines "Light" as the **Torah**. The word that underlies "teaching" is Torah. The "Truth" is the "Word" of ΑΥΑZ, Yahuchanon 17:17. Once again, the "Word" is the Torah, made into flesh in OWYΑZ; as if the Commandments, the personality of ΑΥΑZ, became a man and lived a perfect life without transgressing His own teachings. He gave us the "Keys" to the Kingdom: **TORAH**, which produces LOVE. What is love? *"Love is patient, love is kind. It does not envy, it does not boast, it is not*

proud. It is not rude, it is not self-seeking. It is not easily angered, it keeps no record of wrongs. Love does not delight in evil, but rejoices with the Truth. It always protects, always trusts, always hopes, always perseveres. Love never fails." 1 Cor. 13. The fruit of the Spirit, and the fruit of the Torah, produces: **love, joy, peace, patience, kindness, goodness, faithfulness, gentleness,** and **self-control.** *"Folly is joy to him who lacks sense, but a man of righteousness walks straight."* Pr. 15:21. Something that is "legal" is right. The word is based on "logic", and involves "reasoning". The opposite of legalism is illegalism, and that is what separates us from our Creator! You will recognize a tree by its fruit. The 10 Commandments produce this fruit. Although the Torah is a gift and model for living, we cannot obey it in our flesh ~ we need something more: the New Covenant! What is that? When people read Galatians and other texts, they misunderstand what is being spoken of as "the Law". There is the **MORAL** law that *defines* "sin", and there is the **CEREMONIAL** law, that *atoned* for "sin". A life lived ignoring the MORAL law ~ with murder, theft, adultery, idolatry, etc., is doomed to the second death in the Lake of Fire. But hardly anyone would call it "legalism" if they obeyed certain moral laws. The CEREMONIAL law made atonement, but it could not rescue permanently, because it involved animal deaths, in place of the individual dying for the sins. The ceremonial law that cannot "save" pointed the way to the permanent solution: the death of the perfect sacrifice, OWYΑZ. The blood of the New Covenant covers us permanently, ending the ceremonial law. It is the law of "sin and death" that were ordinances against us, nailed to the wood. It was not the MORAL law that was "done away", but the CEREMONIAL law. How then, can we obey the MORAL laws? This is where the New Covenant comes into play! The Old Covenant was the blood of animals ~ the New is the blood of OWYΑZ. It is our belief in the Resurrection, and the reality of it, that we have eternal life. We receive the Spirit of OWYΑZ when we confess with our mouth and believe in our heart that He was raised from the dead. He comes into us, and WRITES the moral law (Torah) on our hearts and minds, enabling us to LOVE the Commandments! You will not live a life ignoring them, because this "change" inside you causes you to agree with the moral laws. The "Law of Liberty" is our freedom ~ not to sin, but rather our freedom from sin; sinning **against** the moral laws (and we don't have to sacrifice animals). Mashiach OWYΑZ really does save His people from sin, as His Name says! The deciding factor is: do you **LOVE** the Commandments? *"If you love Me, you will obey what I command."* Yn. 14:15. When you can say "I love the Torah", He has "circumcised" your heart. Even Daniel, Dawid, Yesha Yahu, Mosheh, Adam, etc., who lived by the moral law could not obtain eternal life by it; but because ΟWYƎZ resurrected, these captives were delivered from the ceremonial law that was against them. Stop and read Psalm 1, and Psalm 119. *"Oh, how I love your Torah! I meditate on it all day long. Your Commands make me wiser than my enemies . . ."* Ps. 119:97,98.

And, my friend, *THAT* is what "grace" is! It is the gift of ƎYƎZ to receive a LOVE for the Truth.

"For it is by grace you have been saved, through faith (emunah), *and this not from yourselves, it is the gift of* ƎYƎZ—*not by works* (ceremonial offerings), *so that no one can boast. For we are* ƎYƎZ*'s workmanship, created in Mashiach* ΟWYƎZ *to do good works, which* ƎYƎZ *prepared in advance for us to do."* (Those "good works" prepared in advance are the Torah.) Eph. 2:8-10. This has stood in doctrinal opposition to "James" (Ya'akob) 2:17-20, who after explaining that lawbreakers (non-legalists) will be judged, says: *". . . Faith, by itself, if it is not accompanied by works, is dead. But someone will say, 'You have faith; I have works'. Show me your faith without deeds, and I will show you my faith by what I do. You believe there is one Elohim; Good! Even the demons believe that — and shudder. You foolish man, do you want evidence that faith without deeds is useless?"* What he is saying is, obedience is not the thing that saves us, but when we are seen obeying the Torah, it is evidence of our salvation. There is only forgiveness of sins against Torah if there is *repentance*, the turning away from sin, and living by the Torah. Martin Luther was used to spearhead the understanding, but there was more to comprehend. The complete understanding became cut short, no doubt because the adversary saw how close to the Truth people were getting. He began his *INQUISITION*, murdering over 83 million people over a 600-year period. The junkpile of history should now begin to form a picture for you, if we are assembling it correctly. Love is the key! You obey your Earthly father as a child, partly out of fear; but as you mature you begin to obey because you love your father, and do not want to let him down. Our Father says, *"Love Me, and keep My Commandments."* We show Him we love Him when we obey. It's not "legalism", it's LOVE. And that is what worship is.

TITHING: *"Religion that* ƎYƎZ *our Father accepts as pure and faultless is this: To look after orphans and widows in their distress, and to keep oneself from being polluted by the world."* Ya'akob 1:27.

"There were no needy persons among them. For from time-to-time, those who owned lands or houses sold them, brought the money from the sales and put it at the apostles' feet, and it was distributed to anyone as he had need." Acts 4:34,35.

Tithing is the area exploited by the predators (wolves), which 2 Pet. 2 calls "false teachers". They are engaged in religion, and teach it. They would establish a precedent of plundering the flock, and introduce destructive heresies (lies) with cunning seduction. *"Many will follow their shameful ways and will bring the Way of Truth* (Torah) *into disrepute. In their greed, these teachers will exploit you with stories they have made up."* You must read the whole context. He even goes on to say *"It would have been better for them not to have known the Way of Righteousness* (Torah) *than to have known it and then to turn their backs on the sacred command that was passed on to them. Of them the proverbs are true: 'A dog returns to its vomit', and 'A pig that is washed goes back to her wallowing in the mud'."* One of the "stories they have made up" is that we must "tithe" to spread the "Gospel", and to provide a comfortable setting (a building) in which to study and help others worship and come to salvation. This is programming. "Tithe" is mentioned at Lev. 27:30, Num. 18:26, Deut. 12:17, & 14:22. *HEY* ~ isn't that "OLD Testament"? You bet, but you should read it. Altogether, tithing is referred to 16 times in Scripture, and is the *"ma'aser"*, or a 10th of the increase used for 3 purposes. It consists of food only, as you will quickly discover. Clearly, Malachi 1:7 and 3:10 show this. Preachers will select their own "parts" of the texts in order to make the listener believe that money is to be collected and "put at the apostles' feet" to support *them* in their GOD's work. ƎYƎZ*'s* message is *repent*, not pay. The tithe supported (fed) the Lewites, poor, fatherless, foreigners, and widows. Shaul, at 1 Cor. 1-4, & 16:1, is also talking about food, to be taken back to Yerushaliyim to those in need. There was a famine, and gold coins cannot be eaten. If a teacher of Torah is travelling and one of us has him stay at our home for a time, he is able to eat from your table. "You must not muzzle the ox" while it is turning the grindstone, but let it eat the fruits of what it is grinding, for sustenance. The ox doesn't cart off a percentage! The Lewites were not able to own land, but performed the tedious ceremonial law requirements we just discussed. They had to eat, as well as their families. If a preacher tells you he is entitled to 10% of your income, and everyone else's income (numbering 100's or even 1000's of people), remind him that he is not a Lewite. A Lewite had to be a descendant of Lewi, a strict bloodline of priests. Also, the ceremonial law, and the need to support those Lewites who implemented it, is no more. These predators are not the poor, through some physical defect. They are not children without a father to support them. They are not foreigners fleeing a famine or war, or widows in their old age with no husband. They must work! I do, and Shaul did, even though he traveled about.

ELDERS MEETING (Acts 20:13-38)
Shaul called a meeting of the elders in Ephesus (a Pagan town, note the name-ending). He was in a rush to get to Yerushaliyim by the day of Shabuoth (called Pentecost), and knew he would never again see these brothers in his flesh. *"Now I know that none of you among whom I have gone about preaching the Kingdom will ever see me again."* He pas-

sionately pleaded with them, and then mentioned the coming in of savage "**wolves**" among them:

"Keep watch over yourselves and all the flock of which the Ruach ha Qodesh (set-apart Spirit) *has made you overseers* (elders, bishops). *Be shepherds of the assembly of ⰰＹⰰ�--, which He bought with His own blood. I know, that after I leave, SAVAGE WOLVES will come in among you and will not spare the flock. Even from your own number* (that group of men) *men will arise and distort the Truth in order to draw away disciples after them. So be on your guard! Remember that for 3 years I never stopped warning each of you night and day with tears. Now, I commit you to ⰰＹⰰ�--- and to the Word of His lovingkindness*(Torah), *which can build you up and give you an inheritance among all those who are set-apart*(Qodeshim, saints). *I have not coveted anyone's silver or gold or clothing. You yourselves know that these hands of mine have supplied my own needs and the needs of my companions. In everything I did, I showed you that by this kind of hard work WE must help the weak, remembering the words the Rabbi ＯＷＹⰰ�--- Himself said, 'IT IS MORE BLESSED TO GIVE THAN TO RECEIVE'.*

Who was Shaul talking to? Elders! What did he know some of them would eventually begin

to do? He knew it would turn into a **business**, and even mentioned the "wolves" I referenced from 2 Pet. 2. There can be no mistake here, because this is a 2nd witness in the Writings to what we see happening around the world today ~ he even quoted ＯＷＹⰰ�--'s words about "receiving", and this quote is never taken in context. Instead, it's turned around and used *to plunder the flock!* The "merchants" are also mentioned in the book called Revelation (Apocalypse, *uncovering*). These merchants have drunk the maddening wine (*teachings*) of Babylon, taught heresies like Easter / Ishtar, Sun-day, and other Nimrod nonsense, and grown RICH from having done so.

This knowledge, when made known, will rock Babylon to its roots. THIS is the "rebellion" Shaul prophesied to occur at 2 Thess. 2:3! This is the exposing of the *Man of Lawlessness.* Study this thoroughly, because your eyes are being opened. All that has to happen is for a billion people to stop paying these men, and it all comes down. The message is FREE. Now knowing this, how much money will you have spared yourself, and be enabled to help desperate relatives and friends? I certainly don't want any of your earnings, nor do I need your "last will and testament" to leave money to print these books. They will be supported by those who buy the truth, and sell it not. The printing and mailing costs will be covered by each book. Reading 1 Tim. 5:7-9 shows your first duty is to your own relatives, to lessen the burden on the assembly of supporting widows. At 6:5, men of corrupt minds think that religion is a means to financial gain. (Read the context).

The "merchants" use Acts 4:32-36 to trick the listener into believing that money is to be collected and "put at the apostles' feet" to support *THEM* in the Creator's work. If you stop right now and read this in its full context, you will see that this "programming" is completely wrong. The support was distributed among the needy among them, and no one was in want. This is just one area where "inoculating" or "vaccinating" the masses of people against the correct behavior is done. It's almost like everyone is under hypnosis. These merchants are businessmen. To steer you away from obeying Commandments, they will say *"We now have liberty in Christ",* or *"We now live in the Age of Grace".* But, they sure want a lot of your money! It is interesting that Rabbi ＯＷＹⰰⰰ-- threw some merchants out of His Father's House ~ He must not like money being involved in spiritual matters. He also once said, *"Give to Caesar what is Caesar's, and to Elohim what is Elohim's".* The government wants your money, and ⰰＹⰰⰰ-- wants your **obedience**. When the veil in the Temple was torn from top to bottom, it signaled the end of the ceremonial law; but the moral law that defines "sin" is still here. To steal, kill, adulterate, or covet was a sin 10 years **before** He died for sin; and they were still sinful 10 years **afterward** as well. We have to have love for our neighbor, so the suffering poor, fatherless children, widows, and foreigners fleeing wars are everyone's concern. Paul (Shaul) wrote that believing Gentiles must support the needy Yahudim: *"For if the Gentiles have shared in the Yahudim's spiritual blessings, they owe it to the Yahudim to share with them their material blessings."* ~ Rom. 15:27. This is quite a contrast to what Martin Luther wrote three years before he died; *"For the glory of GOD and His Church, Jews' synagogues and holy books should be burned and covered over with soil, and Jewish homes should be likewise destroyed".* His writings were used by Nazi war criminals in their defense at Nuremberg. Giving to the poor is the highest form of tithing, yet "spreading the Gospel" is never associated with a tithe in the Scriptures ~ it's just programmed into peoples' heads that way. Luther knew that "indulgences" were just a big fund-raiser, and that their spiritual benefits amounted to nothing. When OWYAZ told the rich young man to give his wealth to the poor, He clearly didn't want any for Himself, nor did He say to give any to the Lewites. A Gentile convert to Yahudaism (Acts 10) who feared AYAZ and studied Torah at the synagogue is another interesting case. He was Cornelius, a Roman centurion, who sent *3 servants* to go find Peter, and the text says he always gave generously to those in need. A messenger (*malak, angel*) was sent from AYAZ and appeared to him saying, *"Your prayers and GIFTS TO THE POOR have come up as a memorial offering before Elohim."* Acts 10:1-5. This is where the *3 sheets* filled with unclean animals appear to our sleepy Peter, to *prepare him* to go with the *3 Gentile men* who were about to appear at his house gate ~ something he would not have done otherwise! The vision of the 3 sheets of unclean animals wasn't about food, but about Gentiles. One use of the tithe is commanded to be for YOU to bring to the place He has established His Name (Yerushaliyim) and EAT IT before Him. If it is too far and or too much to travel with, He says to sell the food or animals, and put the money in your hand ~ and then come and *buy food, strong drink, or whatever warms your heart,* and eat it rejoicingly before Him, sharing what you have with those who have little. The "merchants" must be thrown out of the Temple again; and WE are that Temple. The time has come now that true worshippers in the Truth worship from where they are, not in Yerushaliyim, as OWYAZ explained to the woman at the well. But, we will see the New Yerushaliyim when He returns, and be with Him! Now for the **MAN OF LAWLESSNESS:**

"For the secret power of lawlessness is already at work; but the one who now holds it back will continue to do so till he is taken out of the way. And then the lawless one will be revealed (uncovered), *whom Rabbi OWYAZ will overthrow with the breath of His mouth and destroy by the splendor of His coming. The coming of the lawless one will be in accordance with the work of Shatan displayed in all kinds of counterfeit miracles, signs and wonders, and in every sort of evil that deceives those who are perishing. They perish because they refused to love the Truth and so be saved. For this reason AYAZ sends them a powerful delusion so that they will believe the lie and so that all will be condemned who have not believed the Truth but have delighted in lawlessness."* 2Th.2:7-12. Who are these people who would "delight" in lawlessness, and refuse the Truth? Well, the Truth is Torah, what they call the Law, and they teach that it has been "done away", nailed to the crux. Then, by their definition, there is no criteria to define what a "sin" is, because if there is no law, then there is no way to sin against it (Romans 4:15). Yet, it says at 1 Yn. 3:4:

" Everyone who sins breaks the Torah; in fact, sin is Torahlessness". By stealth, the "seed" (the Word of AYAZ) was stolen away by the "birds", or trampled under the feet of men, as the parable says (Luke 8:5-15). You see, the words in the Writings we read as *Light, Truth, Word, Voice, Wisdom, Living Water, Commands, the Way, Seed, Life, etc.,* are all metaphors for the TORAH, or teachings of AYAZ. *"'These people honor Me with their lips, but their hearts are far from Me. They worship Me in vain; their teachings are but rules taught by men'. You have let go of the commands of AYAZ and are holding on to the traditions of men. You have a fine way of setting aside the commands of AYAZ in order to observe your own traditions!* Mark 7:6-9, Yesha Yahu 29:13. Do traditions we see in the practices of religion have any basis in the Writings? Can you find "Sun-day" or a worship service on Sun-day in the Writings? Is there any mention that the Shabbat was changed to the first day of the week? Tithing is certainly the work of the predators; and the poor, fatherless, and widows are just overlooked. Legalism is some sort of heresy in the minds and words of most, yet OWYAZ said: *"Do not think that I have come to abolish the Law* (Torah) *or the Prophets* (Nebi'im)*; I have not come to abolish them but*

to fulfull (fill-full) *them. I tell you the truth, until heaven (skies) and Earth disappear, not the smallest letter (yod), not the least stroke of a pen, will by any means disappear from the Torah until everything is accomplished. Anyone who breaks one of the least of these Commandments, and teaches others to do the same, will be called least in the kingdom of 𐤉𐤄𐤅𐤄, but whoever practices and teaches these Commandments will be called great in the kingdom of 𐤉𐤄𐤅𐤄. For I tell you that unless your righteousness surpasses that of the Pharisees and the teachers of the Torah, you will certainly not enter the kingdom of 𐤉𐤄𐤅𐤄."* Mt. 5:17-20. These words sound very much like we should be knowing and acting on the 10 Commandments, as well as all the Moral teachings that the Torah has, which build us up and protect us. A rich young man, (possibly Mark himself), asked Rabbi OWY𐤄𐤅: *"Tob Rab (Good Teacher), what must I do to inherit eternal life?"* (Mark 10:17-27) Rabbi replied, "*You know the Commandments: 'You do not murder, you do not commit adultery, you do not steal, you do not give false testimony, do not defraud, honor your father and mother . . .'"*

As I mentioned, without the Torah to live by, AND the gift of receiving a LOVE for them, you are not under the "New Covenant", and have not received the Spirit of OWY𐤄𐤅; so the wrath of 𐤉𐤄𐤅𐤄 abides on your head. Acts 5:32 says, *"We are witnesses to these things, and so is the Ruach ha Qodesh* (set-apart Spirit, Yahushua)*, whom 𐤉𐤄𐤅𐤄 has given to those WHO OBEY HIM."*

The "man of lawlessness" should be easy for you to identify. His office is the "Vicar" (substitute), also known as "Holy Father". His powers extend to any human being who is deceived, and seeks to deceive others, with the heresy that the Torah is no longer in force. Moral law has been **changed** in their thinking. This beast also has a "mark" (Sunday), which you will find fulfills Dan. 7:25, the "change" of the Torah. The "Covenant Sign" of the 7th-day Shabbat, and the annual appointments, were annulled by this beast. Yet, Mashiach clearly warned us not think that He had come to abolish or alter the slightest stroke of a pen, until the skies and Earth disappear. That's my whole world, because if I look up, there's the sky; if I look down, there's the Earth. Two witnesses again. He called them as witnesses to the **presence** of the Torah, as He had when He gave the Torah to the children of Yisrael: (see Deut. 30:19, 31:28) *"This day,*

I call heaven and Earth as witnesses *against you that I have set before you life, and death; blessings, and curses. Now choose life, so that you and your children may live and that you may love 𐤉𐤄𐤅𐤄 your Elohim, listen to His voice, and hold fast to Him."* And, these two witnesses are still in existence, so the Torah we live by is still in force. And, it is our life. At Mt. 4, OWY𐤄𐤅 uses "the sword" or Word (Torah) to resist Shatan: *"It is written, 'Man does not live on bread only, but on every word that comes from the mouth of 𐤉𐤄𐤅𐤄'"*. The "Bread of Life", is what OWY𐤄𐤅 is, the Living Word made flesh; the Torah became a living, breathing Person ~ the image of the invisible Elohim, 𐤉𐤄𐤅𐤄. The Father is in Him, and spoke to us. His body is a new creation now, never to die; and we will have such a body. Our new body will be our "house" or "tent" that will clothe our spirit, leaving behind the clay vessel we now inhabit that must die. It is appointed for man ONCE to die, and after this, the judgement; He will say **"Well DONE, good and faithful servant"**, not "well believed". What will He say to the people who have never responded to His call, or were deceived by the Babylonian Mother of Harlots (and her daughters)? At Mt. 7:15-23, after explaining that false teachers would be inwardly ferocious wolves, Rabbi tells us we can tell a good tree from a bad tree by their fruit. Then He says, *"Not everyone who says to me 'Adonai, Adonai', will enter the Kingdom of 𐤉𐤄𐤅𐤄, but only he who does the will of My Father who is in heaven. Many will say to Me on that day, 'Adonai, Adonai, did we not prophesy in your Name, and in your Name drive out demons and perform many miracles* (great works)*?' Then I will tell them plainly, 'I never knew you. Away from me, you who practice lawlessness'"*.

You can also look at what He is **NOT** saying. He **never** suggests that those who do their very best to obey Torah are to face a charge of "legalism". Shatan's messengers steer you away from Torah, but appear as messengers of righteousness. These also are the ones who look oddly at you when you bring up the real Name of the Creator. Let's face it; the translators carried over the name for the Yerushaliyim garbage pit (gehenna) very accurately, but couldn't do the same for the Name above every name. There is much to learn from footnotes, but you will notice they steer you away from believing you should obey the "laws" that please our Father. Without Torah, the whole world is filled with violence, as in the days of Noach.

ROSARIES

The prayer beads which monks and nuns wear, and are sold to the "laity" in Catholicism, came into

KEEP YOUR EYE ON EAGLE SYMBOLS, LIKE THE ONE CARVED IN THE UPPER RIGHT OF THIS PHOTOGRAPH. THE SPREADING WINGS WILL EVENTUALLY TAKE ON A SYMBOLIC MEANING. IT IS THE IMAGE OF THE BEAST!

their system around CE 1090, about the same time "indulgences" and celibacy were embraced. Prayer beads originated with Pagans, and are very common among Buddhists and Muslims. The Rudraksha beads of the Buddhists have 108 beads, and are sometimes "seeds". The Muslims use 99 sacred stones on their rosaries, and Catholics have 59.

During the time that Spain was controlled by the Islamic "Moors", a city was established called "Fatima", named after one of Muhammad's daughters. The story is that three little Catholic girls met an apparition of "Mary" in Fatima, and this "Mary" gave one of them the prayer beads, to pray to her with. Mary worship had started in CE 431, and kept growing more and more over the centuries. "Mary" is in the news quite often still, popping up in people's houses, or in the clouds. Catholics rally to see her. It is an odd thing, but Muslims also pray to "Mary", because Muhammad married a Roman Catholic nun named Kadijah, and learned to venerate Mary from her. They only pray to "Allah" and "Mary", yet they don't pray to Muhammad. Both Muhammad and Mary are dead and rotting in the ground.

Pagans' "repetitive" prayers are condemned by Rabbi OWYAZ, since He said at Mt. 6:7: *"And when you pray, do not keep on bab-*

BABYLONIAN WORSHIP   Here we see a Nimrod-influenced ruler ringing a hand-bell. In the upper right, you can see the eagle-sun representing Mithras, the Wise Lord Ahura-Mazda. Note the "tower" head piece he is wearing. The deity Baal is also pictured at the top of the relief.

bling like Pagans, for they think they will be heard because of their many words. Do not be like them, for your Father knows what you need before you ask Him." Also, Dt. 18 and Yesha Yahu (Is.) 8 forbid prayer to any entity other than AYAZ. Contacting the dead is absolutely forbidden. Intercessory prayer may be done by living saints for other saints, but prayers **TO** the dead are an abomination. Any contact with "spirits" is a grievous transgression, and is demonic.

ISLAM

The Arabs are the children of Abraham by his wife Hagar, who lived apart from the tribes of Israel, and became Pagans. They worshipped hundreds of deities. The big black "box" now called the Kaaba was filled with images of their deities, one of which was called "Allah". "Islam" means *submission*. Muhammad was born among the Pagan Arabs, and converted to Yahudaism. He was eventually ejected by the synagogue because of his violence. He sought to convert his mis-guided people from their Paganism, but had to flee for his life from Mecca to his birthplace in Medina in CE 622, because the Arabs were dedicated to their idols. This "flight", or *hejira*, is the beginning point in the Islamic calendar. When he was in his mid 20's, he organized a large band of followers, and attacked the Pagan hierarchy in Mecca, and destroyed the idols in the Kaaba, replacing them with oil lamps. A large black rock inside is believed to be a gift from an angel to their father Abraham, and the Kaaba is considered to be the "holiest" place on Earth today by Muslims. "Muslim" means *one who submits*, and is based on the same word as Islam. He married an older woman in her 40's, Kadijah, who was a Roman Catholic nun. It is believed by many that she had been sent to him by the Vatican, who taught him from the Scrolls of the TaNaKh. In these scrolls, there is a different "transposition" of the names Isaac and Ishmael, indicating that "the Covenant" was really with the firstborn son of Abraham, Ishmael. This may have been with the purpose of causing the Ishmaelites to eventually rise up and re-capture the land of Israel from the Persians. After the slaughter, Rome would make her move, which history shows she did, in the Crusades. The "sign" of the land Covenant is circumcision, which the Pagan Arabs did not practice. The Islams embraced praying to "Mary" because of Muhammad's wife's dedication to her. They consider Rabbi O W Y ꓯ Ɫ to be a prophet, but they pray to His dead mother! The "sacred" writings of Islam are called the Koran (or Quran, from the Hebrew word *qara*, for "proclaim"). Their use of the word "Allah" is known to them as meaning *the god*, and seems to be from the word *elah*, which in Hebrew means *mighty one; but it is not a name*. Muhammad instituted Islam's "Sabbath" as one day before the 7th day, or what is called "Friday". The Ishmaelites and Israelites are both Hebrews, and are brothers, yet they fight over the land given to Abraham. The problem is really their difference of religion. The Romans re-named the land "Palestine", a Latinism for "Philistia", the land of the old Philistines, who came there as settlers. They were "sea people".

When we see the Arabs referring to themselves as "Palestinians", they are calling themselves "Philistines", as if their claim to the land pre-dates the "Jews" because of this. Yet, Genesis 21:34 states **"Abraham sojourned in the land of the Philistines many days."** Obviously, Abraham wasn't a Philistine, so neither Isaac or Ishmael, his sons, were either! The Ishmaelites lived in Arabia, hence their name "Arabs". They were the merchants who bought Yoseph who was carried off to Egypt and sold to Potiphar, Pharaoh's captain of the guard (Gen. 39:1). When all of these things are objectively presented to an Islam, they become very confused. They face Mecca when they pray. When they rise up in their "jihad" (holy war), they are sometimes heard chanting *"first the Saturday people, then the Sunday people!"*. The name "Ishmael" means *Elohim hears*. The descendants of Ishmael have lived in hostility to all their brothers (Gen. 25:18). The name "Ishmael" was given by ꓯ Y ꓯ Ɫ to the boy of Hagar, since she had fled Sarah for being mistreated (Gen. 16), and He told her that Ishmael's hand would be against everyone, and would live in hostility toward all his brothers. There is nothing worse than a religious fanatic. They are taught that if they die in *jihad*, they will be instantly taken into "paradise" and given dozens of dark-eyed women as wives. They actually can't wait to die; they strap explosives to themselves, put their children in the line of fire when they instigate skirmishes, and generally seek to kill everyone who will not submit to their "Allah". The objective of Islam is control of the whole Earth, and the extermination of the "unbelievers". They control the Temple Mount in Yerushaliyim, so the focus remains being hostile to their brothers, even though no one is meddling with their "holiest" place in Mecca.

Now, notice the similarity of this image of the beast with the one on page 17. It represents THE SUN, Mithras:

HOLY ROMAN EMPIRE FLAG!

The above flag was modeled after the old Roman Empire flag, and came into use during the 800's under Charlemagne. Most Pagan nations' flags utilize a "beast" of one sort or another, and the eagle is as old as Zoroastrianism ~ being a symbol of Ahura Mazda, or Mithras. The Pagan priests, "Magi", wore an eagle over their chests. This chapter started out with this old Pagan BEAST image. The Egyptians, Romans, Germans, Americans, and KLA cherished this image of the sun, the great Mithras eagle ~ which is a vulture. Soon, you will see what simple image it later became!

Christmas

BREAKING THE TRUTH BARRIER

A Christian minister once responded to a letter I sent him, admitting that there are many traditions within Christianity that were originally Pagan, but he said they are only in the "background" now. Yes, they certainly are, buried under new meanings, reinterpreted to obscure them! He also said that since we don't intend to be worshipping the sun now, that it's all OK. When a person chooses to believe in something, their heart follows after it. Even if it's a lie, or a fantasy, it matters not to them. Prov. 19:2 says, *"It is not good to have zeal without knowledge, nor be hasty and miss the way. A man's own folly ruins his life, yet his heart rages against ᗩᎩᗩᏃ."* Many believe that "Christmas" is in the Writings, with the stable, manger, star of Bethlehem, shepherds, and Magi visitation. Also, everyone is programmed to celebrate birthdays, so why not celebrate the birth of the most important Person ever born? Please bear with this carefully.

BIRTHDAYS

The popular celebration of one's annual birth-day is acknowledged to be, by all authorities on ancient customs, a Pagan ritual from Babylon. The Babylonians served the sun, moon, planets, and constellations, a Gentile practice condemned by ᗩᎩᗩᏃ. *"Do not learn the ways of the Gentiles, and do not be alarmed by the signs of shamayim* (heavens, skies, outer space) *although the Gentiles are alarmed by them."* Yerme Yahu 10.

Birthdays are mentioned in the TaNaKh a total of 3 times: when Yosef was in prison in Egypt ~ Gen. 40:20, Iyob (Job) 1:4,5, and Herod's birthday when Yahuchanon the immerser (John the Baptist) was beheaded, Mt. 14:6. In the situation described in Iyob 1, Iyob sacrificed an animal because he was aware of his children's idolatry, for which they all died when the house they celebrated in collapsed on them in a violent wind storm. *"His sons used to go and hold a feast in the house of each one on his day . . ."* (the NIV eliminated this phrasing, but you can clearly see it in the KJV, NAV, NAS, and others). The baker was hanged on the Pharaoh's birthday, and the Lewite Yahuchanon (our Savior's cousin) was beheaded on Herod's birthday.

THE BIRTHDAY RITUAL

The ritual of the cake, candles, wish, and presents serve to give thanks to sky luminaries for allowing the birthday celebrant to reach the annual cycle of their birth. The cake was baked for the *Queen of Heaven*. It was decorated, and monogrammed with the celebrant's name. The candles symbolized the sacred

IS HE NIMROD?

SORCERY?

Merry Mithras!

fire, carefully numbered for each annual cycle completed. The prayer chant and all the ritual procedures are carefully preserved, and it is a religious occasion. Witches regard the day of one's birth <u>the most significant event in a person's life.</u> Astrologers base everything on it. If the celebrant can blow-out all the candles, then a secret wish made to a GENIE (or JUNO if the person is female) will be granted. The birthday itself was a time of great superstition to a Pagan, so they were surrounded by their friends and relatives for protection. In the Greek culture, it was believed that personal abilities and talents were bestowed on an individual by being "inhabited" (possessed) by one or more demons, called *MUSES*. A person's "genius" was the gift of the Genie, thought of as the overseer of the Muses. The Muses were 9 female deities believed to endow skills in speech, art, science, memory, scholastics, agility, and *music* ~ a word derived from the 'MUSES" (9 daughters of Zeus & Mnemosyne). The names of these 9 Muses were *Clio, Euterpe, Thalia, Melpomene,* Terpsichore, *Erato, Polymnia, Urania,* and *Calliope.* You may recognize some of their names as having become part of our language, like "Uranus". They are the Greek deities of the **Arts** and **Sciences**, giving us the word **museum**, a showplace of Art and Science. The fairy tale <u>*Sleeping Beauty*</u> directly refers to the gifts and benefits bestowed by the Muses, since the Muses were known as *Fairies* in the Germanic and Gaelic cultures. The *"Three Fates"* were a triad of female deities also known as the *Three Graces,* or *Three Charities.* In the Greek and Roman mythologies, they ruled the lives of men, and determined the **length** of a person's life. *"Clotho"* spun the "thread of life", *"Lachesis"* determined its length, and *"Atropos"* cut it. This is the type of idolatry that Shaul was correcting the Galatians and Ephesians for observing, since they were falling back into these patterns instead of exposing them and excluding them from their lives. He told them that they had lived as Pagans and been in darkness, but now were called-out from such ignorance. This "programming" in these practices became absorbed, and people are either ignorant of them, or too weak to break free of them. Their spiritual leaders aren't going to tell them, because they are hypnotized as well. The reason the Writings don't make much sense to people is because they are not aware, and don't recognize their own behavior as being Pagan. Everything has been pushed into the "background" so well, their eyes are "blinded" to the real truth. Astrology, an ancient Babylonian process of worship, was used to determine the "*sign*" under which a person was born. Everything that happened to a person was determined by "the stars". The position of the sun, moon, planets, and stars at the time of one's birth produced a personal "horoscope", used since ancient times by witches, palmistry experts, fortune tellers, diviners, sorceresses, tarot card readers, magicians, soothsayers, and others who dabble in the "OCCULT". The word "occult" means *hidden*. Such "divination" is idolatry: *"Do not practice divination or sorcery"* and *Do not turn to mediums or seek out spiritists"* Lev. 19, Dt. 18:14. Ex. 22:18 says we are not to allow a sorceress to live. *"Let your astrologers come forward, those stargazers who make predictions moon by moon, let them save you from what is coming upon you . . ."* Yesha Yahu 47:13. These practices from Babylon are tightly woven into our cultural tapestry.

When the people of ⱯY⅂Z mixed Gentile religious practices into their lives, He brought the punishments forth that He had promised would come upon them at Dt. 28, and Dt. 30. The severe punishments for idolatry documented in the TaNaKh are to serve as *examples* for us (1 Cor. 10:5-7). *"This calls for patient endurance on the part of the qodeshim* (saints, called-out ones) *who obey* ⱯY⅂Z's *Commandments and remain faithful to* OWY⅂Z." Rev. 14:12. The Sovereign OWY⅂Z commands us from the skies, to come out of Babylon: *"Come out of her, My people, so that you will not share in her sins, so that you will not receive any of her plagues, for her sins are piled up to shamayim, and* ⱯY⅂Z *has remembered her crimes."* Rev. 18:4,5. The great "dragnet" is the calendar we use based on the solstices. Witches have used it since Babylon. Shatan, by stealth, has this planet worshipping him by diversion. By the process you are about to see explained in the following pages, it will be evident (although in the background) according to the plans of Shatan. He is behind the sun-worship customs: *"How you have fallen from heaven, O morning star, son of the dawn! You have been cast down to the Earth, you who once laid low the nations! You said in your heart, 'I will ascend to heaven; I will raise my throne above the stars of Elohim; I will sit enthroned on the mount of assembly, on the utmost heights of the sacred mountain. I will ascend above the tops of the clouds; I will make myself like the Most High."* Yesha Yahu 14:12-14. Shatan will be exposed as the source of sun worship! If it is in the "background", then it's still there.

"Christmas" is really 2 words: *Christos* (Greek), and *missa* (Latin). *Christos* means "anointed", and *missa* means "depart". Both of these words were inherited from Pagans. The Mashiach was never called "Christ" in His own tongue (language). The "anointing" in the Pagan mind was performed by a physician, who carried a wooden box with various ointments in jars. The medical symbol "Rx" is derived from 2 Greek letters, *rho* (ρ) and *chi* (X). These are the first two letters in the Greek word *Christos* spelled χριστοζ ~ anointed. The sick were anointed for healing, and the letters rho and chi were used as a "logo" for the physician's trade ~ hung up as a sign designed to appear as an EYE (the "eye in the sky"). It was the Egyptian "Eye of Horus", which the Greeks had adopted. Medical students learn this history of the RX symbol in their study of pharmaceuticals. At this point, let me remark that the Mashiach never authorized or invented a new "religion", but rather was upset because of changes already made. He said "repent" ~ turn back. This is what makes all this so bizarre. The word Christos is cognate with the Hindi *Krista*, the sun deity of Hindus. It means *shining one*. The Latin word *Lucifer* means *light bringer*. *Kris* means *shining*. The Hebrew "*Mashiach*" means anointed one, but refers to Him as Sovereign or King, as Samuel anointed Dawid. The "oil" (lamp oil) symbolized the power of LIGHT, or wisdom of Torah, poured on the head (reasoning organ) so that the king would rule wisely in the Commandments. The Torah is "a lamp", and a "light". But, you can still see the way the original word was avoided, and Shatan's "shining" was adopted instead. The word Christmas means *"anointed-depart"*, and is seen abbreviated in "X—mas". The "X" stands for Christos. Let me just say this: *"If men originated any word or idea, then be suspicious of it."* Is nothing sacred? The word "sacred" is Latin, *sakra*, and is used in place of the Hebrew word *qodesh*, meaning *set-apart*. Sakra itself traces back to an *Indo*-European language, "Sanskrit", and turns out to be a Vedic form of an India sun deity, "Indra". It came into Old Persian, and in one of its 12 forms is "Sakra". Another form is Mitra, or the

Persian/Roman "Mithras". OK, then is nothing **qodesh?** Yes! The Name of ㅋㅐㅋ is set-apart, which is in the Name Oㅐㅋㅋ. The Word, or *Torah* (Commandments) is qodesh. The *Temple Mount* ~ which He calls His set-apart mountain forever, where He has placed His Name is qodesh. And finally, *His people*, called *Yahudim*, who bear His Name are qodesh. Pretty much everything else is rock, dirt, metal, water, air, and such. The day we call *Shabbat* is set-apart in time, as a memorial of creation, and is in the Torah. The teachings of Torah are a solid "Rock" on which to build, because they will never change, nor can any man bend them. They were made "straight" by ㅋㅐㅋ.

Missa, Latin for *depart,* was the last word spoken at a Catholic *"Mass"*, and so the word for the liturgical procedure *seems* to be from that. It was tacked-on to the word "Christ" because the Mass ritual on December 25th was called *Christ's Mass*. But, even the "Mass" existed before Catholicism. It was what the Pagan priests of Mithraism and Mandaeanism called their *Mass of the Dead*, which was a ghastly "sacra-mental" ritual of animal and human sacrifice ~ on an indoor "altar", with the Pagan worshippers assembled in two rows of benches with a center aisle. The Pagan priest would be at one end of the room, mumbling obscurely, leading the service to Mithras. At the spring equinox, new "initiates" into the mysteries of the cult were "baptized" (sprinkled) in blood, under a bull being hacked to death. This was the time which the Earth's orbit "crossed" the celestial equator. These sun-worshippers interpreted this as *"Mithras **slaying the bull** "* ~ the sun had "crossed" over the celestial equator, overcoming the "bull", which they called the constellation of **Taurus** (Latin for "bull"). Every "Mass" is truly a Black Mass! The Pagan mind "mixed" this up with the Passover Seder known as "the Last Supper", and POOF! *The 'magic' became our Sun-Day morning* "supper". You have just broken the *Truth Barrier*, as I call it. The word *abracadabra* was used during the Mithraic mystery Mass, when they transubstantiated a sun-shaped disc of bread into the sun, and ate it. You can find this out by digging it up in a library. The Mandaeans also had *"7 sacraments"*, among which were *Holy Matrimony, the "Eucharist" sun-disc bread wafer, "Confession", Holy Orders, and the Mass of the Dead itself.* They were sun-worshippers, from which a "Church Father", Augustine, had come from. Are we still talking about Christmas? Sure! There was never an "indoor" altar in the ceremonial law of ㅋㅐㅋ, and now there is no need for any altar. Our Rabbi had to die but once, and said *"It is finished"*. The RCC (*Roman Catholic Church*) hasn't gotten the message. Catholicism calls the Mass a "**bloodless sacrifice**", offering the "miraculous" transformed bread into the body of Oㅐㅋㅋ to the Father over and over. But, Heb. 9:22 says *"without the shedding of blood there is no forgiveness."* At Heb. 9:28, it says *"Mashiach was sacrificed ONCE, to take away the sins of many people."* (see Heb. 10:12 also). He cannot be sacrificed over again! There was no such term as "Christmas" until the 9th century. Going back to the 6th century, there was a time when our "years" were not even reckoned as we think of them today.

Imagine it is the year 525 CE. No one at that time knew it was "525" though; here's why: There was a real man named **Dionysus Exiguus**. Mr. Exiguus was a pretty Pagan guy, but he didn't know it. He was a "monk", and lived in a part of the world called Scythia, an ancient region of Asia, north of the Black Sea. Remember, "monks" are unknown to the Writings, as are nuns, popes, and cardinals. But, Mr. Exiguus had no idea he was toiling as a monk for absolutely no reason at all, other than ignorance. During his time, and for over 1000 years after him, the city of Rome was venerated above every other place on Earth, even Yerushaliyim. The greatest "pilgrimage" a person could make was to the city of Rome. Finally, the opportunity came for Mr. Exiguus to make his journey to this city of his dreams. Upon arriving, he witnessed things that disgusted his devout sensibilities. The people were drunken, orgies were in full swing; ivy, ribbons, wreaths, garbage, and madness seemed to be everywhere. He was exasperated at the spectacle. What did he witness? He saw the authentic, raw and abominable Pagan festival of the winter solstice: **Saturnalia** (also called Paganalia). It was an ancient belief that the winter sun was slowly dying, because it was seen rising further and further to the south each morning. "Sol-stice" means *sun-stop*. By December 25th, the ancient world's solstice, it could be recognized as beginning to return northward, and was said to be "re-born". It marked the time for a celebration that lasted for days. Carved idols were exchanged (dolls), people hung wreaths on their doors, or wore them around their necks (an echo of the symbol of Nimrod, the branch of a tree, twisted into a circle, symbolic of the shape of the sun, and the annual cycle). Hawaiians use a "lai", a circle of brightly colored flowers as a "sacred" religious emblem of protection and friendship. This "re-birth" of the sun came 9 months (a

32

gestation cycle) after "Easter", when the Earth Mother was impregnated by the sun at the "crossing" of the Vernal (Venusian) equinox, when Mithras (the sun) "slayed the bull" (the constellation of Taurus), and the sun moved into the next constellation ~ bringing on warmer weather. If all of this sounds complicated and wild, that's why it was called the "sacred mysteries". The Writings call it *"folly"*. Folly is the religion of fools, and if what they were doing was foolishness, falsehood, lies, and of no profit, then the Writings explain why people will say: *"To you the nations will come from the ends of the Earth and say, 'Our fathers have inherited nothing but falsehood, futility, and things of no profit'"* (Yerme Yahu 16:19). *"We have made a lie our refuge, and falsehood our hiding place"* (Yesha Yahu 28:15). This is why what you are reading will cause what the prophet says *"The understanding of this message will bring sheer terror"* (28:19). The "world" which the Writings speak of which we are to be set-apart (qodesh) from is the "broad road" of tradition we see everywhere, based on folly. We are called-out of the ignorance, and repent of observing "Easter", birthdays, Christmas, Halloween, Sun-day, the Nimrod based year cycle, and so on. But, we don't show "hatred" for people who are still trapped in them, but love. Nimrod, Constantine, Exiguus, and many others **rule the world from the grave** when practices they established are still observed by people today.

A.D. & B.C.

Under the topic "calendar", your encyclopedia will no doubt mention Dionysus Exiguus. When he became upset by what he saw being practiced when he visited Rome, Mr. Exiguus believed the beginning of the "year" was January 1st, as most do today, but we'll explain why that is under **Nimrod** when his truth barrier gets broken. Mr. Exiguus knew that the Pagan festival of Saturnalia, the re-birth of the sun at the winter solstice, had to go. So, he proposed to simply *change the reason for observing the time*. All the customs, the date, and symbols remained in place, but he camouflaged the behavior by declaring it to be observed as the **BIRTHDAY of OWYAL**. . . . NOT THE SUN. To better "anchor" the idea, he estimated that the actual birth of OWYAL had been **525 YEARS** prior to his visit. He imagined that the end of the Roman/Babylonian year of His birth was "YEAR ZERO", making that year our Rabbi's **525th birthday**. He further declared it be the 525th *year of our Lord*. *"year"* is the Latin word *anno*, and *"our Lord"* is the Latin word *domini*. This produced his main contribution to our present numbering of years. Now, we have embraced his estimate world-wide, and have recorded all history

since his time with references to what *year of our Lord* (A.D.) anything happened. There had never been anyone thinking it was the year "524", because this idea had not yet been established. He referenced everything that happened before the birth as *before Christ*, giving us the term "B.C.". Since the time of Exiguus, scholars have refined the accuracy of his estimate. It turns out that he was **5 years off**, and should have determined that year as 530 A.D. You will see this when you look at any "timeline" in the study versions of the Writings ~ the scholars print the birth of OWYAL as 4 B.C. to 6 B.C. That's really very funny, because that means we entered the 21st century back in "1996 A.D.", roughly. But, no one recognizes it; and besides, it's just a made-up date invented by a man anyway.

The real truth is, our Rabbi was not born on December 25th, but during the fall. It has been carefully calculated that, based on the exact time when Zechariah's duties in the Temple occurred (Luke 1), and the visitation Miryam made to his wife Elizabeth, that Miryam gave birth to the Prince of Peace during "Tabernacles", an annual observance given at Lev. 23, and Dt. 16. He literally "tabernacled" among men, didn't He? The years are all wrong, as well as when they are supposed to start. But, even if the world insists on this system, let's look at more nonsense. For years, the media has "brain-washed" the public into believing that the year "2000" is the beginning of the 21st century. A broadcaster remarked, *"This will be the last World Series Game (US baseball) of the millennium"*. He said this in 1999! The *"20th"* century <u>began</u> on January 1st, 1901, and the Centennial Year 2000 cannot be called the beginning of the 21st century at all. If you can count, consider 2000 pennies. There are 100 pennies in a dollar; and 2000 pennies in 20 dollars. To think that you begin your 21st dollar at your 2000th penny is just bad mathematics. The 19th century included the year 1900. Scholars are not deceived by this, and history will record this blunder. I point this out only to show how easily the masses can be led with blatant errors.

The Satanists and Wiccans know more about the concealed origins of Christian traditions, and often laugh behind their backs. One said: *"The Nazarene Barbarian Church* (the one in the hands of the barbarians) *stole the tradition of the Folk* (Pagan people); *what it could not absorb was turned into their own perverse fantasies"* (signed *Cernunnos><Satan*). I be-

lieve evil is real, and the errors that were absorbed are an outward sign of rebellion against ㅋㅅㅋ乙. It is also true that a deceiver (liar) is in our midst, and has planted his seeds (teachings). *"The great dragon was hurled down ~ that ancient serpent called the devil, or Shatan, <u>who leads the whole world astray</u>"*. (Rev. 12:9). Mr. Exiguus was devout, sincere, and had great zeal, but was deceived and lacked knowledge. Teachers have said that it would not be a good idea to change the calendar to the correct year because *"it would just confuse the children"*. Who is the real "kook": the one who ignores the truth and wallows in fantasy, or the one who exposes the illusions for what they really are? Inventing man-made methods of worshipping ㅋㅅㅋ乙 are not new, and He has given several specific commands forbidding His people from worshipping in Pagan designs, or "adding" anything to His observances. During the Exodus from Egypt, the children of Israel imitated the Pagan Egyptians when they fabricated the Apis (golden calf). It had never been their intention to offend Him, but they constructed an altar and were going to sacrifice to Him on it the following day. But, they "mixed" an Egyptian

custom <u>they were accustomed to</u> into worshipping Him. This "calf" had a sun-disc between its horns. It was also the time of year in the spring when a "calf" or BULL image was an important Pagan item. Remember, the sun was in the "constellation of Taurus" (the bull). If something is Pagan, even if put into "the background" with camouflage, then we should be VERY AFRAID of mixing it into our worship of Him. He doesn't change!

Shaul (Paul) wrote to the Ephesians, people who had been previously Pagans, but converted to walk in the Truth (Torah). He warned them in the following texts, and these are the texts which I am responding to in obedience to warn you about:

"For of this you can be sure: no immoral, impure or greedy person ~ such a man is an idolator ~ has any inheritance in the Kingdom of Mashiach and of Elohim. Let no one deceive you with empty words, for because of such things Elohim's wrath comes on those who are disobedient. Therefore do not be partakers with them. For you were once darkness, but now you are Light in the (Rabbi). *Live as children of Light (For the fruit of the Light consists in all goodness, righteousness and Truth) and FIND OUT what pleases the* (Rabbi). <u>*Have nothing to do with the fruitless deeds of darkness, BUT RATHER, EXPOSE THEM*</u>. *For it is shameful even to mention what the disobedient do in secret. But everything exposed by the Light becomes visible, for it is Light that makes everything visible. This is why it is said: 'Wake up, O sleeper, rise from the dead, and Mashiach will shine on you.' BE CAREFUL HOW YOU LIVE ~ not as unwise but as wise, making the most of every opportunity, because the days are evil."* (Eph. 5:5-16).

We must prove all things, to see if they are being done according to the "Word" (Torah). "Light" is Torah, and "darkness" is lawlessness. Ephesians 6 discusses the *armor of Elohim*. We must buckle on the belt of *Truth* (Torah). We must be steadfast, or possess the shield of *emunah* (faithfulness); we must shod our feet (our walk) in *Peace* (Torah); put on the breastplate of *Righteousness* (Torah); take the helmet of *salvation* (Torah); and **wield the Sword of the Spirit, which is the Word of Elohim** (Torah). This enables us to be able to stand on solid ground in the struggle against the lies sown by the rulers, powers, and spiritual forces of this darkened world. Lies, deceptions, and excuses are the storms and winds that blow against the "house" we have built ~ that skyscraper with missing rivets, or the one with rivets. The foundation, the Torah, is not shifting sand. As it is written, so we walk in it. The wise man will build on it as his foundation! The flesh must be disciplined by *practice* in walking in the <u>Light of Torah</u> (Heb. 5:14). This is so that when lawlessness approaches, we will be steadfast. What a rabbi teaches his students is Torah; so also our Rabbi. A rabbi "binds" and "loosens". If a student goes to ask, *"What does Torah teach about this . . . "*, any rabbi will answer according to his knowledge and skills learned from Torah. If Torah prohibits it, then the action is "bound". If Torah permits it, then it is "loosed". Without Torah, a minister, pastor, or teacher is "blind"; and when the blind lead the blind, both will fall into a pit. ㅇㅆㅋ乙 gave eyesight to us, so we would not be blind. Paganism defiles us.

ㅇㅆㅋ乙 gave us the "Keys" to the Kingdom, the Torah <u>written on our hearts.</u> He left us the authority to "bind" and "loose". I do not "bind" anything alone, but with the Spirit of ㅇㅆㅋ乙, we Nazarenes around the world can bind and loose, and we have bound the items being exposed in this book. We expose them as counterfeit worship. For this, we will suffer, and though we come in peace, some will be killed for it. The merchants have too much to lose. We see that "the Mass" in Christ's Mass (Christmas) is really a song-and-dance operation that has been used for well over 1000 years to take up collections of wealth. This

34

"assembling" on Sun-day has carried over into the Protestant assemblies. They carried-over the collections, the indoor "altar" relic of the Mandaean Mass, Sun-day, steeples, the Roman Calendar with all of the "festivals" dressed up in their bright and shiny clothing to disguise Pagan folly. But they left the images of people behind; but this did not keep them from adopting the sign of the "cross", which began with Constantine. And, then some if not most absorbed the "sacra-**MENTAL**" "dispensation of grace" to some large degree. The weekly plundering of the flock cannot be justified in the Writings at all. There is no "law" *requiring* anyone to attend a weekly assembly either, but Catholicism instituted a <u>Sun-day attendance</u> ordinance which made it a "mortal sin" if one missed it. We are not to forsake the "assembling of ourselves", but this is speaking of the 3 annual appointed times (Passover, Shabuoth, and Sukkot / Tabernacles), not a weekly regulation. Even some of these are only binding on males 20 years old or over. Synagogues are places to study the Torah, Prophets, and Writings to educate people, proselytes as well. The Mashiach's real "religion" is called "Judaism", or more accurately *Yahudaism,* the worship of Yah. Many are shocked to learn He is a Rabbi; but it is even more disturbing to realize He is not even a Christian! He never practiced ~ nor does He now ~ *anything* that Christianity practices. He is not a Catholic, Baptist, Pentecostal, Mormon, or Presbyterian; but He is an orthodox Rabbi of the sect of the Nazarenes. The fact that He is about to return and rule the Earth is not a common message you hear, yet we are told to comfort one another with this knowledge, as we see the day approaching (1 Thess. 4:18). At His return, those who died awaiting Him whose names are written in the Scroll of Life (the one with the 7 seals) will be resurrected. Then, we who are alive will be changed; so fast, it will be like the wink of your eyelids, 1 Cor. 15:52. The rest will be caught by surprise. This will be when the elements will be burned, 2 Pet. 3:7.

You already realize that Santa Claus is not in the Writings, but how did this character get mixed into the stew? A character which has many faces to many people, this enigmatic illusion inspires all ages. Ancient Shamanic cave drawings, Pagan Germanic deities, places of cold and heat alike ~ all have this faceless and nameless one in common since long before history was recorded. Or at least the knowledge extends over the sight-horizon of our knowledge about the past. **WHO** he is was passed down to us from a story from the early Norsemen. That is only true of the English world, because other language groups have a shared cultural memory or such a character as our Santa Claus also. You only get the latest "echo" of what the character was, because the last major change in him happened within the last 70 years ~ one generation, or span of an average life. At adulthood, when it is realized that it's all fiction, most continue to lie to their children, and the cycle continues.

The whole objective of Nimrod worship, and the character of Santa Claus, seems to be intended to divert our worship away from Father ⴰⵢⴰⵣ. Even the cycle of Easter and Christmas itself is the adversary's design, so it's really "satanism" in disguise. When a person turns away from these things, other cultural pressures are brought into play, and the name "Scrooge" is often applied to them. As you "read" this book, it is "sweet" because you are getting your curiosity for the Truth satisfied; but as you "digest" it, it turns your stomach sour, doesn't it? Read Revelation 10:7-11. Most of mankind is worshipping Nimrod still, but they don't know it. Incredible effort is expended by most everyone to conform to the adversary's hidden agendas, but they don't see it happening. The whole world is deceived.

There is a war going on against the Truth! The vast majority believe that in the beginning, there was nothing; then, it exploded. Rain weathered rocks, and in solution developed into the building blocks of life, and eventually became biophysicists, who believe they came from a rock. The second largest rock-carving in the world, Mt. Rushmore in the Black Hills of South Dakota, depicts the faces of George Washington, Thomas Jefferson, Theodore Roosevelt, and Abraham Lincoln (each about 18 meters high). If you ask one of the evolutionists if they think the universe could ever randomly create such a formation by itself, over ANY period of time, they will logically admit it to be impossible. Yet, they believe the universe COULD randomly create the actual men depicted on the rock! The adversary wants people to believe there is no Designer, and this helps him because he can go about manipulating us, because most believe he doesn't exist either.

It is possibility that the memory of the "character" of Santa Claus may lead all the way back to Nimrod, the king of Babylon, Nineveh, and all of Sumer. We sure have received plenty of the other "baggage" from Babylon, and it all seems to be closely related. If the historical time of man could be thought of as an expanding shoreline, the Pagan baggage and the Santa-is-Nimrod idea could be something "washing ashore" together from some ancient, single source. The word "Santa" contains all the letters of the word Satan, perhaps as a little personal joke of his. And the letters are only one off from being in perfect order. If he is dangling that, and we don't believe there's a connection, then we might not get the other one he's "dangling" to see if we'll notice it; SUN-DAY.

THE MAGI ✗⍀✸◔◑☾⠫🜍♒✦◌✧ℂ☪☿

"Magi" was the term used for the Pagan priests of Mithras, and they were "magi-cians", who used fire and eagles as representations of their deity. These are Shatanic designs. Ancient Pagans gave us the worship of Fire, "religious" discs, haloes, or circles, wreaths, (*boughs, branches*), domes with an "oculus" in the top, bells, towers/steeples; candle-altars in front of statues; holy water, wearing black, indoor altars shaped like a flat autopsy table; the idea of dead people's bones being a "relic" that contains powers; tea leaves (scapulas); the dates of Easter/Ishtar and Christmas/Saturnalia being exactly the same; "Easter" being the authentic name for the Pagan event itself; Sun-day; Lent (lengten); Valentine's Day; Halloween; Father's Day, Mother's Day, the ring in marriage; rolling eggs on the grass, or fields; monks; prayer-beads like the Buddhist monks use (also inherited by a separate path to the Pagan Arabs before they converted to Islam); Princes on flying carpets and flying Santas; gurus, popes, "fathers", Asherah poles, obelisks, colossus images of dead men; crosses of candles . . . *(PUFF . . . PUFF),*
It sounds like some wild VooDoo doesn't it?
Let's see if we can establish a difference between the relative advantage of having the Santa myth in our lives, or spinning a dead chicken by its neck over our heads. You go first. OK, you imagined that; which of the two gains you the greater advantages? If you're truthful with yourself, they gain you the very same results ~ *nothing*; in the here and now, as well as in the eternal perspective. (Keep your eye on the Torah, and you'll see it is turning out to be a better foundation and house than any other structure around. Names, beliefs, customs, and teachings all dissolve as shifting sand on the beach of history, but the Torah stands like a ROCK.) Let's pause and look at some of the time-traveling luggage we see "washed up" on the beach. The Magi who visited the young Mashiach O W Y⌐Z came when He was about 2 years old, not the night of His birth. They spoke to Herod first, and he carefully examined them to learn exactly when the star had appeared. The Magi were probably Mandaeans, sun-worshippers, and were watching for this star because they were Babylonians, who had copies of Daniel's writings, and probably other prophets'. The reason the Magi paid close attention was because Daniel was quite a famous and important figure among the

Babylonian "wise men", and his interpretation of Nebuchadnezzar's dream had saved the lives of all of their ancestors. They were what we would call *wizards*, and may have been "keepers of the flame" ~ the sacred fire. Remember that these men were also the primary reason the "clergy" wears black today ~ they played with ashes a lot of the time. They were mumblers who interpreted the "mysteries". No doubt "Nostradamus" had a lot in common with them; he gazed into a fire when writing his quatrains. They engaged in "Magi-c". This logically led to the medieval attempt to "transmutate" metal, like iron into gold. The gifts these Magi brought were gold (a gift for a king), frankincense (a gift for a priest), and myrrh (a burial ointment used to glue the wrappings of the body). But, these costly gifts also provided for the flight and stay in Egypt, since Yosef, Miryam, and the Prince of Peace left that very night, being warned by Gabriel of Herod's design to kill the Child. Speaking of "child" ~ any child can show you which day is the 7th day of the week on a calendar. How is it that we adults find it so difficult to rest on the proper day? At Luke 18:17, O W Y⌐Z said, *"whoever does not receive the Kingdom of ⌐Y⌐Z like a child shall not enter it."* We tend to "read through" the printed text of the Writings, looking for deeper meanings. From Kabbalism, there are 4 "levels" of meaning that certain sects "puffed-up" the Writings with, like leavening expands bread. We are warned to beware of the "leavening" (inflated teachings) of the scribes and Pharisees. These men and others like Kabbalists, "interpreted" Torah on these 4 levels: *PASHAT* (the literal meaning of the words), *REHMEZ* (the simple secondary meaning), *DROSH* (an exotic derivative going "out on a limb", straining the meaning severely), and *SOOD* (let's hope we aren't responsible for this interpretation level!). Anyway, if we "strain" to see past what Torah literally says, this might cause us to overlook it. Straining out a gnat, we could swallow a camel as we drink the milk of Torah. Or, we could find that as we correct another on a small detail, we have overlooked a huge "log" in our own ability to see with clarity what Torah says. So, receive the Words of Torah as if you were a child listening to its father. The remark which O Y⌐ Y⌐Z made must have really been insulting to the puffed-up "interpreters" who heard Him. The Pharisees' Kabbalism had "leavened" or puffed-up their self-image, and added much. Yahushua said a child was superior to them.

NIMROD STUFF & THE "SANTA" DISQUISE

We've heard all the nice stuff; but what entanglements do we have with a man who supposedly flies horned beasts through the air at night? Is it about sorcery? He wears a wizard cap. The red costume is recent, but it's the ancient color of fire. Its our cultural color for danger. The costume is trimmed in sheepskins. He descends into a fire pit at midnight ~ the hearth is directly linked to the idolatry of the Romans. The fire was sacred to them, and its place was the center of the Pagan worship of their deities. Our mythology of him comes to us through Angle-Land (Eng-land), and that traces to Holland, and Germany, and so on. The 3rd-century story about a "Saint Nicholas" never had any mention of "elves", chimneys, flying reindeer, or supernatural feats. Even the "Christmas tree" isn't mentioned in the story. Christianity had made no inroads into the northern areas of Angle Land, Hol Land, Scot Land, Fin Land, and Eire Land, until well into the 5th century. If anyone named "Nicholas" existed in Holland during the 3rd century, he was a Pagan who obeyed his Druid priests. In **the 8th century**, a man named Boniface encountered these Druid-led people of the north, and sought to convert them. He saw them bringing oak trees into their homes at the winter solstice, decorating them with gold balls (note picture on page 3). The word "Dru-id" means "oak-wise", because oak trees were sacred to them. This comes from Babylon. At the death of Nimrod, the wife/mother Semiramis taught the young Tammuz to go into the groves (forests) and place a gift on a tree at the winter solstice. This was an offering to his father, Nimrod, who was now the sun. The custom of tying a "yellow ribbon" around an oak tree represents a prayer to the sun. At this point, branches of trees came to symbolize Nimrod also, so decorating Pagan temples and homes with holly, boughs, and wreaths was the custom. The wreaths are branches twisted into circles, so the branches would be associated with the sun. Ezekiel 8:14-18 shows how the women in Yerushaliyim were "weeping for Tammuz", and the Lewite priests (25 men) were facing the rising sun and putting a "branch" to their nose. These customs were called a detestable thing.

"Do not learn the ways of the Gentiles, and do not be terrified by the signs (zodiac) of the skies, although the Gentiles are terrified by them; for the CUSTOMS of the Gentiles are DELUSION; they cut a tree from the forest, the work of a cutting tool, they DECORATE it with silver and gold; they fasten it with nails and with hammers." Yerme Yahu 10:2-4.

When Boniface saw the people of the Druids bringing oak trees into their homes, he **diverted** them to consider the evergreen tree instead, and used it to teach them about eternal life. He never taught them that the tree or the wreath was a detestable thing. People of other regions use palm trees. Scholars call it "syncretism" when a religious or philosophical behavior is united or combined with another behavior. It is a conscious attempt to DISGUISE one of them in the camouflage of the other by re-inventing a new meaning, and believing in it. Nimrod is lurking nearby at Christmas, so maybe he really is Santa Claus too! The Christmas tree ~ whether an oak, evergreen, or palm, is really Nimrod. Shatan is still using the tree to whisper lies to us. When I go out to stores at the end of the Roman year, I walk by many of these displays, and say, *"Look, it's Nimrod!"* I do the same with wreaths. If there really was a real person named Nicholas, and it's not all just a legend, he sure went through some changes. The oldest account of his existence is vague, and of relatively recent origin. His location places him among the Dutch, but as I mentioned, these people were not yet Christians. The date and location for him makes it an anachronism (the time is "against" it being true). In the 3rd century, the people of the north were barbarians (meaning "bearded Aryans"). They were Druids who burned their enemies and criminals in wicker cages over fires, threw wealth into lakes to water idols (like we still see people do in fountains), burned children as offerings to the sun, and placed jack-o-lanterns outside their homes lit by candles made from the fat of their own children. If they weren't Pagans, nobody was! So, the legendary Nicholas couldn't have been there at that time. Another major problem is this: they claim Nicholas was a "bishop" (presbyter, elder). Yet, at his death on December 6th, he had only reached the ripe old age of 17. "Bishop" means *elder,* from the Greek word *presbus,* "old man". I'm not leaning heavily in favor of believing the tale with all these conflicting facts. The RCC honors him as a "saint". How did we get from **Nicholas** to **Santa Claus**? In the late Middle Ages, the Dutch who told the story of Nicholas to English listeners spoke in a very *pronounced accent.* When they said *"Saint Nicholas",* it came out sounding like this:

" *SAINTNI - CHOLAS* "

The English hearers of this took it down at first as *"Santy Claus",* and it took the more Spanish form *"Santa"* later on. You will sometimes see the form "Santy" in old books from earlier in the 20th century.

Irish Potato Blight

The Irish (*of Eire Land*) had grown very dependant upon the potato during the 18th and 19th centuries. The potato was a transplant to Eire Land from Columbia, South America. In 1846, a **fungus** destroyed the crops, causing widespread famine in Eire Land. Vast numbers of people died, and the decline of the population was catastrophic ~ so much so, that the only hope of escape from death was emigration. It was precisely at this point that most Irish came to the United States, fleeing the Great Famine. What they brought to the United States for the first time was **Catholicism**, since many of the earlier colonizers had fled here from the religious persecution of Catholic and Anglican intolerance. These Irish Catholics had the rich cultural background of Druidism, which they had blended together with Roman Catholicism. Their belief in *elves*, banshees, leprechauns, fairies, luck, and all sorts of Celtic Magic came with them. They brought their pumpkin ritual seen as "Halloween", which had been a Druid festival honoring **Samhain**, their deity of the dead. They also brought their "Christmas tree" tradition, along with Christmas, which had been outlawed as Pagan in many colonies. The Catholics in South America have assimilated the cultural background of the Aztecs. Other Catholics from around the world would **not** recognize many things they do ~ and so it is with them in many other parts of the world. Whatever the Pagans were doing **before** became inter-mixed with the Roman Catholic façade, forming a kind of "crust," **masking the Paganism**. The Haitian VooDoo of Cajun Catholics has produced a spicy "mix" of Pagan and Catholic tradition down in Louisiana, where the alligators grow so mean. So, there were no pumpkins on peoples porches, or Christmas trees in America until that **fungus** drove the Irish people to flee their homeland.

Things, ~ like Paganism ~ *go better with Coke.* In the late 1800's, a pharmacist put some cocaine in a sweetened, bubbling cola beverage, and named it *Coca~Cola*. By the 1930's, it was a major business, and had its own advertising department, strategists, and artists. One of the artists, *Rosenblum*, decided to attempt something new. The Dutch/Irish character called *"Santy Claus"* was beginning to get a lot of attention, so he set his mind on aligning the *Coca~Cola* product with him. In Rosenblum's time, Santy Claus didn't look like he does now. The original character was an Irish transplant, coming from people who had based their beliefs on Druid magic, and **ELVES**. The 19th century poem *The Night Before Christmas* had catapulted our Christmas Elf into the spotlight, because the character was so appealing. Rosenblum used his artistic imagination to change Santy

Claus into what we think he looks like today. Before, Santa was no more that 2 feet tall, skinny, and wore green. He had a long white beard, and for all practical purposes he was a *leprechaun / elf* creature with magical powers to grant wishes, watch you without being seen, and so on. He could also do you harm. The alignment with the hearth is another Pagan syncretism, right down to the stockings hung by the chimney with care. To make this night visitor charming, and more human, Rosenblum made him a full-sized man, jolly and plump, to better assume the distinctive shape of the Coke bottle. He also used the appealing red and white **product colors** to clothe Santa in. The drooping wizard hat was a must. The final art work was combined with a marketing message to encourage customers to leave a bottle of Coke near the hearth when he visits at midnight, Christmas Eve. Now you know why little children say, *"But how can Santa fit down our chimney, isn't he too big?"* Yes, he is now, but they tell the children that Santa has magical powers. When he was less than 2 feet tall, he could fit into many such tight squeezes. The moral implications of telling an outright lie to your own children also has an effect on them later in life. It perpetuates the lie for generations down the line, and cripples them for life regarding believing in things they cannot see ~ such as an unseen Creator. Lying to them about Santa certainly isn't going to help them believe. Who is the father of lies? If you put up a tree, hang stockings by the fireplace, and exchange gifts this coming Roman December, watch for the mistletoe. It's poisonous, and a Pagan spell surrounds its ritual use too. It is just a parasite to a tree (like any government is to its citizenry), but the custom of hanging it up and collecting kisses comes from Druidism. To sprinkle a little "salt" on this whole scheme, there may be a more realistic connection to "Saint Nicholas" that is rooted in the real world. At Rev. 2:15, there is a reference to "Nicolaitans". The messenger to the assembly at Pergamum was to carry a warning about the teachings of "Balaam" that they embraced. *"**Likewise you also have those who hold to the teaching of the NICOLAITANS. Repent therefore!**"* It has been said that these were a sect of religious teachers who *"lorded over the laity"* ~ which is what "Nicolaitan" means. I smell Nimrod all over this, don't you? I don't get the impression that OWYᴈᴢ likes us to mix up our worship of Him with Pagan designs, or wants us to have any contact with it. Light and darkness cannot be mixed.

38

JUDGING OTHERS

As an interlude, let me remind you that as I write this information, I am not condemning or criticizing PEOPLE, but rather exposing the **facts** about why we see them performing the Pagan "format". They were set up; it had me in it's grips, and I am just as easily overwhelmed as anyone. The Torah provides us the Light to enable us to **see** what we're doing, right or wrong. We must NOT look down on others, call them fools, or feel superior because we have the eyesight to see. They may be "blind", at the moment, but now you have the responsibility to tell them the truth. It must be done in a gentle, loving way, otherwise they will be repelled. We must help them to see we do not judge **them**, but rather the customs they have embraced since childhood. The Torah does the judging: *"**For the Word** (Torah) of ᴀΥᴀᴢ is living and active. Sharper than any double-edged sword, it PENETRATES even to dividing soul and spirit, joints and marrow; IT JUDGES THE THOUGHTS AND ATTITUDES OF THE HEART. Nothing in all creation is hidden from ᴀΥᴀᴢ's sight. Everything is uncovered and laid bare before the eyes of Him, to Whom we must give account."* Heb. 4:12,13. I am sure some of you have read that, and it just went past your comprehension. It sounded profound. But now, you can read ANY of the Writings, and comprehend, because His Name has unlocked the secret. *"He who scorns instruction will pay for it, but he who respects a command is rewarded. The teaching of the wise is a fountain of life, turning a man from the snares of death."* Prov. 13:13,14. The Torah is Wisdom (note the feminine-ending as in Sarah). If we "rank" ourselves above others because of their impairments, lack of knowledge, education, race, or poverty, we show contempt for their maker. (Prov. 14:31). ᴀΥᴀᴢ says He HATES certain things: **haughty eyes, a lying tongue, hands that shed innocent blood, a heart that devises wicked schemes, feet that are quick to rush into evil, a false witness who pours out lies, and a man who stirs up dissension among brothers.** Prov. 6:16-19. He also says at Mal. 2:16, *"I HATE DIVORCE".* Let's not go there, OK? Patch up those differences. When a sack of mud (ourselves) becomes angry and filled with pride, we are not very fun to be around. Identify your real enemy! It's not your spouse, but the powers of evil in this world. ᴀΥᴀᴢ seeks righteous offspring, and divorce is not the way to accomplish that. The adversary "divides" and conquers. A kingdom, or marriage, divided against itself, cannot stand.

Now you know a little more about potatoes than you may have before, and how relatively quickly "Santa Claus" rose up and launched into everyone's lives because of the lack of those potatoes. The Germanic term, *"Kris Kringle"* means "Christ Child" - you can see the word "kris" (shining) is right there in the forefront. "Kringle" is a mangling of the word **kindl**, and is the root for "kinder-garten". The vagueness of who this "shining child" really is should cause you to be suspicious. No doubt it is Nimrod "re-born". Nicholas, Nicolaitans, and Nimrod all begin with the same letter, so maybe it is a loose thread pointing to the origin. The Pagan's "shining child" was the re-born sun at the winter solstice. Did you know that "St. Nick" is a popular euphemism for "satan"? One preacher on a radio program once commented that if you removed all the Pagan components from Christianity, there would be absolutely NOTHING LEFT to do. It would vaporize.

THE DRUIDS

The Terror Continues !!!

The word *Germani* originally was the name for a Celtic tribe of Druids, and now is the name of a country, Germany. The Norsemen, such as Vikings, Picts, and even King Arthur were Pagans. The wizard/sorcerer Druid dude *"Merlin"* certainly wasn't trying to convert Camelot to Christianity. The Hollywood versions of history are often *anachronistic* (going against the timeframe). Life for a Pagan under the Druids was like a nightmare. Parents had to endure risking their children's lives because the Druids demanded sacrifices. Children were made to stand in a large **circle** with marker stones, with a tall oak pole at the center. At sunrise, the shadow of the pole would fall upon a single child. This child was tied-up and burned alive on a "bone-fire" (now bonfire), and the charred bones were buried under the stone marker. Given the 2 solstices and 2 Equinoxes, this stone circle with the oak pole shadows produce a familiar symbol: the "peace" sign. This is one of the religious symbols of the Druids, dating back at least 2200 years. The term "Yule Log" means "child log". The Celts have name prefixes like "Mc" and "Mac", which both mean *son of,* which indicated a person was the *son of Donald,* or *son of Kensey.* An "O" prefix meant *grandson of.* Another Celtic/Aryan prefix that indicated a person was an illegitimate child was *"Fitz".* It was common, and when they called someone "Fitz", they were calling them "bastard".

WHY POSTING THE 10 COMMAND-
MENTS IS A PROBLEM FOR THEM:
THEY NEVER COME OUT AND DISCUSS
THE CORE PROBLEM AT ALL, THAT
BEING THE CONFLICT IT CAUSES WITH
<u>EVOLUTION</u>. THE 4TH COMMANDMENT,
BEING OUR DAY OF REST AS A COM-
MEMORATION OF YHWH'S REST AFTER
6 DAYS OF CREATION, COLLIDES WITH
THE GOVERNMENT'S RELIGION THAT
TEACHES <u>THE UNIVERSE CREATED
ITSELF</u>.
"FOR IN 6 DAYS <u>YHWH</u> MADE THE HEAVENS
AND THE EARTH, THE SEA, AND ALL THAT IS IN
THEM, BUT HE RESTED ON THE SEVENTH
DAY — THEREFORE YHWH BLESSED THE
SABBATH DAY AND MADE IT QODESH."
— SHEMOTH/EX. 20:11

HALLOWEEN

(Source material from YNCA, address given in the back). The
two Celtic words *Hallowed Eve-
ning* came from **All Hallowed's
Ev'n**, and now we call it
"Halloween". This is now even

more popular than Easter, and
rivals Christmas. The roots of this festival come to
us from Druid demon worship. Witches were said
to fly brooms over the crops to "teach" them how
to grow. It was a fertility myth. When the first Roman Catholic missionaries encountered these
Druids, they met stubborn resistance because the
inhabitants of Angle Land, Sweden, Neder Land,
northern Germany, Fin Land, and Eire Land were
very nationalistic. The ritual we embrace as Halloween was originally called the Feast of the
Dead, **Samhain** (pronounced *Sa-ween*), and was
on November 1st. These pre-Christian Druids had
the barbarians doing ghastly things. It was a
dreaded occasion, since it was thought that time
stood still, and the souls of the dead walked the
land. Gifts, especially food, were left outside for
these roaming ghosts, with the hope that no harm
would come to the households. The Druids chose
certain children to be burned alive on "bone-fires",
as offerings to the sun. Parents tied yellow ribbons
around oak trees as prayers to the sun to have
their children spared. The fat left over from the
child was fashioned into a candle, and placed into
a carved-out pumpkin, or a hollowed out vegetable
with a "round" (sun-shaped) design. The victim
was called *Jack-of-the-lantern*. Prisoners and
unliked people were burned alive in wicker cages
shaped in the form of animals, hung from trees. All
of this was ultimately to pay homage to the sun,
Woden, or *Odin*. As you now know, this Druid
deity gives us our name for the 4th day of the
week: *Woden's Day*.

FROM SAMHAIN TO ALL SAINTS

Without forcing the Pagans to drop their practices but accept Christianity, the RCC merely
made allowances to accommodate the barbarians,
and called it *"acculturation"*. They *"sanctified"* the

STONEHENGE

Pagan rituals by absorbing and camouflaging
them. In the 7th century, the *Pantheon* at Rome
was extracted from the barbarians, and made
into a *"cathedral"* (Greek, *kathedra,* meaning
seat, or throne). "Pan Theon" means *All Gods*.
They re-named it the **Church of the Blessed
Virgin and ALL MARTYRS**. Thus, it changed
from the worship of *"All Gods"* (Pantheon) to
the center for honoring *"All Saints"*. The day
chosen to honor all the "hallowed" saints was
first observed on the evening of May 13, and
was known as *All Hallows Festival.* This festival
was officially authorized in 835 CE by pope
Gregory IV after it was moved to November
1st, to *coincide* with the festival of *Samhain.* It
began on the evening of October 31st, which
was called *All Halloweds Eve.* "Saints" in Hebrew is the word *"QODESHIM"* based on the
word *qodesh,* meaning set-apart. A "qodeshi" is
a living person, and they don't need the RCC to
"canonize" them after they die to be a "saint".
"Qodesh" has been translated to the word
"holy" and *"hallowed"* which really means
"haloed". Pagans used yellow nimbuses and
floating gold "hoops" in stone carvings, paintings, and stain-glassed windows, as well as
statues ~ to identify their deities and founders
as being inhabited by the sun. When you see a
"halo" about the head of someone in real life,
it's probably ball lightning. But, in any case, get
away from them! The translation "Holy Spirit"
comes from the original Hebrew *ruach ha
qodesh,* the set-apart Spirit. "*Ruach*" is the
Hebrew word for *wind,* and it is the presence of
the helper, OWY∃Z in Spirit. He is not a
Haloed Spook, and after His resurrection dis-
tinctly said He was not a ghost. He first sent
His RUACH to the Nazarenes gathered in the
Temple on the 50th day from the count from
the day after Shabbat to the day after the 7th
Shabbat, now called "Pente-cost" (Greek for
count fifty). This was the annual appointed time
(Lev. 23, Dt. 16) which commemorated the
giving of the Torah at Sinai. It is really called

Shabuoth, meaning *weeks.* The Torah was <u>written on the hearts</u> of the Nazarenes, fulfilling the prophesied "New Covenant" (Yerme Yahu 31, Heb. 8:10).

MYTHOLOGY

A thesaurus will tell you that mythology is the study of fictional traditions, fables, or imaginary stories which sometimes originate from prehistoric times. To keep the Nazarenes from being deceived, our old Pharisee / Nazarene brother Shaul wrote an important letter to his younger pupil Timothy. In the letter, he told Timothy that things were going to be really depraved later on. *"I give you this charge* (order, command)*: Preach the Word* (Torah). *Be prepared IN SEASON, and out of SEASON* ("in season" means during the <u>appointed times</u> declared for assemblies at Lev. 23 & Dt. 16, which were *"done away"* by Constantine, fulfilling Dan. 7:25)*. Correct, rebuke, and encourage ~ with great patience and careful instruction. <u>For the time will come when men will not put up with sound doctrine</u>* (teaching)*. Instead, to suit their own desires, they will gather around them a great number of teachers to say what their itching ears want to hear. They will turn their ears away from the Truth* (Torah) *and turn aside to MYTHS."* (Read all of 2 Timothy, especially chapters 3 & 4).

HEAVEN ~ and the myth of going there.

The word "heaven" stands in place of the original inspired Hebrew word *SHAMAYIM.* This means the skies, or even our modern term *outer space.* It was also used as a customary substitution for the Name of ᴧYᴧZ ~ perhaps to keep from offending Yahudim who considered it "profaning" or "blaspheming" the Name to utter it aloud. All the family of beings created by ᴧYᴧZ are named by the Name of ᴧYᴧZ. He has set His Name upon those He has "called-out" from Babylonian practices, and given them the Family Name, "Yahudim". Israel's wife Leah named her 4th child *Yahudah,* meaning *"worshipper of Yah".* Daniel 9:19 shows also how His people bear His Name. "Yahudah" was corrupted to "Judah", then "Jude", and for the last several hundred years the word "JEW" has come into use. I guess you'll have to answer "yes" if anyone asks you if you are a "JEW". But, will anyone *"go to Heaven"* when they die, or in the resurrection? You will only find the idea of *"the Kingdom of Heaven"* written in the Writings, and this is really referring to the *world-to-come,* the "Reign / Kingdom of ᴧYᴧZ". He fills the Universe, but says His Throne will be in the New Yerushaliyim. Yerushaliyim means *foundation of peace.* "UR" or "IR" means "city", so it also means *city of peace.* The site was at first inhabited by Pagans, and was called "Yebus". They were moon worshippers, but all the Pagans knew about

the TRUE creator ᴧYᴧZ. They simply chose to have fun in their own way. The occupants of "Jericho" knew that the people of ᴧYᴧZ were coming, and their deities wouldn't be able to help them.

The "New Yerushaliyim" will be coming down from the skies, and the meek will inherit the Earth. There is not even a hint in the Writings that anyone will be going to anywhere in the skies. We will be "caught up" and gathered to be with OWYᴧZ ~ but we will not be living anywhere in the sky. Even the dead will be raised, but if they are already "in heaven" with Him, then why are they only then being gathered to Him? They will "sleep" until He returns. Yerushaliyim will be a city of peace, but it will receive a new name: "ᴧYᴧZ Shammah" (YHWH is there). The Earth will be restored, and those who obey the living water that flows from the city (Torah) will enter it. The Kingdom of outer space will be established on Earth among men, with the Throne of the Creator here. The High Priest (Kohen Gadol) ~ a "Jewish" (Yahudi) Rabbi, will be seated on the Throne. So, the dead saints (qodeshim), and the Nazarenes who follow OWYᴧZ, will be here on Earth clothed in immortality.

"Most of us ask for advice when we already know the answer, but we want a different one." Ivern Ball

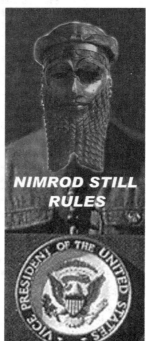

NOTE THE EAGLE EMBLEM; SAME OLD EMBLEM OF MITHRAS. IT JUST DOESN'T SEEM TO EVER GO AWAY, DOES IT?

NIMROD STILL RULES

THE EAGLE: THE SYMBOL OF
THE SUN-SPIRIT; LATIN: *AQUILA.*
HEBREW: *NESHER.   LOOK IT UP
IN A GOOD RESOURCE, AND YOU
WILL DISCOVER IT IS A MEMBER
OF THE VULTURE FAMILY, AND A
BIRD OF PREY.*

WHAT HAPPENS WHEN YOU DIE?

Pagans always believed they would go into the skies to live with their deities. Wizards and magicians have struggled to defeat death, but failed. The Egyptians went to great lengths to ensure that the dead were provided for, and did so according to their "Book of the Dead". Houdini promised to escape and return to the world, but hasn't. A young boy named Eutycus (Acts 20:9) fell and died, a young girl was raised up from her deathbed (Mark 5), and Lazarus was called out of his tomb after several days (Yn. 11). Where did their spirits go? Nowhere! Their spirits were there, but their flesh was unable to walk again under the sun without <u>supernatural</u> help from their creator. El Yahu (Elijah) was used (1 Kings 17:22) to restore the life to a widow's son by the power of ayaz. Those people died twice! The new creation that we will be will not be flesh like we have now, but like the spiritual body Rabbi OWYaz has ~ He is the foremost, first born of a new thing that ayaz is doing. You shouldn't, but if your body is turned to ashes and spread over the ocean, the Creator ayaz will still bring you back.

The parable of the 10 virgins explains that as they waited for the Bridegroom, they all fell "asleep". This means their bodies died. When the "midnight cry" is uttered, "Come out to meet Him", they raise in imperishable spiritual bodies. When we die, we fall asleep. No matter how much time passes, it will be as if we are re-awakening immediately when we are re-born, clothed with immortality. It will seem like no time passed at all. Your spirit doesn't occupy any space at all. A neurologist once said that the human brain is such a sensitive and well designed thing, that it could be operated by a "ghost". It is, in fact, an instrument that we are all equipped with that represents the most sophisticated machine that exists in the universe. Our "life" ~ the nephesh, or breath of life, keeps our body alive, as any animal. We have a spiritual component, created a little inferior to the malakim (angels, messengers, watchers). It cannot be destroyed, except by ayaz. At Luke 12:5, OWYaz told us not to fear those who kill the body, but rather He who can destroy the "real" you in the "lake of fire" (yam esh). You don't want

to get thrown into His garbage can. That's the point, and this points us to the Torah. You cannot inherit eternal life without it, and you cannot obey without the New Covenant ~ having OWYaz come in and write Torah on your heart. You cannot receive Him, and not receive the love for His Torah. *"Multitudes who sleep in the dust of the Earth will awake; some to everlasting life, others to shame and everlasting contempt. Those who are WISE will shine like the brightness of the skies, and <u>those who lead many to righteousness</u>, like the stars for ever and ever."* (Dan. 12:1-4). This means they will endure like the stars, unchanging. If they were already in a place called "heaven", then they wouldn't be "asleep", or coming from heaven, would they? So, if your "pastor" tells you your dead family members are "in heaven with the LORD", kindly remind him what the Writings say. If you really want to stand out, wear white to funerals.

"Let us hear the conclusion of the whole matter; Fear ayaz <u>and keep His Commandments</u> for this is the duty of man." Eccl. 12:13.

The dead know nothing of what goes on in the world after they are gone, but their spirit sleeps. *"If there is a natural body, there is also a spiritual body."* 1 Cor. 15:44. Reading 1 Cor. 15:12 forward will help you see that after the natural body dies, it will be raised later as a spiritual body, and that flesh and blood <u>cannot inherit</u> the kingdom of ayaz. Some teach that a belief in an "immortal soul" is heresy, and a myth that comes from Paganism. It is more important to note what Pagans taught about the "spirits" of the dead being transported to "heaven". That is the heresy that has been accepted. If when we die our life goes to oblivion, then we are no different than a dead dog. It is the reality of the resurrection of OWYaz that we are alive in our spirit. Our spirit is living because of His life in us, so that He may be all in all. At the time the dirt is being thrown on us, we have His seed in us, and He will "clothe" us in a new spiritual body at the resurrection of the saints. This is not heresy; but ignorance of ayaz is shameful. Everyone who believes and is immersed in His Name will be saved.

I'M NOT INFALLIBLE! Just for the record, let me say that I'm learning ~ I haven't nearly arrived at "all truth", and some things I'm saying in this book you <u>must verify</u>. Most are plain facts, which can easily be proven from dictionaries and encyclopedias. Others will require specialized tools like Hebrew lexicons or historical documents. You will only be convinced by personal research, and you <u>should</u> question

42

NOTE THE POLE IN CENTER

SCANDINAVIAN SOLSTICE FESTIVAL AROUND BONFIRE WITH CRUX-POLE

CIRCLE (KUKLUX) KLAN SERVICE TO FIRE CRUX, SYMBOL OF WODEN

basic statements, no matter what their source is, including this one. If I have a personal opinion about a topic, I'll try to be sure to mention is only my opinion ~ and you are welcome to have a different opinion! But, opinions are best when founded on a great deal of evidence.

Things like evolution are opinions, often "decided" on with very little personal research. It is my opinion that frogs only turn into princes in fairy tales.

The "evolution" of Paganism into Christianity (by men) is on display in this book, but the "evolving" of monkeys into people is not. While we're discussing it, the theory of evolution really comes apart when the fossil record is examined from the standpoint that much of the paleontology is really only proving that the **Great Flood** actually occurred. The "layers" of animals show that the larger, more mobile creatures fought to survive the flood better than the smaller, less mobile ones. The smaller critters are naturally on the <u>bottom</u> layers, being the first to get washed away. Often, the so-called "layers" spanning hundreds of thousands of years (ha-ha) will have an upside-down tree, roots-up, penetrating the "layers" for several meters. Also, isn't it interesting that the ancient world had millions of species of plants and animals, and this **total** quantity of species has been continuing to decline in number over

time? No new species are appearing now, and what is here has *always* been here from the fossil record after their kinds. If evolution were true, then there should be MORE species as time progresses, not less and less! Every year, thousands of species become extinct, and **no** new ones are ever seen emerging. At this rate, it won't be long before no species exist, and this doesn't follow the "evolutionary" model very well, now does it? An evolutionist will say that it takes many tens of thousands of years to witness an emerging specie, but it seems that it doesn't take very long to witness the demise of *thousands* of species. They will say these are nature's "experiments"; but again, the total *number* of species is <u>dwindling</u>, not getting larger. If something doesn't make sense, then you should suspect that something is wrong. What makes sense is the original quantity of species were created, and are slowly becoming extinct over time.

How does this relate to "Christ-Mass"? Well, underlying Paganism *turned into something else.* Ancient Nimrod-oriented customs *adapted* because they were already <u>socially-accepted</u>, and "Christmas" is only the surface crust on the old winter solstice festival. "Sun-Day" is another adaptation, as is Easter and Halloween. Nimrod turned into Santa (Satan?). How much of the "smoke-screen" we accept is based on how much we want to <u>conform</u> to the "world" around us.

"He will be successful until the time of wrath is completed, for what has been determined must take place." ~ DAN. 11:36

The Roman Beast

Caesar, Pope, Time Setters
(Watch for "eagle-beast" insignia)

Historians say that Constantine was not of the royal family of Caesars, and Daniel 11:21 refers to such a person. Beginning in the record of Daniel chapter 10, an un-named Being visits him, and His dissertation continues to the end of Daniel's writings. You may be able to guess Who this was. He described many things, including the destruction of the Temple in 70 CE (11:31). At Dan. 11:28-30, an **EVIL KINGDOM** is described that vents its fury against the "Qodesh Covenant" (the Torah, or marriage covenant between ЭYЭ⅂ and His bride, Yisrael). Obviously, this effort was led by Shatan. Any effort brought **against the Covenant** is led by the same. Daniel records the words of the Being, which seem to refer to the "sealed message" called the Gospel:

"Go your way, Daniel, because the words are closed up and sealed until the time of the end. Many will be purified, made spotless and refined, but the wicked will continue to be wicked. None of the wicked will understand, but those who are wise will understand." 12:9,10. This "Being" is described by Daniel (10:4,5), and is identical to the One described by Yahuchanon at Rev. 1:12-16. Of course it was the same Person, OWYЭ⅂. Yahuchanon writes that the reason he was imprisoned on Patmos was because of the **"Word of ЭYЭ⅂"** (the Torah, Covenant), and the **"Testimony of OWYЭ⅂"** (the message, *"Repent, for the Reign of ЭYЭ⅂ draws near"*) - 1:9. One of the biggest stumbling blocks for those who observe "Sun-day" as the "LORD's Day" is Revelation 1:10. *"I was in the Spirit on the LORD's Day . . . ."* The term "LORD's Day" is only found **ONCE** in all of the Writings, and it refers to the **Day of ЭYЭ⅂**, or the great day of wrath ~ which is the FOCUS of the whole 22 chapters; the vision, or Revelation. Yahuchanon wasn't concerned with which day of the week it was, nor can we imagine he was thinking "Sun-day" was anything other than Baal's Day in his time. Of course "Baal's Day" was the LORD's Day, because *Baal means LORD*. The **Time of Wrath** will bring a complete end to man ruling himself, and this Earth will be ruled by the Torah:

"In the last days, the mountain of ЭYЭ⅂'s Temple will be established as chief among the mountains; it will be raised above the hills, and peoples will stream to it. Many nations will come and say, 'Come let us go up to the mountain of ЭYЭ⅂, to house of the Elohim of Ya'a-

kob. He will teach us His ways, so that we may walk in His paths. THE TORAH WILL GO OUT FROM TSIYON, THE WORD OF ЭYЭ⅂ FROM YERUSHALIYIM." Micah 4. These words match perfectly with Revelation 22, describing the "Water of Life", or *living water* (Torah, the Covenant). The "Roman Beast" is set against the Covenant, having altered it by **changing** the day of rest which gives honor to ЭYЭ⅂ for **creation**, as well as the 2nd Commandment which forbids images in our worship. The 7th-day Shabbath is the "sign" of the Eternal Covenant. The idolatry is glaring, and unmistakable. The 4 beasts described in Daniel 7 are all there will be, and the 4th one will endure until the *"Time of Wrath is completed"*, Dan. 11:36. Daniel 7:23—25 describes this 4th beast, which will attack the saints and alter the "set times and law":

"He will speak against the Most High (say his "authority" can change the Covenant) *and oppress His saints and try to change the set times* (annual appointments) *and the Torah."* This was done by Constantine in 321 CE and 325 CE, and ratified by the Roman Council of Laodicea. The 4th Beast enforced the "Sun-day" law under penalty of death, and called the faithful Shabbath-keepers *"Judaizers"*, and pursued "the woman" (ЭYЭ⅂'s wife, bride). Shatan's "wrath" against the marriage Covenant, and the BRIDE who obeys it, has never relented. You see and hear about the struggle on the news constantly. The right to post the 10 Commandments in public view on public property has been a controversy for many years. Which "list" to post is an undiscussed part of the controversy, because Catholics have a different list in their minds than they have in their own translation of the Writings. Also, how can you have a "Sun-day" day of rest when the Commandments say it's the 7th day? How can you misuse the Name of ЭYЭ⅂, when it is not used? Misusing it is one thing; but to *never use His Name at all* is also shaming Him. Certainly snarling "GOD", "LORD" or "JESUS" (being Pagan deities) brings no misuse of the Name of the Maker of Heaven and Earth. The Covenant, and the Bride of the Covenant, are the real target in the war between the sons of Light and darkness:

"Then from his mouth the serpent spewed water like a river, to overtake the woman and

44

"St. Peter's Cathedral" ~ built on one of the 7 hills of Rome, a hill named **VATICANUS**. Note the Dome, chariot wheel, and obelisk of Caligula as its axel.

sweep her away with the torrent. But the Earth helped the woman by opening its mouth and swallowing the river that the dragon had spewed out of his mouth." Rev. 12:15,16—read the context. This means the wife of ayaz fled to safety, and distance provided it. *"Then the dragon was enraged at the woman, and went off to make war against the rest of her offspring ~ THOSE WHO OBEY THE COMMANDMENTS, AND HOLD TO THE TESTIMONY OF* oWYazl." 12:17.
If one can "change" the Torah, then it is not a Rock, but shifting sand. This makes a weak foundation on which to build. The Torah is called the "Word", and the "Word" became flesh, and dwelled with us for a time, showing us perfection. If we build on it, we will not be shaken or carried away by winds of other teaching. What ayaz has made straight, no man can bend or change! Persecution "for righteousness' sake" is written in the pages of history. When ayaz said, *"Everyone is TO STAY WHERE HE IS ON THE SEVENTH DAY; NO ONE IS TO GO OUT"*, He meant what He said (Ex. 16:29). This idea of not traveling any considerable distance is supported by Luke at Acts 1:12:
"Then they returned to Yerushaliyim from the hill called the Mount of Olives, A SHABBATH DAY's WALK FROM THE CITY." If there was some change, Luke would have not mentioned it, or said what *USED TO BE* a Shabbath Day's walk, would he not? He wrote the record many **years** after the resurrection and ascension. If you have ever walked 1,000 cubits (a man's elbow to his fingertips), you know it's a considerable journey. I'm GLAD I don't have to do such a thing on Shabbath. If people in the early times wished to go to a synagogue to hear the Torah, it wasn't nearly as far as we might think. Settlements, and

even cities were only a few acres. Today, we have the increase in knowledge (literacy), as well as printing, so anyone who wants to read the Torah can do so with ease. Yahudaism is a family oriented practice, but we should gather when we have the opportunity. We can't ignore one teaching in order to try to obey another, just because we desire it. Interestingly, if a person rests on the 7th day, other people have no problem guessing their "religion", because this "sign" of the Covenant reveals Who they worship and obey. My best "family" day is Shabbath.
The Beast instituted an ordinance that required everyone to attend "Mass" on the 1st day of each week, without one single verse in the Writings to support either the 1st day as set-apart, or a required gathering. My "gathering" or "convocating" is with my wife and children, who I am to teach **diligently** the Words of the Covenant. If I work six days (a part of the Commandment), then there is only Shabbath left to **diligently** teach them. And because it is such a wonderful family time, they will always love and cherish it, and strive to make it their "custom" as well. This is not evil, although some find it different from their habits. It was our Rabbi's custom, as well as Shaul's, to go to the synagogue ~ surely not far away! Why? To teach, and because that's where the Scrolls were.

THE DEVELOPMENT OF THE DECEPTION
The dragon, who wages war against the Covenant and Bride of Mashiach, controls the "kingdoms" presently. He institutionalized the power of his religion, and centralized the implementation of his plan in the seat of the most powerful empire, ROME.

ROMAN HISTORY
Pagans worshipped the sun, and used fire, the hearth, wreaths, circles, pillars, bells, and many other items seen today as relics of their rituals. Some of the early Roman beliefs came from the Etruscans, Greeks, Egyptians, Persians, and of course Babylonians. The central foundation of Roman nationalism began at Roma, the original name of the city and language of the proto-empire. The mythology of the Romans taught that the empire began with two orphaned boys named Romulus and Remus, who were nurtured by a she-wolf. Their importance to the early Romans was observed by a national day of "purification", associated with the "wolf" (Latin *lupis*) that preserved their lives. Each year on their February 15, a purification festival was held which was called "Lupercalia", or wolf festival. 2 youths (who represented Romulus and Remus) ran around the city in the nude, laughing and whipping around strips of wolf

WHO ARE THESE FOLKS FOLLOWING? ~ ARE STATUES, TORTURES, AND THE KILLING OF HELPLESS VICTIMS THE WORK OF SOME EVIL ENTITY?

TORTURE BY JESUITS AND DOMINICANS

BURNING HERETICS

STATUE OF JUPITER RE-NAMED "PETER".

MILLIONS HAVE KISSED JUPITER'S FOOTSIE, MIS-LED BY POPES.

were settlements on six of these, but the seventh hill was a boggy, swampy place, where the soil was loose. The Etruscans buried their dead there for centuries. Because the graves were shallow, dogs would often go there to dig up and feed on the dead bodies! The Etruscans named this hill **VATICANUS**, meaning *habitation of dogs*. Later, a Roman ruler named Caligula drained this site, and held enormously popular "carnivals" (Latin for *flesh raising*). Caligula was a devotee of Bacchus, and held orgies and drunken parties on a regular basis. The obelisk of Caligula stands today in the center of the chariot wheel design in front of St. Peter's Cathedral (previous page). The Vatican stands on the same hill where the Etruscans buried their dead, so it is an enormous graveyard. The tunnels beneath the Vatican have entire walls made of human bones in certain places.

STATUE OF JUPITER

See the pope in the picture above, puckering-up to kiss the toes of the statue? This very image was made by the Romans, and was their **Jupiter** colossus. It was adopted and **renamed** "Peter", as they will explain to you if you take a tour of the Cathedral. On certain occasions, it is dressed-up in rich robes and crowned as you see it here, and kissed by throngs of Catholic devotees. The toes are worn smooth from the millions of Catholics and previous Romans who have kissed the statue's foot over the centuries. In the days of El Yahu (Elijah), multitudes are said to have *bowed* to Baal, and *kissed him*. Pagan temples often had a colossus idol inside. The "Lincoln Memorial" in Washington is such a colossus, and the inscription on the wall states the place is a "temple". Under the 3-tier miter crown of the image the pope is about to kiss, the statue of Jupiter/Peter has a round "halo", placed there by the sun-worshipping Romans. To associate images with the sun, statues, paintings, and reliefs often had round golden nimbuses or hoops encircling their heads. *"It is not good to have zeal without knowledge, nor to be hasty and miss the way."* Pr. 19:2. If a Naza-

skins, dipped in blood. Unmarried girls exposed their posteriors to be lashed with these bloody wolf hides, supposedly to imbue fertility. As part of the ritual, every eligible girl's name was collected and placed in a large "vat" or jar, and all the young men would "draw" a name from it. This gives us the phrase "luck of the draw". Whatever name a young man would draw out, that girl would be his consort in the festival. This was a very solemn religious process. "Lupercalia" was changed into "**Valentine's Day**" and moved to the 14th after being "Christianized". Instead of having nothing to do with the idolatry, it was simply altered slightly and adapted to the new "universal" religion. This is where we inherit the custom of "Valentine's Cards", and HEART SHAPED symbols. The shape of the heart is an IVY LEAF, the symbol of Bacchus, the male deity of wine and love (orgiastic). He corresponds to Nimrod and Tammuz, and also the archer, Saggitarius or "Cupid". Another name for him is Orion, the hunter. The arrow penetrating the "heart" symbol represented mating. Bacchus is seen in art wearing a wreath of ivy leaves on his head during his mating rituals. So, even the familiar "heart" symbol comes from Pagan Rome, and echoes their idolatry, as the symbol of Bacchus.

Rome is established on seven "hills", and each was originally named by the Etruscans. There rene like Paul were to see this place, he would be traumatized by the spectacle.

PAGAN CLASH

As goes the family, so goes the nation. The fall of Rome had several causes, but all scholars agree that it was fundamentally caused by the deterioration of the family unit. The old phrase, "all roads lead to Rome" was quite true, and it was because of the efficient and extensive road system that the Roman Empire could conquer, control, and trade so effectively. Their quasi-Persian religion, called "Mithraism" was spread over vast distances, but its center was Rome. During the time of Constantine, a more tolerant policy was adopted toward "foreign" religions, as long as everything could be "fused" under one "universal" doctrinal format. With the newly arriving Nazarene faith, there was a clash between it and Mithraism, and the Pagan rule of Diocletian was perhaps the bloodiest one of all. As a young boy, Constantine had witnessed this clash. As a man, he embraced a policy much different from his predecessors, and tried to appease all sides. His Nicene Council established Easter's universal celebration, and blended essential Pagan customs with Nazarene overtones.

THE BEAST'S DEADLY WOUND

During Constantine's rule, he set up a new center for the Empire at what he called "Constantinople", now re-named Istanbul in Turkey. Since this action abandoned the historical center of the Empire at Rome, it accelerated the collapse of the Empire. The well-established "circulatory system" of Roman roads were now useless. Rome fell into ruin, and attackers from the north reduced it to rubble. It became little more than a squatter's camp. By moving the "capital" or "head" of the Empire, Constantine had inadvertently ripped the "head" off the Roman Empire (the head was separated from the heart, the road system). He had also managed to blend the solar religion of Mithraism with belief in the Nazarene Mashiach, which he confused with the sun. Mithras and "Christ" were one and the same to him. The following is an overview of Mithraic doctrine.

THE ROMAN RELIGION:

MITHRAISM

Understanding Constantine, Mithraism, and the fertile Pagan background environment of the Romans will help explain many beliefs and practices seen today. Mithraism is about the worship of the sun, which was titled *Mithras Solis Invictus* (Mithras, the unconquered sun). The "mysteries" of this religion were revealed only to the initiates, who were predominantly soldiers of the Roman army. They spread this religion all over the civi-

lized world by way of the good Roman roads. Mithraism was *the primary religion of the Roman Empire from BCE 222 through the 4th century CE.* It was the chief rival of "Christianity", which history shows compromised radically in order to convert pagans into "believers". By the 4th century CE, the sect of Yahudaism called the *N'tzarim* no longer existed openly, and gnostic clones of it had sprung up and began to compete with Mithraism for dominance. One historian said, *"The entire European continent and New World would be Mithraic today, if Christianity hadn't come along."* Other historians have put it another way: *"Christianity didn't conquer Mithraic Paganism. Mithraism blended in, and CHANGED NAMES."* The doctrines, feast dates, rituals, accouterments, and organizational structure have scarcely changed at all. The religion of Mithraism itself was the result a merger of the astrology of the Chaldean priests of Marduk (Baal) with the Indo-Iranian priests of Mithras. The sun-idol, Mithras, is mentioned in the 'sacred writings' of both cults; the *Avesta* and the *Vedas*. The sun-idol is called *"THE LORD"* in both. The Hindu *Krishna* is called *THE LORD*, as you will recall the syncretistic lyrics in the song, *My Sweet Lord* by George Harrison, where vocalists chant *hare Krishna* interchangeably with *hallelu Yah*. All the while, the song blends the concepts under the impersonal, indefinite, and vague title, "LORD".

MITHRAIC DOCTRINE

1. The center of the Mithraic sun-cult was at Rome.

2. The leader of the ritual service was titled *pater*, Latin for *father* ~ inherited by the priestcraft of Catholicism (against Mt. 23:9), and they wore cruxes as amulets, with costumes of black, having NEHRU collars, originating from the Indo-Iranian roots.

3. There was a *Pater-Patratus* over the paters; a *papa,* or *pope*.

4. The hierarchy initiates below *pater* were called *brothers*.

5. The cult was for *men only*.

6. The cult had the Trinity: *Mithras, Rashnu,* and *Vohu Manah* ~ 3 'persons', but yet 'one'.

7. *Sun-day* was kept hallowed in honor of Mithras, the sun, called *Mithras Solis Invictus*. This has produced our popular name for the first day of the week, *Sunday*. The pattern of resting on Sun-day comes to us directly through what is called the *Blue Laws*, enforced first throughout the Roman Empire, then

through the western traditions into our "New World". The edict was initiated by Constantine I, forbidding officials, artisans, or merchants from engaging in any work on the **Sun-Day**, to give honor to the sun, **Mithras**.

8. There were 5 levels within the hierarchy.
9. **December 25** was observed as **Mithras' Birthday**, called *"Natalis Invictus"*, the rebirth of the winter sun, unconquered.
10. Initiates had to undergo a ritual sprinkling (affusion, which involved being under a bull, or *Taurus*, which being cut to dead allowed the initiate to become saturated. The custom of bloody **bullfights** seen in Spain hearken back to this cult. The custom of performing Christian "baptisms" in the spring at Eastertime will take on greater meaning as you learn the following information).
11. Special value was attributed to the moral virtues of religion, truthfulness, purity, and generosity.
12. Mithraists would enter "paradise" (a Persian word itself, also called *Eleusian Fields, Nirvana, and Nether World*) by the **Three Steps:** A. The Good Thought.
   B. The Good Word.
   C. The Good Deed.
13. The cult supported the **divine right of kings** (including Emperor worship).
14. The **pater** (father) stood at one end of an oblong room, performing mysterious blood rituals; there was an indoor "altar" at his end, on which a victim (Latin, "host") was sacrificed. They had a sun-shaped wafer disc like the Egyptians, and the assembly knelt, sat, and stood in unison.

It was during this time of the "clash" when Christianity and Mithraism merged, that Jerome translated the Greek Writings of the "New Testament" into Latin (391-403). His real name was Eusibius Heirymonius Sophronius. He took the Greek word **STAUROS** (beam, stake, pole) and carried it over to the Latin word **CRUX**. This was an important shift in the meaning of the original word. The Hebrew term was "NAS", used for the word "POLE" that the serpent was lifted up on. To a Mithraist, the CRUX had a significant religious meaning. It could be represented as an "X" or a vertical line crossed horizontally. In the spring, when the Mithraists sacrificed a Taurus (bull), the sun was "CROSSING" the celestial equator, and was in the zodiac sign of the Taurus. ("Zodiac" actually means *animal* figures, related to the word "zoo"). These rabid Pagans "allegorized" or interpreted this as the sun (Mithras) *overcoming the bull, "crossing"* the celestial equator, so the cross was their most cherished religious symbol. The cross symbols of many different Pagan cults from

around the world is what scholars call *"the symbol of the sun, par excellance"*. The words we have inherited from "Jerome's" Latin translation include *cross, crucifixion, and crosier*. So, "cross" is a Latinism. In one of it's Babylonian forms, it was a tilted crux, with an arrow point at the high end, representing Nimrod standing on the tower shooting his hunter arrow at the skies. It was a bow and arrow. He may have even done this, shooting at the constellation Taurus. This is the link with the "Golden Calf". We still call the center of an archery target "the bull's eye". The sign of the "cross" was a Pagan sign of "overcoming". The Babylonian constellation "Orion" the Hunter (Archer) represents Nimrod of Babylon. Pagans practiced Astromancy, Pyromancy, Necromancy, and other occult forms of divination, and the cross was intimately linked to their rituals ~ and still is. A "Black Mass" uses the cross, and was practiced long before Christianity existed. Let's keep our spiritual priorities intact as we move along, and see if the Mark of the Beast can be linked in any way to Sun-day, the sun itself in Pagan worship, and the Pagan's **symbol** of the sun.

Since the Earth Mother was thought to be "fertilized" in the spring (Ishtar, or Easter), the Babylonian symbol for "woman" was also a cross, with the sun circle above it (the sun did the "fertilizing"). If you research Constantine, you will learn he had a vision of the sun with a "cross" beneath it, the same symbol used for "female" today in biology, a type of "ankh". The circle is also interpreted as the sun, and "circuses" like the ones held by Caligula were occultic religious displays, involving animals of the Zodiac, and three "rings". The Olympic Games today use 5 rings as a logo, representing the 5 original planetary deities worshipped in Babylon. In fact, it is still the custom to carry a torch lit by the "sacred fire" altar on Mount Olympus to the site of the games. Where the games are held, an altar dedicated to Zeus is lighted with this torch, so all the nations and athletes who participate are unknowingly worshipping Zeus. That's why this book is titled "Fossilized Customs", to open your eyes so that you can see them. The whole world follows after the "Beast", through the fossilized customs. So, you can see there are many ways we can be found practicing a lie, and having a "mark" or outward sign of following this beast. **Human traditions** may appear innocent, but if you can easily trace their origins to ancient Paganism, they are abominations.

ODD THING: People who are Christians today don't usually ever think of their "Jesus" as being a Yahudi, nor do they realize He is a "rabbi", and was called such by many in the Brit Chadasha. Yet they also use the "excuse" that the TaNaKh (O.T.) was mainly written to "Jews" and by "Jews" for "Jews", so Commandments like observing Shabbaths or making a distinction between the "clean" and "unclean" are now irrelevant for them. Quoting verses from the TaNaKh will often be met with a response like, *"but that's Old Testament"*. Likewise, unbelieving Yahudim will not acknowledge the Brit Chadasha either. Can you imagine Shaul or Peter standing there quoting a passage from the TaNaKh, and being told *"but that's Old Testament"*?

CHRISTIANITY'S PAGAN CONNECTION

Constantine is the connection which bonded Paganism to the belief in the Yahudi Mashiach. Excused as "inculturation", Paganism poisoned the message of repentance beyond all recognition. If you study any aspect of the growth of Christendom, you will only encounter one bloodbath after another. If you go in search of the worst persecution of Christians by Pagans, you will find that it was a picnic in the park compared to what Christians did over many centuries to non-Christians, and even to one another in various struggles for dominance. Constantine made Christianity the Roman State religion, but its form was far from anything known to the first Nazarenes. Constantine had to MERGE the multitudes of Pagans—who were mostly his own soldiers—with the Nazarene faith, in order to control his vast empire. This reconciliation, or merger of the Nazarene faith with Mithraism, produced what we see today as "Christianity". He made the "cross" the primary symbol of this new merger, thus rallying the Pagans around its emotional meaning. The main issue at his Nicene Council in 325 CE centered on the date of "EASTER", again the most important point in the Pagan mind when the sun "crossed" the Zodiac at Taurus. Constantine confused Mithras and "Christ" together, borrowing from the Pagan background of sun-worship for every interpretation. Many of the Pastors in Christendom *know* these things, but never bring them up. Most don't care, it's just a job. A few are afraid that bringing it up will unravel their world. You will notice that if you privately discuss these things with a pastor, he will pluck two or three verses from Shaul's letters, then turn to stone ~ not wanting to pursue the real truth. He really doesn't want to get the "bottom" of it, because it will expose everything he teaches and lives by as being a lie.

The secular population live in their own dream world as well. Some are idealists, blissfully going through life getting the weather reports and sports scores. There are many distractions to occupy yourself with, but very few people can get **real** information, or put it into a meaningful form.

The Roman Beast's most powerful tool is the calendar, as I called it the great "dragnet". When people are made aware that old Babylonian "rhythms" are being kept in the annual cycles of Sun-day, Christmas, Easter, and Halloween, it sometimes endears these rituals to them even more. The "EasterN" religions have become fascinating to many westerners, and they search for hidden secrets in them ~ and call it "New Age". One recent movement of a New Age cult has been the embracing of the Statue of Liberty as an idol. They place lilies near a plaque which displays a prayer to her as the Earth Mother. This enormous colossus is an image of the Babylonian goddess of the dawn, the Earth Mother. The "liberty" she offers the people of Earth is liberty from the Creator's pattern for living: *"Why do the nations conspire and the peoples plot in vain? The kings of the Earth take their stand and the rulers gather together against ᴀΥᴈ⅃ and against his Anointed One. 'Let us break their chains' they say, and throw off their fetters."* This is from Psalm 2, and sums up how people seek to be "free" to choose their own way to happiness. Queen Semiramis remains their image, although she was a witch. The image was a gift to America from the French people, a larger replica of a statue of the sungoddess on a bridge in France. The global "secret societies" linked to the Illuminati know all about this, and they just make sure the common people are manipulated to carry out their agendas. They refer to their armed forces as "cannon fodder", and actually use wars to make more money, and keep populations under their control. The love of money drives the evil. But, remember, we are not called to change any of this; but endure to the end in peace with all men. We love our enemies, they kill us.

Constantine adopted the insignia called the "**labarum**", a cross with a wreath above it with the Greek letters *CHI* and *RHO* inside it. He had it displayed on the shields of his soldiers, as the "Christian" emblem to go forth to conquer in. Later, the "Crusades" were launched with the marauding murderers wearing large red cruxes emblazoned on their chests. The word "Crusade" refers to this crux. The errors overwhelm the world because they and it are in great darkness. Rabbi OWΥᴈ⅃ came to teach the world, but it has not received His teachings. Therefore, when the time comes, it will be punished, convicted of its crimes against Him, and the obedient children of the Father will inherit it. **The saying goes that a wise man pointed at the moon. The idiot only looked at the finger.** Considering the processes and outcomes of Christianity over the last 1600 years, it would appear that early on, the whole point was lost. Constantine's government tried to "fix" a perceived problem, and wound up making it worse. It's a sad commentary, but governments haven't changed much in that respect.

During the Christianization of the Norse areas, and all during the Crusades, people were given the choice:

CONVERT
OR
DIE.

Then came the 600 year reign of terror by the Inquisition.

WHEN YOUR GOVERNMENT TURNS ON YOU

THINGS CAN REALLY PILE UP.

(Dogma from the Catholic Encyclopedia)
ROMAN CHURCH TIMELINE

DATE	DOGMA
CE 300	"Baptism" by immersion changed to affusion (sprinkle).
CE 300	Prayers for the dead. (Against Deut. 18 & Yesha Yahu 8).
CE 310	Making the "sign" of the CROSS.
CE 325	Anathema (death) decreed to anyone who adds or changes the creed of faith of Nice. (See years 1586 & 1560).
CE 370	Council of Laodicea rejects Apocrypha, calls Sabbath observers "Judaizers", worthy of death.
CE 375	Veneration of angels and dead saints.
CE 394	*The Sacrament of the Mass:* *Missa Recitata,* Low Mass, priest + 1; *Missa Cantata,* Sung Mass, " + 1; *Missa Solemnis,* High Mass, " + 2; *Missa Pontificalis,* Bishop + " + ?
CE 431	The worship of Miryam (Mary).
CE 431	Miryam "Queen of Heaven" (against Yerme Yahu 7:18, 44:17, 44:25).
CE 431	Miryam "ever virgin" (against Mt. 1:25, Mk. 6:3, Yn. 2:2-4).
CE 431	Miryam "Mediatrix" (against 1 Tim. 2:5, Mt. 11:28, Ecc. 9:6).
CE 500	Priestcraft began to dress in "priestly garb".
CE 526	Sacrament of "Extreme Unction".
CE 593	Doctrine of "Purgatory" ~ by Gregory (against Yn. 5:24, 1Yn. 1:7-9, 2:1,2, Romans 8:1).
CE 600	Latin language only language permitted for prayer (against 1 Cor. 14:9).
CE 709	Kissing the feet of pope is ordered (against Acts 10:25,26, Rev. 19:10, 22:9).
CE 750	Temporal Power of pope declared (against Mt. 4:8,9, 20:25,26, Yn. 18:38).
CE 754	Council of Constantinople ordered removal of all images and abolition of image worship.
CE 785	Miryam "co-redemptrix" (against Acts 4:12, Ps. 146:5, Yisraelites/Hebrews 7:25).
CE 788	Miryam "worship" (against Romans 1:25, Yesha Yahu 42:8, Yn. 7:10).
CE 788	Worship of cross, relics, and images re-authorized (against Ex.

20:4, Dt. 27:15, Ps. 115).

CE 850 Fabrication and use of "holy water".

CE 890 Veneration of St. Yosef, husband of Miryam.

CE 965 Baptism of the bells ~ ceremony of actually "baptizing" bells to ward off demons and to call the elect to vespers when blessed bells are rung.

CE 995 Canonization of dead saints (against Romans 1:7, 1 Cor. 1:2).

CE 998 Fasting on "**Fri-days**" & during "**Lent**" (against Mt. 15:11, 1 Cor. 10:25, 1 Tim. 4:1-8).

CE 1079 Celibacy of priesthood/priestcraft declared (married priests ordered to cast off wives, against 1 Tim. 3:2-5, 3:12, Mt. 8:14,15).

CE 1090 Institution of **rosary prayer beads**, or "chaplet" (against Mt. 6:7, Dt. 18, Yesha Yahu 8 ~ also, Buddhism, Shinto, and Islam practice prayer bead counting).

CE 1190 **Sale of indulgences** (against Eph. 2:8-10). For those of you who don't know, this was a practice of people actually paying the clergy money to have punishment time taken off from burning in "Purgatory" after their death. They probably weren't swimming in their own gene pool to be swindled so easily, but they were just kept uneducated.

CE 1215 Dogma of "**trans-substantiation**" declared (against Luke 22:19,20, Mk. 13:21, Yn. 6:35, Mt. 24:23-28, 1 Cor. 11:26 ~ this was truly a case of the idiot looking at the finger!).

CE 1215 Confession of sins to priest ordered (against Ps. 51:1-10, Luke 7:48 & 15:21, 1 Yn. 1:8,9).

CE 1220 **Adoration of the wafer "host"** (matzah adoration! Against Yn. 4:24).

CE 1229 **Scriptures forbidden to "laymen"** (against Yn. 5:39, 8:31, 2 Tim. 3:15-17).

CE 1265 Miryam's **house moved** by angel to Lorento Italy. (as fishy as this smells, I don't think they violated Torah, unless they were lying ~ what do you think?).

CE 1287 **Scapular protection** decreed (brown cloth talisman with picture of virgin packed with tea leaves proclaimed to contain supernatural powers or "virtues" to protect wearer. Sure, like Miryam and "St. Christopher" are omni-present,

and can speak and hear you. They're DEAD, Jim).

CE 1414 "Chalice" forbidden to laity at "communion" (a radical distortion of the Passover Seder, the annual remembrance of O W Y ᖳ Ƶ's death).

CE 1439 Dogma of **seven sacraments** (against Mt. 28:19,20, & 26:26-28).

CE 1439 **Purgatory** declared valid dogma (against Mt. 25:46, Luke 23:43).

CE 1508 Miryam "Mother of GOD" (against Mt. 12:46-50, Mk. 8:19-21, Acts 1:14).

CE 1545 **Church tradition equal to Scripture** (against Mt. 15:6, Mk. 7:7-13, Col. 2:8 ~ also **adds** all of above and many other dogma to Council of Nice!).

CE 1560 Creed of pope Pius IV decreed (against Gal. 1:8).

CE 1580 Pope declared to be "**LORD GOD**" (that ought to just about be enough to get some people roasted).

CE 1593 "Ave Maria" adopted.

CE 1710 **Stuffed donkey** in Verona, Italy, at Church of the Madonna of the Organs, *decreed to be the actual animal Rabbi Yahushua/ Yahusha ha Mashiach entered Yerushaliyim on.* (This is the idiot looking at the finger again. I'm ashamed to say, but when I first heard about it, I couldn't stop laughing for about 10 minutes.)

CE 1854 **Immaculate Conception** of Virgin Miryam (against Romans 3:23, & 5:12, Ps. 51:5, Yerme Yahu 17:9).

CE 1864 Miryam "sinless" (against Luke 1:46,47, Romans 3:10-19, & 23).

CE 1870 **Papal infallability** decreed (against 2 Thess. 2:2-12, Rev. 17:1-9, 13:5-8, 18).

CE 1907 All sciences condemned.

CE 1922 Pope declared to be "Jesus Christ".

CE 1930 All public schools condemned.

CE 1950 Declaration of the bodily assumption of the Virgin Miryam into Heaven.

The dogma of "**trans-substantiation**" that popped-up in **1215** caused many people to lose their lives. The idiot was looking really closely at the finger, because when our Rabbi said "*This is My Body*", and "*This is My Blood*", He was picturing what was soon to be. The matzah

FASCISTS SALUTE THEIR CAESAR IN ROME IN 1938

is pierced and bruised, and the blood of the grape is red. These emblems are to remind us once every year at Passover, OF HIS DEATH. First of all, this remembrance isn't done every day, or every week. Second, the "metaphor" for "eating" and "drinking" His Body and Blood was mistaken to be *literal* by several Pagan rulers, so they killed as many of these "believers" as they could find, *because they thought there was some sort of cannibalism involved.* The believers being killed didn't even understand *why* they were being killed! But the "believers" were led astray also by their enchanters, thinking the "priests" had some supernatural ability to call out certain Latin words, wave items in the air, and by some superior powers in them LITERALLY CHANGE BREAD AND WINE INTO THE ACTUAL LIVING BODY OF THE MASHIACH. Rabbi meant that He would be *IN US* like the food we eat, not *BE* the food we eat. The New Covenant is receiving the Spirit of OWYヨL, where He writes His Covenant Torah on our hearts, and we walk in the Commandments obediently. Our mind of the "flesh" no longer controls us, He does. We don't receive Him by eating bread. The bread we eat at Passover is to **remember His death** by, at *that* time of year (Passover). People need to stop looking at the finger. Millions are entranced, and can't wake up from this bad dream! No one has explained it to them, because no one "gets it" in the circles they find themselves in. The pope himself doesn't understand. But I pray he will learn, and then teach everyone who is Catholic what they need to comprehend. It's still a huge "mystery" to most Protestants too ~ many have an indoor "altar" left over from the Catholic "bloodless sacrifice of the Mass". But, remember ~ without the shedding of **blood**, there is **no remission** of sins. Throw out the "altar", tear down the "steeple", and start over again is my advice to pastors. Tell the congregation *THEY ARE THE TEMPLE* ~ if the Mashiach dwells in them. If He does not, they are not His!

NATSARIM - not "Nazi"
"There will be a day when WATCHMEN *cry out on the hills of Ephraim . . ."* ~ this is from 31:6 of Yerme Yahu (Jeremiah), and in the same chapter as the prophesied New Covenant. The word

"watchmen" is *NATSARIM*. Those today who "see" are announcing that the world is off course, and out-of-bounds.

THE BEAST'S DEADLY WOUND: HEALED
After Constantine's action of moving the head of the Roman Empire to Constantinople, the Empire faded into what is called the Byzantine Empire. Rome was in ruins, wounded to death. By the 6th century CE, the bishop at Rome was regarded more highly than any other by reputation, simply because the name "Rome" was a profoundly stirring one. During the 7th century, the bishop of Rome took on the Mithraic title, "pope", or papa. The title "Pontifex Maximus" was also bestowed on him, the Caesar's title. ("Caesar" is also spelled Czar and Khasar.) By the end of the 8th century, Rome was resurrected back to life in the leadership office of the "pope", and in the year 800 this bishop crowned King Charlemagne the "Defender of the Faith", and announced the beginning of *The Holy Roman Empire*, or *First "Reich"*. This remained intact for 1000 years. The pages of history record the evil "fruit" of death and destruction of this empire. The **symbol** of Caesar's authority can be seen on the front of a US coin, the dime, or 10-cent piece. It is a bundle of reeds, wrapped in red leather strapping, called a **FASCIS**, from which we derive the term *fascist*. Caesar's throne had this symbol under the armrests on the left and right. It symbolized complete unity, and the power to control and punish all opponents to magistrates and Caesar's universal authority. (Thomas Jefferson designed US currency).

The men in the picture above include Adolf Hitler, Mussulini, and Hitler's inner circle of fascist henchmen. Who would Hitler himself salute with the old Roman soldier's salute? These fascists marched with a swastika crux inside a golden wreath modeled after the old Roman style banners in their military parades. The word "Reich" means "realm", and the First Reich was the "Holy Roman Empire", as your dictionary will explain. This "3rd Reich" was planned to last 1000 years, like the 1st one. Shatan was unleashing his "Final Solution" on the Earth, establishing Catholicism, with Hitler as the "Defender of the Faith".

CONCORDATS

Individual nations signed a "Concordat" with the Vatican, a written arrangement which officially recognized only Catholicism as the national religion. All other religions were banned, and severely persecuted by the power of the state which signed the Concordat. "Concordat" means the state was in accord, or agreement, with the Vatican. To a citizen in such a Catholic nation, their ultimate authority was the pope, then the leader of their nation, local civil authorities, teachers, and parents. The pope wielded both "temporal" and "spiritual" authority over the citizens, which is the secret behind the "hand-sign" of two fingers you often see in religious art, and lifted in the air by the pope as he "blesses" his votaries. Germany and Italy had a Concordat with the Vatican.

[The US Constitution stands in the way of ever having a Concordat with the Vatican, since it safeguards complete freedom to practice one's religion; the state cannot restrict religious practice in any way under the US Constitution. The Constitution controls the **government**, not the free citizens.]

At the end of World War 2, thousands of Nazi fascists fled to Brazil, the world's densest concentration of Catholics. War criminals are still hiding there in their old age. The pope visited this country in 1999. He was born in Poland, and his real name isn't "John Paul II", but Karol Wojtyla. As a young Catholic man, he worked for a large chemical firm which manufactured the deadly gas which the Nazi fascists used to kill 6 million Yahudim men, women, and children. Leaving the chemical firm, he became a Catholic priest, and in a surprisingly short time became a Cardinal. The hidden history of this man is well-documented. He was in attendance at the signing of the Concordat with Germany as a "prelate", and has been much closer to the "action" than most ever get. If you would like to get more acquainted with just how close Hitler was to the pope, Pius XI, find the new book "Hitler's Pope" at a bookstore.

CRUSADES

They were called "crusades" because the rampaging murderers wore a large red "crux" on their chest. They were sent off by various popes, to re-capture the "holy land" from "the infidels". Killing, raping, looting, and burning libraries in their path, these 13 "divine campaigns" defy description. They flung the civilized world into the dark ages, and made no small contribution to the spread of the Black Death. Sure, fleas on rats carried the Plague, but 25% of the continent perished in part because the fleas were being carried by these travelers as well. [Several organized secret societies were spawned within Catholicism during this time period, which you can independently research: Curia, The **Society of Jesus**, (Jesuit Order, founded by Ignatius de Loyola), **Jesuit General** (the "Black Pope", the real power behind the pope), **Alumbrados**, **Opus Dei**, **Knights Templar**, and **Ecole Biblique**.]

(The following was received by internet in CE 1986, from an anonymous source):

ILLUMINATI

In recent years, there have been hushed whispers about the secret society called the "illuminati", and their conspiracy to control the world. The Order of the Illuminati was founded May 1, 1776 by Dr. Adam Weishaupt. Born a Yahudi, he converted to Roman Catholicism and became a professor of Canon law at the University of Ingolstadt in Bavaria. He became

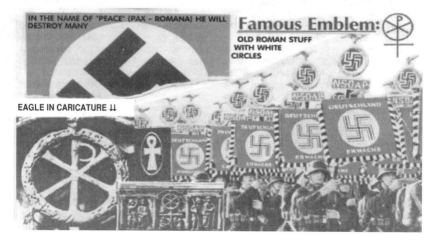

IN THE NAME OF "PEACE" (PAX - ROMANA) HE WILL DESTROY MANY

Famous Emblem:

OLD ROMAN STUFF WITH WHITE CIRCLES

EAGLE IN CARICATURE ⚔

a Jesuit priest, and then formed his own secret organization. The secret order began with 5 members, and each had a secret name. Weishaupt was "Spartacus", and his chief assistant, Herr Von Zwack, took the name "Cato". Weishaupt hoped to attract the German Freemasons, but was unsuccessful. Finally a few prominent citizens joined in Munich, to receive the mysterious title, "Areopagite".

3 CLASSES ~ In 1779, Weishaupt divided his secret organization into 3 classes: **Novice, Minerval, and Illuminatied Minerval** ("Minerva" is the Pagan name for the "Mother of the Sun", from *The Mystic Hymns of Orpheus*—the hymns which are the basis of "Gregorian Chant"). Each candidate had to swear an oath to secrecy plus unconditional obedience to Weishaupt. One feature of their society was a most unusual system of "mutual espionage". Every member spied on every other member. When the Novice was promoted to the Minerval stage, a solemn initiation ceremony was performed. In a dimly lit room, the identities of other members of the society were revealed to him, up to and including the Minerval grade, but not the upper grades. By the time he reached the grade of Illuminated Minerval, he learned the ultimate aims of the order:

THE ABOLITION OF: *all governments, inheritance, private enterprise, patriotism, religion, the family unit, and the creation of* **A NEW WORLD ORDER**. (Fascism had much the same objectives, since the leader was the "Father", and there was no room for any other allegiance).

Weishaupt wrote to his chief assistant "Cato": *"The most admirable thing of it all is, that great Protestant and reformed theologians who belong to our order really believe they see in it the true and genuine mind of the Christian religion. Oh, man! What can not you be brought to believe?"*

Weishaupt knew how to lure the unsuspecting, and at one time wrote:

"These people swell our numbers and fill our treasury; get busy and make these people nibble at our bait . . . But do not tell them our secrets. They must be made to believe that the low degree that they have reached is the highest."

Weishaupt gradually infiltrated the

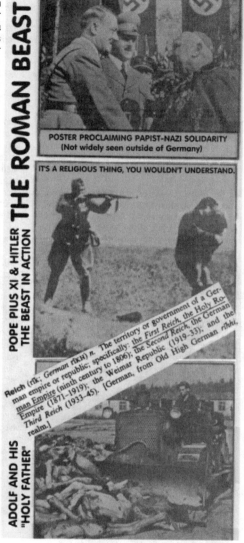

THE ROMAN BEAST

POSTER PROCLAIMING PAPIST-NAZI SOLIDARITY
(Not widely seen outside of Germany)

IT'S A RELIGIOUS THING, YOU WOULDN'T UNDERSTAND.

POPE PIUS XI & HITLER
THE BEAST IN ACTION

Reich (rîk; German ríKH) n. The territory or government of a German empire or republic; specifically: the First Reich, the Holy Roman Empire (ninth century to 1806); the Second Reich, the German Empire (1871-1919); the Weimar Republic (1919-33), and the Third Reich (1933-45). [German, from Old High German *rîhhi*, realm.]

ADOLF AND HIS
"HOLY FATHER"

Freemasons. On July 16, 1782 at the Congress of Wilhelmsbad, an alliance between Illuminism and Freemasonry was finally sealed. On that day the leading secret societies were infiltrated, and to some degree, *united*, numbering more than 3 million members. Eventually, the Bavarian government banned both the Illuminati and Freemasonry on March 2, 1785. Weishaupt was forced to leave the country. The Bavarian government heard 4 leading members of the Illuminati testify before a court of inquiry, exposing the Luciferic nature of its aims. A voluminist array of documents were found in the Illuminati headquarters. The Bavarian government published them, to warn all other .countries of Europe. The name of the document was: *The Original Writings of the Order and Sect of the Illuminati*. ("Lucifer" is a Latin word based on lucia, "light", and means *"light—bringer"*. The word Illuminati means *"holder of the light*). By the time the document was published, 15 lodges of the Order of the Illuminati had been established in the 13 American colonies. There was a lodge in Virginia that was identified with Thomas Jefferson. In 1797, Professor John Robison published *Proofs of a Conspiracy*, in which he warned the world of Illuminati infiltration into Masonic Lodges. (Perhaps there is a connection between the American Revolution and the Illuminati?).

Dr. Adam Weishaupt, the Illuminati founder, adopted the familiar *All Seeing Eye* symbol when he first set up operations in Bavaria. This symbol is found on the back of the $1.00 US bill. The Roman numerals at the base refer to 1776, the date he founded the Illuminati ~ and it conveniently corresponds to the year of the US Declaration of Independence. This "eye" symbolized a "big brother", and the mutual spying system of the domain. The Latin words above and below the eye on the dollar bill in translation mean *"Announcing the Birth of a New World Order"*. The All Seeing Eye is seen in the meditation room at the United Nations building in New York City. The "Great Seal" was designed under the authority of Thomas Jefferson and John Adams (both Freemasons), and Benjamin Franklin (a member of another secret society, the Rosicrucians).

THE GREAT SEAL

(Masons revere Nimrod, the eye above, as their founder)

After Adam Weishaupt died, an Italian revolutionary leader became the director of the Illuminati: **Giuseppe Mazzini**, who held the position from 1834 to 1872. "Mazzini" gives the first letter to the acronym, **M.A.F.I.A:**

Italian word	English meaning
Mazzini	Mazzini
Autorizza	Authorizes
Furti	Thefts
Incindi	Arsons
Avvelemanti	Poisonings

This "Mafia" acronym developed in about 1859. The organization was previously called "Camorra" since 1800, and was an Italian criminal society. This information is supplied in the 1945 Encyclopedia Americana. Shortly after Mazzini took control, an obscure intellectual joined a branch organization called "The League of the Just". His name was Karl Heinrich **Marx**. Marx denounced the Messianic Judaism of his parents, and embraced atheism, studied at the Universtiy of Bonn and Berlin, and wrote the book *Das Kapital*, laying the foundation of the communist movement (set against private enterprise and property ownership). In 1847 Marx wrote the *Communist Manifesto*, which was basically a rehash of the writings of Adam Weishaupt. At this time, Mazzini selected Albert Pike to head the Illuminati activities in the US. Pike was an admirer of the Secret Hebrew Cult of Cabala (Qabbalism). Mazzini, in a letter dated January 22, 1870, wrote to Pike:

"We must create a Super Rite, which will remain unknown to which we will call those Masons of high degree whom we shall select. With regard to our brothers in Masonry, these men must be pledged to the strictest secrecy. Through this supreme rite, we will govern all Freemasonry which will become the one international center, the more powerful because its direction will be unknown."

This letter was published in the book, *Occult Theocracy*, by Lady Queensborough, pgs. 208, 209. Supreme councils were formed in Charleston, South Carolina (US), in Rome, and in Berlin. Known secretly as "Palladism", it is the cult of Satan in the inner shrines of a secret ritual to surpass all other secret rituals. On July 14, 1889, Pike issued this statement to the 23 Supreme Councils of the world:

"That which we must say to the CROWD is: 'We worship a god, but it is the god that one adores without superstition.' To YOU sovereign Grand Inspectors General, we say this, that you may repeat it to the brethren of the 32nd, 31st, and 30th degrees: 'The Masonic Religion should be, by all of us initiates of the high degrees, maintained in the purity of the Luciferian doctrine. If Lucifer were not god, would Adonay (Yahushua) *calumniate him? . . . Yes, Lucifer is GOD . . .'"*

~ *General Albert Pike, 33rd degree*
(Quoted from *The Freemason*, the organ of English Freemasonry, 19th January 1935).

In 1871, Giuseppe Mazzini issued a remarkable letter in which he graphically outlined plans for **3 world wars**. Until recently, this letter was on display in the British Museum Library in London. Pike aided in making this plan known in the US. It was a blue-print for 3 wars. Called ***The Mazzini-Pike Plan***, its ultimate goal was eventual ***world domination***. The letter outlined three relatively simple strategies. It called for communism, fascism, and the struggle for the Mid-East to foment three global wars and at least two major revolutions. WW1 was to destroy the Czarist government of Russia, and replace it with militant atheism. WW2 would begin by manipulating Great Britain and Germany to achieve a global war, which was done almost single-handedly by Adolf Hitler. WW3 of the Mazzini-Pike blue-print called for the firing up of the controversy between the Israeli and Moslem world. They hoped that the "Zionists" and the Moslems would destroy one another, and bring the rest of the world into a final conflict. The "Great Battle" would usher in a complete social, political, and economic chaos. To fill the void created by the "Great Battle" would come a world government, headed by the Illuminati. In Illuminati doctrine, "Lucifer" is "GOD", and Satanism is heresy.

— END OF INTERNET DATA —

(If you research a man named Ignatius de Loyola, you will find he founded *The Alumbrados*, which eventually became *The Inquisition*).

I don't wish to turn this book into a critique on politics, but the world is controlled presently by ha Shatan, and you can see that the conflicts around the world are ROOTED in religious differences caused by his "divide-and-conquer" methods, and driven by greed. [Here in the US, Norman Thomas ran for President in 1936 on the Socialist ticket, and stated: *"The American people will never knowingly adopt Socialism, but under the name of Liberalism, they will adopt every fragment of the Socialist program, and America will be a Socialist nation without ever knowing how it happened."*] The word "NAZI" is short for *National Socialist Party*. The objective of fascism and National Socialism is <u>government control</u> of business, religion, the family, and the economy. Look up the definitions for "fascism" and "Nazi" in a dictionary, and you will be amazed that they are identical to the aims of the socialism we find ourselves surrounded by. Where is the "Illuminati" today? Let's find out.

THE ILLUMINATI AND THE COUNCIL ON FOREIGN RELATIONS (excerpt) by Myron Fagan:

"Now then, this satanic plot was launched back in the 1760's when it first came into existence under the name 'Illuminati'. This Illuminati was organized by one Adam Weishaupt, born a Jew, who was converted to Catholicism and became a Catholic priest, and then, at the behest of the then newly-organized House of Rothschild, defected and organized the Illuminati. Naturally, the Rothschilds financed that operation and every war since then, beginning with the French Revolution, and has been promoted by the Illuminati operating under various names and guises. I say under various names and guises because after the Illuminati was exposed and became notorious, Weishaupt and his co-conspirators began to operate under various other names. In the United States, immediately after World War 1, they set up what they called the "Council on Foreign Relations", commonly referred to as the **CFR**, and this CFR is actually the Illuminati in the United States and its hierarchy."

So, watch the behavior of the **UN** and the World Bank. Food control is one of their objectives. This is brought about by undermining foreign governments, using Jesuit priests under "deep cover" to create religious conflicts. The Vietnam war was fought over religion. The president of South Vietnam (Diem) was a Catholic, and was persecuting his Buddhist subjects. North Vietnam was Buddhist, and sought to come to the aid of their Buddhist brothers. You'll recall headlines with images of Buddhist monks in South Vietnam burning themselves in front of their pagodas to attract the world's attention! Religious bickering is causing civil unrest in Northern Ireland, the Balkans, India, Africa, and Indonesia. They "plant" the seeds of unrest, then come in with their "international peace keepers", and on the surface appear to be "the good guys". But, the soldiers who work to restore the peace are what they internally call "cannon fodder". All the while, they develop and test new deadlier weapons at secret facilities like Area 51, and encircle the globe with nuclear submarines. They have weapons in orbit, which can target individual persons, or shoot down planes which carry the people they wish to eliminate. Mysterious crashes for unexplained reasons occur all the time; but if you check the record of those who were on board the planes, you will find people of prominent influence every time. Planes which suddenly explode for no reason, or crash into the sea like John Kennedy Jr's did, might not be the "accidents" they appear to be. I became aware of this possibility several years ago when I heard about a plane going down that had the US Air Force Procurement officer on board. The

56

Illuminati controls political leaders with money and sex, as you see these two issues swarm around them constantly. But, we must live in peace, and trust that all these wars, conspiracies, storms, earthquakes, firestorms, and other record-breaking natural disasters are signs that the end is near for Shatan. Where ever you see eagles or "obelisks", Shatan cannot be far away.

THE SEAL OF MASONRY

The "fraternal club" of masonry is for men only, but they started a women's chapter for the wives, called the "Eastern Star". Masonry is a very old craft, really. It didn't involve all the convoluted "secrets" it has today, but only had one objective: BUILDING. Yes, the men who designed and built all the ancient and modern temples and government buildings were **stone masons**. They took on apprentices, or students, who eventually became journeymen, and finally master craftsmen. They had to learn how to lay foundations, measure, and cut stone. The graduates of schools wear a flat square-topped hat, which is really a "mortar board", attached to the round hat of "Hermes", an idol of the Greeks, which scholars wore as a badge of learning. (This "beanie" hat was imposed on the Hellenized Yahudim, and now "Jews" wear them when they attend synagogue).

The "seal" of modern masonry has a compass open above a square, which are two tools used in the geometry of their craft, with a capital letter "G" in the center. The letter is "interpreted" to stand for "GOD", and Christians who join see it this way. Some see it as standing for "Great Architect". It really stands for the Greek word "gnostic", which means "knowledge" ~ the knowledge of the craft. But it also stands for "GUILD". During the Middle Ages, stonemasonry formed into organized groups of men called "guilds", which were pre-cursors of unions. The building trades were monopolized by the guilds. Their most cherished item was their apron, which they wore when laying stones. Without this apron, they could not work, and it became their "badge" of approval, or "righteousness". The emblem of each guild was displayed on the apron.

THE GREAT ARCHITECT

Originally, Masonry was a trade, but after Adam Weishaupt, people with no building skills were accepted into the organizations, and advanced in grade as they acquired knowledge carefully "fed" to them over time. Hideous blood oaths, some involving murder, are sworn to maintain control and secrecy. In the original guilds, mathematical formulas were held as secrets ($\pi r2$, $2\pi r$, $4\pi r3$, etc.) but Masonry today doesn't involve architecture anymore. To be a Mason, a man has to believe in a deity who is referred to as "the Great Architect", who they must invoke for blessings and protection. Salvation is taught by Ma-

sonry to have many roads, and all religions are believed to lead to the "Great Architect". They meet in what are called "Masonic Temples", and call their leaders "Worshipful Masters".

Knowledge is power, and the skills of a master stonemason enabled him to rise above a common person. He knew the formulas and ratios necessary to construct great buildings. Naturally, you wouldn't want everyone to control such "secret" information, if your trade could be more secure by withholding it. Today, with engineering schools teaching the detailed formulas for architecture, chemistry, and electronics, the old "guilds" have no secrets anymore. But, the gullible members of today's Masonry are led to believe they will achieve some secret knowledge if they remain members.

PENTAGRAMS

Masonry uses the five-pointed star as one of its "secret" symbols, and it is used by the women's organization, which is called "the Eastern Star". Christians see it as an evil sign, especially when it is displayed point-down, because they understand Satanists use it to worship "Baal". It is said to outline the features of a goat head, which represents a Pagan deity called "Baphomet". Many of these ancient names are two or three deities' names joined together. Masons call on "Jabulon", which is supposed to represent "Jehovah", "Baal", and "On" (the "On" part is an Egyptian deity).

In reality, the pentagram is an ancient building tool, a geometric figure which contains what is called "the golden section", or "golden mean". This is a repeating mean RATIO. It was used like a ruler in the ancient world in building design. It is **61.25%** of any given length. It is the division of a length, such that the smaller part is to the greater as the greater is to the whole. Pentagrams' lines intersect one another at these key places. It is much used as a "key" or **proportion** in design. The main measurements in many arches, bridges, and buildings have used this "golden mean" since early times. Artists, architects, sculptors, and engineers frequently use the **golden mean** in industrial design. This proportion is found in all living things; the rate of curve in the nautilus, the placement of the eyes on the head, the location of the heart in man relative to his height, the knees, the elbows in the arm span, etc.,. Beauty is determined by how close to the golden mean one's features approach! It was discovered by the Greek mathematician Euclid II in the mid 5th century BCE, and later used by the Pythagoreans as a sign of salvation and secrecy. The Italian mathematician Luca Pacioli called it *divina proportione* (divine proportion), and Johannes Kepler (d. 1630) called it *sectio divina* (divine section).

Since we know that the proportions found in the pentagram are used by the true Creator, ᄏᎩᄏᘔ, there is no need to fear the symbol. If Pagans adopted it, then they only show their ignorance by not knowing its true origin. Pagans also adopted the "serpent on the pole" as the sign for healing! Originally, the bronze serpent "Nehushtan" (2 Kings 18:4, Num. 21:8, John 3:14) was a sign to be looked upon, and those bitten by a snake were healed. But, the serpent on the "staff" became a Greek sign of a healing deity, Aesculapius, a symbol embraced by the medical sciences, and called a "caduceus". The "Seal" of those who worship the True Creator is the Name: ᄏᎩᄏᘔ.

Paul exhorts us: *"Examine yourselves TO SEE WHETHER YOU ARE IN THE FAITH; TEST YOURSELVES."* ~ 2 Cor. 13:5. If you have the Spirit of OᎳᎩᄏᘔ, you pass the test. When you are able to **closely examine** the trappings and observances you are programmed to follow in Christendom, you will discover unsettling truths. This book is written for those who have wished to learn the truth, and want to progress to the next level. The practices like Christmas, Easter, Sunday, steeples, holy water, the wearing of black by "clergy", wreaths, trees, etc., are all customs "fossilized" from Paganism. The meanings behind them have been put "out of focus", to keep the masses from discovering how they are camouflaged counterfeits. Look closely at them, their true origins become clear.

Here's a practical example of how to see the "fine print" that often gets people into trouble for not reading it: (It's a *"pin-hole lens"*) **Take your first finger, and put your thumb below the "crease" of the first knuckle, making a tiny "pin-hole" to look through right up close to your eye. Now, find some really small print that you find difficult to read, like on a cassette or CD. Hold the print in good lighting about 5 to 6 inches away from your eye, and look through the "pin-hole" you make with your first finger and thumb, very close to your eye. You will discover you can read a word very clearly through this pin-hole, and by opening the pin-hole too much, the small print will become blurred.**

The pin-hole you make becomes the lens, or primary focal point; your eye lens is taken out of the picture. Now, it is just the fine print focused through the pin-hole, onto your retina in the back of your eye. The reason you can "focus" better on fine print in a bright light is because your iris closes to make a smaller "hole", but this thumb-and-finger "pin-hole" makes a much more powerful lens than your iris can make.

The physics of this practical example should also apply to the close scrutiny we give to what's behind our customs. Look closely, and test everything. Just because the origins are "out-of-focus" doesn't mean you can't look closely enough to see them clearly. Christendom has "blurred" quite a few things, wouldn't you say? Remember that we fight NOT AGAINST FLESH AND BLOOD, but against **spiritual forces** of evil. Rabbi OᎳᎩᄏᘔ was not hateful or mean-spirited when He spoke with Pilate, even when He knew this man would pronounce His death-sentence. Surely we can be patient with those who disagree with us. The Church of Rome, and her daughters, are the "beast" upon which rides **Mystery Babylon**. This Roman Beast is the 4th and last beast prophesied at Daniel 7, and will be successful *"until the time of wrath is completed"* Dan. 11:36.

"This calls for wisdom. The seven heads are seven hills on which the woman sits." ~ Rev. 17:9. Rome was founded on 7 hills. It is often referred to as *the seven hills of Rome.* *"Mystery Babylon, the Great Mother of Prostitutes and of the Abominations of the Earth."* This "title" is written on her forehead, so says Rev. 17:5. What is her name, or how can we identify her? Her name is the same as it was in ancient Babylon:

ISHTAR

As we have already covered, this name became Astoreth, Asherah, Astarte, Eostre, Eastre, and she is now embraced (or blurred) in the festival called *Easter.* Find *Easter*, and you find *her*. She's a bit *fossilized*, but nonetheless still around. The "beast" is here, and has been here for many centuries. If you are waiting for a "beast", then you will miss it, because it has been here deceiving ~ even the very elect ~ since it's deadly wound was healed, since the bishop of Rome became Pontifex Maximus. You will know them by their fruits. If you can honestly say that Rome isn't the beast, in the face of the wars she's waged, the Inquisition, the Crusades, the Roman Catholic Hitler, Concordats, Pogroms, and the bloody "convert-or-die" policy from Constantine onward, then many men before me have been wrong. If, on the other hand, Rome is not masquerading but is in fact doing the deeds of the Father, ᄏᎩᄏᘔ, would she be capable of such evil fruit? No, she is doing the work of her father ha Shatan. ᄏᎩᄏᘔ would not "change" His Shabbath to the Pagan Sun-day, nor use the Earth Mother's name for a celebration of His Son's resurrection, or re-invent by deception the Pagan festival for the rebirth of the sun, and call it His Son's birthday. He would not promote "Halloween", called such because it was *"all Halloweds' Eve'n,* the night before *All Saints' Day,* a re-invented Druid feast of the dead. ᴙᵞᴙ𝘇 would not continue to "sacrifice" His beloved Son <u>over and over</u> in a ghastly "mass" ritual ~ but ha Shatan would. ᴙᵞᴙ𝘇 would not have us "praying" to anyone but Himself in His Son's Name, but Shatan guides the Church of Rome to pray to Miryam, and many other so-called dead "saints" for blessings, protection, guidance, and intercession. I can go on and on. But, if there is the chance that these things are being misunderstood, perhaps the pope would like to **discuss** some of these issues with myself or any other Nazarene, then let it *be televised world-wide in the City of Yerushaliyim.* We'll bring OWᵞᴙ𝘇 with us.

Below, some Egyptian "priests" are honoring an image of the sun that looks very familiar. The

Egyptian Sun Worship

priests in the picture below are also offering to an image that is sun-like. The Roman Catholic "Monstrance" in the picture at the above right looks quite a bit like these other images. There is no such item mentioned in the Scriptures, so they must have borrowed it from the Pagans. (Many share this opinion).

Sun worship in Peru.

GOD OF MANY NAMES Shatan conceals his identity, and uses many names — while ᴙᵞᴙ𝘇 only needs one. Shatan is not omnipresent, and uses a network to gather information. Among his names like Baal, Molech, and Woden, he also uses the "female" forms like Ishtar, Frigga, Venus, or Aphrodite. Masons revere Nimrod, whose eye it is at the top of the pyramid on the back of the US $1 bill. "IN GOD

Monstrance

WE TRUST" takes on new meaning when one discovers Shatan, the "shining one", is the "GOD of this world". He uses the "reins" of old customs to rule us. So, it is really not Nimrod ruling us from the grave!

See the "Monstrance" above? Catholicism has taught that these display the actual "presence" of the literal body of Mashiach. Millions were killed for denying it was. Yet, Rabbi OWᵞᴙ𝘇 told us:

"At that time, if anyone says to you, 'Look, here is the Mashiach!' or 'There He is!', <u>do not believe it</u> . . . So, if anyone tells you 'There He is, out in the desert', do not go out; or, 'Here He is, in the inner rooms', do not believe it." ~ Mt. 24:23.

RELIGION HAS BEEN THE "DISNEY WORLD" OF MANY CENTURIES, DISPLAYING WONDROUS SIGNS AND MARVELS, WHILE PILFERING THE IGNORANT.

A funny quote:

*"Isn't Disney World a **people trap**, operated by a mouse?"* ~ Steven Wright

A famous quote: *"That which you find hateful to yourself, do that not unto your neighbor."* ~ Hillel, 1st century Pharisee

Many Christians are *awaiting* a one-world "government" they call the "beast" system. The text doesn't say there will **suddenly** be a "beast" government ruling the whole world prior to OWᵞᴙ𝘇's return, but rather it says,

"The whole world was astonished (overwhelmed) **and followed the beast . . . All inhabitants of the Earth will worship the beast . . ."** Rev. 13. This is not just a government, but a religious system ~ people are not <u>legislated</u> to worship this beast, they are tricked into it through *tradition, the establishment.* The intoxicating "wine" is the calendar, as you will see on page 110. It doesn't appear suddenly.

INTERMISSION

In view of the fact that some readers may be developing facial twitches, shuffling walk, smacking lips, neck-jerking, twisting movements, or other assorted character-istics, let's try to calm down. We should reassess, and reevaluate a bit.

Where does all this information we are gathering place us in the grand scheme? What "religion" or way of living does all of this point to? Since the "broad road" can be exposed as diverse "sects" traced to individual men who came out of one or another sect themselves, let's just look past them all, and only look at the One Who walked out of His tomb. What is His religion? Not only is He a **Rabbi**, but also the High Priest, and our Bridegroom. **One** of the reasons He died was to end the marriage vow of the previous Covenant, which ended in His divorcing Yisrael for harlotry (idolatry). He discusses this, before the New Covenant happened, at Yesha Yahu 50. At Yerme Yahu 3, "faithless Yisrael" (His wife) was given a "certificate of divorce" ~ that's what the 70-year Babylonian Captivity beginning in 586 BCE was all about. The Husband pleaded, "Return to Me, and I will return to you." But, remember, before a wife can re-marry, **her Husband must die!** In latter times, these times, we finally under-stand. He has taken the SAME Covenant people (His bride), and Gentiles who graft into them, and made a NEW COVENANT with His bride. He-brews chapters 8 & 9 help explain this. Yes, Elo-him died, and remained so for 3 days and 3 nights. The bride is now free to re-marry, because the Husband died. It's not a new bride, nor a new Husband; yet He died, ending the older Covenant. By making the New Covenant in His own blood, our Maker calls-out His bride, and writes the Covenant on their HEARTS, not stone. The blood of bulls and lambs did not change their hearts to obey, but in the power of the resurrection, OWYAZ's Spirit comes into us, enabling se-lected ones to repent, be immersed, and become a new creation as children of AYAZ.

NAZARENES

Some "handle" is commonly used for different groups, so that others will know what "bunch" or "compartment" to put them in. There are thou-sands of sectarian groups; Roman Catholic, East-ern Orthodox Catholic, Quakers, Shakers, Bap-tists, Mennonites, Amish, Pentecostals, Church of GOD, Christian Church, Mormons, Jehovah Wit-nesses, 7th Day Adventists, and so on. Each views all the rest as having serious doctrinal er-rors. Yet, the Mashiach is nothing even close to any of them. Now, we come to the "Nazarenes". We are not "organized" as a financial corporation. There's only a Spiritual "Head", and we are all members of His Body, with diverse gifts. We are all so different, we would not recognize each other necessarily by anything but how we live.

MESSIANICS

This is another "handle", sometimes com-monly understood to be a descendant of Abra-ham who believes in the Messiahship of Rabbi OWYAZ. All Nazarenes are Messianics, but not all Messianics are Nazarenes. Sure, many Gentiles are Nazarenes, and Messianics. Some "Messianics" are really practicing Christianity (Constantine's invention), but using Hebrew terms and symbols. The "elect" can even be deceived, as it was prophesied. Many of them have NO CLUE of the message of the Reign of AYAZ, nor know what the NEW COVENANT is. If you can read this book and still not know what these are, then I've failed miserably. I am a Nazarene, and a Messianic. I am also a "Yahudi", or worshipper of Yah. My son, Adam, has to attend school where he is often made fun of by Christians, because the other children have no idea what a Messianic is. Their "handle" is a Greek term, and they are taught by their parents, teachers, and community at large to celebrate Christmas, Easter, Halloween (some of them), and keep Sun-day as their "day of worship". We worship by obeying, everyday. What about "tithing"? Our giving is as the Writ-ings require; and part of this is explained at 1 Tim. 5. At 5:16, the assembly of believers not only helps support the needs of "elders" (those who are aged), but widows (and their children). It even says that the assembly should not be "burdened" with legitimate widows, **if she has a family that can help instead** (5:16). In fact, it says at 5:8:

"If anyone does not provide for his RELA-TIVES, and especially for his immediate family, he has denied the faith and is WORSE THAN AN UNBELIEVER." Elders, who need to eat also, are worthy of "double honor" if they direct the affairs of the assembly well. But, this is not for them all, such as myself, who have **no need for help**, since I am gain-fully employed, as I should be. I'm still young enough to work for food! It certainly doesn't mean the "elders" receive the WHOLE TITHE, nor is it for "spreading the Gospel". YOU are the letter; YOU spread the message of the Reign of AYAZ. We elders are here to teach

you, so many of you can become elders. The word "elder" in Hebrew is ZAKAN, and is the same word for "beard", with only a vowel sound changed. It came into the Greek using the word "PRESBUS", the root of "Presbyterian". It then took another turn in the word "BISHOP". We're just brothers with a responsibility, we're not any more important! Shaul considered Timothy an elder, and told him not to be hasty in the laying on of hands. Armed with knowledge, anyone can objectively see that most have wandered from the faith. The stubborn and ignorant cannot repent, until they are changed inside, spiritually.

Instead of unity in the Body of Mashiach, what we have is "compartmentalism"; each claiming to be following OWY∃Z, but actually each "compartment" follows a man who founded their "denomination". They don't actually come out and say "I am of Herbert Armstrong", or "I am of John Smyth", but that's still the result of it. An elder named Daniel Botkin who publishes a newsletter (see Resources in the back), very effectively explained this. He quoted C.E. Tozer, who observed the same thing. Mr. Tozer noted that if 100 pianos are tuned to the same tuning fork, then they are tuned together perfectly. If each of us "tunes" himself to Rabbi OWY∃Z, then we are automatically in unity! That's one of the reasons I'm using the palaeo-Hebrew when I write the Name; men have "monked" with things, but the original cannot be denied by any honest scholar.

FLESH: A BODY OF DEATH!

As you know, we are approximately 83% water, and 17% dust. We are the sum total of what we eat; plantlife, or animals who ate the plantlife. What are plants made of? Dirt, and water! As we age, our cells divide about once every 7 years. When they do, they lose information each time. In our DNA molecules, there are "telemeres" at each end, which the DNA uses as a building platform to begin assembling another cell when it's time to. Each time a new DNA strand is assembled, roughly every 7 years, a "telemere" is lost. They act as "counters", counting down to the point when there are no more, and the cell cannot divide, because there are no more telemeres! We're all gonna DIE! Inside this body of death, we have our spiritual body, which doesn't age. Sometimes, more often these days, people develop clusters of rapidly reproducing cells called **cancer**. As our cells divide, sometimes a molecule is plugged in where it should not be, but still "fits". This is a mis-reading, and cellular information is lost. So, cancerous cells are more "stupid", and are not as stable as normal cells. We can eat what we think is good food, but since the farmlands have been depleted of vital nutrients over the many decades of overuse, vitamins and minerals that should be there in our food just aren't there anymore. Eat wheat grass tablets—cows just eat grass, so how can this supplement hurt? The land is supposed to lie "fallow" for one year in every 7.

Normally, when a cell goes "foul", our body issues an order telling it to self-destruct. Because cancer is a **mutated**, stupid cell, it doesn't understand this command. Normally, cells have "receptors" on their outer cell walls which convey this message to self-destruct when they are detected by our body to have problems. The outer cell wall of cancer cells lack the ability to "hear" the message to self-destruct, because they are mutants. Medical science uses "cell poison" (Latin: cytoxin) to attempt to destroy these mutants. But, it also kills normal cells indiscriminately, attacking the immune system, arterial walls, bone marrow, hair follicles, fingernails, and sensitive cells in the eyes. Cancer can be caused by a variety of types of **damage to DNA:** electromagnetic "ionization", where strong magnetic fields can snatch-away an electron from one of the DNA molecules; radiation, such as being bombarded by or ingesting radioactive elements, or being subjected to cosmic rays, X-rays, or even solar radiation! Chemical abrasion can easily occur to DNA as well, as with nicotine or alcohol. . . And, simple trauma, or ripping away the DNA in tearing cuts and wounds can cause a cell to mutate.

IF YOU HAVE CANCER

Find a healthfood store, and buy a "tea" called **Flor-essence**. Get it fast, and use it. Waiting too long, or trying it after the point-of-no-return (like after the chemo-therapy has destroyed your ability to recover), makes it useless. Not using it after being told about it doesn't help either. Every **hour** counts without it in your body. For some reason, the mutant cells respond to it, and the "message" to self-destruct begins to work. Cancerous tentacles recede, and the "tumors" shrink away. Skin cancers fade away to nothing. **IF** it's used as directed, as **EARLY** as possible, you will absolutely not believe what 3 to 6 months will do. Find it on the internet. I have it in my store, and have used it for skin cancer (caused by the sun) personally. You cannot even tell the cancer was ever there!

ANTIBIOTICS AND ANTISEPTICS

To better care for this 'mudbag' of death we live in, we should strive for proper nutrition, exercise, safety, and proper hygiene. Back in the late 1800's, a doctor named Joseph Lister revolutionized surgery with his study of antiseptics. Better than 50% of those patients who underwent surgery died of infections, caused by the surgery itself. Joseph Lister succeeded in popularizing the idea of hand-washing before surgery, and in the use of antiseptics, such as alcohol. Cinnamon is an antiseptic too. Today, the mouthwash **Listerine** bears his name. If you would like to have the use of your teeth for most or all of your life, *pre-rinse* with a mouthful of Listerine full strength, then brush your teeth with a good anti-plaque flouride toothpaste. Then, rinse well. **Always** brush your teeth each night before bed, after breakfast, and especially immediately following candies, desserts, and gooey foods. Tooth decay occurs within the first 15 minutes of eating sweets, and progresses rapidly. Soft drinks will cause you to lose every tooth in your head. "Diet" soft drinks with sugar substitutes contain a nerve toxin in their ingredient **aspartame**, which when it reaches 86 degrees, releases methanol. It is linked to neurological damage, birth defects of every description, and seizures. The phenylalanine in aspartame breaks down the seizure threshold; and its depletesserotonin causes manic depression, panic attacks, rage, and violence. The mysterious "Gulf War Syndrome" was no doubt caused by the thousands of pallets of diet drinks sitting for weeks in 120-degree Arabian heat. Our own bodies are 98.6 degrees, well above the required 86 degrees that chemically changes the aspartame! Men from the Gulf War came home, and produced children with no arms, brain damage, and they themselves had "shaking", seizure-like symptoms for months. Now you know why you can't "cook" with sugar substitutes ~ it becomes chemically altered by heat. It only seems sweet until it gets past your tongue ~ but it's deadly. Over 20 years ago, it was suspected to cause long-term memory damage. If you are on the internet, search for "aspartame disease". You don't have to believe me, the evidence is overwhelming!

MAD COW'S DISEASE

This deadly disease is caused by a molecular "crystal" which replicates itself much like rock candy does in a glass of sugar solution. It goes after the **nervous system** in animals and humans. Only this crystal is not sugar; it's a **non-living** crystalline molecule (It's an epidemic of a fatal brain disease called bovine spongiform encephalopathy, or BSE). Animals which are only fed **plants** don't get it. But, the cattle industry "supplements" the diet of the vegetarian animals (cattle) with food pellets manufactured from the waste products of **other animals' bodies**. This molecular crystal cannot be "cooked-out" because it is not alive. Eating "kosher" ensures that you will not be exposed to such meat, nor will you receive the toxins contained in the blood, or the antibiotics, steroids, and growth hormones, because the diet of kosher animals is strictly controlled. Pigs are out of the question; not only are they declared "unclean" to consume, but they will eat anything.

(We'll look at Mark 7 and Acts 10, to see if we really can eat pigs). You are what you eat. [Something tells me you may not be relaxing during this intermission, but bracing even more!]

CURE FOR VIRUSES

Dr. Madeleine Mumcuoglu, doing research at the Hebrew University ~ Hadassah Medical center in Jerusalem, has found the answer to the influenza virus, and the common cold. It is a syrup derived from the plant *Sambucus Nigra*, better known as the black elderberry (she calls it **Sambucol**). The man who discovered **interferon**, Dr. Jean Lindenman, was the supervisor at the virology lab when Madeleine was looking for a topic for her doctorial research. He suggested elderberries: *"They have possibilities"*, he said, *"In any case, I've got 10 kilos of them in my deep-freeze"*. As viruses cannot replicate themselves outside of living cells, they have to **invade** cells to survive. *"If you can stop them from invading cells, you've defeated the disease"*, she said. She tested the black elderberry proteins against the Influenza B virus first, and discovered that *"they actually prevent the virus from invading the cell"*. The influenza virus invades cells by **puncturing** the cell wall with the tiny spikes of hemaglutinin that cover its surface. The active ingredient in the elderberry disarms the spikes, binds to them, thus stopping them from piercing the cell membrane. *"This was the first discovery"*, says Dr. Mumcuoglu. *"Next, we found evidence that elderberry proteins fight the influenza virus in another way, too. The viral spikes are covered with the enzyme, **neuraminidase**, which helps break down the cell wall. The elderberry inhibits the action of the enzyme. My guess is, that we'll find that elderberry acts against viruses in other ways, as well."* Clinical trials have proven that this 'healthfood product' actually works, and requires no medical approval because it is not a drug! For example, in a study of patients with influenza, half were given four doses daily of **Sambucol** (the name given to the product), and half were given a placebo. Within 24 hours, the symptoms of 20% of the **Sambucol** patients had significantly improved (fever, cough, muscle pain). After the second day, 735 declared themselves *cured*. Among the placebo group, only 16% were improved after two days, and it took most of them six more days to feel well again. **Sambucol** is no more than a 'health food' officially, but interest is snow-balling all over the world. In Hadassah's virology lab, it has been seen to inhibit the AIDS virus, and encouraging results are being seen now against the herpes and Epstein-Barr viruses. You can probably find this product in any good health food store; I stock it in lozenge form in my retail store (address on page 2) for $11. per bottle. I spent almost two years trying to get in touch with the suppliers when it first came out, so that people would have access to it. A friend of mine came down with chicken pox (as an adult, it could have been fatal or severely damaging to him) ~ and he was covered from head-to-toe with sores. Two days later, after taking **Sambucol**, he was not only completely well, but had no signs of the sores. Another case involved a mother who had been suffering from a flu for three months. She was getting worse in spite of antibiotics and the best in medical care, and was about to be put in the hospital. She talked to my wife Phyllis, and began taking **Sambucol** immediately. She was well in two days. How much money and suffering can be saved from not treating "symptoms"? Think of the lives to be saved, especially the fragile elderly ~ time lost from work, and so on. I've lost two close friends in their 70's over the years before this product was available, who both caught a flu and perished within 2 weeks from it. Once you've tried this product, you'll wonder why it isn't on the cover of every magazine. Why hasn't Madaleine won a Nobel Prize? If you think about it, the answer will come to you: it upsets too many money-making endeavors, exactly like this book does.

We've discussed how cancer is caused by abrasions and damage at the cellular level. Nicotine and estrogen-substitutes cause cancer. ("Estro-gen" is named after "Easter", the Babylonian Ishtar). Proto-cancer cells are in all of us. From now on, we can only expect the incidences of cancer to increase; currently *2 out of every 5 people will develop cancer* sometime during their lifetime. That's 40% of everybody, and only about half of those will survive the traditional **therapy**. I've watched them die, that's why I'm telling you. Avoid cheese, or at least treat it like you would chocolate, because it clogs your arteries and intestines, making the absorption of nutrients greatly reduced. Also, clots break free and block blood-flow to the heart or brain. Buy a jug of cranberry juice every month, and force yourself to drink it. It cleans your system out.

Now, for a bit of more calming news. During this relaxing intermission, it's nice to be able to go outside and breathe in some fresh air, and gaze up into the peaceful universe above us. While we're doing this, let's consider the 5th planet, called "Jupiter".

JUPITER STAR

Jupiter -- 5th planet, named for Roman idol meaning "Zeus-father" (IU-PITAR). NOTE: It's a pagan name, folks, forbidden by Ex. 23:13, Ps.

16:4. This giant ball of mostly hydrogen has always been intriguing to scientists, since it would have been the **second star** in our system if it had only a slightly larger bit of mass. It has the same make up as our sun. With only a LITTLE more mass, the core temperature would be sufficient to cause a fusion effect; the nuclear reactions of the hydrogen cycle -- to ignite the star! For all practical purposes, it is an **unignited star**. This is the premise of the movie 2010 (the sequel to 2001 A Space Odyssey). This movie was based upon a real possibility, however.

In the real world, a controversial book called Behold a Pale Horse by Milton William Cooper has revealed many unsettling government secrets, and has quite an extensive historical perspective of events world-wide. This book is not fiction! He discusses the spacecraft Galileo which orbited the 5th planet, and how its decaying orbit was expected to deliver its payload into the dense inner regions of the planet sometime about December 1999. So what? Well, the book goes on to say that the dangerous power plant on board Galileo generates from a nuclear source: 49.7 pounds of weapons-grade **PLUTONIUM**. The pressures it may encounter in the deep, hot regions of the planet could simulate the conditions created by an implosion detonator. There is no worse place in our solar system for such a set of circumstances to exist, since the possibility of igniting the planet into a sun is very real. Just how long it would burn is unknown, because sustaining the nuclear reactions is linked to the stability of the hydrogen cycle in the core. But, it could explode so violently that it actually destroys the planet, causing a chain-reaction that turns the planet into a huge hydrogen bomb. The plutonium is encased in ceramic chips to keep it from going 'critical', and it is undergoing fission to generate the heat necessary for electrical production for on-board systems. But, if the ceramic chips are subjected to intense heat and pressure, they will **melt** -- and they could take their time to do it. It could sink into the liquid planet, drifting into hotter and hotter regions. It could take years, or even decades to explode, or maybe nothing will ever happen. There is also the **asteroid belt** to consider (between the 4th & 5th planets); if the star ignites, the explosive action would disrupt millions of chunks from this belt, sending them right at us, and distributing them into the entire inner solar system! That would be '**stars**' falling from the sky, burning as they enter our atmosphere, and impacting on our planet! The asteroid belt may have been put there for this very purpose, as the waters of the FLOOD were.

Planets do not emit energy, as a star does. Yet, the 5th planet is radiating twice as much infra-red (heat) as it receives from the sun! Something is _already_ happening inside it -- scientists estimate that only several hundred miles down, the metallic hydrogen is liquid, and is thousands of degrees. The core could be tens of thousands of degrees, or hotter. The Earth is one "AU" (astronomical unit) from its center to the center of our sun. The 5th planet is about 5.2 AU from the sun, making it 4 AU from Earth at its closest position. Double stars are more common than our system's single sun, and it appears that we could be responsible for igniting the giant gas bag. The additional radiant heat from a second star in our system would completely melt the Northern and Southern polar ice of Earth, flooding the lower elevations and coasts -- many islands would be no more (another prophetic occurrence). Then we really would have to "flee to the mountains", high ground! When you take it all in together, with the added situation of the asteroid belt to pelt us, the final days of distress were created beforehand to fulfill their purpose; like the frogs, flies, locusts etc., that plagued ancient Egypt! Being children of light (Torah), we will understand these things, while many others' hearts will fail from fear of the things coming upon the Earth.

If and **when** any of this happens, this Earth will be in distress. "And the fourth _angel_ poured out his bowl upon the sun, and it was given to it to scorch men with fire. And men were scorched with fierce heat; and they blasphemed the name of Elohim who has the power over these plagues, and they did not repent so as to give Him esteem." - Rev. 16:8,9. There is no indication which 'sun' is being referred to! People will "blaspheme" His Name (not use it), thus not giving Him esteem. The saints will be on Earth during the Tribulation, counter to the Christian Rapture Myth, and it will be the 'weeds' who will be taken first. The 144,000 are being sealed with the Name in their foreheads right now: the palaeo-Hebrew four letters YHWH (Yod-Hay-Waw-Hay).

According to the book, scientists have already chosen the name for the new star: _LUCIFER_, which means _light-bringer_ in Latin. Our Nazarene Rabbi, OWYAL, told us of a prominent sign or signal that He is coming: _"But pray that your flight may not be in winter, or on a Shabbat; for then there will be a great tribulation, such as has not occurred since the beginning of the world until now, nor ever shall. And unless those days had been cut short, no life would_ _have been saved; but for the sake of the elect, those days shall be cut short."_ -- Matt. 25:20-22. As a prelude to the final days of the 'times of the Gentiles', a world-wide message is to go forth, called the 'Gospel' or message of the Kingdom:

"Repent! For the Reign of AYAL draws near".

This report was the same message spoken by Yahushua's cousin called 'John the Baptist'. 'John' just prepared the way for it, and the One Who will be our Ruler one day soon. The whole Earth will be in distress. **And then, the end will come.**

(You might have guessed, but "John" wasn't a "Baptist", but rather a Torah-observant Levite priest. Being a priest, they didn't stone him when he said the Name ~ it was only a problem for non-priests. But, no one else was ever saying it, and many probably didn't even know he was saying it, not realizing what it was).

WHAT COULD IT MEAN?

MITHRAS SLAYING THE BULL

NOTICE the above stone carving of Mithras as a lion standing on a "sphere" with a cross on it? Plato wrote that the universe was created in the shape of an **X**, being the intersection of the celestial equator with the axis of the **Zodiac** (constellations of "living animals", since "zoo" and "zodiac" are related words). Could this "X" be the image of the beast? To the above right, we have a Pagan altar piece depicting Mithras slaying the bull, or overcoming the constellation of Taurus the bull. This is reverently cared for in the Vatican museum. Mithras, the sun deity, is shown in the act of *tauroctony*, slaying the bull. This act showed Mithras to be the supreme power in the universe, able to move the spring equinox out of the Age of Taurus (really caused by the precession of the Earth ~ a wobble). In this photo, the zodiac animals are represented along with the sun and moon (upper corners); the bull is Taurus, the dog is Canis Minor, the snake is Hydra, the raven is Corvus, the scorpion is Scorpio, and the stars around Mithras' head are thought to be planets, but could also be the Pleiades, or seven sisters. The lion motif represents the constellation of Leo, the lion. The universe is illustrated as a sphere with the cross on its surface, depicted above with Mithras standing on it as its supreme ruler with a lion's head. Atlas is seen holding this same sphere with the intersecting axis on its surface. Hopefully, this book has successfully slain some "bull" too.

Leaving all this Pagan Mithraic nonsense behind, what can we turn to? We can't follow after the Roman calendar, because it is like a dragnet trapping the whole Earth in its tentacles. You may wish to pick up a "Jewish calendar" at a synagogue or funeral home, to roughly familiarize yourself with Yisrael's Scriptural time system. Although there are a few technical glitches, they are mostly correct. Some Messianic groups have very good calendars available, and I recommend the one issued by Petah Tikvah, listed in the *Resources* portion in the back of this book.

Before Chris Koster died, I asked him to summarize the annual appointments for us, so here is what he provided. *(My additions will be in italics) :*

ᴀΥᴀℲ's APPOINTMENTS
A GENERAL OVERVIEW

THE APPOINTED TIMES

The Hebrew word is mo'edim, and in the traditional versions of the Scriptures, it was mistranslated as "festivals". The Hebrew for festival is "chag". Although many a "mo'ed" is also a "chag", this is by no means always the case. Elohim legislated these Appointed Times to be just that; a time that He has appointed for us to draw near to Him to serve Him, to worship Him. In 3 Mosheh 23 *(Lev. 23)*, we find these Appointed Times listed. The very first and most important one is the weekly **Shabbat**, of course. The weekly Shabbat, as well as the yearly Shabbat, the Day of Atonement *(Yom Kippur)*, are "mo'edim", but they are not festivals. The other Appointed Times in 3 Mosheh 23 are also called "festivals". If we turn our attention to these "Festivals of ᴀΥᴀℲ", we naturally ask two questions: What is their significance, and secondly, why were they done away with by the Church? Before we discuss this, please note that the seven festivals are grouped in three groups:
1. The festivals of the first moon, Abib,
2. The Festival of Weeks (Shabuoth)
3. The festivals of the seventh moon.

THEIR SIGNIFICANCE They were instituted "as a law forever", as we repeatedly read. In the first Scriptural month, Abib, we find the

PASSOVER

Pesach, also called Unleavened Bread. *(These are 2 separate things. One is an observance at twilight on the 14th, while Unleavened Bread begins the next evening ~ but some will differ on this).* Certainly having been fulfilled in the Messiah, our Passover Lamb slaughtered for us (1Cor. 5:7) ~ why insist that we still keep it? *(While the firstborn died in Egypt on the Passover, the blood on the doorposts pre-figured the Firstborn Son of* ꓷYꓷ꒒ *dying to cover our Torah-breaking).* The Passover was instituted forever, but as *(Rabbi)* Yahushua fulfilled it, His Body and His Blood took the place of the Passover lamb and its blood. Therefore we still observe the Passover, but with its Messianic emblems, the unleavened bread and the cup of the vine. Suffice it to say, the apostles kept on observing Unleavened Bread *(Matzah)* (Acts 12:3 and 20:6), and *(Rabbi)* Yahushua also promised that He will again drink of the fruit of the vine when the Reign of Elohim is physically set up, here on Earth (Mt. 26:29). *(The 1st and 7th days of Matzah are "rest days" from work. The 7th day is traditionally believed to be the day that Yisrael crossed the yam suph, or Sea of Reeds. The mightiest army on Earth perished that day, and Egypt has not recovered from it and the 10 plagues even to this day).*

The second group actually consists only of

SHABUOTH ~ The Festival of Weeks

(Called "Pentecost", Greek for "count-fifty", 7 weeks from a count of Shabbats from Passover). Traditionally this is thought to commemorate the giving of the Torah on Mt. Sinai. *(This is the event recorded at Acts 2, and saw the fulfillment of the promise of the New Covenant given at Yerme Yahu 31, where the Torah given at Sinai was written on the **hearts** of the 120 Nazarenes assembled in the upper room at the Temple. If they had not been observing this, they would not have received the Ruach ha Qodesh. Constantine re-designed its determination at the first Council of Catholicism, at Nicea in 325 CE, and involved the Vernal Equinox in setting it. He also set up the policy that if ever "Easter" and Passover occurred on the same day, "Easter" would be observed the following "Sun-day", so as not to have anything "in common with the hostile rabble of the Yahudim.")* When the taught-ones were assembled on Shabuoth, as we read in Acts 2, the Set-apart Spirit was poured out on them. Nevertheless, they simply kept on keeping Shabuoth year by year, e. g. Acts 20:16 and 1Cor. 16:8.

The third group, those of the seventh Scriptural month, are most interesting, because they have never been fulfilled. The Appointed Times of the seventh month consist of **Trumpets** *(or shofar/ram's horn blowing, called Yom Teruah),* **Day of Atonement** *(Yom Kippur),* **Festival of Booths** *(Sukkot, or Tabernacles),* and the **Last Great Day**. Interestingly, the Festival of Booths also has the name "Festival of Ingathering".

In Col. 2:16,17, we read that these festivals, new moons, and Shabbats ***"are a shadow of what is to come"***. Notice, it is not past tense "were". No, it is present tense, "are". Some years ago, the editor of <u>Midnight Cry</u>, a well-known prophetic magazine, said; "The Church has been robbed of its festivals." He then went on and elaborated on the great prophetic significance of the festivals of the seventh moon in particular. What do these Appointed Times of the seventh moon foreshadow? By the way, we all know that the weekly Shabbat is a shadow of the seventh millennium, yet to come. Nevertheless, we still keep the Shabbat for it is the sign of the Eternal Covenant (Exodus 31:13-17 and Ezekiel 20:12-20).

TRUMPETS ~ Yom Teruah

This is generally interpreted as being a shadow of the Last Trumpet—1Cor. 15:52, Mt. 24:31, 1Thess. 4:16, Rev. 11:15—heralding the Second Coming of Messiah and the establishment of the Reign of Elohim here on Earth! *(This is also called Rosh Hashanah, and is the 1st day of the seventh moon).*

DAY OF ATONEMENT ~ Yom Kippur

Yahushua has certainly atoned for us as individuals when He died in our stead. However, as a nation, Yisrael is still awaiting its national atonement. Yisrael is still to be reconciled to Elohim, through Yahushua, the Sovereign of the Yahudim, the Shepherd of Yisrael. *(This is the 10th day of the 7th moon, called "the Fast" at Acts 27:9).*

FESTIVAL OF BOOTHS ~ Sukkot

This is a shadow of Elohim setting up His Booth as the New Yerushaliyim comes from heaven. *(Outer Space, Shamayim, or skies. Dwelling in tents ourselves for 7 days, we are reminded of the wilderness experience of Yisrael, but more importantly the spiritual teaching that we are sojourners in these bodies of flesh, and we will move into a "permanent" or immortal "house" when we put on incorruption).* Let us read Rev. 21:3; ***"See, the Booth of Elohim is with men, and He shall dwell with them and be their Elohim."*** But, in spite of Him dwelling among His people, the Festival of Booths continues to be observed ~ read all of ZekarYah 14! Even those who are left from the Gentiles *(goyim, v. 16),* after YHWH had fought against all the Gentiles who came up to fight against

A TIMELINE TO CONSIDER

"But do not forget this one thing, dear friends; with � a day is like a thousand years, and a thousand years are like a day . . . But the Day of ᴧYᴧ⅂ will come like a thief. The heavens will disappear with a roar; the elements will be destroyed by fire, and the Earth and everything in it will be laid bare . . . But in keeping with His promise we are looking forward to a new heaven and a new Earth, the home of righteousness." 2Pet. 3:8-13. Life's lessons are repeated until you learn them, and ignoring them will only cause you to go through old lessons again and again.

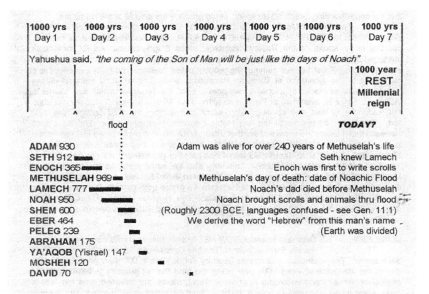

Yerushaliyim (vv. 2,3), shall be compelled to worship YHWH and to observe the Festival of Booths (vv. 16-18).

THE LAST GREAT DAY

This is a shadow of what Yahushua will do in the Last Day, as we read of its fulfillment in Rev. 7:17, 21:6, and 22:1,2. As Messiah was observing the Festival of Booths in Yoch. 7, we read in Yoch. 7:37-39 how He will give us to drink from the fountain of the river of life, sometimes called the fountain of living waters. Already this has had a *partial* fulfillment in the lives of the True Believers, but the final consummation of the prophetic promise is still future! *(Get ready for Y6K).*

The seventh Scriptural month is the time when the ingathering from the threshing-floor and the winepress has been completed (read Deut. 16:13). This ingathering includes those truly converted Gentiles who joined themselves to YHWH (Yesha Yahu 14:1, 56:6-8, ZekarYah 2:11), *"even all the Gentiles on whom My Name has been called"* (Acts 15:17).

Why did the Church do away with these festivals? The answer is given to us at Daniel 7:25 ~

the little horn (generally interpreted as Rome) *"intends to change Appointed Times and Law."* This is exactly what took place when the Roman Church was set up to lay waste the True Worship, to trample underfoot that which is set-apart. The Festivals of YHWH were done away with and they continued with their old Gentile customs and festivals ~ Christmas, Easter, Sunday, etc.,. *(Let's not forget the Pagan underpinnings of Halloween, Valentine's Day, Lent, and the "feasts" dedicated to particular "saints" that were all re-interpreted Pagan days).*

Chris Koster

Brother Chris fell asleep in the Spring about 5 years ago. Wilhelm Wolfaardt is carrying on the work of *ISR* (Institute for Scripture Research), which is listed in the back, under *Resources.*

Note: Chris died from cancer. Everyone needs to be taking the very BEST vitamins and minerals . . . This gives your cells the right stuff so they can divide without "errors" from free radicals. Remember your *VITAMINS, VITAMINS, VITAMINS!!!*

MIND OF THE FLESH
VS.
MIND OF THE SPIRIT

The Testimony of Yahushua
THE GOSPEL
MESSAGE OF THE REIGN

THE MOST IMPORTANT
DATA IN THIS BOOK!
READ CAREFULLY;
IT'S A
SECRET

THE WORD "GOSPEL" AN ANALYSIS

The word "Gospel" is 𝔒𝔩𝔡 𝔈𝔫𝔤𝔩𝔦𝔰𝔥. It's really 2 words crammed together: GOD + SPEL. We have already seen that the Teutonic Celts worshipped the sun with the word "GOD", and it was a proper name. It was used because it was already a familiar word to them, coming from the Greeks' translation. The Greeks used THEOS instead of "Elohim", because they were already familiar with their old word also. The Greeks called Zeus "Theos", and their letter "theta" Θ was originally a circle with a dot in the center, representing the sun running across the sky. They called all their deities by the title "Theos". Some scholars believe that using "GOD" and "THEOS" to refer to �богㄱㅈ is the prophesied abomination of desolation. Pillars of Jealousy (steeples), Sun-day, calling OWYㄱㅈ "Yeh-Zeus", Easter, and more yet to be exposed follow in that line of thought.

The second part of the word "Gospel", SPEL, is also Celtic in origin. It means incantation, speech, spiel, news, message, or report. It is the "spell" spoken to others.

In 1948 CE, A. W. Tozer wrote the following words, underscoring how we can become swept up in mindless devotion by imitating others:

"Christian literature, to be accepted and approved by the evangelical leaders of our times, must follow very closely the same train of thought, a kind of 'party line' from which it is scarcely safe to depart. A half-century of this in America has made us smug and content. We imitate each other with slavish devotion and our most strenuous efforts are put forth to try to say the same thing that everyone around us is saying."

The true "Gospel" is virtually unknown by most people on Earth today, yet "collections" to "spread" the "Gospel" are being donated to men who don't know what it is. It's all wasted, because like cancer researchers, they stumble in great darkness. The original followers of OWYㄱㅈ carried its free message, but it died out (on the surface) with the last of the Nazarenes and Ebionites before the 4th century. The Writings reveal that it is a SECRET, and a mystery, and will one day be revealed just before the end of men's kingdoms. It is directed only for the understanding of those whose names are written in the Scroll of Life, sealed with 7 seals. These are the BRIDE of Mashiach. The wedding betrothal occurred at Sinai, when the children of Israel listened to the Voice of the Groom, and agreed to obey Him. Other "sheep"

not of this fold (Gentiles) will also take the Name of the Groom. We'll discuss this in greater detail here. The word "Gospel" is one of many words we have inherited from dead translators that has taken on a kind of life of its own. Even encyclopedias admit that it is a bit "fuzzy". Scholars accept the term, but both what it is, and how the term came into use, are not clearly understood. The word's meaning and use is the result of our imitating each other for centuries, or our attempting to say the same thing everyone around us is saying. People who want to defend the altered names and other words they are conditioned to use by imitation sometimes will say, *"Well, I speak English, and not some foreign language."* English is like a wide river with many other languages flowing into it. "Gospel" is Celtic. "Evangelical" is Greek (from *euangelion*, meaning *message, or report*). It became the Latin word *evangelium*. You can see the word *angel* in both, which simply means *messenger*. "Epistle" is Greek for *letter*. Many words we think of as English are really *Celtic, Latin, Greek, French, Hebrew, or aboriginal tongues* spoken by the natives of an area prior to English settlers. Rivers, states, and countries are often named by "foreign" terms. They're not "English", but our familiarity with them causes us to believe they are.

When Rabbi OWYㄱㅈ was in the synagogue (Mt. 11) and read from the TaNaKh, He read aloud in Hebrew the words of Yesha Yahu 61. He told them that this prophecy had been fulfilled in their ears! He announced the fulfillment of the prophecy of the awaited Mashiach, as His listeners comprehended. He proclaimed the *"acceptable year of ㄱㅈYㄱㅈ"*, known as the year of *Jubilee* (every 50th year, native-born Yahudim are to be freed, and land is to be returned to the heirs according to their tribes). He was also proclaiming the *"Gospel"*: the announcement that the *"Reign of ㄱㅈYㄱㅈ"* had come into their midst. If you read all of Yesha Yahu 61 & 62 (as He probably did), you'll discover that it promises the day when the *"Bridegroom"* will rejoice over His BRIDE. At Mt. 11:5 where this passage of Yesha Yahu is being quoted, the word "Gospel" appears in our *translation* from the original Hebrew word BASAR (ㄱㅈ Ψ 𐤁 or ㄱ ש ב), meaning *tidings, message, report, or news*. You must know what the message is, to carry it to others.

THE REIGN OF ᴀYᴀZ

(Otherwise known as the "Kingdom of GOD")

How do we know it's a **secret**? At Mark 4:11,12: *"And when He was alone, those about Him, with the 12, asked Him about the parable. And He said to them, 'To you it has been given to know the SECRET of the REIGN OF ᴀYᴀZ, but to those who are outside, all are done in parables, so that seeing they see but do not perceive, and hearing they hear but do not understand, lest they should turn* (repent) *and their sins be forgiven them'".* (He was quoting Yesha Yahu 6:9). The "secret" or "mystery" is really the "Gospel" itself. At Romans 16:25: *"Now to Him who is able to establish you according to my (GOSPEL) and the preaching of* OWYᴀZ *ha Mashiach, according to the revelation of the MYSTERY which has been kept SECRET for long ages past . . ."* So, the *"GOSPEL"* isn't something new, but was first spoken to **Abraham** (see Gal. 3:8, Gen. 12:3). Abraham was *called-out* from among Pagans and Gentile practices, and was ultimately to become a blessing to the Gentiles because of his *"fidelity"* (faithfulness, *emunah*). Paul had to sternly warn the Gentiles who had converted at Galatia, and to those at Ephesus (4:17,18) he said: *"This I say therefore, and affirm together with ᴀYᴀZ, that YOU NO LONGER WALK AS THE GENTILES WALK, in the futility of their thinking, being darkened in their understanding, excluded from the Life of ᴀYᴀZ, BECAUSE OF THE IGNORANCE THAT IS IN THEM, because of the hardness of their heart."*

They were just overwhelmed by the Pagan patterns of everyday living. When Paul stood before the Greek idolators in Athens, he stood as Yonah had in Nineveh:

"Therefore having overlooked the times of ignorance, ᴀYᴀZ is now declaring to men that all everywhere should REPENT, because He has fixed a day in which He will judge the world in righteousness through a Man whom He has appointed, having furnished PROOF to all men by raising Him from the dead." Acts 17.

The Reign of ᴀYᴀZ will be to most like a trap springing shut, and catch the majority by complete surprise. They are in a Roman system, ignorant of the annual observances they are taught are "Jewish". Weekly Shabbat, Passover, Shabuoth (Pente-cost), Yom Teruah, Yom Kippur, and Sukkot (Tabernacles) all picture the redemption of ᴀYᴀZ's Bride, but they are kept from the knowledge of the plan, and what to watch for. (For those unaware, Paul used to be "Shaul").

Paul explains it is a mystery to the Ephesians at 6:19: *"and pray on my behalf, that utterance may be given to me in the opening of my mouth, to make known with boldness the MYSTERY of the (GOSPEL) . . ."* (see also Eph. 3:3-9). In Col. 1, Paul states his goal is *"That I might fully carry out the preaching of the Word of ᴀYᴀZ, the MYSTERY of which has been hidden from the past ages and generations, but has now been manifested in His qodeshim* (set-apart ones, saints) *TO WHOM ᴀYᴀZ willed to make known what is the riches of the esteem of this SECRET among the Gentiles* (the Torah written on your hearts) *which is: MASHIACH IN YOU, the expectancy of esteem, Whom we announce, WARNING every man and TEACHING every man in all WISDOM* (Torah, Commandments), *in order to present every man perfect in Mashiach* OWYᴀZ *..."*

Shaul's reference to _Mashiach in you_ indicates that the believer is *ENABLED* to *LOVE* the Torah, and thus obey it (ᴀYᴀZ's Word), because His "seed" (the Commandments) came into the Nazarenes literally, fulfilling Yerme Yahu 31, implementing the *New Covenant:*

"'But this is the Covenant which I will make with the house of Yisrael after those days', declares ᴀYᴀZ, 'I will put my Torah within them, and on their HEART I will write it . . .'" This prophecy is quoted at Heb. 10:16, and 2Cor. 3:3, and it first occurred at "Pentecost" (the commanded convocation called "Shabuoth", which commemorates the *giving of Torah at Sinai*).

Paul is quoted very often by today's preachers when they need to justify their "freedom" from the Commandments, making "sin" more of a state of the heart than a tangible, definable thing. Sin is definable, because 1 Yahuchanon 3:4 says:

"Everyone who sins breaks the Torah; in fact SIN IS TORAHLESSNESS." (anti-nomia, *lawlessness*). OWYᴀZ came to *destroy the devil's work* in us, and Yahuchanon goes on at 3:9 saying: *"No one who is born of ᴀYᴀZ will continue to sin, because ᴀYᴀZ's seed remains in him; he cannot go on sinning, because he has been born of ᴀYᴀZ. This is how we know who the children of ᴀYᴀZ are and who the children of the devil are: Anyone who does not do what is right is not a child of ᴀYᴀZ; nor is anyone who does not love his brother."*

2Pet. 3:15,16 discusses how this lawlessness was being propagated by *DISTORTIONS OF PAUL'S WRITINGS*:

"Our beloved brother Paul wrote to you according to the wisdom given him, as also

in all his letters, speaking in them concerning these matters, IN WHICH SOME ARE HARD TO UNDERSTAND, WHICH THOSE WHO ARE UNTAUGHT AND UNSTABLE TWIST, as they do also the other Writings, to their own destruction. Therefore, dear friends, since you already know this, BE ON YOUR GUARD so that you may not be carried away by THE ERROR OF LAWLESS MEN and fall from your secure position." The "merchants" draw away your attention to the fact that Peter is calling Shaul's words "Scripture", but they cause you to overlook the serious warning of Peter *talking about the very men you are listening to!* Paul is always the one they quote to "prove" the Torah is no longer in force, yet here is Peter warning us of "falling" for that lie. (Paul is speaking of the "ceremonial" law coming to an end). The "Message", called the "Gospel", is very simple. The Writings are very clear about what it is, but listening with "lawless" ears, it is *veiled* to those who are perishing:

"'*The time has come, He said. 'The Kingdom of ᴧYᴧ𝘡 is near. Repent and believe the good news'*". Mark 1:15.

"*The Torah and Nebi'im* (Law, or *Teachings,* and prophets) *were proclaimed through Yahuchanon. Since that time, the good news of the Reign of ᴧYᴧ𝘡 is being preached, and everyone is forcing his way into it. It is easier for heaven and Earth to disappear than for the least stroke of a pen to drop out of the Torah.*" (Luke 16:16,17). What "Gospel/good news" have you been taught all your life? Commonly, it involves not being condemned for disobedience to the Torah. This is partly true, but it overlooks what the resurrection means to us, and what receiving OWYᴧ𝘡 accomplishes, by His writing His Torah on our hearts! Shaul said to the Galatians, who were falling back into their old Pagan customs:

"*But even though we, or a messenger from the skies brings a message* ("Gospel") *to you besides what we announced to you, LET HIM BE ACCURSED.*" - Gal. 1:8.

THE REAL MEANING

The *real* "Gospel" (message) is not the popular one. It is *"Repent, for the Reign of ᴧYᴧ𝘡 draws near."* Mt. 3:2, 4:17, Luke 16:16, Mark 1:15, Acts 8:12, etc.,. In fact, **ALL THE PARABLES** describe it in great detail. The message of the Reign of ᴧYᴧ𝘡 is the subject matter of the parables, which veil its meaning from those not called. (Many are called, few chosen).

"*I will open My mouth in a parable; I will utter dark sayings of old which we have heard and known, and our fathers have told us.*" Ps. 78. You can praise the Living ᴧYᴧ𝘡 till you drop; but if you will not *obey* Him, your prayers and praise are an abomination, Pr. 15:8,9, 28:9, Yesha Yahu 1:15.

At 2Cor.4:3, Shaul states that he does not distort the "Word of ᴧYᴧ𝘡", and says: *"Even if our (Gospel) is veiled, it is veiled to THOSE WHO ARE PERISHING. The elohim (Shatan) of this age has blinded the minds of unbelievers, so they cannot see the Light of the (Gospel) of the esteem of Mashiach, Who is the Image of ᴧYᴧ𝘡."* At 2Cor. 2:15-17, Shaul speaks also of those perishing, and says something that might really open your eyes:

"Unlike so many, WE DO NOT PEDDLE THE WORD of ᴧYᴧ𝘡 FOR PROFIT."

The "WE" would be the ones called the *Nazarenes,* who follow the Lamb where He leads us, into Truth.

The **"Gospel"**, or *glad tidings,* announcing that all men everywhere should REPENT (turn from sin, and obey Torah), is our commission:

"And these good tidings of the Kingdom shall be preached in the whole world for a testimony to all the nations; and then shall the end come." Mt. 24:14.

(Those who are perishing do not understand the message, and they are being plundered by false teachers who are profiting from the faith).

The **first thing** a person must do is be con-victed of their sin against the Torah. Hearing first that their "sins are covered" doesn't emphasize repentance from sin, it sounds like they can live in their mind of the flesh, "believing".

Where is it written, that we will be punished for attempting to obey the Torah? Your enemy wants you to ignore the Torah, just as he tricked the first woman. If we think she goofed over such a simple thing, then we should look at how we find ourselves in the very same situation. Shatan is a liar, and has many people following his masquerading messengers of lawlessness. "Legalism" and the accompanying criticisms cannot be found in the Writings anywhere. The merchant messengers will tell you *"rest any day you like, just try to do it about every 7 days".* They still "program" you to come to a Sun-day morning assembly, so you will be able to feel good about contributing to their wonderful "work". They are the "priests of Baal" (the LORD), wearing black. "The LORD's Day", Baal's Day, is Sun-day. Start obeying the 7th day Shabbat, and watch what they say to you. It's the sign of the Eternal Covenant, which we will see details of later. I picked the 7th day Shabbat to rest, and do it without fail. I'm "marked" now, with a mark called the Sign of the Eternal Covenant Ez. 20:12, Yesha Yahu 56:4-8, Ex. 31:12-17, Gen. 2:2, Heb. 4.

THE EVERLASTING COVENANT

The Everlasting Covenant establishes a new relationship between ayaz and mankind. It's the relationship of a **Husband** and His **wife**. It's metaphoric, or a figure of speech that draws an analogy. Like a marriage, there are two processes involved: **betrothal** and **consummation**. 50 days after leaving Egypt, representing the bondage of sin, the children of Yisrael (the chosen wife of the promise) were at Mount Sinai. This was the first "Shabuoth", now called "Pentecost". The elements found in the Everlasting Covenant correspond to Yahudim wedding traditions. ayaz refers to Yisrael as His "wife", because He has engaged in a formal betrothal. Sinai was this betrothal, and two written copies of the Torah (teachings, written in stone on front & back) were the marriage "ketuba". One for the Husband, and one for the wife. These were placed into a special container, called **The Ark of the Covenant**. The Husband chose His wife, Yisrael, to care for, provide for, and protect. The wife agreed to **obey**, *forsaking all others*. *Two witnesses* were called forth to hear the Covenant: *shamayim* (heavens, skies), and *Eretz* (Earth). They are the witnesses to the wife making her vows: *"All the words which ayaz has spoken we will do."* Ex. 24:3. At this point, the 70 elders of Yisrael (the Sanhedrin of the time) ate and drank with the Husband, Bridegroom, Creator, and Sovereign. The "wife" provided her contribution to the marriage covenant, a type of property brought by a bride to her husband at a marriage: the gold, silver, bronze, fabrics, oils, and precious stones for the construction of the ark and dwelling of the Husband among them. The terms of this formal covenant (the written wedding agreement, or *ketuba*), were burned into stone with the finger of ayaz. The **NAME** of the Husband was taken by His wife; and so they (we) are called: **YAHUDIM**. This was corrupted to *Judah*, by translators, then *Jude*, and for the last several hundred years, it has been *Jew*. ayaz speaks of His Covenant without ceasing, reminding His wife of the marriage. *"For your Maker is your Husband ~ ayaz Shaddai is His Name"* (Read all of Yesha Yahu 54, 55 & 56).

GENTILES ALSO CALLED

"Blessed is the man who does this, the man who holds it fast; who KEEPS THE SHABBATH without defiling it, and keeps his hand from doing any evil. LET NO FOREIGNOR who has bound himself to ayaz say, 'ayaz will surely exclude me from His people'. And let not any eunuch complain, 'I am only a dry tree'. For this is what ayaz says: "To the eunuchs who keep my Shabbaths, who choose what pleases Me and hold fast to my covenant ~ to them I will give within My Temple and its walls a memorial and a name better than sons and daughters; I will give them an everlasting name that will not be cut off. And FOREIGNERS who bind themselves to ayaz to serve Him, to love the Name of ayaz and to worship Him, ALL WHO KEEP THE SHABBATH without defiling it and who hold fast to My covenant, these I will bring to My qodesh mountain and give them joy in My house of prayer . . . . For My house will be called a house of prayer for all nations.'" Yesha Yahu 56:2-7.

All of the "converts" underwent an immersion, called now a "baptism", which is a logical progression for us to turn to now. Any body of water can be used; the Hebrew term is "MIKVA". Traditionally, a mikva is a place to wash away "uncleanness", as a woman would bath after her monthly cycle before having contact with her husband. Likewise, our "Husband" doesn't wish contact with us until we have washed away our past sins (ignoring Torah). Our immersion is an outward sign of our commitment to obey from that point on, and the New Covenant promises the Spirit (our "helper") which writes the Torah (Covenant, marriage vows to obey) on our hearts. This pledge identifies us with His Name, His burial, and His resurrection from the dead. At 1Peter 3:18-22, Cephas (Peter) states that the 8 persons on the ark were also *saved through water*, and that water symbolizes our immersion that now saves us. Those who came through the water fleeing Pharaoh came through the sea, along with "foreigners". All were saved through water. Immersion is our outward sign of a good conscience toward ayaz, and now represents our "circumcision", Col. 2:11,12:

"In Him you were also circumcised, in the putting off of the sinful nature, not with a circumcision done by the hands of men, but with the circumcision done by Mashiach, having been buried with Him in (baptism) and raised with Him through your faith in the power of ayaz Who raised Him from the dead." Obviously, not comprehending this at the time of one's immersion means it was not anything but a "fake", and probably wasn't in the correct Name! An infant cannot possibly be considered capable of knowing what is happening. Immersion is an act of your own personal will; You covenant with owyaz.

LAYING ON OF THE HANDS

You can immerse yourself, but it is my advice to find an elder if possible to attend. After immersion, you should seek to have an elder's hands laid upon your head, reciting the priestly blessing which places the Name of ﬡYﬡZ on you (Num. 6:22-27). At this point, you may bring others to the water, and lay hands on them. The students (disciples) of Rabbi OWYﬡZ did this, but He immersed no one ~ it is our duty to make converts and immerse them into His Name. At the time of the laying on of hands, you will receive a greater "measure" of OWYﬡZ's Spirit, or gifts; not that the man touching your head has any "power" of his own, but rather by your obedience, our Beloved OWYﬡZ witnesses your actions; and brings you an increase in His power. Do you feel driven to the water now? This knowledge is free, and the "Kingdom" of ﬡYﬡZ is not a thing to "go" to, because it is in our hearts, unseen. We are the set-apart (qodesh) "Temple", not a building dedicated to the financial plundering of the lost. I was immersed in a creek here in Louisville, with only my 8-year-old son present, when I was 39 years old. I had been immersed as a baby, and by a Christian minister a couple of years before, but I called on Yahushua when he said "Jesus". He looked pretty shocked when I said it. But, I did it again myself in the creek, because I felt disturbed over the other situation. The Blood of the Lamb covers our sins, but we inherit eternal life by the resurrection of OWYﬡZ ~ which is what our immersion pictures. Although my son and I were the only people present at the creek, I felt the presence of ﬡYﬡZ, and other beings in His presence who witnessed my immersion. You will also, when you obey, and undertake this "circumcision". Romans chaps. 7 & 8 are a must-read! Read the whole context without a "lawless mind". The secret is unlocked for you. Shaul explains the whole struggle with "sin", and how we, with the Spirit, delight in ﬡYﬡZ's Torah in our inner being. The "law" is spiritual; but while we remain in an unspiritual condition, it produces death. The "law" was created to produce LIFE, but can only do so if we become spirit-minded by having Mashiach in us, destroying our sinful, lawless nature. *"Those who live according to the sinful nature have their minds set on what that nature desires; but those who live in accordance with the Spirit have their minds set on what the Spirit desires. The mind of sinful man is death, but the mind controlled by the Spirit is life and peace; the sinful mind is hostile to* ﬡYﬡZ. *IT DOES NOT SUBMIT TO* ﬡYﬡZ's *TORAH, NOR CAN IT DO SO. Those controlled by the sinful nature cannot please* ﬡYﬡZ. *You, however, are controlled NOT by the sinful nature, but by the Spirit, IF THE SPIRIT OF* ﬡYﬡZ *LIVES IN YOU. And if anyone does not have the Spirit of Mashiach, he does not belong to Mashiach."* Rom. 8:5-9. Please read

Romans chapters 7 & 8. You will be confronted by many people in the future who struggle to understand what Shaul really means. Men attend B-ble colleges, seminaries, and spend their entire lives without being able to "crack" the secret, nor can it be done ~ unless your mind gives up, and you ask OWYﬡZ for the TRUTH. As I said on page 4 of this book, you must have asked Him for the TRUTH, because now you have it. I asked, and I received. "The Truth Is Out There" ~ but now it can be **IN** you. You have just found the treasure of eternal life, if you will only pick it up and put it on! That is what the ("Gospel") message of the Reign of ﬡYﬡZ is, and the 1st part of the secret:

REPENT. *FOR THE REIGN OF* ﬡYﬡZ *DRAWS NEAR.* This means He reigns in our hearts and minds, and we obey Him because we love the Covenant (the marriage vows, the 10 Commandments). We show our love for Him by our faithfulness. We change, they don't. The "change" in the "law" between the Old Covenant and the New concerned the ceremonial animal sacrifices, which were imperfect, and could not justify us permanently.

The New Covenant: This is the 2nd part of the secret. It was "cut" in the Blood of the Lamb of ﬡYﬡZ, when ONE sacrifice put an end to atoning for lawbreaking. Having become convicted of our sinfulness, we "turn" or repent to the Torah. Our belief in Him as our substitution, convinces us of our sinfulness and need for a debt payer. However, we cannot be perfect, because of our mind of the flesh. This is where the New Covenant brings us eternal life. Showing our repentance to the marriage vows by obedience, we go to the water in full submission to our Husband, and wash clean spiritually. We actually "die" to sin. We are then "raised" with Him, and He comes into us ~ you will feel Him, it is like a "wind" grabbing you from the inside, filling you. You will feel something change in your will, and have a new clarity of mind. Your flesh will no longer rule your mind, but your spirit will rule your flesh. By His resurrection, we have eternal life also. We are atoned for by His death; but we are SAVED by His LIFE, the resurrection from the dead. This is the complete Truth, and it is absolutely free. You don't have to pay for it, by going to a steeple for decades giving a man 10% of your money, because he doesn't even know it.

As you continue to learn, you will see that Christianity is a man-made religion, and absolutely nothing like the faith (religion) that was delivered to the saints. The Nazarenes existed for centuries before a "Christianity" did.

THE 10 COMMANDMENTS

CALLED THE "DECALOGUE", DECA (TEN), LOGUE (WORDS), Ex. 20:1-17

1. I AM 𐤉𐤄𐤅𐤄 YOUR ELOHIM. HAVE NO OTHER BEFORE MY FACE.
[NO FOREIGN NAMES, RITUALS, CUSTOMS OF PAGANS]

2. YOU DO NOT BOW TO IMAGES.

3. YOU DO NOT BRING THE NAME OF 𐤉𐤄𐤅𐤄 YOUR ELOHIM TO NAUGHT.
[NO MISUSE OR NONUSE, BRINGING HIM SHAME]

4. REMEMBER SHABBATH, TO KEEP IT SET-APART.
[SIGN OF EVERLASTING COVENANT OF LOVE, EX. 31:13, EZ. 20:16-20. CHANGED (DAN. 7:25) BY CONSTANTINE TO HIS "DAY OF THE SUN" IN 321 CE FOR CHRISTIANS, CHANGED BY MUHAMMAD TO 6TH DAY, CIRCA 622 CE. SHABBATH ACKNOWLEDGES 𐤉𐤄𐤅𐤄 AS **CREATOR**, HEB. 4. IN THE WORLD BEFORE SIN CAME, AND REMAINS FOR ALL ETERNITY, IS. 66:23, PS. 119:152, EX. 31:13.]

5. YOU RESPECT YOUR FATHER AND YOUR MOTHER.

6. YOU DO NOT MURDER.

7. YOU DO NOT ADULTERATE.

8. YOU DO NOT STEAL.

9. YOU DO NOT BEAR FALSE WITNESS AGAINST YOUR NEIGHBOR.

10. YOU DO NOT COVET YOUR NEIGHBOR'S HOUSE, WIFE, SERVANTS, OX, ASS, OR ANYTHING THAT BELONGS TO YOUR NEIGHBOR.

THESE ARE TO BE DILIGENTLY TAUGHT TO YOUR CHILDREN, AND POSTED ON THE DOORPOSTS OF YOUR HOME. (Dt. 6).

NOTE: Roman Catholics eliminated the 2nd (so as to continue the Pagan behavior of bowing and kneeling before images), and split the 10th Commandment into two, so as to maintain 10. They briefly outlawed images during the 8th century, but after 34 years without them, reverted back by wiping out the dogma. (At the Council of Constantinople in 754, image worship and images were abolished. In 788, worship of the cross, relics (dead bones), and images were re-authorized. Source: _The Catholic Encyclopedia_ When Rabbi O W Y 𐤄 𐤅 warned us that _"a little leaven_ (yeast) _leavens the whole lump_ (bread dough), He meant that a "little" error will spread and corrupt the entire group, if it is ignored. "A rotten apple spoils the whole barrel". Constantine "spoiled" the true day of rest, and turned it into his "Baal's Day", Sun-day. He brought in the Pagan festival of "Easter" to obliterate Passover. If you were Shatan, wouldn't you "possess" the man with the most power, and divert things? Where do you think Shatan is today? It's easy to figure out.

The **Covenant** is the 10 Commandments, Dt. 4:13. If you read Galatians chaps. 4 & 5, you will see that "Sinai" represents the slave woman. The slave woman is fleshly, carnal, and non-spiritual. But the "free" (spiritual) woman represents those **born of the Spirit**, having the Covenant written on their hearts, not stone. The "law" that could **not justify** us was the ceremonial law of animal sacrifices (Heb. 10:1-4), but the New Covenant is able to justify us, being in the Blood of the Lamb of 𐤉𐤄𐤅𐤄 (one sacrifice for sins, Heb. 10:12). The 10 Commandments are called the "**Covenant of Love**" (1Kings 8:23, 2Chr. 6:14, Ne. 1:5). Look over the list of them at the left; is there **ONE** that is not good? If your inner being AGREES with them, then you are being called! When you can say "**I _LOVE_ these teachings**" ~ you have crossed-over into a Spirit-led realm, controlled by the Spirit of O W Y 𐤄 𐤅 ~ and you will not sin against them, because they are now your personality, as they are His. _"If we deliberately keep on sinning after we have received the knowledge of the truth, no sacrifice for sins is left, but only a fearful expectation of judgment and of raging fire that will consume the enemies of Elohim. "_ (Heb. 10:26, 27). These Commandments are your marriage vows. You change; **they don't!**

HOW DO GENTILES BEGIN?

THE ANSWER IS AT ACTS 15. At the Yerushaliyim Council, the issue of fleshly circumcision (the sign of the land covenant) was debated, and called "a yoke that neither we nor our fathers have been able to bear". Peter told them of how he learned that no man is "unclean" (the 3 sheets, Acts 10). He saw that "unclean animals" alluded to **MEN**, not food, as he explained at Acts 11. When Gentiles heard the **message**, Peter said their hearts were purified by belief, and **they received the gift of the Spirit**, and were immersed (spiritual circumcision). Then "James" (Ya'akob) decided the beginning steps for Gentiles:

"It is my judgment, therefore, that we should not make it difficult for the Gentiles who are turning to Elohim (no fleshly circumcision). _Instead we should write to them, telling them to :_
(1) abstain from food polluted by idols, from (2) sexual immorality, and from (3) the meat of strangled animals and from blood. For Mosheh (Moses, the Torah) _has been preached in every city from the earliest times and is read in the synagogues on_

every Shabbath." (Acts 15:19-21). Because few could read and write (being illiterate), and because scrolls were not widely available, the converts needed to attend the readings of the Torah, Prophets, and Writings at synagogues (houses of study) in order to **learn more**. The Nazarenes remained a part of the wider group of Yahudim, and even many "synagogue rulers" were Nazarenes. The main disruption of this "oneness" was caused by the Romans (a "war" conducted by Shatan), when they destroyed the Temple in 70 CE, and again crushed the Yahudim 60 years later. Shatan managed to kill millions of us, and dispersed us into the surrounding regions. Because our Rabbi had warned us beforehand that when we saw armies surrounding the city to "flee to the mountains", the Nazarenes were "shunned" because they **did not stay and fight**. Without the Temple and the ceremonial sacrificial system, "rabbinical" Yahudaism developed among the dispersed Yahudim. Shatan pursued "the woman" (ayaz's bride, wife): **"Then the dragon was enraged at the woman and went off to make war against the rest of her offspring ~ THOSE WHO OBEY ayaz's COMMANDMENTS AND HOLD TO THE TESTIMONY OF OWYaz."** (Rev. 12—read it all). What is the "TESTIMONY" of OWYaz? It is: **"Repent ~ for the Reign of ayaz draws near".** We are engaged in a war, and wear the Torah as our armor. We are the meek. Our sword is the Word of ayaz, His Torah. The true elders who serve our Rabbi do not plunder the flock, but serve and feed the flock. You can recognize us by our "fruits" ~ whether or not we **keep** and **teach others** the Commandments. Read all of 1 Yahuchanon carefully. We also carry the true "message". We have been saved by "grace", the unmerited lovingkindness of the GIFT of the Spirit of OWYaz, Who has written His Torah on our hearts and minds. Now, having the ability to LOVE the Commandments, we do not sin against them. We are led by the Spirit (the spiritual seed), not the flesh (Hagar, the mind of the "flesh"). The Commandments are spiritual, but the mind of the flesh wars against them. How do we show our love for ayaz? We obey His Torah, teachings, Covenant of Love! We are the "wise virgins" who await our Bridegroom, having the "oil" (Torah) that lights our way. If you have been raised in, or converted to Christianity, you should by now be starting to see the "rotten" decay that Paganism brought into the barrel of apples long ago. The Torah (teachings) is the "Rock" that the wise man will build his house on. You need no other "rabbi", or the approval of any man, to convert to the religion of OWYaz. We do not beg for money, but work ourselves. The love of money is the root of all kinds of evil. The wisdom of Torah is more precious than gold or rubies! It must not be "sold". The New Covenant makes you an heir of the promises, and you will be included at the Wedding Supper of the Bridegroom, not locked outside. It doesn't matter how much you pay your pastor to spread the message of the Reign; you must do it **yourself!** His **Name** and the **Covenant** is the "buried treasure", so apply your whole heart and mind to remain steadfast. You can trust your Husband to be faithful, and He will say, "well done, good and faithful servant". If He gives you 5 pieces of **"silver"** (wisdom, knowledge, understanding), and you return to him 5 **additional** pieces at His return (you have invested and helped **others convert**), you will be greatly rewarded. Your money cannot help. People who misunderstand the parables, or are tricked by their pastors, not only are blocked from the **Covenant**, but they are also plundered. The reason so many men can peddle the Word of ayaz for profit is because the message is veiled. The harvest is great, because there are billions alive **right now** who need to hear the true message of the Reign of ayaz. The harvest of the Earth is coming very soon, probably **within** the generation (70 years) of the re-gathering to Yisrael (1948 CE). But no man knows the day or hour of His coming; we will know the "season" however. First, you must be **immersed**, calling upon the Name of OWYaz for the forgiveness of your past uncleanness (sins), then walk in the Truth (Torah, the Covenant). You will know you are ayaz's Bride.

THE "ONENESS" OF MARRIAGE

The "message" (gospel) of the Reign of ayaz is **LINKED** to the idea of a marriage covenant, and begins with ayaz's CALL. If we agree to His COVENANT (the 10 Commandments), then we love Him and obey Him as a Husband is to be obeyed. He loves, provides for, and protects us as a wife. The immersion into the waters (called baptism now) removes our "uncleanness", and we are then enabled to become ONE with our Maker. He only seeks the love of a faithful bride, and He is not bashful about telling us He is JEALOUS. He calls us out from **ancient Paganism** which pollutes His bride. This is why the prophet Hosea was told to make a prostitute his bride, to illustrate how we make ayaz feel. At our resurrection, He will inhabit us fully. It is most important that we be **immersed** in His **NAME**, then **sealed** in His **NAME** with the laying on of hands. A faithful wife is an obedient wife, who obeys out of LOVE. It's a Covenant of Love.

74

PAGANISM EXPOSED

It's very important that we consider the impact that Constantine had on our accepted customs, **because he acted as a "lens" which filtered-out the (Jewish) roots of the faith.** The habits of the western Pagan Gentiles like Sun-day, Easter, Saturnalia, Samhain, towers, and many familiar symbols were carried along and blended into the Nazarene faith as a matter of state policy. O W Y ᕀ Z's death and resurrection occurred at the time of **Passover**. Since the Gentiles of the western localities were in the habit of their Earth Mother fertilization festival, Easter, they continued to keep it in a new perspective when they converted to Christianity. The eggs and rabbits, rolling eggs on the fields, egg "hunts", etc., should be more than enough evidence to show this. The early Nazarenes who were less inclined to "inculturate" the Paganism were disturbed as they witnessed the Gentiles' changes. Since they continued to observe the **Passover**, it meant even more to them than ever before. O W Y ᕀ Z had revealed the mystery that Passover had foreshadowed. We know there was a controversy concerning the alterations made by Constantine when he set up "Sun-day", and "Easter", replacing the Covenant Commandments. In Eusebius' *Ecclesiastical History*, there is the record of the following letter written by an **elder**, **Polycrates**, to Victor of the Church of Rome:

"We, therefore, observe the genuine day; neither adding thereto nor taking therefrom. For in Asia great lights have fallen asleep, which shall rise again in the day of the (Rabbi's) *appearing, in which He will come with esteem from Shamayim, and will raise up all the saints; Philip, one of the twelve apostles, who sleeps in Hierapolis, and his two aged virgin daughters. His other daughter, also, who having lived under the influence of the Ruach ha Qodesh, now likewise rests in Ephesus. Moreover, Yahuchanon, who rested on the bosom of our* (Rabbi); *who also was a priest, and bore the sacerdotal plate, both a martyr and a teacher. He is buried in Ephesus; also Polycarp of Smyrna, both elder and martyr of Eumenia, who is buried at Smyrna. Why should I mention Sagaris, elder and martyr, who rests at Laodicea? Moreover, the blessed Papirius; and Melito, the eunuch, whose walk and conversation was altogether under the influence of the Ruach ha Qodesh, who now rests at Sardis, awaiting the episcopate from Shamayim, when he shall rise from the dead. ALL THESE OBSERVED THE 14TH DAY OF THE PASSOVER ACCORDING TO THE WORD, DEVIATING IN NO RESPECT, BUT FOLLOWING THE RULE OF FAITH. Moreover, I, Polycrates, who am the least of all of you, according to the tradition of my relatives, some of whom I have followed. For there were seven, my relatives elders, and I am the eighth; and my relatives always observed the day when the people threw away the leaven."*

There it is, friends. An elder who saw the changes, and wrote to another elder who was being carried away by "winds" of doctrine. He mentioned the throwing away of the leaven for the 7 days of the feast of unleavened bread (Matsah), as Shaul also mentioned at 1 Cor. 5:7-10. Shaul even said *"Let us therefore celebrate the Feast"*, speaking of **Matsah**. Remember how Shaul said he wept and pleaded with the elders for years (Acts 20), knowing that these things would come after he was gone. The assemblies were turning aside to "myths". The heretics have distorted the true walk to suit themselves, and created a powerful hierarchy which has killed tens of millions, and is still in place causing human catastrophes. The current "times of the Gentiles" will not be set right by human means, but will be obliterated by our returning Mashiach, as a roaring lion from space, as lightning from one end of the sky to the other. You have to be a "saint" while you are alive, if you expect to enter the New Yerushaliyim in the resurrection. There is no religion in the Writings that requires us to meet together on Sun-day morning, or observe "Easter", or "Christmas". To follow "leaders" who are blind, you will fall into a pit. Many trust their own hearts, saying *"I believe in my own way"*, or *"I worship the Creator in my own personal way"*. They do what seems right in **their own eyes.** *"You are NOT to do as we do here today, everyone as he sees fit . . ."* Dt. 12:8.

Following your own heart, you will be deceived also: *"The heart is crooked above all, and desperately sick ~ who shall know it?"* Yerme Yahu 17:9.

At 18:12, the prophet wrote that the people said to themselves, *"It's no use. We will continue with our own plans; each of us will follow the stubbornness of his evil heart."* People find comfort in cliches like *"When in Rome, do as the Romans do."* Is this what our Rabbi taught us to do? *"And the fire shall prove the work of each one, what sort it is. If anyone's work remains, which he has built on, he shall receive a reward. If anyone's work is burned, he shall suffer loss, but he himself shall be saved, but as though through fire."* 1 Cor. 3:13-15. The prophesied "apostasy", or falling away from the Torah, has happened. Be warned.

"Blessed are those who wash their robes, that

they may have the right to the tree of life and may go through the gates into the city. Outside are the dogs, those who practice magic arts, the sexually immoral, the murderers, the idolaters and EVERYONE WHO LOVES AND PRACTICES FALSEHOOD." Rev. 22:14,15. *"It would have been better for them not to have known the way of righteousness, than to have known it and then to turn their backs on the qodesh command that was passed on to them. Of them the proverbs are true: 'A dog returns to its vomit', and 'A sow that is washed goes back to her wallowing in the mud'."* 2Pet. 21,22. "Dogs" is the term used for Gentiles without any hope (see Mt. 7:6, and 15:26). The 'vomit' a dog returns to is his old Pagan ways.

Although there are a number of things that don't effect our salvation, some people place a great deal of emphasis on them, so I'd like to discuss one of them. My own opinion about the "Last Supper" is that it was at the beginning of the 14th of Abib, and was the Passover Seder, since Rabbi Yahushua called it that. He said *"Go and make preparations for US to eat the Passover"* (Luke 22:8), and *"I have eagerly desired to eat this Passover with you before I suffer.* (Notice that He said He desired to eat "this Passover" before I suffer?) *For I tell you, I will not eat it AGAIN until it finds fulfillment in the Kingdom of YHWH."* (Luke 22:15,16). This reinforces John 19:31, which states it was the Day of Preparation (as I understand the Passover is observed at the beginning of this Preparation Day), since the next day was a **special** (annual) Shabbat, beginning at sunset. There is no "lamb" mentioned, but our Rabbi is the Lamb. *"It was the Day of Preparation of Passover Week, about the sixth hour"* (John 19:14), being what we would call "noon" when Pilate sentenced Yahushua. Luke records that it was about the sixth hour that darkness came over the whole land until the 9th hour (3 p.m., Luke 23:44). This agrees with Mark 15:33, but Mark 15:25 says it was the 3rd hour when they hung Yahushua up on the tree. These errors could have been made by copyists, since no two sentences in the Greek manuscripts are uniform among the many copies; or Yahuchanon actually wrote the wrong time, recalling the events as an elderly man from his boyhood memory of it. But, if the translators can wipe-out whole phrases to suit themselves, and add phrases as they have done to many texts, and leave out the Name of the Creator, and change the Names of everyone recorded (except Shatan), then who are we going to blame for the discrepancy we see between Mark and Yahuchanon's record of what time of day it was our Rabbi was hung up?

Although there is a chance of 14% that an annual Shabbat can coincide with a weekly Shabbat, both kinds have a "Preparation Day". Mark also records *"It was Preparation Day"* (15:42). To me, this was the day before the 1st Day of Matzah, the 7 days of Unleavened Bread. The struggle we deal with is from John 18:28, where our Rabbi is being brought to Pilate from Caiaphas: *"By now it was early morning, and TO AVOID CEREMONIAL UNCLEANNESS, the Jews* (Sadducees) *did not enter the palace; THEY WANTED TO BE ABLE TO EAT THE PASSOVER".* I could be wrong, and the Last Supper may have been just a meal, and Rabbi didn't eat the Passover, but He said looked forward to eating this Passover **before** He suffered.

I will offend people no matter which side of this I come down on, but I observe Passover at the beginning of the 14th of Abib at twilight, the same day our Rabbi was executed. The Yahudim *combined* the observance of Passover with the beginning of the 15th of Abib, although Passover is not a "day", or a Shabbat in itself. Lev. 23:5,6 says: *"ایۀۀ's Passover begins AT TWILIGHT on the fourteenth day of the first month. On the fifteenth day of that month ایۀۀ's feast of Unleavened Bread begins; for seven days you must eat bread made without yeast."* These are two separate things, on 2 different days. "Twilight" is just after sunset, between sunset and darkness. At the time these events occurred, the Sanhedrin and the Temple observances were controlled by the Sadducees, the priests. The Pharisees, who were more attentive to what Scripture required, had a different opinion about certain "times" things were done. This may account for the seeming contradiction, since our Rabbi fraternized with the more popular "Pharisees" rather than the Sadducees. It was the Sadducees who were in control of the Sanhedrin, and the ones who were leading the campaign to execute Yahushua because of His threat to their authority. (The Pharisees had no power, but were popular with the common people.)

[You know, Shatan hates marriages.]

Do you see a face or 3 little raccoons? I drew this from a photo I saw on a book of animals, and added the rest to make it appear as a face. The line is an adaptation from a Simon & Garfunkel song.

MEN SEE WHAT THEY WANT TO SEE, AND DISREGARD THE REST.

THE LAST SUPPER

Most people have come to understand the final meal of the talmudim (disciples, students) and our Rabbi OWY⅃Z the night before He died was something new. Catholicism has taught it to be the model for what they call the "consecration" and "offertory" of the "mass". They instituted this annual observance of "Passover" into a **weekly** "morning" observance. The Mithraists were already holding a Sun-day morning service to worship the sun deity, and used a flat disc of bread. The moment the Pagan priest would lift it into the air to receive the sun's rays, it became "tranformed" with the words "hocus-pocus", and "abracabra". Although these words are now used to ridicule superstitious nonsense, the sun worshippers would have died for them. They believed the bread had "transubstantiated" into the actual presence of the sun, and by eating it, they would possess the powers of the deity. The Egyptians laid the round wafers out in the sunlight at their "consecration". To a Nazarene, these rituals are an abomination, and the wafer is a "death cookie".

PASSOVER SEDER

Many of you will differ with me, and that's fine, but it is my opinion that the "Last Supper" was what our Rabbi said it was: *"I have eagerly desired to eat this Passover with you before I suffer."* Luke 22:15. There is confusion on this. It is possible that this was what was called a _teaching seder_, as rabbis would commonly hold a seder the evening before the actual Passover, so the students could be with their families as required for the real Passover. We just don't really know. But, how Christendom has NO Passover is what is amazing, but now some are beginning to.

The "Last Supper" was not a "Mass", but a very familiar observance. The students of Rabbi OWY⅃Z were talking about it for days before it came. The word "seder" means **order**. The primary objective is to remove all "**chametz**" or leavened bread from our homes (no doubt an inherited activity we now call "spring cleaning"). It has been said that it took Leonardo De Vinci almost **20 years** to paint this famous picture, known as

THE LAST SUPPER:

The actual word for "Passover" is **PESACH**. If something is "Kosher" (appropriate, approved) for Pesach, then it doesn't contain yeast or anything that makes it "rise". This is to remind us of the hasty departure from the bondage of Egypt (Mitzraim) by the mighty hand of ⱥY⅃Z. It is always observed in the evening (darkening) at the 14th of the 1st month of the year, determined by the appearance of the "green ears" of the barley crop in Yisrael. This pictures the beginning of the redemption plan for OWY⅃Z's bride, since He is the "first fruits" of the Reign of ⱥY⅃Z, our "wave offering". Other neglected observances will be discussed in sequence. This "wave offering" occurred after the <u>most significant event in the history of mankind</u>: The resurrection from the dead of Rabbi OWY⅃Z. The "first-born" from the dead, of what <u>will be a great **harvest** of mankind</u>, was like grain, cut-down; then, upon resurrecting, was "waving". He is literally the first to be "born" of the spirit, because He doesn't have a body like we do any more; He's something completely NEW. We receive a small "seed" of this rebirth upon being immersed, but while we are still in our flesh, we are not yet "born of the spirit" in the complete way we will be. We are, however, re-born in a spiritual way, even while we are in our flesh. We must be born of water, at our immersion, and later, raised as spatial beings like OWY⅃Z is. *"Dear friends, now we are children of ⱥY⅃Z, and what we will be has not yet been made known. But we know that when He appears, WE WILL BE LIKE HIM, for we shall see Him as He is."* ~ 1 Yn. 3:2. This painting of the Last Supper is widely recognized, and most think it is linked in some way to what they do on "Sun-day" <u>morning</u>. Not true. "Supper" and "morning" are oxymoronic.

IF IT'S TWILIGHT, WHY IS IT STILL LIGHT OUTSIDE?

WELCOME TO OUR PASSOVER SEDER

Jubilee Year

When Rabbi said, *"Do this in remembrance of Me"* (Luke 22:19), He was referring to the observance of Pesach. **Once** every year, we are to remember Him and His *death*, as our Passover Lamb. The unleavened bread, known as "MATZAH", reminds any observant Yahudi of our Lamb. If you look at one of these flat, square pieces of cracker-like bread, it is **PIERCED** and **BRUISED**. During the annual cycle of reading the TaNaKh in synagogues, Yesha Yahu 53 is skipped. This is no accident! *"But He was PIERCED for our transgressions, He was BRUISED for our iniquities; the punishment that brought us peace was upon Him, and by His wounds, we are healed."* v. 5.

With no "Passover", how is it that Catholicism and her daughters have a "Passover Lamb"? Sounds like some serious mental acrobatics, or folly is afoot. Whose transgressions did He die for? His bride's! The penalty for her idolatry (harlotry) was death. (The bride's name is "Daughter of Tsiyon" but her new name will be **HEPHZIBAH** *(my delight is in her, 62:4.)*

A little entertaining background concerning Leonardo's portrait of *The Last Supper* gives perspective to what a life **without Torah** is like. It is said that as Leonardo began his painting, he studied the text of the Writings for who was present, and he imagined their appearance. Naturally he had to search for subjects to pose for each person in the portrait. He **began** by looking for the most "angelic" and pure features he could find for the face of our Rabbi. After a thorough search, he finally found a young boy with the face of **absolute innocence**. Leonardo kindly asked the boy if he would pose for him, and compensated him for his time. Over the years, Leonardo carefully selected models to pose for each of the men. This took almost 20 years. Finally, he was down to the last man in the painting, known as "Judas" (really *Yahudah*). He spent months searching for the perfect model, but there just didn't seem to be anyone who looked evil enough for this terrible job. At long last, he discovered a man who had sunken as low as any man had ever gone. He was in a tavern, drunk, and had lines of pain and sin in his face that reflected the kind of life he had lived. Leonardo knew at once he had to get him to pose. Offering the man compensation, Leonardo had him pose for the most famous betrayer in the world. As Leonardo busily arranged his model, and was mixing his paints, the man spoke to him saying, *"You know me."* Leonardo was sure he had never been around *anyone* who was like this man, and replied, *"Oh no, I'm sure you're mistaken, I've never laid eyes on you."* The man, sure of himself, replied saying *"Oh yes, sir, it was me, when I was very young, who posed for this portrait. I was the first, you said."* Hearing this, Leonardo put his hands to his face, and wept over the young boy he had crossed paths with so long ago.

Each of us have people we cross paths with, who need something from us. We either help them, ignore them, or push them down lower. I work in a store that for over the past 20 years has had a wide mixture of people coming into it. Most everyone who comes in is "searching" for something to embrace; or fulfill a need or emptiness within them. With your daily contacts, neighbors, co-workers, clients, etc., there are many who are looking for guidance which you can inspire them with. One of my missions in life is to dispel error, and replace it with Truth.

Concerning this Passover Seder known as "The Last Supper", there was a Medieval superstition that arose, based on error. Most have become convinced (hypnotized) into the thinking that O W Y З Z was executed on a "**Fri-Day**", the day of preparation for the weekly Shabbath, and resurrected at SUNRISE on "**Sun-Day**". This is not anything like what the memoirs reveal to us. This is just a traditional misinterpretation, propagated by Rome. In fact, there is no phrase "last supper" in the Writings, but only this "Passover" which our Rabbi said He had looked forward to observing **before** He suffered, and He had observed it every year of His life. He also said he would observe it again, drinking again the fruit of the vine, in His Father's Kingdom/Reign. Shatan de-railed the train, folks. The only "sign" (like "tongues", a sign for unbelievers, 1 Cor. 14:22) to prove that O W Y З Z is the Mashiach was the "sign of Yonah". As Yonah was 3 days and 3 nights in the belly of the fish, so O W Y З Z was **3 days** and **3 nights** in the tomb. The year O W Y З Z was executed, he observed Passover on what Pagans today would call a "Tues-Day" evening at twilight. Later that night He was arrested, and by the 3rd hour of the next day (our 9 a. m.), Rabbi O W Y З Z was being pierced. At the 6th hour (our "noon"), darkness fell on the land until the 9th hour. With a loud cry, O W Y З Z breathed His last, and the 60-foot-high curtain in the Temple was ripped from top-to-bottom, as a man tears his robes in grief. Because the meal we call the "Last Supper" was, according to some, a Passover observance, then it is observed at the *beginning of the 14th day of the moon*, at the "darkening" between sunset and night (twilight). There is some controversy about this, and you should study all sides thoroughly. However, the "superstition" I mentioned that developed, from the Christian ignorance of what "preparation day" we are dealing with, gave rise to what is called **"FRI-DAY THE 13TH".** "Preparation day" indeed includes every sixth day of the week. Six of the seven "annual appointments" are movable, one of which is the **1st Day of**

Matzah, or _Unleavened Bread_, and also have preparation days. Obviously there are not **3 DAYS AND 3 NIGHTS** between "Fri-Day" night at sunset and "Sun-Day" morning. Shatan's "spin-doctors" twisted it for us, to "bend" things toward a "Sun-day" morning "supper". That's not just quaint, it's goofy. Because the entire Christian world has been "programmed" to believe that the annual observance of the day of our Rabbi's **death** is somehow linked to the days of the week, and not Passover (a movable appointment), **"FRI-DAY"** just before "EASTER" is _celebrated_ as "Good Friday". OUCH! Good? In a selfish way, yes, for us; but it is the day on which Shatan pierced our beloved O W Y ᴚ Z. (Only it wasn't a "Fri-Day"). In fact, if you asked Shatan what was the most significant thing he's ever accomplished, nothing else could compare to it. It fulfilled the prophecy at Gen. 3:15. The "myth" that it was a "Fri-Day", and not the preparation day for the High Shabbath of "Matzah" (Yn. 19:31) is part of the superstition of "Fri-Day the 13th". The "13" represents the fact that there were **13 MEN** present at the meal the previous evening. The 13th day of each Roman month has no connection with the real moon, nor the number of men present at the meal. Not only that, but what day the resurrection occurred has _nothing to do with what DAY is the Shabbath, our day of rest_. It's hard to understand how such obvious "smoke and mirrors" masked so much of the truth, and could be propagated by so many scholars over so many centuries. Shatan successfully blinded the eyes of populations with his "teachers", and desolated the correct pattern of observances. The "head" (Shatan) of this fiendish scheme controlled Constantine I, and the office of the papacy, BECAUSE HE RULES THIS WORLD.

CHRISTIANITY'S PAGAN CONNECTION
THE TRICK: APOSTASY

It's the same old trick: the **LIE** that "we don't really have to OBEY". The FALSE "Gospel" is what most understand, woven into their minds by the "merchants" who masquerade as messengers of righteousness. It's partly true, but it leaves out the core of the New Covenant, "**Mashiach IN you**". Here's how they usually teach it: "_You don't have to obey, your sinning is atoned for. Besides, NO ONE can possibly obey the Commandments perfectly. J-sus obeyed them FOR us, and died to atone for all our sins, past, present, and future. You cannot out-sin the grace of G-d. When the Father looks at us, He only sees the righteousness of His Son_". So, just _believing_ on this "Gospel" message makes a person extremely grateful to their J-sus, and they think they will show him how grateful they are by going to "Church" every Sun-day. This is a false, COUN-TERFEIT, and incomplete message, and they don't know the True Mashiach. The soul that sins will die (Ezek. 18). The New Covenant is having **Mashiach in us**, allowing us to love and **agree** with the Torah; we no longer live in the "mind of the flesh". Catholicism taught for centuries that this "Mashiach in you" was achieved by receiving "communion", a man-made "sacrament" they associated with the symbols of bread and wine at the Passover seder the night before He was put to death. It's true that the emblems represented what the New Covenant pictures, but it's only a model for what was to literally take place when He came into them with power, as He does when we accept the TRUE message of salvation. The Protestant sects carried this out of the Mother, leaving behind the belief in the bread and wine _trans-substantiating_ (changing into His literal Body by the mystical "powers" endowed in the "priest"). Never learning that they are empowered to obey by having the Ruach ha Qodesh (the set-apart Spirit of O W Y ᴚ Z) in them, they keep coming back week after week. They want to learn more, but never do. The tragic thing is, Shatan has turned this into a world-wide business, and his messengers go to the bank thinking "The Lord" is blessing them. Remember, a liar tells part truth, but withholds important information.

Do we go on sinning, that "grace" may abound? **_"Shall we go on sinning so that grace may increase? By no means! We died to sin_** (at our immersion)**_; how can we live in it any longer?"_** Romans 6:1,2. **_"Shall we sin_** (break and ignore Commandments) **_because we are not under law but under grace? By no means! Don't you know, that when you offer yourselves to someone to obey him as slaves, you are slaves to the one whom you OBEY ~ whether you are slaves to sin, which leads to death, or to OBEDIENCE, which leads to righteousness?"_** v. 15,16.

If you carefully read Romans 6, 7, and 8, you will eventually see that Shaul is looking at the Torah from 2 perspectives; the mind of the flesh, and **the mind controlled by the Spirit**. Since the "law" is spiritual, our inner being must be controlled by the Spirit of O W Y ᴚ Z in order to live by it. Shaul says **_"For in my inner being, I delight in ᴚ Y ᴚ Z's Torah"_** Rom. 7:22. He also makes it clear that without the Spirit to change us, we are doomed:
"For if you live according to the sinful nature, YOU WILL DIE." Rom. 8:13.

PILLARS OF JEALOUSY

Ezekiel saw Paganism mixing into the worship of ایﬃﬤ. *"Then He said to me, 'son of man, look toward the north'. So I looked, and in the entrance north of the gate of the altar I saw this <u>pillar of jealousy</u>."* Ez. 8:8.

"HIGH PLACES" which harken back to the tower of Babel, are ziggarats, obelisks, pyramids, poles, pagodas, spires, stupas, and a whole array of sky-pointing structures. Try to find any such thing as a steeple in the Writings. All Pagan temples utilized a tower, and bells or gongs to summon the sun-worshippers. Hand-held bells were also used in their worship, sometimes made in rows which they would shake like rattles. In the worship of Circe, altar bells were rung periodically during the "services", inherited by Roman Catholicism and their "Mass".

One of the oldest relics of Pagan worship is the pillar of jealousy called an **OBELISK**. Any ancient Pagan would recognize one. They were interpreted to be a ray of the sun, but also the image of male generative power, the phallus. Pagans also stood stones up in circles, and prayed within the area they defined. Most of the time the stones were only a few inches tall, but Stonehenge was one exception. In the time of Daniel, in Babylon, Nebuchadnezzar constructed an image ninety feet high, and nine feet wide, and this obelisk was to be bowed to when the "national anthem" sounded (Dan. 3). If you were able to ask Shadrach, Meshach, and Abednego if they would accompany you to most Christian places of worship, what do you think they would have to say about the big "steeple" near the entrance? I'd wager they wouldn't go near the place. You can even see obelisk shapes in the building designs, signs, and window shapes of many of these buildings. They are also very partial to "circles", which related to the sun in Pagan temple design. Some Christian congregations have torn down the steeples of their meeting places, after learning of the origin of these "high places".

CHURCH

Circe, a Greek deity who turned men into pigs, is the origin from which springs our English word **KIRCHE**, producing the word "Church". In the very first English translation of the Brit Chadasha (New Covenant Writings), a Catholic priest named John Wycliffe used the word "congregation" for the Greek word *ecclesia* (ek-la-SEE-a), not "Church". It really means *called-out ones*. These are those who have submitted to immersion in His Name, and repented of sin. The Hebrew word is QAHAL,

the congregation of Yisrael. We get our English word "call" from *qahal*. There is no covenant with "Christians", only Yisrael, and foreigners must engraft into Yisrael to partake of the Covenant:

"Therefore, remember that formerly you who are Gentiles by birth and called 'uncircumcised' . . . . At that time you were separate from Mashiach, excluded from citizenship in Yisrael and foreigners to the covenants of promise, without hope and without ایﬃﬤ *in the world. But now, in Mashiach* OﬃYﬃﬤ *you who once were far away have been brought near through the blood of Mashiach. For He Himself is our peace, Who has made the two ONE, and has destroyed the barrier, the dividing wall of hostility, by abolishing in His flesh the law with its commandments and regulations."* Eph. 2:11-15.

"Consequently, you are no longer foreigners and aliens, but FELLOW CITIZENS with ایﬃﬤ*'s people, and members of* ایﬃﬤ*'s household, built on the foundation of the apostles and prophets, with Mashiach* OﬃYﬃﬤ *Himself as the chief cornerstone."* - 2:19,20.

The "commandments and regulations" referred to here are what the ceremonial law required for <u>atonement and cleansing</u>, they don't refer to what defines sin. Not eating blood (Acts 15), or disregarding Shabbath (Heb. 4), or murder (Ex. 20) etc., are still "Commandments" in force. "Foreigners" can now call themselves Yisrael, if they are immersed in His Name and live in the Covenant. If they don't "engraft", they are outside the Covenant promises, and Shatan knows it!

"The <u>way of peace</u> they do not know . . ." Yesha Yahu 59:8. *"Truth has stumbled in the streets, honesty cannot enter. Truth is nowhere to be found, and whoever shuns evil becomes a prey."* 59:14,15. The "Truth" and "way of peace" is the Torah, the Word. The invitation to the "feast" shown in the parables represent the Shabbats of ایﬃﬤ. At Yesha Yahu 58:11-13, once again we see the Torah is what is called the "ancient ruins", and those who obey are like a well-watered garden (see also Ps. 1). *"You will be called Repairer of Broken walls, Restorer of Streets with Dwellings ~ if you keep your feet from breaking the Sabbath, and from doing as you please on My Qodesh Day; if you call the Sabbath a delight, and* ایﬃﬤ*'s Qodesh Day honorable."*

"I GAVE THEM MY SABBATHS"

"Also, I gave them My Sabbaths as a sign between us, so they would know that I ⲀⲨⲀⳐ made them qodesh." You may want to read all of Ezekiel chapter 20. We've learned that a mere man was responsible for instituting the change from the 7th day to the 1st day of each week, and the "Sun-day Sabbath" has been the "Christian Sabbath" ever since. Let's just take a brief overview of the Sabbath, and determine if there is one, and if so what "choice" we should make in observing it.

MASTER OF THE SABBATH

Please take this only as from a lover of the Commandment, not as any condemnation or personal criticism, bearing in mind, "He who answers before listening ~ it is to his folly and shame" (Pr. 18:13). I was once in denial and rebellion against Gentiles needing to follow the 4th Commandment, but I listened to all of what Scripture says, not men, or Constantine's establishment of "Sunday" as the new Christian day of rest. Hebrews 4 has been "allegorized" to mean our "rest" in Mashiach, but really the whole section deals with the disobedient, and mentions the "Gospel". **The message of repentance is of no value to the lost**, and it says *"He has spoken about the seventh day in these words: 'And on the seventh day Elohim rested from all His work.'"* At v.9: *"There remains, then, a Sabbath-rest for the people of Elohim; for anyone who enters Elohim's rest also rests from his own work, JUST AS ELOHIM DID FROM HIS. Let us, therefore, make every effort to enter that rest, so that no one will fall by following their example of DISOBEDIENCE. For the Word of Elohim (Torah) is living, and active. Sharper than any double-edged sword, it penetrates even to dividing soul and spirit, joints and marrow; it judges the thoughts and attitudes of the heart . . ."* With the New Covenant, we receive the Torah written on our hearts, and His "Word" is the Torah. If the Sabbath is for only Hebrews, not Gentiles, then why would Gentiles be punished for not observing the Feast of Tabernacles after Yahushua's return, cited at Zech. 14? Also, there is no difference now between a Hebrew and a Gentile, **as a follower of Mashiach**. The Replacement Theology has lulled us into thinking Gentiles (or the "Church") are now "Israel", but it is rather these wild olive tree branches **grafted into** the original olive tree, Israel (Rom. 11). This is far more than a "Pharisaical" issue. There is no "Covenant" in Scripture with "Christians", only Yisrael!

BINDING OURSELVES TO YHWH

At Is. 66, in the Millennial Reign: *"FROM ONE SABBATH TO ANOTHER, ALL MANKIND will come and bow down before Me, says YHWH. And they will go out and look upon the DEAD BODIES of those who rebelled against Me".* (Is 56): *"Blessed is the man who does this, the man who holds it fast: who keeps the Sabbath without desecrating it . . . . "Let no foreigner who has bound himself to YHWH say, 'YHWH will surely exclude me from His people'. . . . .To the eunuchs who keep My Sabbaths, who choose what pleases me and hold fast to My Covenant ~ to them I will give within My Temple and its walls a memorial and a name BETTER THAN SONS AND DAUGHTERS . . . . AND FOREIGNERS WHO BIND THEMSELVES TO YHWH, to serve Him, to LOVE THE NAME OF YHWH and to worship Him, ALL WHO KEEP THE SABBATH WITHOUT DESECRATING IT, and HOLD FAST TO MY COVENANT, these I will bring to My holy mountain and give them joy in My house of prayer . . . . for My house of prayer will be called a house of prayer for ALL NATIONS."*

JERUSALEM COUNCIL CONCERNING GENTILES

After deciding that fleshly circumcision is not a requirement, the Gentiles who BEAR THE NAME are told to begin by abstaining from idolatry, sexual immorality, FOOD STRANGLED, AND BLOOD. *"For Mosheh* (the Torah) *has been preached in every city from the earliest times, AND IS READ IN THE SYNAGOGUES EVERY SABBATH."* The Nazarenes studied next to the other sects in the places where the Scrolls were read, until after the destruction of Yerushaliyim, then were shunned for having fled the city instead of defending it, as they were obeying what Rabbi Yahushua had warned them of. Many of the synagogue rulers were believers in the Mashiach! At Acts 1, Luke records *"Then they returned to Yerushaliyim from the hill called the Mount of Olives, A SABBATHS DAY'S WALK from the city."* Even the "day of Pentecost" , called Shabuoth (weeks), is an annual Sabbath ~ one of **seven**, and is the **memorial of the receiving of Torah at Sinai** (the Nazarenes received it in their hearts, circumcised by Mashiach on that day, fulfilling the prophecy at Yerme Yahu 31). Paul even states that we should "keep the feast", speaking of the **7 days of unleavened bread**, at 1 Cor. 5:8. "The Fast", or **Yom Kippur**, is referred to at Acts 27:9, because the weather was turning bad because of the lateness in the year. I completely understand the turmoil this causes in your mind; I remember it well. I endured it when I had to weigh all the evidence, but I received Him; and the Sabbath, and all His Commandments fill me with extreme joy. Will YHWH punish you for resting on Sabbath, or is it really the "bad seed" (teachings) of ha Shatan that inoculates most people from repenting? It is only Israel, YHWH's obedient Bride, who will enter the gates into the city. There is no gate named "the Church", or "Christianity" ~ only gates bearing the names of the 12 tribes of Israel. I am of His Bride. Please receive this oil into your lamp, before we all slumber (the sleep of death).

THE DRAGON RECOGNIZES SABBATH-KEEPERS BY THEIR OBEDIENCE

"Then the dragon was enraged at the woman (the Bride) and went off to make war against the rest of her offspring ~ those WHO OBEY ELOHIM'S COMMANDMENTS, and hold to the TESTIMONY OF YAHUSHUA (which is: 'repent - for the Reign of YHWH draws near.')." The 4th Commandment tells us all to **remember the Sabbath**, and it's the 7th day of every week. As a regular observer of Sabbath, I stay home and rest, and study with my wife and children. Obedience is worship. Can we "obey Elohim's Commandments", and not have His Sign of the Covenant, His Sabbath? If Rabbi Yahushua is **"Master of the Sabbath"**, and it was made for man, will ignoring it bring us closer to Him in our walk? If the 4th Commandment is only for "Jews" to obey, then the Creator has 2 different sets of rules ~ or, an enemy has sown weeds among the wheat! The parables are "dark sayings" that only the Bride will understand, and Proverbs 9 even refers to the 7 annual appointments: *"Wisdom* (Torah) *has built her house; she has hewn out its seven pillars."* From Passover through Tabernacles and the Last Great Day, there are "7 pillars" or high Sabbaths. These outline the redemption plan of YHWH's Bride. The parable about the "Great Banquet" (Luke 14:16-24) illustrates how many are just not interested in coming to the appointed observances of ﬡYﬡוּ.

As you can readily see, there is no "break" between what is meant by the "Sabbath" in the TaNaKh and Brit Chadasha, as many would lead you to believe. If you'd really like to learn how this rift occurred, you can look up a man named **Marcion** in a good encyclopedia, or go to a library. He was a heretic, who taught that we need to completely disregard the "Old Testament". However all scholars realize that the New Covenant authors consistently used the "Old" as their foundation, and never taught the changes we see today.

HOW TO BEGIN

If you are a Gentile, you may have a little knowledge already, but you should re-ground yourself by starting with Acts 15. Then do as it says, and study the writings of Mosheh, the Torah (Ten Commandments). Read all of Exodus 20, Lev. 19, Lev. 23, then Deut. 16, understanding that you are about to enter into a Covenant with your Creator, ﬡYﬡוּ. When you know and understand how you are to live, you must be *immersed* in water as your 'circumcision'. Your 'Husband' doesn't wish to dwell in the vessel of your body before you have washed, and this immersion signifies the death of your mind of the flesh, the washing away of your sins by your trust in Rabbi OWYﬡוּ's death which covers your sins against Torah, and the resurrection in kind with OWYﬡוּ, so you will obey the Torah. This is only the beginning.

1. Pronounce your belief, "I believe Rabbi OWYﬡוּ (Yahushua, Yahusha) of Nazareth is the Mashiach, and that He raised from the dead 3 days and 3 nights after His execution for my past sins."

2. "OWYﬡוּ please save me."

3. Going under the water, think of your mind of the flesh "dying" , no longer controlling your actions against Torah. Your sins are left behind you, lifted from you, and you are now a "new creature". The "old person" is now dead.

4. Coming up, you have committed to the Covenant: to obey OWYﬡוּ, hold to His Testimony, and you will show Him you love Him by observing the Torah. Having obeyed Him, you will now receive the promise of the New Covenant: **His Spirit**, which will write His Commandments on your heart and mind, **enabling you to love them and obey them**.

This is the way you give yourself to the Bridegroom. As a woman will bath after her period of uncleanness before contact with her husband, so we wash away our uncleanness (past sins), and COVENANT to obey our Husband. We are His virgin bride! The unrepentant and the very young cannot be immersed, because they have not been convicted of their sinfulness. Next, you need your "gift", that which you are to use to serve the Body with. This is received by an elder laying hands upon you and reciting the priestly blessing (Num. 6:22-27). This must be performed by an elder who knows what the Covenant is! At Acts 9:17, Shaul had the hands of Ananias placed upon him before immersion. You can receive your "anointing" without an elder, but eventually you should submit to the laying on of the hands when you encounter an elder. The "power" comes from OWY︎AZ, not the brother; the Ruach ha Qodesh is given to those who obey Him (Acts 5:32). As I said, the MYSTERY of the Kingdom that we all hope to be partakers of is revealed in all the parables. One of the most misunderstood parables speaks about how OWY︎AZ will "go away on a journey", and entrusts His property to His servants. At Mattit Yahu 25:14-46, the parable of the "talents", our Rabbi illustrates Himself as a man who went away for a long time, and returned to see what his servants had done with the various "talents" He had left them in charge of. According to their abilities, each servant was given 5, 2, or 1 talent each. The "talents" represent the number of Torah-observant people, and the objective was to produce more by the time the Master returned to "settle accounts". (It's not about "money", but PEOPLE). If we go through life without "investing" in others the Word of Life, but rather "bury" the "talent", we produce no growth in those around us, and we are as a dead branch ourselves.

TEN MINAS The "talents" are one illustration, and at Luke 19:11-27, a similar parable is given. Again, *"A man of noble birth went to a distant country to have himself appointed king, and then to return."* Before leaving, this man gave ten (the 10 virgins?) of his servants a mina each, and told them to put the "money" to work, until he returned. While he was away, the servants "invested" such that one gained 10 more, another 5; but one of them just wrapped up his mina and hid it. In other words, one gained 10 converts, another 5, and the other NONE. While he was away, the man heard that the "subjects" he had left (all the people of the Earth) proclaimed *"We don't want this man to be OUR king."* Upon his return, the new King of the Universe proclaimed, *"But those enemies of mine who did not want me to be king over them ~ bring them here and kill them in front of me."* That's exactly what will happen to the "weeds" when He returns as a roaring Lion. You had better get busy, my friend, because the servant who hid his "mina" lost his "mina", and was not found to be worthy of his Ruler any longer. If we are not spreading the "seed" (Torah, and the message of the Kingdom), then we have not understood that it is US, not the preachers, who must be actively engaged in reaching those around us. *"Unless you repent, you too will all likewise perish."* Luke 13:3. Why people will perish is clearly explained at 2Thess. 2. The return of our Sovereign OWY︎AZ ha Mashiach will not come until **the rebellion** occurs, and the **man of lawlessness** is revealed. The rebellion is the Nazarene

sect, exposing the lie; the whole world is in the power of lawlessness, and religious merchants have taught lawlessness for centuries. We rebel against the lie, and the work of Shatan *"displayed in all kinds of counterfeit miracles, signs and wonders, and in every sort of evil that deceives those who are perishing. They perish because they refused to love the Truth, and so be saved. For this reason, AY︎AZ sends them a powerful delusion, so that they will believe the LIE, and so that all will be condemned who have not believed the Truth, but have delighted in lawlessness."* The "lie" is clearly lawlessness, and it is everywhere taught that "legalism" is evil. How amazing, because this is the *strong delusion.* The "delusion" is taught by twisting Paul's writings, EVERYTIME! Peter warned us of those who use Paul's writings to support their error: *"Just as our dear brother Paul also wrote to you with the wisdom that AY︎AZ gave him; he writes the same way in all his letters, speaking in them of these matters. His letters contain some things that are hard to understand, which ignorant and unstable people DISTORT, as they do the other Writings, to their own destruction. Therefore, dear friends, since you already know this, BE ON YOUR GUARD, so that you may not be carried away by the error of lawless men, and fall from your secure position."* ~ 2Pet. 3:15-17.

At Luke 8:11,12, the parable of of the Sower, the Torah is sown by the Master of the harvest: *"The seed is the Word of AY︎AZ."* The adversary, Shatan, steals the Word from people's hearts, so they will not believe and obey, and so be saved. Shatan's messengers are disguised, masquerading as messengers of righteousness. Be careful how you listen! We must produce a crop, by spreading the true seed, not the seed of weeds. Psalm 119:152 says, *"Long ago, I learned from your statutes that you established them to last FOREVER."* 119:160 says *"All your words are TRUE; ALL your righteous LAWS ARE ETERNAL."* With David, we who love the Torah say, *"Streams of tears flow from my eyes, for your LAW is NOT obeyed."* 119:136. He's not talking about the CEREMONIAL LAW, but the MORAL LAW. That's why Paul is not properly understood.

History was "revised" over and over, making it appear that "Christianity" was "founded" by OWY︎AZ. But, in truth, He founded the sect of the Nazarenes, and these remained in the true faith. Pursued by the "dragon", this "woman" had to endure many severe trials.

TURNING THE WORLD UPSIDE DOWN
(How They Used To Get "Stoned" In The Old Days)
THEY USED THE NAME ALOUD!

The Book of Acts (the book of "**Action**") records how the early students of O W Y⅁Ⱬ "turned the world upside down". Put yourself in that lifesetting. The **Name** of the Creator had been concealed from the common people for centuries, since the Babylonian Captivity. Learning this truth, everyone was **astounded**, and a natural curiosity swirled among everyone. When Peter stood up and addressed the crowds at Acts 2, he quoted Yah El 2 (Joel) and told them to be immersed into the Name. Today, just before the end of the "times of the Gentiles", the world is being turned upside down once again by the growing knowledge of the Name, which has been concealed for many centuries by the religious merchants. Like today, it was the **Name** of the Creator that caused the religious establishment to be turned on its head.

NAME OR NO-NAME? People are quick to label others with "handles". Christians in general are called by a Greek term, having no idea that the term was used by Pagans first, as worshippers of Serapis, or that it is cognate with "cretin" (see your dictionary). They hang their hat on one translated verse from the Scriptures (Acts 11:26), while scholars know they were called **Nazarenes**, as a sect within Judaism.

Many today are apprehensive of groups that use the Hebrew personal Name of the Creator, calling them "sacred name" groups. These who would criticize those who use the Hebrew Name should remember our Rabbi's prayer at John 17, where He said He had revealed the Name to them, and that they be kept as one by the power of the Father's Name. Now, I'm going to initiate a new "handle" ~ the "NO-NAMERS". The **no-namers** use traditional terms in place of the Name, as most prefaces of the Scriptures will acknowledge. The words "GOD" and "LORD" are used as traditional replacements for the Name, a regrettable situation considering John 17. In review, the Encyclopedia Americana has this to say about the word "GOD":

GOD (god, gawd) A common Teutonic word for personal object of religious worship, formerly applicable to superhuman beings of heathen myth; on conversion of Teutonic races to Christianity, term was applied to Supreme Being, and to Persons of Trinity."

Swell. So, what does this mean ~ are we calling on the Creator with a word originally used by Pagans, to avoid the "ethnic" Name for the Creator? Look up the word "BAAL" in Webster's. It is defined as "LORD". Belial is a form of BAAL, and is another term for Satan. What's going on?

The over-looked issue here is this: at the time our Savior came, Whose Name is Yahushua, the Name was concealed, and any who spoke it aloud could be stoned to death for saying it. He said He revealed it to those given to Him out of the world, and that we be kept as ONE (in unity) by it. Are we in unity? He criticized the Pharisees for withholding the "Key of Knowledge" (Luke 11:52), and what they withheld was the Name! Why did they constantly want to stone Yahushua? He kept saying the Name. At Luke 19:38, the crowds were crying out a verse from Psalm 118:26 which contained the Name, and the Pharisees told Yahushua to rebuke them ~ because they were using the Name. Why were the disciples called to stand before the Sanhedrin? The Name! Why was Stephen **stoned** (Acts 7)? When he said the Name, they screamed and put their hands over their ears, and killed him. Yahushua Himself was condemned because He spoke the Name before the Sanhedrin, which caused the High Priest to tear his clothes, saying, "He has spoken blasphemy!" Blasphemy only involves one thing: **the Name**. Why was Paul on his way to Damascus to arrest Nazarenes? To carry them back to the Sanhedrin to see if they would say the Name and be similarly condemned to death. Why were the Dead Sea Scrolls buried in the first place? Because worn-out scrolls were treated with respect and buried in jars instead of being profanely burned or discarded, because they had the Name written on them. The book of "Esther" isn't among them, because the Name is not written anywhere in the text. Even at Acts 2, Peter quoted Joel 2:32, emphasizing the importance of calling on the Name ~ and then to be immersed calling on it. No-namers insist it is of no importance, and don't use it in their immersions. Falsehood and futility is what the prophet Jeremiah says the Gentiles have inherited: **"YHWH . . . To you the nations will come from the ends of the Earth and say, 'our fathers have inherited nothing but falsehood, futility, and things of no profit' . . . This time I will make them know My power and My might; and they shall know that My Name is YHWH."** -16:19-21.

84

At Romans 10:14, after quoting Joel 2:32, Paul asks, *"How then shall they call upon Him in whom they have not believed? And how shall they believe in Him whom they have not HEARD?"* They don't know, or call, on His Name. *"HALLELU-YAH "* means *"praise Yah".* It's easily seen that monks and translators **sterilized** the Scriptures by removing the Name from the texts, especially when you look at Acts 7 and the stoning of Stephen, or even read your preface. Taken as a whole, the <u>main controversy</u> in the New Testament seems to be the Name issue, and the announcing of the Kingdom of YHWH. Yahushua's own Name contains the Name. Revelation 7 and 14 connect together, because the "seal" in the foreheads (minds) of the 144,000 is this Name of the Father. Taking His Name "in vain" means to bring it to nothing, missing it, or wiping it out. The "Sinai Autograph" of the original Name YHWH written by His own hand was in what is called palaeo-Hebrew. All the prophets wrote it in this script.

PAUL HAD NAZARENES KILLED FOR PRO-NOUNCING THE NAME!

The Yahudim were hoping for the Mashiach to come, and Rabbi O W Y ∃ Z was not going around telling anyone He was ~ but rather kept that an inside secret. The only thing He did that caused the law teachers and priests to pick up stones to kill Him was what they called "blasphemy". It was against *their* law to say the Name of ∃ Y ∃ Z ~ and the penalty was death. This is not usually mentioned by the merchant preachers, because people would naturally start to search it out, and the "Key of knowledge" would be widespread. The Name of O W Y ∃ Z contains the Name of the Father, so even His Name was part of the problem for them. The name "Yeshua" means *salvation,* and was a rather common name at the time; however "Yahushua" means *Yah is our salvation,* and had the Name being clearly heard by all.

Paul explains how he fought against those who were found in the synagogues that proclaimed O W Y ∃ Z. At Acts 26:9-11, Paul explains:

"I truly thought with myself that I ought to do many things contrary to the Name of the Mashiach of Nazareth. And this I also did in Yerushaliyim: and I both shut up many of the saints in prisons, and having received authority from the chief priests, and WHEN THEY WERE PUT TO DEATH I GAVE MY VOTE AGAINST THEM. And punishing them constantly in the synagogues, I STROVE TO MAKE THEM BLAS-PHEME; and being exceedingly mad against them, I persecuted them even to foreign cities." They weren't being killed for any other reason than that they were going against the "law" of pronouncing the Name. After "Shaul" was knocked-down on his way to Damascus, and encountered the risen O W Y ∃ Z, he began to pronounce the Name, and did what he had watched others die for! This is no small side-line issue, but is really central to what the entire Brit Chadasha reveals to us. After Shaul was immersed by Ananias, (who was himself very afraid at first when he learned he was to be visited by the infamous Shaul), he took the name of "Paulos". The name "Shaul" and his reputation was terrifying to the Nazarenes, and you can well understand why. For some time, Nazarenes were still afraid and distrustful of Paul: *"... Is not this he that in Yerushaliyim made havoc of them that <u>called</u> on this Name? And has he come here for the intention that he might bring them bound before the chief priests,"* (Acts 9:15,16).

Yes, pronouncing the Name was a REALLY big deal. Paul was nabbed by the Yahudim of Achaia, and they wanted him dead so much that they rushed him to the Roman proconsul Gallio. Gallio, no doubt a Pagan, must have thought they were crazy when he heard the reason they were so murderously enraged, and he said:

"If indeed it was an act of injustice or reck-less evil, O Yahudim, according to REASON I would bear with you; BUT if it be a question concerning a WORD, or NAMES, and that law which is among YOU, see you to it, for I will be no judge of THESE things." (Acts 18:14,15). Paul had to be locked up to protect him. He claims he was stoned on several occasions over pronouncing the Name. Men had sworn oaths to see Paul dead before they would eat again. Paul had to hide, and sneak out of the city in a basket. How many Christians really know why Paul was imprisoned? Now, you know. Believe it or not, there is quite a bit of "shunning" against those of us who use the Name, even among Messianics who observe the appointed times. Paul's life, and many other Nazarenes' lives were taken for simply pronouncing the Name, and yet believers today shun and demonize those of us who seem to be making a "big deal" out of it. We can't help ourselves, the Name burns inside us. We would die for it too. If we are misguided, then those who have died over the Name have done so needlessly, including Paul and all the early Nazarene followers. O W Y ∃ Z revealed the Name to them, and He has done so to us as well. There are always 2 sides to most issues, but since the Name is the strong tower, that's the safer bet to go with. The Name turned the world upside down once, and here in the days of the final message, it is doing it again.

85

The Early Church Fathers

(Excerpts from: _A History of AntiSemitism_)

["For almost a century, the early believers in Yeshua the Messiah were culturally and ethnically the same as, and worshipped alongside, mainstream Judaism. The first believers in Messiah Yeshua were Jews. The Torah was of great importance to them and they kept its laws, keeping the Sabbath and performing circumcision. They did not follow 'another religion', but remained within the framework of Judaism. This Messianic movement spread largely among Jews to begin with, and for some time it remained as a **sect** within Judaism, mostly known as the sect of the Nazarenes (Acts 24:5). Thousands of Gentile 'converts' and 'God Fearers' joined themselves to the Nazarene sect. It is important to say something about the Nazarenes, as documentation of their existence and beliefs gives us much insight on how the early believers in Messiah thought and lived. The fourth century 'Church Father', Jerome, described the Nazarenes as _"those who accept Messiah in such a way that they do not cease to observe the Old Law"_ (Jerome; On. Is. 8:14). Yet another fourth century Church Father, Epiphanius, gave a more detailed description of them: _"We shall now especially consider heretics who.. call themselves Nazarenes; they are mainly Jews and nothing else. They make use not only of the New Testament, but they also use in a way the Old Testament of the Jews; for they do not forbid the books of the Law, the Prophets, and the Writings... so that they are approved of by the Jews, from whom the Nazarenes do not differ in anything, and they profess all the dogmas pertaining to the prescriptions of the Law and to the customs of the Jews, except they believe in Messiah... They preach that there is but one God, and his son Yeshua the Messiah. But they are very learned in the Hebrew language; for they, like the Jews, read the whole Law, then the Prophets... They differ from the Jews because they believe in Messiah, and from the Christians in that they are to this day bound to the Jewish rites, such as circumcision, the Sabbath, and other ceremonies. They have the Good news according to Matthew in its entirety in Hebrew. For it is clear that they still preserve this, in the Hebrew alphabet, as it was originally written"._ (Epiphanius; Panarion 29; translated from the Greek). There is evidence that the Nazarene Sect continued to exist until at least the 13th century. The Catholic writings of Bonacursus entitled 'Against the Heretics', refers to the Nazarenes, who were also called 'Pasagini'. Bonacursus says: _"Let those who are not yet acquainted with them, please note how perverse their belief and doctrine are. First, they teach that we should obey the Law of Moses according to the letter - the Sabbath, and circumcision, and the legal precepts still being in force. Furthermore, to increase their error, they condemn and reject all the Church Fathers, and the whole Roman Church."_]

(Most spell the Name "Yeshua", which is Hebrew for "help", however "Yahushua" means "Yah is our salvation").

You will notice this quote states that the Nazarenes practiced "circumcision". Some may have; not understanding Acts 15, and other writings stating circumcision of the flesh is nothing. But, the Nazarenes rejected Rome's change of the 7th day Shabbat to Sun-Day. The 4th Commandment actually **states** that the reason we are to keep the 7th day set-apart is because ⴽYⴷ-Z created the skies and Earth in 6 days, and He rested on the 7th. Thus, we honor Him as Creator by resting as He did (Heb. 4). There is no peace for the wicked. **"But the wicked are like the tossing sea, which cannot rest"** Yesha Yahu 57:20. Epiphanius also claims that the writings of "Matthew" were originally written in Hebrew.

Epiphanius, Bonacursus, Jerome, and later records up to the 13th century speak of these "Nazarenes", who were constantly castigated and repelled by the "new" revisionary doctrines, replacement theology, and supercessionism of the Universal Roman State religion. The gates of the grave have not prevailed. Benjamin Franklin wrote, _"History is the record of the winners."_ History is the written record of events; the struggles people recorded through their eyes. Rarely do we read about history from the point of view of the losers, or the conquered. The "father of history", Herodotus, was objective in his report, but his "bias" still comes through. The Nazarenes almost vanished from recorded history, since they had to flee to the mountains to survive. Their outposts were discovered at times, forcing them to stay on the move. Some of them influenced the peoples around them, giving rise to little groups like the Anabaptists and Waldenses, who were persecuted by the Roman religion. Anyone who was not "Catholic" yet trusted in Rabbi ⵔWYⴷ-Z was termed a "heretic", and exterminated, being a threat to the teachings of Catholicism. So, naturally Jerome, Bonacursus, and Epiphanius would call them "heretics". Now, we Nazarene Yisraelites are on the internet! The first settlers to America came to flee religious persecution. In early America, there were civil laws enacted which prohibited the celebration of "Christmas", because they knew it to be a Pagan festival counterfeited as a "holy" day (holiday). George

Washington crossed the Delaware to attack the British on Christmas Day. George knew that because the British celebrated on Christmas, they would be drunken and unprepared to defend themselves. But, as history will show, George was not a nice guy. When George was 25, he caused the French and Indian war by killing the French Ambassador. Then, George started *another* war with his own King over taxes on tea; taxes intended to help pay for the previous war! Our "history" is only written from the point of view of the winner. George was a Mason, and had his "apron" of righteousness to cling to. I'm not "judging" George, but these facts are easily researched for all to see. What will judge George? It will be the Living Word.

THE LIVING WORD

At Hebrews chapter 4, it is made very clear that those whom ᴧYᴧZ is angry with *will never enter His rest.* "THE WORD" of ᴧYᴧZ is His Torah, the instructions for how His wife/bride is to live. Those who hear THE WORD, yet do not profit from hearing it, are the ones who are not steadfast, but **disobedient.** The Yisraelites disobeyed in the wilderness, and wandered for 40 years until their bodies fell dead. *"For who provoked Him when they had heard? Indeed, not all those who came out of Egypt with Mosheh? And with whom was He angry for 40 years? Was it not with those who sinned, whose bodies fell in the wilderness? And to whom did He swear that they should not enter His rest, but to those who were disobedient?"* Heb. 3:16-18.

These "disobedient" did not **believe**, therefore they did not **obey.** Billions today "believe", but they believe the wrong thing; THE LIE. The enemy has sown "weeds" among the wheat, which are false teachings. He did it long ago. He said Shabbat was now "Sun-Day", and we can ignore the appointed times, because they are just "Old Testament Jewish Stuff". Shatan also taught the world that the Creator was so angry with Yisrael, that His New Covenant was with a new wife; THE GENTILES. This is called "Replacement Theology", and it is a lie.

The "sign" of ᴧYᴧZ's Everlasting Covenant is His "rest": (Go read all of Exodus 31:12-18)

". . . . So the sons of Yisrael shall observe the Sabbath, to celebrate the Sabbath throughout their generations, as a perpetual covenant. It is a SIGN between Me and the sons of Israel FOREVER; for in six days ᴧYᴧZ made Shamayim and Eretz, but on the seventh day He ceased from labor, and was refreshed."

"And also I gave them My Sabbaths to be a SIGN between Me and them, that they might know that I am ᴧYᴧZ who sanctifies them." Ezek. 20:12.

"There remains therefore a Sabbath rest for the people of ᴧYᴧZ. For the one who has entered His rest has himself also rested from his works, as ᴧYᴧZ did from His."

"Let us therefore be diligent to enter that rest, lest anyone fall through following the same example of disobedience."

"For THE WORD of ᴧYᴧZ is LIVING and active, and sharper than any two-edged sword, and piercing as far as the division of soul and spirit, of both joints and marrow, and ABLE TO JUDGE THE THOUGHTS AND INTENTIONS OF THE HEART." Heb. 4:9-12.

This "WORD" that is "living and active" is the Torah; it "judges" the thoughts and intentions of our hearts, and there is no way to hide how we feel about it from ᴧYᴧZ. The Torah is ALIVE, because it came to life and walked this Earth as a man. It is now His Spirit living in His bride, and He has circumcised our hearts with this "LIVING WORD", enabling us to LOVE His Covenant Law. If we sin, it is not our spirits in agreement, but our flesh at war with our spirits.

PROTESTANT CONFESSIONS

This is from a tract published by the Bible Sabbath Assoc., 3316 Alberta Dr., Gillette,WY 82718, which is called *ROMAN CATHOLIC AND PROTESTANT CONFESSIONS ABOUT SUNDAY,* part 2, which I ran across re-printed by the *PETAH TIKVAH* (address in Resources section in the back of this book).

Protestant theologians and preachers from a wide spectrum of denominations have been quite candid in ADMITTING that there is no Biblical authority for observing Sunday as a Sabbath:

ANGLICAN / EPISCOPAL

Isaac Williams, *Plain Sermons on the Catechism,* vol. 1, pp. 334, 336:

"And where are we told in the Scriptures that we are to keep the first day at all? We are commanded to keep the seventh; but we are nowhere commanded to keep the first day . . . The reason we keep the first day of the week holy instead of the seventh is for the same reason that we observe many other things, not because the Bible, but because the church has enjoined it."

T. Enright, C.S.S.R., in a lecture at Hartford, Kansas, Feb. 18, 1884:

"I have repeatedly offered $1000 to anyone who can prove to me from the Bible alone that I am bound to keep Sunday holy. There is no such law in the Bible. It is a law of the Holy Catholic Church alone. The Bible says, 'Remember the Sabbath day to keep it holy'. The Catholic Church says: 'NO. By my divine power I abolish the Sabbath day, and command you to keep holy the first day of the week'. And lo! The entire civilized world bows down in a reverent obedience to the command of the holy Catholic Church."

Canon Eyton, *The Ten Commandments,* pp. 52, 63, 65:

"There is no word, no hint, in the New Testament about abstaining from work on Sunday . . . Into the rest of Sunday no divine law enters . . . The observance of Ash Wednesday or Lent stands exactly on the same footing as the obser-

vance of Sunday."

Bishop Seymour, *Why We Keep Sunday:*
"We have made the change from the seventh day to the first day, from Saturday to Sunday, on the authority of the one holy Catholic Church."

Dr. Edward T. Hiscox, a paper read before the New York ministers' conference, Nov. 13, 1893, reported in *New York Examiner*, Nov. 16, 1893:
"There was and is a commandment to keep holy the Sabbath day, but that Sabbath day was not Sunday. It will be said, however, and with some show of triumph, that the Sabbath was transferred from the seventh to the first day of the week. Where can the record of such a transaction be found? Not in the New Testament—absolutely not. To me it seems unaccountable that Jesus, during three years' intercourse with His disciples, often conversing with them upon the Sabbath question . . . Never alluded to any transference of the day; also, that during forty days of His resurrection life, no such thing was intimated. Of course, I quite well know that Sunday did come into use in early Christian history. . . But what a pity it comes branded with the mark of Paganism, and christened with the name of the sun god, adopted and sanctioned by the papal apostasy, and bequeathed as a sacred legacy to Protestantism!"

William Owen Carver, *The Lord's Day In Our Day:*
"There was never any formal or authoritative change from the Jewish seventh-day Sabbath to the Christian first-day observance."

Dr. R.W. Dale, *The Ten Commandments* (New York: Eaton & Mains), p. 127-129:
"It is quite clear that however rigidly or devoutly we may spend Sunday, we are not keeping the Sabbath . . . The Sabbath was founded on a specific Divine command. We can plead no such command for the obligation to observe Sunday . . . There is not a single sentence in the New Testament to suggest that we incur any penalty by violating the supposed sanctity of Sunday."

Timothy Dwight, *Theology; Explained and Defended* (1823), Ser. 107, vol. 3, p. 258:
The Christian Sabbath [Sunday] is not in the Scriptures, and was not by the primitive Church called the Sabbath."

DISCIPLES OF CHRIST

Alexander Campbell, *The Christian Baptist*, Feb. 2, 1824, vol. 1, no. 7, p. 164:
"'But', say some, 'it was changed from the seventh to the first day'. Where? When? And by whom? No man can tell. NO; it never was changed, nor could it be, unless creation was to be gone through again; for the reason assigned must be changed before the observance, or respect to the reason, can be changed! It is all old wives' fables to talk of the change of the Sabbath from the seventh to the first day. If it be changed, it was that august personage changed it who changes times and laws EX OFFICIO– I think his name is DOCTOR ANTICHRIST."

First Day Observance, pp. 17, 19:
"The first day of the week is commonly called the Sabbath. This is a mistake. The Sabbath of the Bible was the day just proceeding the first day of the week. The first day of the week is never called the Sabbath anywhere in the entire Scriptures. It is also an error to talk about the change of the Sabbath from Saturday to Sunday. There is not in any place in the Bible any intimation of such a change."

LUTHERAN

The Sunday Problem, a study book of the United Lutheran Church (1923), p. 36:
"We have seen how gradually the impression of the Jewish Sabbath faded from the mind of the

Christian Church, and how completely the newer thought underlying the observance of the first day took possession of the church. We have seen that the Christians of the first three centuries never confused one with the other, but for a time celebrated both."

Augsburg Confession of Faith., art. 28; written by Melanchthon, approved by Martin Luther, 1530; as published in *The Book of Concord of the Evangelical Lutheran Church*, Henry Jacobs, ed. (1911), p. 63:
"They [Roman Catholics] refer to the Sabbath Day, as having been changed into the Lord's Day, contrary to the Decalogue, as it seems. Neither is there any example whereof they make more than concerning the changing of the Sabbath Day. Great, say they, is the power of the Church, since it has dispensed with one of the Ten Commandments!"

Dr. Augustus Neander, *The History of the Christian Religion and Church*, Henry John Rose, tr. (1843), p. 186:
"The festival of Sunday, like all other festivals, was always only a human ordinance, and it was far from the intentions of the apostles to establish a Divine Command in this respect, far from them, and from the early apostolic church, to transfer the laws of the Sabbath to Sunday."

John Theodore Mueller, *Sabbath or Sunday:*
"But they err in teaching that Sunday has taken the place of the Old Testament Sabbath and therefore must be kept as the seventh day had to be kept by the children of Israel . . . These churches err in their teaching, for Scripture has in no way ordained the first day of the week in place of the Sabbath. There is simply no law in the New Testament to that effect."

METHODIST

John Wesley, *The Works of the Rev. John Wesley, A.M.*, John Emory, ed. (New York: Eaton & Mains), Sermon 25, vol. 1, p. 221:
"But, the Moral Law contained in the Ten Commandments, and enforced by the prophets, he [Christ] did not take away. It was not the design of His coming to revoke any part of this. This is a law which never can be broken . . . Every part of this law must remain in force upon all mankind, and in all ages; as not depending either on time or place, or any other circumstances liable to change, but on the nature of God and the nature of man, and their unchangeable relation to each other."

DWIGHT L. MOODY

D.L. Moody, *Weighed and Wanting*, pp. 7, 48:
"The Sabbath was binding in Eden, and it has been in force ever since. This fourth commandment begins with the word 'remember', showing that the Sabbath already existed when God wrote the law on the tables of stone at Sinai. How can men claim that this one commandment has been done away with when they will admit that the other nine are still binding?"

PRESBYTERIAN

T.C. Blake, D.D., *Theology Condensed*, pp. 474:
"The Sabbath is a part of the Decalogue-the Ten Commandments. This alone forever settles the question as to the perpetuity of the institution. Until, therefore, it can be shown that the whole Moral Law has been repealed, the Sabbath will stand . . . The teaching of Christ confirms the perpetuity of the Sabbath."

What happened? By denying the "roots" of the faith, the engrafted Gentile assembly gradually became so anti-Torah, that there was no connection with 𐤀𐤉𐤄𐤆, and they became an

88

instrument of death. When a few "reformers" began to crawl away from it, they were pursued to their death. The Christian assembly turned to fables and mythology:

"Preach the WORD; be ready in season and out of season. Reprove, rebuke, and exhort with great patience and instruction. For the time will come when they will not endure sound doctrine, but after their own lusts shall they heap to themselves teachers to tickle their ears, and they shall turn away their ears from the Truth, and shall be turned aside to myths." 2Tim. 4:2,3. The "Word" is the Torah, and the "in season" - "out of season" refers to the annual appointed times like Passover, Shabuoth, and Sukkot (Tabernacles). False security is fostered in order to fleece the flock, and MANY will utter these words from Matt. 7:22,23:

"Many will say to Me in that day, 'Lord, Lord, have we not prophesied in your Name, and in Your Name done many wonderful works?' And then I will profess to them, 'I never knew you. Depart from Me, you who practice lawlessness.'"

What are we to do? *"Come out of her, My people, so that you will not share in her sins, so that you will not receive any of her plagues; for her sins are piled up to Shamayim, and ᴀYᴀꝫ has remembered her crimes.* Rev. 18:4. The "merchants" will mourn because no one will "buy" their lies anymore. Babylon, soon your doom will come. Armed with this knowledge, you can study on your own, and put the showmen preachers out of business by telling others who will listen. Support the orphans and widows, and especially your own family members in need (such as elderly parents). *"The woman you saw is the great city that rules over the kings of the Earth."* Rev. 17:18. The calendar and customs of the whole Earth are following the beast, seated in the ancient city of Rome. When your eyes are opened to this fact, you will be absolutely astonished. If you wonder what the "image" of the beast is, all you have to do is objectively open your eyes, to watch what it is that billions of people alive today bow down to. This is covered under **"QUESTIONS & ANSWERS"**, in the next section. (Truth can be a paradox.)

Something very curious happened when the detachment of soldiers came to arrest O W Yᴀꝫ in the olive grove at Yahuchanon (John) 18:5,6:

"When O W Yᴀꝫ said, 'I AM HE', they drew back and FELL TO THE GROUND." Many believe He spoke the <u>Name</u> of the Creator, and the power of the Name repelled them with a physical force. At 17:11,12, He prayed: *"Qodesh Abba, protect them by the power of Your Name ~ the Name You gave Me ~ so that they may be one*

as We are one. While I was with them, I protected them and kept them safe by that Name you gave Me." He told us: *"I tell you, you will not see Me again until you say, 'blessed is He who comes in the Name of ᴀYᴀꝫ."* ~ Luke 13:35. At Mattit Yahu 24:20, He said *"Pray that your flight will not take place in winter or on <u>the Sabbath</u>."* Very few, if any, Christians are praying for this, but Nazarenes are. When all the changes that have been made are corrected, Scripture begins to make much more sense. It takes a great deal of dedication to the Truth for a person to step out from their family and preacher even after learning about the false deceptions. Most everyone who does will have no one around them at first who shares a love for the Name and the Torah. In fact, they will be bombarded with twisted quotes from Paul's writings that seem to annul the Sabbath or other appointed times. This situation is described in the Parable of the Sower at Luke 8, where the "seed" is stolen away, choked by weeds, or has no root. But, they must bear in mind the words of 2 Pet. 3:15-18, where it states that <u>Paul's writings</u> are twisted by unstable and ignorant men, leading to their destruction. We are each placed where we are as "salt"; so we are not intended to be "bunched up", but rather must reach the few around us who **will** listen to the Truth.

EAGLES & CROSSES REPRESENTED THE SUN TO ANCIENT PAGANS —
THIS MAKES THEM SYNONYMOUS. JUST STUDY THE DEVOTION IN THE FACE OF THE GENTLEMAN IN THE PICTURE AT LEFT. HE WOULD LIKE TO KNOW THE TRUTH, BUT IT WASN'T HANDED TO HIM LIKE IT WAS TO YOU. THERE ARE MANY OTHERS JUST LIKE HIM ALL AROUND EACH OF US.
(THAT'S NOT A CHRISTIAN POW-WOW STICK JUST BECAUSE IT INVOLVES A CRUX).

GREAT SPIRIT EAGLE CRUX

EAGLE SUN-SPIRITS EVERYWHERE!

IMDUGUD OF EL

Questions & Answers

ALWAYS LOOK TO SCRIPTURE, NOT TRADITION

QUESTION from Dawna: You say in your book that we should not give our tithe to help support our leaders (Rabbi). Well if that is their full-time job (teaching Yeshiva, leading Shabbat services, traveling, then how should they be supported? Furthermore we meet in a building that we are renting and somebody has to pay for the electric bill! Yes, we could meet in a house, but there are more than 500 of us. What's your view on this? We put our tithe in the box every week. I'm not sure how every penny is spent. Our leader says it's also from the Torah (I don't remember where) to publicize who pays their tithe and when each year. They print out a list with everyone's name on it declaring who gave their tithe and how often. What do you think about that? - [from e-mail]

ANSWER: ~ What your e-mail described was not a "tithe", but a social decision, which is fine, but it's not the purpose of the commanded tithe. The electric bill, and rent to house 500 people, are costs to run a school or club, and the payment being made is more like tuition, or club dues. The elders who teach are worthy of part of the tithe, in fact, a "double portion" (1 Tim. 5:17) of the meal fed to support the poor, widows, and fatherless children. Actually, no where in Scripture did any apostle take the whole tithe (10th part, ma'aser) for himself, to support him and his family! Paul said he supported not only himself with his own hands, but those who traveled with him. Sure, an elder is able to eat from his labors, but eat only, not pay mortgages, and personal support above and beyond staying with those he is teaching. The record at Acts 20:17-35 describes how Paul pleaded with the elders at Ephesus, which you should read very carefully, because it describes the situation we see today, which Paul wept over. Note carefully verses 20:32-35. He was speaking to the elders. Generosity to the poor gets YHWH's attention (Acts 10:4). But, one should first see to the support of their own family in need, such as parents, or close relatives, rather than have them be a burden on the assembly of saints (1 Tim. 5:3-11). Here, there was a "list" mentioned (5:11) that one had to be on to receive support. I would emphasize 1 Tim 5:16, which says: "If any woman who is a believer has widows in her family, she should help them, AND NOT LET THE AS-SEMBLY BE BURDENED WITH THEM, SO THAT THE ASSEMBLY CAN HELP THOSE WIDOWS WHO ARE REALLY IN NEED." We are all to progress in knowledge, and although we never become greater than the one who teaches us, we

should become like them. I teach and work a job, like bro. Paul. We are to feed the sheep of Yahushua, not fleece them. If one man has a group of 100 people who regularly "tithe" 10% of their income to him, that one man gains an income that is TEN TIMES greater than that of any one of those who "tithe" to him. You see, this is the "business" of the merchants. They often attend seminaries, which train them to be extremely successful at this, and they pay a percentage to their denomination. It mush-rooms like an MLM, or pyramid organization. As long as one knows they are not paying a "tithe", but supports the costs of the group meeting, there's no problem. If there's 500 people, and each one gives 75 cents per week, that's $375 for a meeting place once a week. But, if 250 of them pay $20 each week, then that's $5000 a week. That's a big business, not the rental and electric bill. An elder is not to receive the whole tithe, but SHARE in eating with the poor among the assembly, if he doesn't work for a living like everyone else. I'm sure any man who is able to have the size income from an assembly as large as yours is, or even larger, would be very much against everything I teach on this subject. I could easily have 2000 or more attend a weekly meeting here in Louisville, and bilk them out of many thousands, but I have to teach the truth, and face my Rabbi one day. "In their greed, these teachers will exploit you with stories they have made up." ~ 2 Peter 2:3. [Actually, we already pay quite a bit more than 10% to support the needy, just through Social Security, Medicaid, and various other public support mechanisms in place. There is no "tithe" to "spread the Gospel" in Scripture. Also, when we give, we are not to let our left hand know what our right hand is doing, so our Father who sees in secret will reward us. Our giving is "anonymous"].

Reading all of Acts 4:32-35 shows that those in need received the proceeds, and there were no needy among the Nazarenes. "James" 1:27 says " *Religion that ⴰⲨⴰⱫ our Father accepts as pure and faultless is this: to look after or-phans and widows in their distress, and to keep oneself from being polluted by the world.*" 2Cor. 2:17 says "*Unlike so many, we do not peddle the Word of ⴰⲨⴰⱫ for profit*".

QUESTION: Christianity has always taught salvation is a free gift through faith, not works. Wasn't the "Law" done away with in the Messiah's atoning sacrifice, so we can now eat pigs, lobsters, blood, and ignore Sabbaths?

ANSWER: What OWYAZ's death accomplished was bringing an end to the *ceremonial law*, which required the shedding of blood for the forgiveness of sin. Our faith is in His atoning blood ~ we're covered! Animal sacrifices were not a permanent atonement, as the precious blood of OWYAZ is. Nor could animal blood change the inner man. Our "faith" is in OWYAZ's shed blood covering our past sins, which is what all the animal sacrifices **pointed to**. Our life is in His resurrection, and His Spirit comes into us to dwell, circumcising our hearts with His MORAL Law. Allowing Him to write His Covenant Moral Law on our hearts is the New Covenant, promised at Yerme Yahu 31:31-34, and Heb. 8:10. This is commemorated each year at Shabuoth, called "Pentecost" (meaning *count* fifty). This is the 50th day after the Shabbat following Passover. This was when Yisrael was at Sinai in Midian, receiving the Torah Covenant, and took the marriage vows "I do". It is very fitting that the Spirit of OWYAZ came into the 120 Nazarenes on this day!

The model prayer, called "The Our Father", asks for AYAZ's "will" to be done on Earth, and His Kingdom to come. His "will" is His Covenant Laws, the Torah, or 10 Commandments (the marriage covenant). The eating of blood is even prohibited (Noahide law) at Acts 15:19-21, and it goes on to mention Shabbat, when Gentiles went to synagogue to learn more Torah. The "Sabbath" was changed to Sun-day by Constantine, in his attempt to "universalize" his Empire. At Mark 7, the text is twisted backwards with the **addition** of the words ("He thus declared all foods clean"). Our Mashiach was really saying that we sin because "evil" comes out of our hearts, it doesn't enter into our mouth from unwashed hands. Sin defiles us. The copyists added the words in *parenthesis*, to fit their lawless theology. (At Mark 7, the Pharisees were washing their hands because of a Kabbalistic superstition). Our "works" (actions) are evidence of our faith, as "James" says, *"You see that a person is justified by what he does, and not by faith alone."* (2:24). Read all of James chapter 2. Of course "legalism" is always taught as a bad thing, but only Shatan would teach people **not** to obey ~ remember the deception of Adam's wife, Chuwah. No Scripture condemns anyone for obedience, but rather all Scripture teaches that we must obey.

"For not the hearers of the Law are righteous in the sight of Elohim, but the doers of the Law shall be declared right." (Rom. 2:13). The Spirit is only given to those who obey (Acts 5:32). Of course this will get you labeled as a "cult", but that's OK.

QUESTION: What is sin?

ANSWER: *"Everyone who sins breaks the Law; in fact, sin is Lawlessness"*. (1 Yahuchanon 3:4). (The Gentilized name for Yahuchanon is "John".) Another way to translate the verse is *"Everyone practicing sin also practices Torahlessness; and sin is Torahlessness."* Paul answers it also: *"Is the Law sin? Let it not be! However, I did not know sin, except through the Law."* Rom. 7:7. Rabbi OWYAZ Himself said: *"Whoever then, breaks one of the least of these Commands, and teaches men so, shall be called least in the reign of AYAZ (the heavens); but **whoever does** and **teaches them**, he shall be called great in the reign of AYAZ"*. Mt. 5:19. The teachers of Torah today are thought to be cultists, or heretics, because great darkness has spread over the Earth, and the Torah is Light (see Prov. 6:23). The "Word" of AYAZ is the Torah, His teachings: *"Your Word is a lamp to my feet, and a Light for my path."* Ps. 119:105. Psalm 1 begins, *"Blessed is the man who does not walk in the counsel of the wicked, or stand in the way of sinners, or sit in the seat of mockers; but his delight is in the Law (Torah) of AYAZ. On His Torah he meditates day and night."* Torah has a feminine ending in Hebrew, and is called "Wisdom" in Proverbs. This "woman", Wisdom, is supreme; therefore get wisdom. It will unlock the mystery of Revelation 13:18, and many other veiled secrets. Sin is lawlessness, living outside the Covenant. While the Commandments of the Creator were known and applied, the "vineyard" was green and fruitful because the "living waters" kept it alive. The symbol of the Torah is the Tree of Life, memorialized in the lampstand called a "menorah". Removing the "living waters", the vineyard has become dried up, and the dead branches will be burned in the fire. The "oil" that lights the lamps of the menorah is the Torah, the personality of AYAZ. The 10 virgins in the parable at Mt. 25:1 illustrate the difference between the "5 wise" and the "5 foolish". They all "slept", meaning they died. When the Bridegroom comes, He will call them out, but the lack of oil will impede the "5 foolish" virgins. Man-made rules have caused most to be deceived.

QUESTION: What is "The Gospel"?

ANSWER: Simply put, *"Repent, for the reign of AYAZ draws near."* This "message", also called "testimony" is not popular, because it involves "repenting", or turning from sin. We must obey the Covenant, or Commands and teachings (Torah), but we cannot while in the "mind of the flesh". The carnal person "dies" at their immersion, calling on the Name of Yahushua, Who cleanses or washes the past

Torah-breaking from them, and He comes into them, enabling them to "walk in the Spirit", because He changes their attitude about the Commands ~ they love the "Word" from that point. The writing of the Torah on our hearts is the New Covenant. That would be your next question.

QUESTION: Why are we here, and what is the meaning of life?

ANSWER: We were created to be companions to AYAZ, and rule the universe He created with Him. This really sounds like Mormonism, but it's not that at all. We will "inherit" the Earth, and OWYAZ will rule the universe from here. In the here-and-now, our purpose is to make "righteous offspring". That's not easy, believe me. Everything you see is passing away, and everything you can't see is eternal. We will become spatial beings, able to interact with the physical world as well as the unseen "space" or spirit energy, when the "children of AYAZ" are finally revealed. "Going to Heaven" is a Pagan myth; it's not an idea found in Scripture. (By the way, when you read the phrase "Kingdom of Heaven", the word "heaven" was used to avoid saying the Name. It was probably changed by copyists.)

QUESTION: Where is sin?

ANSWER: Sin exists in the heart. Yerme Yahu 17:9 states: "The heart is deceitful above all things and beyond cure. Who can understand it?" The good news is at Ezek. 36:26, 27: "I will give you a new heart, and put a new spirit in you; I will remove from you your heart of stone, and give you a heart of flesh. And I will put My Spirit in you and move you to follow My decrees and be careful to keep My Laws." When a person builds a thermonuclear bomb or landmine, a sin was committed. The idea itself was a sin if even the intention was there. AYAZ doesn't make such things. Why? Because these things kill without selection! A gun or sword is not a sin to build, but their use can be. Automobiles and dynamite have killed, but they are not "sin". Sin is not outside us, it's in our hearts. OWYAZ told His students to arm themselves with a sword the night He was arrested, so a sword or gun is not the sin, but the use it is put to. The same logic applies to "images". If you bow down to a statue, picture, or object (like a national icon) for any reason, it is an abominable act, and the object also becomes an abomination, and must be destroyed. This happened to the serpent on the pole, Nehushtan, so it had to be destroyed (Num. 21:8,9, 2Kings 18:4). Also, food, money, gold, silver, or other valuables become defiled (in men's hearts) if they were offered to foreign elohim. But, the person must know this, or there is no problem. Paul explains this at 1Cor. 8. We know that foreign elohim are as nothing at all, but all people do not know this. The LOVE of money is the root of all kinds of evil, not the money itself.

QUESTION: Who is OWYAZ?

ANSWER: He is the "Word of Life", and anyone who acknowledges the Son of AYAZ has the Father. "And this is the testimony: AYAZ has given us eternal life, and this life is in His Son. He who has the Son has life; he who does not have the Son of AYAZ does not have life." (1John 5:11,12). The reason He appeared was to destroy the devil's work. "We know we have come to know Him if we obey His Commands." (1John 2:3). His indwelling _enables_ us to do no sin. OWYAZ is the Mashiach, Who came in the flesh, "Who, being in very nature AYAZ, did not consider equality with AYAZ something to be grasped, but made Himself nothing, taking the very nature of a servant, being made in human likeness." (Philippians 2:6,7). OWYAZ "is the image of the invisible AYAZ, the firstborn over all creation. For by Him all things were created: things in Shamayim and on Earth, visible and invisible, whether thrones or powers or authorities; all things were created by Him and for Him . . . He is the beginning and firstborn from among the dead, so that in everything He might have the supremacy. For AYAZ was pleased to have all His fullness dwell in Him, and through Him to reconcile to Himself all things on Earth or things in Shamayim, by making peace through His Blood, shed on the stake." (Col. 1:15-20). He is the Spokesman Who made all the Covenants with Yisrael. He is the Ruach ha Qodesh, or "set-apart Spirit", the resurrection and the life. "When he looks at Me, he sees the One Who sent Me." (John 12:45). Philip said, "'Rabbi, show us the Father, and that will be enough for us.' OWYAZ answered, 'Don't you know Me, Philip, even after I have been among you such a long time? Anyone who has seen Me has seen the Father.'" (John 14:8). He is the living Word (Torah) ~ the personality of AYAZ, made flesh. The physical body of OWYAZ being the "Son", and the mind being AYAZ is a better "grasp" for our limited abilities to comprehend. I guess that makes me a monotheistic modalist. But, so were all the prophets.

QUESTION: Is AYAZ a "Trinity"?

ANSWER: The Shema (meaning "hear"):
"Hear, O Yisrael: AYAZ our Elohim, AYAZ is _one_! **Love** AYAZ your Elohim with all your heart and with all your soul and with all your strength. These Commandments that I give you today are to be upon your hearts. Impress them on your children. Talk about them when you sit at home and when you walk along the road, when you lie down and when you get up. Tie

them as symbols on your hands and bind them on your foreheads. Write them on the doorframes of your houses and on your gates." (Dt. 6:4-9). The words *"EhYah asher EhYah"* mean *"I will be whom I will be".* YHWH, Yahueh, Yahuah, Yahuwah, Yahweh, IAUE, IAOUE, etc., are transliterations from the Hebrew letters ᴧΥᴧZ / יהוה. This Name means all three of the following: *I was, I am,* and *I will be.* *"'I am the alef and the tau', says the Sovereign* ᴧΥᴧZ, *'Who is, and Who was, and Who is to come, the Almighty* (Heb. *Shaddai)'".* (Rev. 1:8). The speaker was OΨᴧZ, speaking to "John" (Yahuchanon) on the island of Patmos. Men who "interpret" the Writings with their own preconceived ideas can put a "spin" on them, making them seem to say things they don't say. They will admit that Mosheh and Daniel didn't think there was a "Trinity", but claim there was "progressive revelation" later on. If there were a "Trinity", then surely there would have been a great deal of explanation given in the Writings, because it goes against everything the Scriptures ever taught. You can't have monotheism, and trinitarianism! *"I am* ᴧΥᴧZ; *that is My Name!"* (Yesha Yahu 42:8). *"I am the First and I am the Last; apart from Me there is no Elohim."* (44:6). *"Is there any Elohim besides Me?"* (44:8). *"I am Elohim, and there is no other; I am Elohim, and there is none like Me."* (46:9). *"Before Me, no elohim was formed, nor will there be one after Me. I, even I, am* ᴧΥᴧZ, *and apart from Me there is no savior."* (43:11). He is infinite in power, space, and time. He is not a multiple personality, but can be anything He wills to be. Zechar Yah 12:10 reveals Who died at Golgotha: *"They will look upon Me, the One they have pierced, and they will mourn for Him as one mourns for an only child, and grieve bitterly for Him as one grieves for a first-born son."*

TRINITIES WORLD-WIDE Since Pagan religions were (and are) based on sex, the *father-mother-child* triad were common to them all. The four seasons were interpreted as manifesting a great cosmic cycle from impregnation (spring) to birth (winter, at the solstice). The power or control over the masses was in the hands of the very few who were "initiated" in the mysteries, and could tell when to plant, when to reap, and when to sacrifice their children to the deities. "deity" comes from the word "diva", and produces the words divine, deis, and day; it means *to shine.*

Here are a few of the Trinities from the past:

Babylonian: **Baal, Semiramis, Tammuz.** (alt. Bel, Ishtar, Duzu). Ishtar was also known as Easter, Asherah, Astoreth, Astarte, Aphrodite, etc.

India: **Brahma, Shiva** (or Devaki), **Vishnu** (or Krishna). The family name of "Brahmans" may have stemmed from one of Abraham's descen-

dants, due to the close spelling, so some say.

Egypt: **Amon Ra, Isis, Osiris** (or Horus).
(Note: E.G.Y.P.T. is said to be short for *the Genie of Ptah.)* **I.H.S.** originally stood for *Isis, Horus, Seb.*

Greece: **Zeus** (or Apollo), **Demeter** (or Athena, Artemis), **Porsephene** (or Nike).

Rome (Roma): **Deus** (form of Zeus, also known as *Zeus-Father,* or *Iu-piter, Jupiter*); **Venus** (or Astarte, Biblia, Charis); **Cupid** (or Bacchus, Nike).

Celtic: (also known as Druid, Wiccan, Norse, Gaelic); **Baal** (or Woden, Teutates, Heil); **Ceridwen** (or Freya, Frigga, Eostre); **Thor** (or Balder, Taranis, Dero). (alt. Esus, Taranis, Teutates).

Canaanite: (and Phoenician); **Baal** (or Moloch); **Asherah** (or Ishtar, Easter, Tanit); **Rompha.**

Chaldean: (and Zoroastrian); **Baal Mithras** (known as "wise-lord" *Ahura Mazda,* or *Ohrmazd*); **Astoreth**; **Haoma.**

Persian: **Shamash, Ishtar, Sin.**

Macedonian / Asian: **Dagon** (fish idol); **Cybele** (or Ceres); **Deoius** (or Janus).

Mithraic: (Chaldean fusion with Indo-Iranian); **Mithras** (or Marduk, called *Sol* by Romans); **Rashnu; Vohu Manah.**

Mandaean: **Joshaman, Abatar, Hibil Ziwa.**

Manichaean: **Ohrmazd, Maitreya** (New Age "Christ"); **Zurvan.**

In Japan, the Shinto religion has the phrase, *"San Pao Fuh",* which means *"one deity, three forms".* The Irish use one of their ancient Druid symbols, the trifolium clover leaf, as a symbol of their Celtic pride, but also as a secret symbol of their Trinity. The male and female symbols used in Biology are the secret Babylonian signs of Nimrod (Orion, Sagittarius ~ the mighty archer/hunter), and his wife/mother Semiramis (Great Mother, Magna Mater). All of these things and many more, were the "interpreted" mysteries of the Pagan religions, overseen by Wizards, sorcerers, warlocks, shamans, and priest-magicians who exploited the masses. (The "Magi" from Babylon were priests of Ahura-Mazda (Mithras), the sun deity. They arrived when the Mashiach was about two years old, and the gifts they bestowed enabled the family of Yosef, Miryam, and little Yahushua to live in Egypt until Herod died.)

Trinitarianism and Replacement Theology

Replacement theology, or *supersessionism, resulted from un-converted Pagans becoming part of the early assembly of believers.* The educated men were influencial and wealthy, and they swayed doctrines to conform to the mold of the Pagan mind, simply because it was the easiest thing to do. It also preserved their control over the masses. The Pagan mind was already skilled at "spiritualizing" everything through interpretation, and the early Church Fathers had all come from this mold. Augustine had been a Manichaean, which is a sun worshiper. Anti-Semitism (from the word *Shem*, a son of Noach) developed from the writing of the Church Fathers. By the 4th century, it had become conspicuous; the record bears witness to it in this letter of **Faustus**, who wrote to Augustine:

*"You have substituted your love feasts for the sacrifices of the Pagans; for their idols, your martyrs, whom you serve with the very same honors. You appease the shades of the dead with wine and feasts; you celebrate the solemn festivals of the Gentiles, their calends, and their solstices; and as to their **manners**, those you have retained without any alteration. Nothing distinguishes you from the Pagans, except that you hold your assemblies apart from them."* The change-over to Paganism is right here on the record, witnessed by Faustus as it happened. Again during the 4th century, the learned **M. Turretin** wrote this into the record as he saw the changes occur:

"It was not so much the (Roman) Empire that was brought over to the faith, as the faith that was brought over to the Empire; not the Pagans who were converted to Christianity, but Christianity that was converted to Paganism."

In the year CE 439, the historian **Socrates** wrote:

"Although almost all assemblies throughout the world celebrate the sacred mysteries on the Sabbath of every week, yet the Christians of Alexandria and at Rome, on account of some ancient tradition, have ceased to do this."

In the year CE 440, the historian **Sozomen** wrote:

"The people of Constantinople and almost everywhere, assemble together on the Sabbath, as well as on the first day of the week."

The "love feasts" referred to by Faustus were the original commanded appointed times from Scripture, called **Pesach, Shabuoth,** and **Sukkot** (Passover, Pentecost, and Tabernacles, Lev. 23,

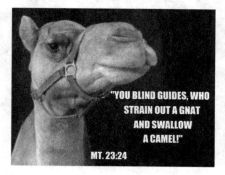

"YOU BLIND GUIDES, WHO STRAIN OUT A GNAT AND SWALLOW A CAMEL!"

MT. 23:24

Dt. 16). Today, those of us who observe these and the correct weekly Shabbaths are thought of as some kind of "cultists", or heretics. In reality, who are the real cultists and heretics?

"ERROR, INDEED, IS NEVER SET FORTH IN ITS NAKED DEFORMITY, LEST, BEING THUS EXPOSED, IT SHOULD AT ONCE BE DETECTED."

~ IRENAEUS (c.130-c.200)

The APOSTASY is here, folks, and has been for a long, long time. They missed the big picture, and became overwhelmed by all the small Pagan details. They didn't want to be accused of substituting Pagan customs, so they "re-invented" them by revisionism over time.

Coming out of this Pagan background, it is no wonder Protestants carried out so many things from their "Mother", like Sun-day, altars, steeples, Easter, Christ-mass, trees and wreaths, the Trinity, and the fake name they use for the true Creator. It's also no wonder the "Jews" are so appalled by the Christian religion! Abandoning the Torah, and calling the Mashiach by a Greco-Roman Name might not be the best way to begin introducing the Savior to a Yahudi.

QUESTION: What about Paul's letters? Doesn't he clearly say that all days are special, and observing Sabbaths were "shadows"?

ANSWER: Paul's letters, especially Galatians, Romans, and Colossians have been used to "prove" certain things he was not saying at all. When Paul discusses the "Law", he is often speaking of the *Ceremonial Law* which dealt with *atonement*. When atonement for sin was made one time for all in Mashiach's death, the Ceremonial Law came to an end. The **Moral Law**, which defines sin, will be in force for all eternity. Consider what Rabbi OWYᑛZ said at Mt. 5:17,18:

"Do not think that I came to destroy the Torah (Law) *or the Nebi'im* (Prophets)*. I did not come to destroy but to fulfill* (fill full)*. For truly I say to you, till Shamayim and Eretz pass away, not one yod or tittle shall by any means pass from the Torah till all be done."*

The skies and Earth are still here, so the Moral

KAMPUCHEAN BUDDHIST
TRIUNE GODHEAD
(c. 1100 CE)

RA, ISIS, OSIRIS

Louvre Museum, Paris

BRAHMA
SHIVA
KRISHNA

Law is in force ~ every <u>letter</u> of it. Also, if you read Acts 6:13, and 7:53, the stoning of Stephen, there is concrete evidence that the "Law" is in force, AFTER the "crux", and the resurrection of Mashiach. Acts 1:12 states *"then they returned to Yerushaliyim, from the hill called the Mount of Olives, <u>a Sabbath day's walk from the city.</u>"* This not only mentions a "Sabbath", but also mentions a maximum distance (1000 cubits) one can walk on a Shabbat. Even the day called "Pentecost" (Acts 2) is **Shabuoth**, the 50th day after the weekly Shabbat, following the weekly Shabbat after Passover, <u>every year</u>. See Lev. 23:15,16 to see that it is the day AFTER the seventh Shabbat. (To me, Shabuot/Pentecost/Feast of Weeks is always on the 1st day of the week, and there are some who disagree on this.) The "Fast" (Yom Kippur) is mentioned at Acts (27:9— the "Fast" being the 10th day of the 7th moon, in the autumn, when the storms at sea make traveling hazardous).

When Paul writes at Romans 14 about "fasting" and special days, he is addressing <u>traditions</u> of the Yahudim that arose, not Commandments. When the Temple was destroyed in 586 BCE, it became a custom to fast each year on the "9th of AV". The Temple was destroyed both times on this day! Ferdinand and Isabella's expulsion of the Yahudim from Spain occurred on this same day. At Col. 2:8, Paul says, *"See to it that no one makes you prey through philosophy* (commentary) *and empty deceit,* **according to the <u>traditions</u> of men** . . ." At Col. 2:21,22, Paul condemns **ascetism** (obsessive self-denial, austere living) because these are the commands and teachings of <u>men</u>. Another place Paul's writings are used to negate Commandments is Col. 2:11-23. If you read the various *translations*, you will see huge differences in the texts, and even sentences that say the opposite of other transla-

*Jupiter image,
re-named Peter,
in Vatican*

Circe

Devaki and Krishna

Buddha with HALO

tions. The text says, *"Let no one judge you . . . BUT the body of Mashiach."* The KJV shows the added word, "IS", to the phrase, *"but the body (is) of Christ."* At 2:16, it is being stressed that only the body of Mashiach should "judge" what you eat or drink, or regarding a religious festival, New Moon celebration, or a Shabbat Day. Then at 2:17, he says these things are **shadows** of things to come. The NIV butchered the text, and men over the years have read into the text what they wanted to see.

QUESTION: Should we use crucifixes with, or without, the body of the Savior on them?

ANSWER: Many things thought, done, and said within the various denominations of Christendom can be traced to Constantine I. He set the pattern for Sun-day and Easter, and gave us the labarum emblem, a circle with a crux beneath it. This symbol, complete with the chi-rho letters in the circle, are on coins that date back to the 2nd century BCE. Tradition says that his aging mother, Helena, traveled to Yerushaliyim to find the actual wooden "cross" which the Savior hung on. It is claimed that she dug it up! Today, supposedly the pieces of this "discovery" are scattered all over the Earth. If brought together, there would be enough splinters to fill several railroad cars. Catholic "altars" contain 5 relics each, which the priest-craft kiss during their rituals. These relics are anything from human remains to clothing fragments of "saints", and often there is also a splinter of "cross wood" in the "altar". We have already seen that Pagans used the crux as their symbol of the sun, and the word in our translations came from the Latin Vulgate. Thanks to Constantine, the symbol of Christianity is the cross symbol. The 1965 *World Book Encyclopedia* vol. VII states:
"Cross forms were used as symbols, religious or otherwise, long before the Christian era in almost every part of the world . . . This symbol had a wide diffusion before the Christian era in Europe, Asia, and America, and is commonly thought to have been an emblem of the sun, or fire; and hence, of life."

The ancient symbol of life to the Egyptians was the **crux ansata**, or ansate cross (ankh or anchor), and began to be embraced by Coptic Christians from their Pagan surroundings. The 1945 *Encyclopedia Americana* states,
"The symbol of the cross was used throughout the world since the later Stone Age; Greek pre-Christian crosses were the tau and swastika; the cross first became a symbol of Christianity during the reign of Constantine."

The swastika is four Greek *gamma* letters, and it is also seen prominently displayed on the entrances of Hindu and Buddhist temples, as an emblem of the *"wheel of Samsara"*. The 3rd Reich used it to identify itself with Christianity in Nordic caricature (runes), as all scholars agree. The use of halos, steeples, statues, candles, holy water, magic relics, spells, bells, amulets, necklaces, magic rings, scapulas, talismans, rosaries, and crosses enabled the designers of Christianity to appeal to masses of Pagans. The specimens on the previous page illustrate pre-Christian religious uses of the cross.

The 1945 *Encyclopedia Americana* continues:

"Prescott says that when the first Europeans arrived in Mexico, to their surprise, they found 'the cross, the sacred emblem of their own faith, raised as an object of worship in the temples of Anahuac'. The cross as a symbol dates back to an unknown antiquity. It was recognized in all countries throughout the world at all times. Before the present era the Buddhists, Brahmans and Druids utilized the device. In Eire Land, great monoliths beautifully carved into elaborate crosses are found everywhere. They date from the early Celtic period and they are freely decorated with Runic inscriptions. Constantine adopted the "labarum" as his standard. In CE 680 at the Council of Constantinople, the bleeding Lamb on the symbolic crucifix was forbidden, and the dying Savior's image on the cross was ordered to take its place, thus originating the present form of crucifix to be displayed to the public."

We find the word *"TREE"* used at 1Pet. 2:24:

*"He Himself bore our sins in **His body** on the tree, that we might die to sin and live to righteousness; for by His wounds you were healed."*

Here we see it was His **body** lifted up and wounded, not the object He hung on, that is the central point. Many teach that the palaeo-Hebrew letter "TAU" (see back of book—"X") was the "mark" placed on the servants spared at Ezekiel 9:4. Well, the Roman Catholics place an "ash crux" on their congregations' foreheads every "Ash Wednesday". If you reflect on the fact that the **mark** placed in the foreheads of the elect that protects them from harm at Rev. 7:3 is also called a "seal", the smoke and mirrors begin to clear up. There are 144,000 **sealed**. A seal is usually a Name, as seals in wax served as security checks. Again, at Rev. 14, this "seal" is identified as the Name of the Father in their foreheads: ﾀYﾑﾆ, and the 144.000 are mentioned **again**. How likely is it that YHWH would use a TAU (X) in one instance, and His Name in another?

Since the emblem of the **crux** has always been, and continues to be, a symbol to which the people of Earth bow down to, it is more likely that it, in what ever form it comes in, is the "**image of the beast**". Considering its source, this is the only symbol that makes sense, being a "blind-spot" of sorts for everyone. Add up what we know: it was used throughout all times and places by Pagans, and it was thrust upon the masses very early in Christianity's development. The adversary has used Christianity as an implement of death, and

it's symbol is Pagan. 100 years ago, Alexander Hislop recorded more on this in his book, *The Two Babylons*. The fire worshippers raised a cross of candles in their temples, and this is done today by the Roman Catholics, in St. Peter's Cathedral. The Ku Klux Klan also use a fire cross, and when indoors, they use a cross of candles. The emblem of our Rabbi O W Y ﾑ ﾆ ~ the Light of the world, is a lampstand, called a MENORAH. So, I would think you would not want to go near a place displaying a crux, or wear one of any kind. Pagan priests wore them as talismans! Maybe "Dracula" is only afraid of it in the movies because it reminds him of the sun. Think about it. It's Shatan's symbol, and it's used in Black Masses! What agreement is there between light and darkness? When people are programmed with Pagan rituals and designs, and taught to ignore the Torah, Shatan effectively "disarms" them of the "sword of the Spirit", the thing that makes him flee. *"I have hidden Your WORD in my heart, that I might not sin against You."* Ps. 119:11. *"Have nothing to do with the fruitless deeds of darkness, but rather EXPOSE them."* Eph. 5:11. *"Put on the full armor of ﾀYﾑﾆ, so that you can take your stand against the devil's schemes."* Eph. 6:10-17. The armor is the belt of Truth, breastplate of righteousness, shodding our feet in the message of peace, the shield of faith, helmet of salvation, and the sword of the Spirit, which is the Word of ﾀYﾑﾆ. The Torah is the "seed" of the Kingdom.

THE MENORAH The actual word "menorah" was avoided by copyists, and we have inherited the word "lampstands". At Revelation 1:12, O W Y ﾑ ﾆ is clearly associated with the menorah, because He is standing in the center of "seven golden lampstands". At Revelation 1:20, the text says the menorah is the seven congregations, His body. At Revelation 2:5, He threatens to remove the menorah (Himself, the Light) from the congregation at Ephesus. So, the sign of the Son of man is a menorah, not a crux.

A menorah is essentially a **TREE**, with seven branches holding sources of light. It is the symbol of Yisrael, more so than any other. The 7 branches signify the 7 days of the week, the 7 annual appointed times, the 7 congregations mentioned at Rev. 1:20, and the 7 millennia. The 7th millennium will be a "rest", corresponding to the weekly "rest". In Yahudaism, the worship of Yah, the menorah is a symbol of the **TORAH**, and the Torah is called a "Tree of Life". At Proverbs 3:18, "Wisdom" (the Torah) is the "woman" we must embrace:

"She is a Tree of Life to those who take hold of

her, and happy are all who hold her fast. *Treasure My Commandments within you, make your ear attentive to Wisdom . . ."*

The "Tree of Life" is mentioned in Genesis, Proverbs, and Revelation. Its leaves are to be used to heal the nations, and its fruit enable one to live forever. This is the Torah, which O W Y ∃ Z gave answer to the rich young man when asked how he might acquire eternal life. The Torah will go forth from Yerushaliyim, and it is also called *Living Waters*. When someone receives a LOVE for the Torah, they have received a precious gift, not a burden. Metaphorically, O W Y ∃ Z is the root, and we are the branches of the menorah, lighting the world with the Torah. The hatred of the Torah was put to death by O W Y ∃ Z's execution, so that both the sons of the Covenant and engrafted Gentiles could be reconciled in one body to ∃ Y ∃ Z. The Commandments weren't abolished, the hatred of them was. You will not be punished or lose the promise of eternal life by obeying the Torah. You WILL be unable to obey Torah without O W Y ∃ Z, and for this you will be cast into the Lake of Fire. Shatan is NEVER going to tell you to obey the Torah, but he WILL tell you that you don't have to obey it. It's the wedding Covenant, which he is at war against. "Legalism" is not condemned in Scripture, lawlessness is. Shatan is in the business of religion. O W Y ∃ Z told us we cannot find the Kingdom by looking around for it, because it is within His people (Luke 17:20,21). In other words, you cannot go to it. It is within you, or it is not.

QUESTION: How long did Cain hate his brother?
ANSWER: As long as he was Abel.

QUESTION: What is greater than ∃ Y ∃ Z, more evil than Shatan, the poor have it, the rich need it, and if you eat it, you will die?
ANSWER: (When asked this question, only 17% of Stanford University seniors knew the answer. Yet, 80% of kindergarten children had the answer right away.) To give you time to think, the answer will be given in the answer to the next question.

QUESTION: If a child is lost in the woods, and the rescue team wanted to hunt for him all night, what would you use to help?
ANSWER: Nocturnal operations, though hazardous, involve night goggles. (The answer you seek is the acrostic within the last sentence.)

QUESTION: Why is the penalty so severe for calling anyone a "fool" or an "idiot"?
ANSWER: The "lashon hara", or evil tongue, is any remark that puts down or belittles another person, and if said to their face, causes them to be harmed in a number of ways. If said behind their back, the harm is conveyed through others, ruining their reputation. The main insult, however, is directed toward their MAKER, and this puts the insulter in a very serious position. *"Set guard, O ∃ Y ∃ Z, over my mouth; keep watch over the door of my lips."* ~ Ps. 141:3.

QUESTION: What is a cult?
ANSWER: One definition in Webster's Dictionary says it's *"a religion regarded as unorthodox or spurious* [and] *its body of adherents."* People who are not totally in line with "mainstream" Christianity in every way are often labeled a "cult". But, the word has only recently taken on a negative meaning, and it is defined as a "sect" also. Webster's also calls a cult *"a group of followers, sect.."* Just reviewing the evidence provided in this book, it should be very apparent that the gross errors that came to overwhelm Christianity over the centuries makes it the most extravagant and over-blown "cult" one could possibly imagine. As I said, if you shoe-horned just a little bit more Paganism into it, it would pop. A considerable amount of "brain-washing" is certainly employed. But, without being persecuted, I would fear that I was not on the "narrow way". We must not seek the praise of men. Standing up for the Truth will cause men to shun us. The Light of Torah drives away those who will not repent. *"But everything exposed by the Light becomes visible, for it is Light that makes everything visible. This is why it is said; 'Wake up, O sleeper, rise from the dead, and Mashiach will shine on you.'"* ~ Eph. 5:13,14.

"Everyone who does evil hates the Light because their deeds are evil. Everyone who does evil hates the Light, and will not come into the Light FOR FEAR THAT HIS DEEDS WILL BE EXPOSED. But whoever lives by the Truth comes into the Light, so that it may be seen plainly that what he has done has been done through Elohim." ~ Yahuchanon 3:19-21.

Simply calling yourself a "Christian" is a generic reference, and could be applied to any follower of any "Christ". The Nazarene Mashiach, O W Y ∃ Z, has followers who do not wish to sin, but they understand this is not what delivers them. *"My dear children, I write this to you so that you will not sin. But if anybody does sin, we have one who speaks to the Father in our defense ~ Yahushua haMashiach, the Righteous One. He is our atoning sacrifice for our sins, and not only for ours but also for the sins of the whole world. We know we have come to know Him if we obey His Commands. The man who says 'I know Him', but does not do what He commands is a liar, and the Truth is not in him. But if anyone obey His Word, Elohim's love is truly made complete in him. Whoever claims to live in Him must walk as Yahushua did."* 1Yoch. 2. Those who sin, of course, do not continue to sin, thinking they are living in "grace", because their spirit does not agree with sin. We will, at times, say or do things we shouldn't, but these things are not our "pattern" for living.

QUESTION: What does the word "nature" mean?

ANSWER: "Nature" is based on the Latin word, *NATURA*, and means *birth*. It is the root of the word nativity. "Mother Nature" refers to the Earth Mother, also called *Regina Coeli* (Queen of Heaven). This is the root of all Paganism, and she was known as the SKY to the Egyptians, who called her NUT. Nut means *nurture* in Latin. Really, the sky was the time-clock used to determine when the fertilization cycle of events occurred. The calendar is the "stage" on which the Babylonian Pagan Mysteries are played-out on.

QUESTION: Why do people say "GOD bless you" when someone sneezes?

ANSWER: Pagans believed that when someone sneezed, their heart stopped, or at least skipped a few beats. Being that the sun was called "GOTT", the Celtic peoples would call on their highest deity to come to the aid of anyone sick, or leaving on a journey. When we say "good-bye", we are really saying "GOTT bless ye".

QUESTION: What is the "Gospel" of Yahushua ha Mashiach?

ANSWER: The word "Gospel" is two Celtic words, "GOD" + "SPELL". It came from the Greek word *evangelion*, and means "acceptable report" or "message". The Hebrew word is *BASAR*. The message brought by Yahushua, and carried by His cousin Yahuchanon, Paul, and all the students, was simply: *Repent, for the reign of YHWH draws near.* This simple message was the core idea of what Paul spoke to the Greeks at Athens. At a meeting of the Areopagus, these Pagans wanted to know about what Paul was trying to say. (Read Acts 17:18-34.)

"In the past, Elohim overlooked such ignorance, but now He commands all people everywhere to REPENT. For He has set a day when He will judge the world with justice by the man He has appointed. He has given proof of this to all men by raising Him from the dead." - 17:30,31.

Here, Paul said it in a more elaborate way. The "Good News" also contains "Bad News", at least for those who do not understand and obey, because they will not REPENT. Their sinfulness must first be made apparent to them, then they must turn away from sinning, be immersed in the saving Name of O W Yᴧ⅃ for the forgiveness of their sins, then walk in the Commandments of freedom, having O W Yᴧ⅃ "circumcise" their

hearts, and causing them to love the Torah. This is the New Covenant (Jer. 31, Heb. 8).

"But he is a Yahudi who is one inwardly; and circumcision is that of the heart, in the Spirit, not in the letter; whose praise is not from men, but from ᴧYᴧ⅃". - Romans 2:29.

QUESTION: How can I prove to myself that the Name of our Creator was removed from the translations commonly used?

ANSWER: Check any encyclopedia under the Name "YAHWEH", and especially the preface and dictionary of your translations. You will see the Latin letters "YHWH". These stand for the Hebrew letters YOD, HAY, WAW, HAY. Also, the KJV slipped it in as the short form "JAH" at Psalm 68:4, and the letter "J" is less than 500 years old, being a YOD in Hebrew. *"Everyone who __calls__ on the Name of ᴧYᴧ⅃ will be saved"* ~ This text at Yah el (Joel) 2:32 is quoted at Acts 2:21 and Romans 10:13, and the Name is spoken of thousands of times as central to our salvation throughout Scripture. His people bear His Name, Daniel 9:19. He declares *"This is My Name FOREVER, the Name by which I am to be remembered from generation to generation."* (Ex. 3:15). You hear it in the phrase *hallelu YAH*. The Covenant Name is contained in the Name of our Redeemer, Yahushua. Husha or hushua means *save*, and you will recall the crowds shouted *"Husha nu"* (meaning *save us*) at John (Yahuchanon) 12:13. They also shouted *"baruch haba baShem ᴧYᴧ⅃"*, meaning *blessed is he who comes in the Name of Yahueh,* Yahuchanon 12:13 and Luke 19:38. This caused the Pharisees to scold our Rabbi because they were saying the Name aloud, which was to them "blasphemy". At Yahuchanon 17:6, He said: *"I have __revealed__ Your Name to those whom you gave Me out of the world."* At Rev. 2:3, He says *"You have endured hardships for My Name, and have not grown weary."* We are "sealed" with the Father's Name (Rev. 14:1): *"Then I looked, and before me was the Lamb, standing on Mount Tziyon, and with Him 144,000 who had His Father's Name written on their foreheads."* (See also Rev. 7). Malachi 3:16 says *"Then those who feared ᴧYᴧ⅃ talked with each other, and ᴧYᴧ⅃ listened and heard. A scroll of remembrance was written in His presence concerning those who feared ᴧYᴧ⅃ and honored His Name."*

To enter into His Covenant with Yisrael, and to have our sins removed and give ourselves to Him, we must be immersed in the Name above Names, O W Yᴧ⅃.

Since ancient Babylon, the tongues (languages) of the nations have been babbling. The pure language, **HEBREW**, was undisturbed because Shem and his clan settled apart from his brothers' clans, the Babylonians. The babbling nations of today have in excess of 2,600 languages. They will be purged of their blasphemous terms, and one day call upon the Name of ᐊYᐊZ. Zeph. 3:8,9: *"I have decided to assemble the nations, to gather the kingdoms, and to pour out my wrath on them ~ all my fierce anger. The <u>whole world</u> will be consumed by the <u>fire</u> of my jealous anger. Then I will <u>purify the speech of the peoples</u>, that all of them may <u>call</u> upon the Name of ᐊYᐊZ, and serve Him shoulder to shoulder."* See? He knew the "wrong" wouldn't be using His Name.

ABBA Hebrew for male parent; this is what Rabbi OWYᐊZ also called His Father. **ABINU** is Hebrew-Aramaic for *our father.* The ending "u" is plural possessive.

ADONAI Hebrew, meaning *my sovereign.* The ending letter " I " (yod) makes it mean "my" ~ as expressed in *Eloi* (my mighty one, *rabbi* (my teacher), and *ani* (myself, me, my). Adonai was used in place of the Name.

AGNOSTIC Greek for *without knowledge;* A = against; GNOSTIC = knowledge.

APIS A "sacred" bull worshipped as Aton by the ancient Egyptians, having horns with a sun-disc between them. The Yisraelites made a golden calf, or apis, to worship the Creator, ᐊYᐊZ Elohim. He's on the record as being against images, and He was especially disturbed they used a previously Pagan image to represent Him. In fact, He hates to be worshipped in any Pagan way.

ARCHAEOLOGY From Greek, *ARKHAIOLOGIA, archaeo-* (ancient, beginning) + *logy-* (study, reason). It's the study of antiquity, customs, structures, etc.,.

ASCETICISM A severe, self-denying, austere way of life, supposed to permit union with the divine— a practice condemned as useless by Paul at Col. 2:21,22. Pagan monks and hermits often lived this way, most often celibate, and they still practice it. This was used by Catholicism, accompanied by "vows", to control literate men who copied and translated the Scriptures. In these monk factories, sentences from Scripture were divided, so the men could not make sense from them as they were copied and translated; a "vow of silence" was imposed so they could not discuss what they had worked on with others, so the sentences would remain incomplete in their minds.

ATHIEST Greek for one who subscribes to the belief there is no Creator, or spiritual being of any kind. A- (without), + *THEOS-* (deity, deus, elohim).

BAAL Hebrew for "LORD". This word was used as a proper name for the sun deity by the Canaanites, Phoenicians, and even the Druids. The familiar word *Beelzebub* is more accurately the Hebrew **BAAL-ZEBUL**, meaning *LORD OF THE FLIES.* The names containing **BEL** are references to the Pagan deity, as in *Jezebel* and *Belshazzar.* Another name for Shatan (Satan) is *Belial.* So, to say "the LORD is my shepherd" doesn't relate to the Creator, but rather Shatan! Shatan "deleted" the true Name, and put in a <u>generic term</u> referring to himself. The main point is that the SUN was what the ancients related this term to, and we see it camouflaged in words like *bell, ball, and Cybele.*

BAPTISM From the Greek *baptizein,* to dip. Originally, it referred to dyeing fabric, but came to be used by Pagans for initiation ceremonies, using water or blood in <u>sprinkling</u>. The true Hebrew word is *TEVILA,* where a person is <u>immersed</u> in a body of water, called a *MIKVAH.* It also signifies repentance, and it is the most important event in one's life in the conversion of a Gentile, to become engrafted into Yisrael. It is a <u>covenant sign</u> to obey ᐊYᐊZ, and identifies the convert with the death and <u>burial</u> of OWYᐊZ, and is the death and burial of one's <u>mind of the flesh</u>. Rising up from the water of Tevila, a convert is identified with the resurrection, and walks in obedience, *enabled* to obey by the Spirit. OWYᐊZ gave us His example.

BELLS The world's oldest bell was unearthed in Babylon. Bells are among the oldest items used in Pagan worship, and were one of several noise-makers used. They were employed to give worship to the sun, and were usually placed in or near the top of an obelisk or high-place. Orientals use gongs as well as the familiar bell shapes. They were brought into Christian worship along with "steeples" from Paganism. Augustus Caesar is on record as having dedicated an enormous bell, placed in the entrance tower to the temple of Jupiter.

BELIEF   A mental act or habit of placing trust or confidence in an opinion, or the acceptance of something as true or real. To expect or suppose. When something believed-in is exposed as being false, a **reaction** is aroused. How an individual reacts depends on how well-equipped they are, and the degree to which they want to believe the falsehood. Dresden James wrote *"A truth's initial commotion is directly proportional to how deeply the lie was believed. It wasn't the world being round that agitated people, but that the world wasn't flat. When a well-packaged web of lies has been sold gradually to the masses over generations, the truth will seem utterly preposterous, and its speaker a raving lunatic".* The Smith Ministry in Abilene, Texas has stated, *"It isn't the fact that the Savior's Name is* Yahshua (**OWYAZ** - Ya-husha, Yahushua) *that agitates people, but that His Name is not Jesus (Jhesus, Hey-Zeus, Yeh-Zus, Hesus)".* This means that people may think they have the facts, but all they really have are beliefs. If we are imputed "righteousness" by our belief alone, then why did Ya'akob (James) write *"show me your belief without deeds, and I will show you my belief by what I do. You believe that there is one Elohim—good! Even the demons believe that—and shudder . . . You see that a person is justified by what he does and* ***not by belief alone.***" We can believe "He knows my heart"~ but without LOVE, shown by our obedience, we have profited nothing. We can believe otherwise, but when we call Him "Jesus" or Hay-Zus, in Hebrew He hears "Yeh-horse", because the Hebrew word *SOOS* means "horse".

BIBLE   This word was originally Phoenician, then passed into Greek, then Latin. It means *books* in Greek. It is no where to be found in the inspired text of Scripture ~ it's just put on the cover. If your Scriptures have maps in the back, check for a Phoenician port city called "BYBLOS". This city was named Byblos because the Phoenician fertility idol **BIBLIA** was worshiped there, in a temple dedicated in her honor. The city was later re-named *Gebal*. This port city exported papyrus, or the writing paper of the ancient world, so scrolls came to be called after the name of the city ~ which was named after an idol. It might not be wise to continue to call the Word of **ᴀYᴀZ** "The Bible" now that you realize this. He calls His Words to mankind the **Torah** (Teachings), **Nebi'im** (prophets), and **Kethubim** (writings). This is abbreviated to the acronym: TaNaKh. The Hebrew word for "scroll" is *megillah*, and His Words are called *debarim*. Remember Ex. 23:13.

BINDING and **LOOSING**   At Mt. 16:19, Rabbi **OWYAZ** told His students whatever they would "bind" or "loose" would be honored by the heavenly throne also. The idea of BIND means *to forbid*, and LOOSE means *to permit*. They had been fully trained in Torah by the Torah-Giver! He was going away, and his students would have to judge things as OK or not.

CATHEDRAL   Latin, *cathedra*, for *throne*.
CEREAL   Latin, *Cerealis*, the grain of Ceres, a Pagan deity.

CHARIS   From Greek, *Kharisma*, a Pagan deity's name, *Charis*, wife of Hephaistos, the fire deity. "Charred" means burned. Other words produced from this are *charity, charisma, and charismatic*. The *"Three Graces"* or *Three Charities*, were a Pagan trinity known as the *Three Fates*. Their names were *Clotho* (our word "cloth", was the producer of the "thread of life"), *Lachesis* (carrying rods which she shook to determine the fate of mankind), and *Atropos* (who cuts the thread, determining the length of a person's life).

CHURCH   The Old English word was *CIRICE*, and you will see it spelled *CHIRCHE* written above many old "church" entrances throughout England. This is from the West Germanic *KIRIKA*, which is based on the Greek deity's name, *CIRCE*. Circe was famous among Pagans for turning men into pigs, or other animals, using drugs. The original English translation from the Greek text by John Wycliffe (about CE 1380) used the word *congregation* for "ecclesia", the called-out body of believers. The original set-apart ones who studied and "did" the Word (Commandments) were called *qahal* in Hebrew, from which we get our word "call". The "saints" were the set-apart ones, known as *qodeshim*.

COMMANDMENTS   The original Hebrew word is *MITZVAH*, both singular and plural. The Old English meaning is "edict". "Bar Mitzvah" means *son of the Commandments* (Torah), and "bat mitzvah" is the feminine. In the TaNaKh, there are 613 Commandments, but in the Brit Chadasha (NT) there are 1,089 technically specified. All of them are "summed up" in the 10 words, or Decalogue, called the 10 Commandments. These are further summarized into the "2 greatest Commandments", which Rabbi **OWYAZ** quoted to a lawyer who was testing Him: ***"Love* ᴀYᴀZ *your Elohim with all your heart and with all your soul and with all your mind"*** (Dt. 6:5), and ***"Love your neighbor as***

yourself" (Lev. 19:18, Mt. 22:37). **OWYƷZ** warned us not to set aside any of the Commandments, *"Whoever, then, breaks one of the least of the Commandments, and teaches men so, shall be called least in the Kingdom of Shamayim; but whoever does and teaches them, he shall be called great in the kingdom of Shamayim"* ~ Mt. 5:19. "Shamayim" is skies, outer space, or "heaven", often used as a substitution for the Name of **ayaz**. Our Rabbi restored the Name, but monks subsequently removed it again from the texts. We know this, because at Acts 7:56, the Sanhedrin covered their ears, and stoned Stephen to death ~ for saying the Name aloud. Shaul, later called Paul, was there giving approval for his death. **OWYƷZ** told us to become **sons of light**, and the Torah is Light (see Pr. 6:23). Our eye must be filled with Light, or it is darkness (without Torah). The Commandments sum up how the wife (bride) of **OWYƷZ** is to live, and is the Covenant. The "Ark" of the Covenant was the box which carried the Commandments, and now each of us who are of His bride are the "box", having them written on our hearts (the "New" Covenant). If we love Him, we will obey Him, and love His Laws. Read 1 Yoch.

CLERGY This word comes from the Greek *clericos*, and went into the Latin as *clericus*. It means "literate", or having the ability to read and write. Peter couldn't read and write, so he had to enlist the help of Silas (1 Pet. 5:12) to record his words. He was illiterate, or *not clericus*. The words *cleric, clerk, and clergy* all refer to a *"man of letters"*. Literate men could read "literature", and those who could read were given status, and therefore became known as "clergy". The Church of Rome divided their clergy from the "laity", by the distinction of being literate or not. They burned books and libraries in part to control literacy, and therefore power. Another reason to destroy records was so their revision of history could remain uncontested. People who threatened their control were exterminated by the Inquisition, implemented by the Jesuits and Dominicans.

CROSS *(See QUESTIONS & ANSWERS)* The word "cross" is derived from the Latin word, **CRUX**, (stem, *cruc-*), perhaps originally Phoenician. The word "cross" came into the Latin translation when Jerome translated the Greek word **stauros**. His real name was Eusebius Hieronymus Sophronius, and he did this during the years CE 391-403, calling his translation *The Latin Vulgate*. Catholicism considers this to be "inspired". The Greek word *stauros* means staff, stake, pole, or beam, corresponding to the Hebrew word **NAS**, which the serpent Nehushtan was lifted up with in the desert (Yn. 3, Num. 21:9, 2 Kings 18:4). Many scholars strongly suspect this term and symbol were introduced from Paganism, because the use of the cross is so commonly found in Pagan religions world-wide. It usually symbolized the **SUN** (an eagle), which Constantine seemed to identify with "Christ". The 1934 *Encyclopedia Britannica* states:

"In every part of the world, crosses were used both as religious symbols or as ornaments long before the Christian era . . . It did not become the symbol of Christianity until 400 years later, during the time of Constantine."

IMAGE OF THE BEAST! If you think about it, what possible meaning could the words *"Take up your CROSS and follow Me"* have meant to a listener of Rabbi **OWYƷZ** BEFORE His execution? All He was saying was *"Take up your STAFF (a walking stick) and follow Me."* These words meant to walk (Hebrew, *halak, halacha*) in His example, since He is the living model of Torah.

Images that we are programmed to embrace as "holy" need to be thoroughly researched, to see if they originated from Paganism or not. Catholics "genuflect" before a box with bread inside, before a crux with a statue figure of a dying person, supposed to represent our Rabbi. *"In the past, **ayaz** overlooked such ignorance, but now He commands all people everywhere to repent. For He has set a day when He will judge the world with justice by the man He has appointed. He has given proof of this to all men by raising Him from the dead."* Acts 17:30, 31. If you place no image before your eyes, you will not be found guilty of any wrong doing, but Scripture says FEW are going to make it (see Luke 13:22). *"Why do you also transgress the Command of Elohim because of your tradition?"* Mt. 15:3. *"But in vain do they worship Me, teaching as teachings the commands of MEN."* v. 9. The cross is really a solar eagle symbol.

ELOHIM Hebrew, enlarged from **EL**, meaning *mighty-one*. The ending of many Hebrew names use the short form, as in *Micha**EL*** (who is like EL), *Rapha**EL*** (healing EL), *Yisra**EL*** (prince of EL), *Gabri**EL*** (warrior of EL), *Yishm**EL*** (EL hears), *Shemu**EL*** (Name of EL), *Imman**EL*** (EL with us), *Yah**EL*** (Joel, Yah is EL). We see that **OWYƷZ** referred to Psalm 22 as He continued to teach as He was dying on the stake, saying *"Eloi, Eloi, lama sabachthani?"* Eloi means *my mighty one*. EL is a pronoun, not a name. In translating this pronoun into various vernacular terms in Gentile languages, commonly they substituted the Pagans' principal deity's name, as was done in the English word "GOD" (GOTT, the sun). The Hebrew term

ELAH became "Allah", but it is not a name. Elohim can mean *mighty one of oaths*. It's the "oaths" that are plural, explaining the ending "im".

EMUNAH   Hebrew for fidelity, faithfulness, steadfastness. It is usually translated to our word "faith". This is a rabbi's foremost concern: that his pupils will remain steady and unswerving to their teachings of Torah. *"If you are* (unswerving) *in the small things, you will be* (unswerving) *in the greater things also."* The meaning points to obedience. The flesh must be disciplined, and the one trained and walking in the "light" will remain steadfast. *"Your Word is a lamp to my feet, and a light for my path."* Ps. 119:105. *The righteous* (tzedek) *will live by his EMUNAH."* Hab. 2:4.

ERETZ   Hebrew for Earth, soil, land. *Eretz Yisrael* means *Land of Yisrael.*

EUNUCH   Greek, a castrated man, meaning *bed-watcher.* (*"Woman"* means *womb-man*).

EUROPA   The Greek deity (mythology) who was abducted by Zeus disguised as a white bull, and taken to Crete. The continent of "Europe" is named for her.

GEMATRIA   This is the use of letters as numbers, because Hebrew (and others) letters carried numerical values. The numerical values of each letter of a word are added up, so a word or name can be expressing a number. The Name of YHWH has a value of 26. If you would like to calculate the number of the beast, first find the Hebrew letters, then add it up.

GETHSEMANE   Two words in Hebrew, *gath + semane*, meaning OIL PRESS.

GOLGOTHA   Hebrew for *place of the skull.* The Latin word "Calvary" means *cranium, skull, or bonehead.* Let's leave it the name Golgotha. "Japan" means *rising sun,* but we call it Japan.

GRACE   Based on the Latin word, *gratia,* this word comes from the Hebrew word *chasid,* which means *unmerited loving kindness.* Preachers often give people false security by claiming we live in the *"Age of Grace",* but this is not supported by any Scriptural verse. Actually, the Creator has always been praised as the Elohim of forgiveness, and showed lovingkindness to all who would acknowledge sin and REPENT. We are of course under ᲐᎩᚨᏃ's *chasid* by the once-for-all atoning death of His Son, but this is not a license to sin. Catholicism set up a "dispensational" method of "dispensing" grace through 7 "sacraments". This gave the "clergy" complete control over the "laity". First of all, the sacraments are a sham, only a trick used to mislead people. Second, we are ALL priests, and there is not a division in Scripture called "clergy" and "laity".

HANUKKAH   Amazing fact: *if there had been no Hanukkah, there would never have been a* Christianity. Prior to 186 BCE, a ruthless Greek ruler named Antiochus Epiphanes was forcing Greek customs and religion on the nation of Yisrael, and outlawed the Torah. People were slaughtered, and children were tortured to death in front of their parents, *forced to work on Shabbat,* eat swine flesh, and wear the little "beanie", a Greek hat of Hermes (scholar cap). The Temple was polluted with images of Zeus, swine was offered on the altar, and new brides were deflowered first by the Greek ruler. Only in extreme secrecy could the young study Torah. During such study, children would hide the Torah scroll and pull out a little "top" called a *dreidel* when they heard soldiers coming ~ thus they would appear to be playing an innocent game. A Hebrew family, the **Maccabees**, succeeded in over-powering the Greek forces, and Antiochus was stricken with a fatal intestinal malady. He suffered a lingering, torturous death ~ his rotting body was such a foul stench that his own men could not bear to go near him!

The Dedication   The word "Hanukkah" or Chanukkah is Hebrew, meaning *dedication.* What was dedicated (or re-dedicated) was the Temple, after a thorough cleansing after the Pagans were ejected. It took **8 days** to cleanse it. The **Menorah**, or 7-branched lampstand, burned its lights for the 8 days of clean up, even though only enough oil was found to last for ONE day. Every year since this dedication, we remember the deliverance from the Pagan oppression which almost wiped out the observances of the Commandments, which the Yahudim have preserved as priests of the nations.

At Yahuchanon (John) 10:22, our Rabbi ᎣᎳᎩᚨᏃ was walking in the Temple area during this festival called Hanukkah:
"Then came Hanukkah in Yerushaliyim. It was winter, and ᎣᎳᎩᚨᏃ *was walking around inside the Temple area, in Shlomo's Colonnade."*

HEBREW   This is what is called the Qodesh Lashon, or set-apart tongue, which will be restored during the 7th Millennium, Zeph. 3:9. The word comes from Abraham's great, great, great-grandfather, **Eber**. It was the language our Rabbi spoke to Shaul when he was thrown to the ground, and at Acts 26 Paul explains to Agrippa that he heard a voice speaking to him in Hebrew. Actually, that's the only language Yahudim spoke to each other, except for those who were living in foreign lands. Aramaic is a dialect of Hebrew. Paul spoke many tongues.

HOLY   This word became used instead of the Hebrew term *qodesh,* which means "set-apart". To a Pagan, "holy" related to the sun's glow, and relates to the word "halo", a glowing nimbus seen on statues and pictures. The Pagans called shrines "hallowed". The holy "halo" was to associate the statue of the glowing deity with the yellow sun. At Ps. 51:11, Dawid wrote *Ruach ha Qodesh* in Hebrew, which we see translated "Holy Spirit". Ruach means wind, or spirit. Even the gold ring used in marriage was inherited from Pagan priests who worshipped the unconquered sun. Ministers hold it up and say things about eternity and endless devotion. The Latin word *sacrare* means "dedicated", and is very close in meaning to qodesh, or holy.

J   The letter "J", amazingly, didn't exist in any language until the 15th century, at which time printing styles differentiated the letter " I " when it was used at the beginning of a sentence, or the first letter in a proper name. They gave the " I " a little tail, and now we have a new letter. Since there was no letter in Greek or Latin like the Hebrew "yod" (𐤆), these languages opted for the " I " called "iota". The first letter in the Rabbi's Name is best transliterated as a " Y " in English.

JEHOVAH   this is the formulation of the Creator's Name which was promoted by a man named *Petrus Galatinus* during the 15th century. Encyclopedias will explain this is a double error, since it is both a hybrid and a mongrel word. The four letters of the Name 𐤀𐤉𐤄𐤆 are YOD, HAY, WAW, HAY, and are read from right-to-left. In modern Hebrew, they appear as 2 ה (HAY), 1 ו (WAW), and 1 י (YOD). Clement of Alexandria transliterated these letters into the Greek alphabet as IAOUE. The word is called the Tetragrammaton, which is Greek for "four letters".

Since there is no letter " J " or " V " in ancient Hebrew, the Tetragrammaton YHWH was altered to JHVH, and the vowels were another mistake. The 10th century vowel pointing by the Masoretic copyists added little marks under the four letters, which were intended to "cue" a reader to pronounce "adonai" instead of pronouncing the Name. "Adonai" is Hebrew for *my lord*. **The pronouncing of the Name was prohibited, and therefore considered unutterable.** (This is a man-made law, and was central to the problem faced by our Rabbi and the apostles.) Our Mashiach was never called "Jesus", but rather "Yahushua" (yah-HOO-shua). This is the **same name** as the successor of Mosheh, known by most as "Joshua", as can be proven in various literary sources, as well as the underlying Greek text at Acts 7 and Hebrews 4, where both names *Jesus* and *Joshua* have the Greek letters IESOUS as their basis. The Hebrew phrase, **HALLELU-YAH** means *praise you* (plural) *YAH*. Most don't realize they are saying the short form of the Name, and it is used in many prophets' names: *Yesha Yahu* (Isaiah), *Obad Yah* (Obediah), *Yerme*

Yahu (Jeremiah), *Zechar Yah* (Zechariah), and others with an ending ~ **iah**.

JUBILEES   This word comes from the original Hebrew YOB-HEL, and means "ram's horn" or *leading animal*. The late Greek word *iobelaios* was based on the Hebrew. The measurements of time in the Scriptural model are not "centuries", but rather "Jubilees", or groups of 50 years. The 10th day of the 7th moon of every 50th year being the time that all property is returned to the original owner or heirs according to primogeniture. A Jubilee also requires the release of all Hebrew slaves. The land is given a rest also. (Land is to rest every 7th year anyway). Since Adam died before he lived a complete "day" (a day is 1000 years to 𐤀𐤉𐤄𐤆), he lived 18 Jubilees plus 30 years, or 930 years (70 short of 1000). 20 Jubilees is 1000 years. The year of Jubilee is referred to in the inscription on the **Liberty Bell** at Independence Hall in Philadelphia, Pennsylvania: *"Proclaim liberty throughout the land to all its inhabitants"* ~ being words taken out of context from Lev. 25:10. The complete sentence says, *"And you shall set apart the **fiftieth year**, and proclaim release throughout all the land to all its inhabitants, it is a Jubilee (Yob Hel) to you."* The text at Genesis 6:3 says that mortals will be given 120 years, then 𐤀𐤉𐤄𐤆 would bring about a complete change because He will not contend with man (the ADAM) forever. The allotted time for man before the Messianic Age of rest will be 120 Jubilees (6000 years!). Then fire will be brought upon the Earth, and the very **elements** themselves will burn (2Pet. 3:12). The Messianic Age will occur at the beginning of the "7th Day", as foreshadowed by the still unfulfilled pre-figurements of the feasts of the 7th month's appointed times of Yom Teruah (now called Rosh Hashanah), Yom Kippur, and Sukkot. Our Mashiach was sacrificed approximately 80 Jubilees from Adam's beginning, and we are about 80 Jubilees away from the Noahic Flood right now. I wonder if these are related, since 𐤏𐤅𐤔𐤉𐤄𐤆 said *"The coming of the Son of man will be just like the days of Noach."* He is called the "second Adam".

KNACK   People say, *"You've really got a knack for doing that".* A "Knack" was a spirit demon that was thought to possess a person like the 9 Muses, enabling them to have certain abilities.

KORAN   The sacred text of Islam, believed to contain the revelations by Allah to Mohammed. It is also called Alcoran. The Arabic word *qur'an* means *reading* or *recitation*. It comes from the original Hebrew word, *qura'a*, which means read or recite. **QARA** is the Hebrew for "*proclaim*". Israel's half-brothers, the Ishmaelites or Arabs, use lots of Hebrew words. The word "arab" is from *ereb*, which is Hebrew for *evening* or *darkening*.

KOSHER   This is from a 3-letter Hebrew word, *kasher*, and means *approved, proper,* or *appropriate*. The consumption of "approved" animal flesh is stressed at Gen. 9:3,4, Lev. 3:17, 7::26, 27, 11:1-47, 17:10-14, **and Acts 15:20 & 15:29**. Acts 10 and Mark 7 are often used to "annul" the distinction of the clean and unclean. Those who permit themselves to be misled this way should read "Isaiah" 66:17. On the Day of ᕠYᕠZ, those who "approve for themselves" to eat whatever they wish from the "garden" (farm), *"who eat swine's flesh, detestable things, and mice, shall* **come to an end altogether**". Your Writings, especially the KJV, will put the added words in parentheses from Mark 7. At Acts 10, Peter woke up and *"was greatly perplexed in mind as to what the vision which he had seen might be; behold the men* (3 Gentiles) *who had been sent by Cornelius . . . Appeared at the gate."* Acts 10:17. The "3 sheets" of unclean animals related to the <u>3 Gentiles</u> who were at his gate, whom Peter would otherwise never have gone with, or entered their residence without this vision. This is explained by Peter himself at Acts 11.

MARK OF THE BEAST   Without the Torah to make one wise, this "mark" or sign cannot be determined. This calls for WISDOM. The Covenant, the Torah, which is the marriage Covenant with Yisrael, contains a "mark" or sign, called the sign of the Eternal Covenant. It is mutually exclusive with the beast's mark. All covenants made by ᕠYᕠZ have such a sign. Babylon, the Mother of Harlots, has established a sign, and it has remained the same within Catholicism, and her daughters which follow after her. This system is called a "beast" because dumb animals, or beasts, have no regard for ᕠYᕠZ's appointments, processes, or invitations. The "feasts" of ᕠYᕠZ which He proclaims at Leviticus 23 and Deut. 16 are described in the parables, like Luke 14:15-24. The wife of ᕠYᕠZ carries the "sign" of the Sabbath, and Shatan is waging WAR against this woman and her offspring, and the <u>Covenant </u>(Rev. 12:17). This outward sign or "mark" of ᕠYᕠZ is how we **acknowledge Him as Creator** (Gen. 2:3, Ex. 20:11, Heb. 4:4). Exodus 31:13 declares that Shabbat (the weekly and annual appointments) are a sign between ᕠYᕠZ and His people FOREVER. Shabbat is celebrated *from evening* (twilight) *to evening*. Yesha Yahu (Isaiah) 66:23 speaks of a future time when, after the burning of the Earth, the people of all nations who serve ᕠYᕠZ will bow down *"from Shabbat to Shabbat"*. Converts, like Cornelius, became engrafted

to Yisrael, and rested on Shabbat. Gentiles in general are referred to as "dogs", or figuratively as "beasts" - like the Canaanite woman was at Mt. 15:26. The Babylonian "Sun-day" was imposed as a MARK under the penalty of death by Constantine I, and unknowingly the mark of the beast has been placed on everyone who follows after the beast. In the days of the "7th Angel" (Rev. 10:7), the mystery of these things is to be revealed, exposing Shatan, *"who leads the **whole world astray**"* (Rev. 12:9). *"Then I saw another angel flying in mid-air, and he had the eternal message to proclaim to those who live on the Earth—to every nation, tribe, language and people. He said in a loud voice, 'Fear Elohim and give Him esteem, because the hour of His judgment has come. Worship Him* **Who MADE the heavens, the Earth, the sea**

The Oriental Institute, The University of Chicago

THE MOABITE STONE

This stone contains the Name of the Creator, and is written in palaeo-Hebrew!

The "monstrosity" (man-made from different parts) word "**Jehovah**" contains a <u>terrible</u> coincidental meaning in Hebrew. The word "hovah" in Hebrew is based on a word that means *ruin, calamity, destruction, and wickedness* according to Strong's concordance dictionary. Has the adversary done this to make our Creator's Name mean "I am ruin, wickedness"?

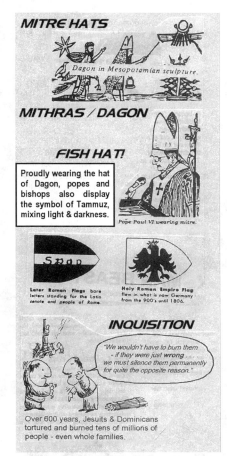

MITRE HATS

Dagon in Mesopotamian sculpture.

MITHRAS / DAGON

FISH HAT!

Proudly wearing the hat of Dagon, popes and bishops also display the symbol of Tammuz, mixing light & darkness.

Pope Paul VI wearing mitre.

Later Roman Flags bore letters standing for the Latin senate and people of Rome.

Holy Roman Empire Flag flew in what is now Germany · from the 900's until 1806.

INQUISITION

"We wouldn't have to burn them - if they were just *wrong* . . . we must silence them permanently for quite the opposite reason."

Over 600 years, Jesuits & Dominicans tortured and burned tens of millions of people - even whole families.

and the springs of water." ~ Rev. 14:7. The "sign" of this "worship" is <u>Shabbat</u>, and is seen prominently in *"those who obey Elohim's Commandments, and hold to the Testimony of* OWYƎꟻ." ~ Rev. 12:17. No lie is found in the mouths of His redeemed, those who have been sealed with the Father's Name. (Read all of Rev. 14).

MITRE   This is a Pagan religious hat, originating in the worship of Dagon, the chief deity of the Philistines, a sea people. Its name, *mitre*, comes from the name *Mithras*. Popes, bishops, and cardinals wear them in the Church of Rome, and the Anglican Church uses them also.

MOABITE STONE   This large stone over 3 feet high was discovered in 1868 CE, and was broken by Arabs in order to fetch more money for each piece. It contains the palaeo-Hebrew script, and the Name of ꟻYƎꟻ is written on it.

MOSHEH   This is the name distorted to "Moses", and it means <u>draw-out</u>. He was born during a time when all male children of Yisrael were to be destroyed at birth in Egypt / Mitsraim. Pharaoh's daughter named him this Hebrew name because she *drew him out of the water*. He *drew out* the children of Yisrael from Egypt. (Hold it—is that a Christmas tree at left?)

RABBI   Hebrew for *my teacher.* OWYƎꟻ was called Rabbi by His pupils and others at Mt. 26:25, 26:49, Mk. 9:5, 10:51, 11:21, 14:45, Yn. 1:38, 3:2, 3:26, 4:31, 6:25, 9:2, 11:8, 20:16, and many other places where the word "teacher" or "master" were translated. He's the ONLY one we call "rabbi", as He directed us at Mt. 23:8.

ROME   The language of the Romans was called *Roma*. The Empire was called by the capital (head) of it, after an Etruscan myth of two orphaned boys name *Romulus and Remus*. This city is located in what is called Italy, where the pre-Roman civilazation of Etruria used to be (5th century BCE).

TZITZIT   Hebrew for *tassels*. At Num. 15 and Deut. 22, we are commanded to wear tassels at the 4 corners of our garments, attached with a blue cord. The Throne of ꟻYƎꟻ is on a sea of blue sapphire, and the color blue is to remind us of the Torah each time we see our tassels. OWYƎꟻ wore them, and continues to; at Mt. 9:20 and 14:36, the text states that His tassels were touched by many people, and they were healed by doing so. He criticized the Pharisees for *lengthening* their tassels to make a show of outward righteousness. This is not a "talisman" like a Pagan would use. Pagans relied on objects to confer protection or powers over evil with runes, amulets, stones, tags, scapulas, necklaces, rings, and wands. This is idolatry. Wearing cruxes, medals, making magic signs, waving in the air, splashing water, or counting on a "rosary" is no different from VOODOO. They may as well twirl a chicken over their heads. Tzitzit are to remind us to obey the Torah always.

YARMULKE   This is a Yiddish word for the kipa, or skullcap seen worn by the pope, and most orthodox Yahudim on the street, in the classroom, and in the synagogues. Mosheh would not know what it is. Alfred J. Kolatch, an orthodox author and "rabbi", states: *The skullcap* **has no religious significance in Jewish law**." He goes on to say that it has no basis in Scriptural or Rabbinical law. To trace the use of the cap to its source, we find that it came into wider use only in the 17th century, where before that only a very few Yahudim used it. Did Rabbi OWYƎꟻ wear a kipa? All researchers and historians say NO, and there is no evidence of its use in any data or archaeological finds at all.

106

The pope of Rome and his cardinals wear them, but that is because it was originally a Greek hat of a scholar, called the "hat of Hermes" (Hermes is a Pagan idol, of course). You will recall the "cap and gown" of graduates from schools and universities employs this "hat of Hermes", topped with a square mason's board. A mason is a layer of bricks, and the mason's board holds the cement mix. These were scholars who graduated to different levels in their guilds; from apprentice to journeyman, then journeyman to master.

In ancient times, just prior to 186 BCE, the land of Yisrael was ruled by a Greek Seleucid, Antiochus Epiphanes IV. He was extremely cruel, and outlawed the Hebrew religion, forcing his Greek customs on them. In the record of 2 Maccabees, an apostate high priest (named "Jason" in translation, but really named Yeshua) helped this Greek ruler *impose* the Greek ways of living:

"And abrogating the lawful way of living, he introduced new customs contrary to the Torah; for he willingly established a gymnasium right under the citadel (the Temple), *and he made the finest of the young men **wear the Greek hat**."*

Paul writes at 1Cor. 11:7 that a man is not to have his head covered in the assembly, but a woman is required to, to keep from dishonoring one another's headship. ⵔⵓⵣⵣ is the man's 'head', while a woman's 'head' is her husband. We are to follow the Torah, and not add to it in any way: *"Do not add to nor take away from it".* Dt. 12:32.

Man-made customs, including all the camouflaged Paganism found in Christendom, are traditions that are forbidden in the worship of ⵣⵓⵣⵣ. They represent more than a "strange fire", but are like the **golden calf**. It is forbidden to worship Him after the customs of the Pagans. *"The one who says he abides in Him ought himself to walk **in the same manner as He walked**."* ~ 1 Yoch. 2:6. Walk in Light ~ the Torah.

Human traditions run unchecked from generation to generation. The word "Bible" is not found anywhere in the text of the Writings, but they are called by this name of a Pagan deity, *Biblia*. They will tell you it's a "translation" from the Greek word for "books", but stop there. It's been traced further back than the Greek.

VIKING EAGLE

BIBLOS, THE ORIGIN OF WORD "BIBLE"

Gebal (Byblos)

Be

Sidon

D

Mt. Herr

Tyre

Dan   AR/

Kedesh

Hazor

Acco

Sea of Kinnereth

Megiddo

Beth

Ashta

Taanach

Shan

Edre

Gilboa

Ramc

MITHRAS SUN SPIRIT

MORE EAGLES?

EAGLES SYMBOLIZED THE SPIRIT OF THE SUN TO THE BABYLONIANS, PERSIANS, EGYPTIANS, ROMANS, VIKINGS, AZTECS, MAYANS, INCAS, HOPI, AND MANY OTHERS. LOOK FOR EAGLES AND CROSSES, AND YOU'VE FOUND A LITTLE PIECE OF BABYLON.

ANY DIRECTION BUT
STRAIGHT

"They have left the straight way and wandered off to follow the way of Balaam" ~ 2Pet. 2:15
"Teach me Your way, O ⟨ YHWH ⟩, lead me in a straight path" ~ Ps. 27:11

Now that you've come this far, you may realize almost everything about society is based on the Roman time system, and our lives are framed in a dragnet. Whether you're an atheist, agnostic, or believer, you live under the rule of a global system that originated in a Babylonian system of sun worship. Fish are not smart, but they travel in groups, and move in perfect order. But have you ever watched sheep? They wander off, and become prey. We are very much like them. An evangelist on TV can hypnotize many of us to send money to him, and all he has to do is tickle the right emotions in us. The mega-churches use music and lighting to well-up emotions in their audiences. They use tried-and-true methods to pilfer your purse, with a rigid order of sequenced liturgies. People are surrounded by smiles, kindness, and gain a feeling of belonging to their special group. But, they learn very little. A showman merchant throws out the meaning of a Greek word here and there, leading people to believe he is very competent. They will often use the conversation between Peter and OWYAZ at Yahuchanon 21:15-19, and describe the <u>Greek</u> words for "love", paying great attention to the difference between eros, phileo, and agape "love". It never occurs to the listeners that the resurrected OWYAZ and Peter weren't speaking Greek, but the Hebrew dialect of Syriac Aramaic. It's all done to make the preacher look very knowledgeable. Actually, the reason Peter was asked **3 times** if he loved the Rabbi was because he had denied Him **3 times**. Peter was instructed to **feed** His sheep, meaning teach them, not **fleece** them.

The serious offense against the man-made law of not speaking the Name of AYAZ aloud made the Nazarenes easy prey. Shaul traveled far and wide to cities, and arrested Nazarenes in synagogues, bringing them back to "blaspheme" before the Sanhedrin, the elders of Yisrael. The assembly at Philadelphia, spoken of by OWYAZ at Rev. 3:7-13, remained steadfast in the Word, and His Name:
*"I know that you have little strength, yet you have kept My Word, **and have not denied My Name**."*
People will go to many extremes to show they are sincere and dedicated, yet even when confronted with the "straight" truth, it's more than they can bear to drop the nonsense they are pro-

grammed with. The praise and acceptance of men is more important to them than the changes required in abandoning Halloween, Christmas, Sun-day, and Easter. The largest group of Christians in the US is the Pentecostal sect, concentrated heavily in rural areas. Emotions and experiential "faith" seem to motivate them, and this makes it very simple for the showmen merchants to exploit them, cashing-in on their human nature. Yet Paul says *"Tongues, then, are a sign, NOT FOR BELIEVERS, but for UNBELIEVERS; prophecy, however, is for believers, not for unbelievers. So, if the whole assembly comes together and everyone speaks in tongues, and some who do not understand or some unbeliever comes in, will they not say that you are out of your mind?"* 1Cor. 14:22,23. He goes on to say that *prophecy* will convict us in our hearts of our sinfulness. "Prophecy" here really means *explaining what the Scriptures mean*, teaching us how to live. "Edify" means *educate*.

Our ears must be "tuned" to discern a lie. When people are not taught, but just undergo emotional experiences, they are trapped and stagnant. "Tongues" are <u>known languages</u>, and require interpreters for those who don't understand them. If everyone already speaks the same language, then foreign languages are unnecessary to use in an assembly. If you really want to sprinkle-in some "foreign" words, <u>use the correct Name</u>! Yet, I've heard Pentecostals say they use the name "Jesus" because *"it's His name in English"*. With just a little research, you can find that Pagan deities were called **ESUS, HESUS,** and **IEUSUS.** Since DEMONS are behind the worship of false deities, then there is a demon named "JESUS". They can manage to keep the word "Satan" relatively intact across the language barriers, and the word for the Yerushaliyim *garbage pit* unmolested, but the **Name** above all names they will not accept. This blindness is no doubt caused by programming to a large extent, but it is also possible they are not being sealed with the Name. Nazarene Messianics are coming out of the Paganized assemblies in large numbers today, beginning with their love for the Name. *"Salvation is found in no one else, for **there** *is no other name under heaven given to men by which we must be saved."* ~ Acts 4:12.

PAGANISM IS VOMIT

You now have more than enough evidence that the calendar, customs, objects, symbols, and words used by popular religion overwhelmingly originated from Babylonian sun worship. Religion has become socialized, Gentilized, and sterilized of all Scriptural recognition. Every excuse under the sun is used to avoid actually living according to the directives given in the Torah. The Apostasy, as prophesied, is all around us. People have been tricked into following after the beast, and don't even know it. The religious merchants *"promise them freedom, while they themselves are slaves of depravity— for a man is a slave to whatever has mastered him. If they have escaped the corruption of the world by knowing our Rabbi and Savior ⵁ W Y ⴰ Ⳑ ha Mashiach and are again entangled in it and overcome, they are worse off at the end than they were at the beginning. It would have been better for them not to have known THE WAY OF RIGHTEOUSNESS* (Torah), *than to have known it and then to turn their backs on the sacred command that was passed on to them. Of them the proverbs are true: A DOG RUTURNS TO ITS VOMIT, and a pig that is washed goes back to her wallowing in the mud."* ~ 2Pet. 2:19-22.

The religious merchants are experts in greed. Only a small handful of them can even recite the 10 Commandments, especially in order. The only thing we will carry beyond the grave will be the Torah. Without preparing by having this "oil", our lamps will go out, and we will not be ready when the Bridegroom calls *"Come out".* Without this light to lead our way, and knowing His Name, we will be shut out from the Wedding Supper of the Lamb. This is not the popular message, so that, in itself, should testify that something is wrong. In fact, the Truth is so bizarre-sounding to most, those who follow it are labeled a "cult". The "familiar" and "popular" behavior of the majority provides a false security blanket. The odd thing is, Christendom is packed tight with so much Paganism, it would be difficult to imagine it containing more! This was done so slowly over time that the average person never questions anything. We need to question everything, and prove all things from Scripture. People who have preconceived notions of what the Scriptures are saying have to take sentences out of context, and "spin" them to mean what they are not saying. They say they KNOW why man is separated from his Creator, but they still make excuses for not doing what He requires, written over and over in

His Word. They are messengers of Shatan, not ⴰ Y ⴰ Ⳑ, or they would warn you.

MYSTERY BABYLON
The Great Mother of Harlots
And of the Abominations Of the Earth:
IDENTIFIED.
BRIDE OF SHATAN: *EXPOSED!*

The goddess of the dawn, queen of heaven, abomination of desolation: *Easter / Ishtar* is her name. Astarte, Venus, were others.

The thought of the altar of Zeus being set up on the Temple Mount is unthinkable; but if the Olympic Games are ever held in Yerushaliyim, this could happen as part of a big "peace ceremony". Or, a "May Pole" could be utilized, which for all we know is an Asherah pole. Babylon is the origin of all false worship, and it is called a "harlot" because it draws us away from our Husband, and we pollute ourselves with its Paganism.

THE GREAT MOTHER

In ancient Babylon, the Pagans began to worship a trinity of father Sun, mother Earth, and the re-born "son", who was interpreted to also be the father, come back to life each winter solstice, beginning a "new year". The Sun was thought to be "dying" as it rose lower and lower on the horizon, until it "stopped" (sol-stice means "sun-stop"). By December 25th, it was evident that it had reached its stopping point, and in the ancient world this was the solstice. December 25th was celebrated by Pagans from all over the world, and has been the "birthday" of Nimrod, Baal, Moloch, Dagon, Hercules, Atlas, Mithras, Krishna, Zeus, Osiris, Tammuz, Horus, Apollo, Amon Ra, Bacchus, Ju-piter (Zeus-father), Hermes, Indra, and Buddha (Guatama Sidhartha was born on a different date, but as "Buddha", his birth is celebrated on Dec. 25). "Buddha" means *light-bringer,* just as the Latin word "Lucifer" means. This evidence only shows who is really lurking behind "Christmas", because there was a *Nativity of the Sun* already long established. But, since any "nativity" is a birth, the Pagans thought of it as the *Nativity of the Son,* followed by a "new year" in the dead of winter.

Nimrod established Babylon and Nineveh, in what is now Iraq. The making of bricks and building a tower in order to "make a name" for themselves became the Babylonians' nationalistic obsession. It was believed that the objects in the skies could be reached if one could build high enough. So, they constructed a "high place" on the highest ground they could find. Other than fire, the lights in the heavens were the only luminous objects around. The descendants of Ham and Yapheth wanted to communicate with these heavenly bodies. The principle deity (shining one) was the sun, worshipped for its life-giving warmth. The Babylonians had left the truth behind, and produced their own system of religion based upon **SEX**. The changes in the seasons were "interpreted" by the ancient Pagan mind in a sexual way. They pictured the Earth Mother Ishtar / Easter being "impregnated" in the spring near the Vernal (Venus) equinox. Then, *nine moons later*, the Sun was said to be "re-born" at the winter solstice. Nimrod's mother, Semiramis, was probably the first "witch" ~ as a person who possessed secret knowledge and powers to manipulate the natural world (*wikkerie*). The "Great Mother", or Magna Mater, was a title given to her.

DEATH OF NIMROD

According to traditional accounts, Noah's son Shem had settled with his clan apart from his 2 brother's clans in Babylon. Nimrod was a descendant of Ham, and the abominations that he committed caused Shem to destroy him. To shock the Babylonians even further, Shem delivered Nimrod's body parts to the far reaches of his Pagan kingdom. This indeed caused the Babylonians to mourn, and is the origin of what is called "weeping for Tammuz" ~ as recorded in Ezekiel 8:14. Nimrod's mother began to comfort the people by telling them that she was pregnant with Tammuz, who was also "Nimrod", because he was the father of her child. And, she explained, Nimrod had gone into the heavens, and was now the Sun itself. People were led to believe that after death they too would go into the heavens. This is still the belief of many Christians, even though there is not a scrap of evidence contained in Scripture to support this belief (it's Babylonian). Actually, the "saints" (Hebrew: "qodeshim") will inherit the

EAGLE BAAL-POLES
BAAL/MITHRAS CARRYING SUN ACROSS SKY ---
THE WHOLE WORLD SALUTES HIM TO MUSIC

"AWK ! ! ---- I'M EXPOSED!!"

"THE LONGER IT GOES ON, THE WEIRDER IT GETS."
---- RALPH DOUGLAS WHITE

WATCH-OUT FOR FLAGPOLES ---- MITHRAS IS **NIMROD.**

Earth, not heaven (see Ezek. 37:12, Isaiah 65:17, Mt. 5:5). The universe will be ruled from this Earth, restored to its Edenic state.

MAGNA MATER

The Great Mother was translated as *Magna Mater* in Latin, and is this very same "sungoddess" or witch, Semiramis. To the Greeks, Zeus was the sun, and his mother was Lydia, shown riding a swan earlier in this book, with spikes on her head. The Egyptians depict Isis holding Horus, who is somehow also Osiris, in art that looks **exactly** like the "Madonna and Child" art seen in Christendom. Shatan has been a very busy character, keeping us all in his control over the many thousands of years.

The Phoenicians called Semiramis **Ishtar**. The Hebrews recorded her name as **Asherah**. She has been known throughout the world by many other names; Oster, Easter, Eastre, Eostre, Austron, Eostra, Astoreth, Ostara, Astarte, Artemis, Aphrodite, Tanit, Diana, Nana, Maia, Gaia, Devaki, Ceres, Cybele, Circe, Indrani, Venus, Isis, Frigga, Frey, Biblia, Usha, Eos, Aurora, Ausra, Ushastara, Stella, Aster, Nut (the sky), and others. Astarte, or Venus, was said to have fallen to Earth in a huge EGG ~ Ster; from the word *aster*, (e**Aster**), Latin *stella,* for **STAR**. By diverting people from worshipping the true Creator, Shatan has designed traps to lure people to worship *him* through stealth. Most don't do it consciously. He removed the Name from our worship, so we won't know specifically who it is we honor: ***"They think the dreams they tell one another will make My people FORGET MY NAME, just as their fathers forgot My Name through Baal worship."*** This text from Yerme Yahu (Jer.) 23:27 is from a time that lying prophets were misleading the people by avoiding ᴀYᴀZ's great Name. They had begun to just call Him "LORD" (Baal). Read Yerme Yahu 11.

The Magna Mater or "mother & child" worship doesn't mean Shatan is a "he" or "she", because he wasn't created as a male or female. But, he will accept any worship we can spare, as long as we don't do what ᴀYᴀZ asks of us. As the "Queen of Heaven" (Yerme Yahu 44:17) the Magna Mater is represented in sculpture with radiant sun-rays around her head. Carved images of her associated with "sacred pillars" rallied multitudes of Pagans to the seasonal observances, because these were the times their Pagan religion ordered grand sexual "services" to be conducted. Many of these people were "shrine prostitutes", both male and female, as can be determined from Gen. 38:21 (where Yahudah *thought* Tamar was a shrine prostitute). The "sacred pillars" were obelisks,

110

like seen in Babylon, Egypt, Rome, London, and the "Washington Monument" in Washington, D.C. They are also the very same Pagan pillars seen on most Christian meeting places today ~ now they're called "steeples". The ancient mind interpreted these religious pillars as a male reproductive organ.

MYSTERY BABYLON: "Queen of Heaven"

The Great Earth Mother, and the religious customs inherited from Babylon, are richly entangled within our world-wide observances, though veiled to the average person on the street. Revelation 17 explains how this great prostitute will be brought down, and how she has deceived the nations ~ or caused them to be "intoxicated". Her title remains the same:

MYSTERY BABYLON
The Great Mother of Harlots
And of abominations of the Earth

This religious "system" sits on seven hills, called the Great City. Almost all scholars understand this is Rome, which is in fact built on seven hills from the early Etruscan period. The scholars confuse the issue by claiming this is only ancient PAGAN Rome, and draw a distinction there. This is done so as not to "offend" of course, and keep blinders on everyone. Let's consider if there is anything Pagan still there, shall we? Let me think. The "Great Mother" is what she was called? Well, the Church of Rome calls itself "Mother Church", which is literally "Mother Circe". Do they perform anything remotely Pagan? Yes, the name **Ishtar** became Astoreth, then Eastre, Oster, Astarte, and **Easter**. Easter was a Pagan spring observance brought into Christianity by Constantine I at Nicea in 325 CE. A Webster's Dictionary will tell you quite a lot about the word itself. If this is in fact the *personal name* of Mystery Babylon, the Great Mother, why is it the most celebrated observance of Christianity? The answer of course is, Constantine re-invented the meaning behind Easter in order to desolate Passover. He also established the practice of Sun-day, superseding the Scriptural day of rest, Shabbat, which is the "sign" that we worship the true Creator, *as* Creator. He claimed the resurrection as the reason for both Easter and Sun-day, and he got away with it!

EARTH MOTHER IN ROME

The statue of the Great Mother is in the Vatican Museum, and was called Artemis to the Greeks, and Diana to the Romans. "Di" means *to shine*. Diana means *bright one*. That's why she faces the rising sun; she's the dawn deity. The Statue of Liberty in New York Harbor even has seven sunrays, or horns, extending from her *TOWER* headpiece. Many statues of the Earth Mother throughout history have this tower emblem on her head, thus harkening back to Babylon. The torch is an old emblem of fire worship, and even the Greeks' lighting the altar of Zeus at Olympic Games owe this Pagan eccentricity to the ancient Babylonians. Child sacrifice was their real purpose for the torch and altar, and the Sun started the "sacred" flame for the offering.

COME OUT OF HER

WHO IS "SHE"?
WHAT IS THE "GOLDEN CUP" FILLED WITH ABOMINATIONS? (NOTE "ABOMINATIONS")

Well, what do we know already, and what is employed to lead or guide everyone astray?

MAINLY, IT'S THE BABYLONIAN

CALENDAR

The whole Pagan system is based on SEX. "She" is fertilized in the spring, and gives birth at the winter solstice, and the years are based on when the SUN is re-born. Take the calendar away, and the whole system falls apart! The Roman calendar is based on the same processes established in Babylon. If people live their lives by it, they will not recognize the "seasons" or appointed times that the lights in the sky were put there for us to know them (Gen. 1:14). The calendar of Babylon holds all the "abominations" together! This dragnet, or "gold cup" intoxicates the people of Earth, and they can't see clearly. The Pagan observances are "abominations", and they "desolate" the Scriptural observances, as Constantine intended.

THE ABOMINATION OF DESOLATION
HAS BEEN SET UP

I've been telling people for years that the Roman calendar is a "dragnet" that guides everyone into *indirectly* worshipping the sun, or-dering their lives according to the old Babylonian mysteries. It really fits when you consider the title "Mystery Babylon, the Mother of Harlots, and of the Abominations of the Earth". Since the calendar "regulates" *when* everyone does *what*, it has to be the dragnet that intoxicates us with the filth of the harlotries in the golden cup in the woman's hands. The woman in this case is Satan's bride, riding the beast. "Coming out" of her will indeed keep us from participating in her sins, as Rev. 18 describes.

EGYPTIAN "SKY" QUEEN OF HEAVEN CALLED "NUT". THIS CLEARLY SHOWS IT IS A WOMAN, AND SEX WAS USED TO INTERPRET THE SEASONS AND PAGAN RITUALS.

LET'S GET OUT OF IT

This "**Queen of Heaven**" and her daughters deceive the nations even today. Babylon masquerades today even as recorded at Yerme Yahu 44:17. Christianity assimilated her **ways** very early, and abandoned the true straight path of obedience to the Creator, Whose Name is ∃Y∃Z. As Peter put it, *"a dog returns to its vomit . . . "* ~ 2Pet. 2:22. Being called away from Paganism and idolatry, early Gentiles *fell back* into their old ways by mixing them together with the Messiah message. OWY∃Z commands us saying *"Come out of her, My people . . . "* at Rev. 18:4. (Get ready for "**Y6K** ".)

"Formerly, when you did not know ∃Y∃Z, you were slaves to those who by nature are not elohim. But now that you know ∃Y∃Z ~ or rather are known by ∃Y∃Z ~ how is it that you are turning back to those weak and miserable principles? Do you wish to be enslaved by them all over again? You are observing special days and months and seasons and years! I fear for you, that somehow I have wasted my efforts on you." Gal. 4:8-11.

Being that the name of the Great Mother is in fact **EASTER**, you need to come out of the mother and her daughters, since they practice Easter, Sun-day, Christmas, and many other intoxicating filth from the golden cup in the Harlot's hand.

Alexander Hislop, in his work *The Two Babylons*, has written about this same topic over 100 years ago, explaining how this fusion occurred with Christianity long ago:

"To conciliate the Pagans to nominal Christianity, Rome, pursuing its usual policy, took measures to get Christian and Pagan festivals amalgamated, and by a complicated but skillful adjustment of the calendar, it was found no difficult matter, in general, to get Paganism and Christianity ~ now far sunk in idolatry ~ in this as in so many other things, to shake hands."

Ezekiel 8:12-17 discusses how 25 men (the 24 courses of priests + 1 high priest) *"bowed down to the rising sun and put a branch to their nose."* The Pagans used branches, wreaths, trees, and became really excited when a sprig of new growth sprang from a tree stump. To them this symbolized their slain Nimrod, and the new life of a branch growing from this stump symbolized Tammuz. In truth, this is how we came to be bringing trees into our homes at Christmas, carried over to the US by the Irish.

BRIDE OF SHATAN

The Great Mother, Easter, has been the main deception for mankind as recorded throughout Scripture. She was called the "Queen of Heaven". Even the words "east" and "estrogen" refer to this abomination. "eAstrology", and "eAstronomy" contain her name as well. At Sinai, what happened was a wedding betrothal as Yisrael became ∃Y∃Z's WIFE, as He claims repeatedly. The Covenant was in two stone copies, one for each partner. The wife agreed to obey, and ∃Y∃Z promised to provide. Yisrael was to show her love for ∃Y∃Z by her obedience. Gentiles who convert and begin with the decision reached at Acts 15 engraft into Yisrael. Through belief, and obedience to OWY∃Z, they become part of the natural olive tree, Yisrael. Shatan's bride is deceived. They have not taken the name of the husband, but adhere to several Pagan titles such as GOD, LORD, and yes, even "CHRIST" (Kristos, Kris, Krishna, are only a few deities). They flounder aimlessly paying, observing Sun-day, Easter, and Christmas, and have no clue of their true origins. They call our Rabbi "Yeh-Zeus" (but He knows who they mean, right?). They blindly follow the traditions, forsaking the teaching (Torah) given for Yisrael as her marriage Covenant.

"You are servants to the one whom you

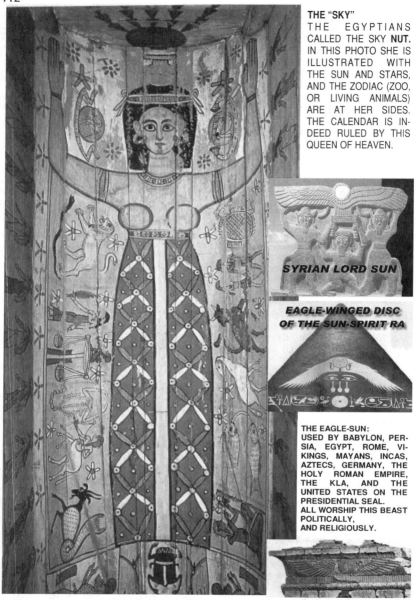

SYRIAN LORD SUN

EAGLE-WINGED DISC OF THE SUN-SPIRIT RA

THE EAGLE-SUN:
USED BY BABYLON, PERSIA, EGYPT, ROME, VIKINGS, MAYANS, INCAS, AZTECS, GERMANY, THE HOLY ROMAN EMPIRE, THE KLA, AND THE UNITED STATES ON THE PRESIDENTIAL SEAL.
ALL WORSHIP THIS BEAST POLITICALLY, AND RELIGIOUSLY.

obey ~ whether you are slaves to sin, which leads to death, or to obedience, which leads to righteousness . . . "Romans 6:16.

If you are obeying Shatan by keeping the traditions he's using to deceive the whole world, then you are embedded in Mystery Babylon, and are his bride, not OWYAZ's. The abominations set up look and feel good, but they are the way of death, because they were not commanded by AYAZ. Their origins in Paganism should expose their Shatanic design. These counterfeit works and wonders were discussed by Paul:

"And then the lawless one will be revealed . . . The coming of the lawless one will be in accordance with the work of Shatan, displayed in all kinds of counterfeit

miracles (great works), **signs, and wonders, and in every sort of evil that deceives those who are perishing. They perish because they refused to love the Truth and so be saved. For this reason Elohim sends them a powerful delusion so that they will believe the lie, and so that all will be condemned who have not believed the Truth, but have delighted in lawlessness."** ~ 2 Thess. 2:5-12. Is "Sun-day" a delusion? Paul means these people will not obey the Commandments, and condemn "legalism", which the true bride obeys gladly. Those perishing *delight* in **not** obeying the law (Torah). *"Come out of her, My people."* Do just a little research on *The Inquisition*, and find out what an "iron maiden" is ~ you will be very enlightened to see these things go completely against the *"love your enemies"* philosophy we were commanded to live by. You will recognize a tree by its fruit. In everyday life, you will find that if you pray for someone who is giving you a difficult time, there will be a change in their treatment of you. It actually works!

When we are not humble, we can walk around with a "chip" on our shoulder, and not even be aware of it. When we gossip or ridicule others who are poor, physically impaired, different from us because they're white, black, yellow, red, or some "ethnicity" (*ethnos* means "foreign"), **we insult their Maker**. I've always tried to make it clear that when I teach or write about Pagan customs, I am not judging people at all, but rather the philosophies themselves. Invariably, some receive the information as an "unloving" criticism of people. In a popular magazine called BAR (*Biblical Archaeological Review*), a reader wrote in saying,

" *I understand your position on reporting the facts, but I do not have to read such drivel.* "

The reader may as well have said, " *My mind's made up; DON'T CONFUSE ME WITH THE FACTS!* "

It's easy to steer children down the path of error with Pagan programming. Growing older, many lose their belief because they see through a few things, and realize the shallowness of what they were taught. Others never have the opportunity to comprehend the basis of why the "world" does the things it does. They're "set in their ways". I'm not right about everything, and as I stated earlier, you may differ with me on some details. But, there is a "restoration" taking place, as prophesied at Acts 3:21. A French philosopher, Jean Paul Sartre, said,

"The more sand that has escaped from the hourglass of our life, the clearer we should see through it."

It's scary to think about, but the Scriptures we place our trust in are only translations made by fallible men. In many places they put into the text words and phrases that reflected their doctrinal understanding, and "monked" with it. This is why there are so many different versions. Even the Greek underlying the English has many versions, and no two sentences agree perfectly. This is evidence that the "New Testament" in Greek is only a translation itself!

Christianity today is so fully-packed with Paganism, that if you TRIED, you couldn't get any more in! But, if you took a shoe-horn and forced in a little more, it would POP. When we confront Christian ministers, evangelists, apologists, and so-called "men of GOD" with just a few of the issues brought up in this book, they become cold, and even hateful of us for being critical in our thinking. The bottom line is, their livelihoods are being threatened, because they are profiting from the ignorance of those who remain unaware of the truth.

"'Is not My Word like fire', declares ⱯΥᴣႨ, *'and like a hammer that breaks a rock in pieces?'"* ~ Yerme Yahu 23:29.

Too bad, but the Truth *will* be shouted from the rooftops! In the *Resources* section in the back, you can contact elder Jacob O. Meyer at the *Assemblies of Yahweh* for a book he has written on the topic of the Name. I know of no other work done on the subject that compares with it. If we can't learn the unadulterated Truth from institutionalized Christianity, then we have to turn to others. A Messianic Nazarene from Australia (who recently moved to Tasmania) named John Steed is another elder who I list in the back. He has a wonderful web site with links to others in the Truth. The following is an article he published, re-printed as written:

NEPHILIM
WHEN GIANTS STALKED THE EARTH!

We are all well aware of the story of David and Golyath, how David as a young man killed Golyath who was a giant, around three metres tall. But rarely do we stop to consider how this giant came to be. Giants belong in stories for children like "Jack and the Beanstalk" don't they? Or do they? The idea that a race (or races) of giant semi-human being once lived on Earth certainly sounds preposterous to most people. Certainly the scientists. When they uncover the skeletons of what appear to be 3-4m tall humans (as they do) they prefer to remain silent, instead speculating over a few bones of some deceased person! But the story of the giants, the Nephilim and the Repha'im, is clearly found in the Scriptures. It is also attested to by Josephus and other ancient Jewish literature. But surprisingly few people are aware of this.

You may, of course, question the spiritual value of knowing the story of the Nephilim ~ it lies in the fact that this forgotten facet of our history holds the answers to many questions that have been asked about the Scriptures. Just a few of the points it enlightens us on are:
1. Why the flood came.
2. Why Noach was chosen.
3. Why Israel was told to slaughter certain Kena'anite peoples ~ men, women and children.

Also it gives greater understanding of the following texts: 1Cor. 6:3, 11:10, & 2Kepha 2:4 ~ to name just a few. But, if nothing else, it like much in Scripture, is an important chapter of the history of sin's destructiveness which should be known by all. The story begins in 1 Mosh. (Gen.) 6:1,2:

"And it came to be, when the Adam began to increase on the face of the ground, and daughters were born to them, that the sons of the Elohim saw the daughters of the Adam, that they were good. And they took wives for themselves of all whom they chose."
(This is a very literal translation from Hebrew). Who were the "sons of the Elohim"? This expression is used only a few times in Scripture and always refers to a being which came into existence by the direct act of Yahueh. Adam himself is called such in Luke 3:38. Yahushua is such, and indeed He opens the way for us to become "sons of Elohim" by being "born again" (born *from above*) ~ Yoch. 1:12. But generally it is used in reference to heavenly beings ~ messengers or "angels" ~ as we see in Iyob (Job) 1:6 and 2:1. This usage is evident here in 1 Mosh. 6:1,2 as the "sons of the Elohim (Yahueh)" are shown in contrast to "the Adam" (mankind).

Some have objected to this concept ~ heavenly beings mating with human women ~ because of what Yahushua said in regard to those who are raised in the resurrection being "as messengers (angels)" and not marrying (Mark 12:25 and Luke 20:34-36). However it is not the meaning of this text in 1 Mosh. ~ That the heavenly beings marry, rather it shows that they departed from their proper role. Indeed other literature that we'll examine shortly supports Yahushua, and says that Yahueh did not intend for the messengers to take wives, but that this action on their part was rebellion against Yahueh. We may wonder how it is possible for heavenly beings to cross-breed with humans. We are not told how this was done, but in an age of in-vitro fertilization and genetic engineering, when human genes have been put into pigs, it should not be difficult for us to imagine how this could be done ~ as indeed it was!

We read further in 1 Mosh. 6:4 the following:

"The Nephilim were on the Earth in those days, and also afterward, when the sons of the Elohim came in to the daughters of the Adam and they bore children to them. Those were the mighty men who were of old, the men of name." Nephilim (Strong's #5303 from #5307 *"to fall"*) probably means "fallen ones" in reference to these heavenly beings who fell ~ physically and spiritually. Or alternatively it means "fellers" or "slayers" due to the fact that these beings brought slaughter to the Earth. This first occurrence is prior to the flood, and indeed as is mentioned in the chapter (v. 6) is the reason why the flood occurred. Mankind became so genetically mixed with the Nephilim that few of the pure race of Adam remained, and it probably would have become extinct if Yahueh had not intervened. We read in verse 9 of this chapter that Yahueh chose Noach because he was a "righteous man, *perfect in his generations* (descent, family history)". In other words, Noach and his family were of the pure race of Adam, able to carry the line into a new beginning.

Notice how in 1 Mosh. 6:4 it says that not only were the Nephilim on the Earth "in those days" but also "afterward", that is, after the flood. In 4 Mosh. (Numbers) 13:33 we strike the Nephilim for the second time in the report of the spies regarding the land of Kena'an ~
And we saw there the Nephilim, sons of Anak, of the Nephilim. And we were like grasshoppers in our own eyes, and so we were in their eyes."
This is the first direct reference to them being of large size (see previous verse also). Back in 1 Mosh. 6:4 we were only told that they were "mighty men . . . Men of name." Undoubtedly the actions and exploits of these Nephilim were the basis for the Pagan deities and mythology. These giants were also called Repha'im; we find this name used not only for the Anakim, but also the Emmim (5 Mosh. / Deut. 2:10,11, and Zamzumim (v. 20). Og, who you will remember was the giant of Bashan, was of the Repha'im (5 Mosh. 3:11). His bed was over 4m long! Indeed Bashan had formerly been a land of the Repha'im, the remnants of their giant-sized cities can still be found there today. They were there in the time of Abraham as we read in 1 Mosh. 14:5.

We are not told how this second outbreak of Nephilim came about. Those sons of Elohim who were reponsible for the pre-flood outbreak had been imprisoned in the Earth to await the day of judgment as we read in 2 Kepha 2:4:
"For if Elohim did not spare the messengers who sinned, but sent them to Tartaros, and

delivered them in chains of darkness, to be kept for judgment."

However, the Adversary undoubtedly had other heavenly beings at his service to corrupt the "seed of the women" ~ for this seems to have been the aim ~ to prevent the coming of the Messiah, the promised "seed" (1 Mosh. 3:15) by corrupting the genetic line. Yahueh Himself intervened by means of the flood in the first instance, and in the second He used the children of Abraham and Lot to destroy them (see 5 Mosh. 2). And He instructed Yisrael to completely destroy those peoples who had mixed with them (5 Mosh. 20:16,17). Of course it was David and his men who finally finished the job, killing the last of the giants ~ Golyath and his family (2 Shemu'el 21:15-22).

As mentioned earlier, ancient Jewish literature upholds these facts. Josephus the Jewish historian mentions it briefly ~ but I don't have his works at hand to quote them ~ check this for yourselves. The book of Jubilees 5:1-6 says the following:
"And it came to pass when the sons of men began to increase on the Earth, and daughters were born to them that in the first year of the jubilee the angels of Elohim looked on them and saw that they were beautiful; and they took wives from as many of them as they chose. And they bore them sons: and they became giants . . . And against the angels He had sent on Earth His anger was so great that He uprooted them from their dominion and commanded us to imprison them in the depths of the Earth; and behold they are in prison there and separate".

The book of Enoch, which comes to us from the Ethiopian version of the Scriptures, and from which comes the quote in Yahudah / Jude 1:14,15, contains extensive material on this subject. Enoch, or more properly Chanok, was given a special mission to bear witness against these rebels and to record their actions to the end of time. Chanok records that these messengers were of the order called "Watchers" (see Dan. 4:13 & 23), so-called because their task was to watch over mankind ~ guardian angels. Chanok writes: *"And it came to pass when the sons of men had increased, that in those days there were born to them fair and beautiful daughters. And the angels, the sons of heaven, saw them and desired them. And they said to one another, 'Come, let us choose for ourselves wives from the children of men, and let us beget for ourselves children.' And Semyaza who was their leader, said to them, "I hear that you may not wish this deed to be done, and that I may alone pay for this great sin.' And they all answered him and said, 'Let us swear an oath, and bind one another with curses not*

to alter this plan, but to carry out this plan effectively.' Then they all swore together and all bound one another with curses to it. And they were in all two hundred, and they came down on Ardis which is the summit of Mount Hermon." He then records a list of the names of the leaders of these two hundred, followed by:
"And they took wives for themselves, and every one chose for himself one each. They began to go into them and were promiscuous with them . . . And they became pregnant and bore large giants . . . These devoured all the toil of men, until men were unable to sustain them. And the giants turned against them in order to devour men. And they began to sin against birds, and against animals, and against reptiles, and against fish, and they devoured one anothers' flesh and drank blood from it. Then the Earth complained about the lawless ones." Further on he tells of Yahueh's judgment against them, this being first the sending of the flood ~ in the future ~ which Noach is informed of; then:
"Further Yahueh said to Raphael, 'Bind Azazel (who had taught mankind the making of weapons of war) *by his hands and feet . . . And split open the desert which is in Deudael, and throw him there. And cover him with darkness; and let him stay there forever . . . That on the day of judgment he may be hurled into the fire.' And Yahueh said to Michael, 'Go inform Semyaza and the others with him . . . When all their sons kill each other, and when they see the destruction of their beloved ones, bind them for seventy generations under the hills of the Earth until the day of judgment . . . And in those days they will lead them to the abyss of fire.'"*

As mentioned previously, Yahueh also speaks of how the Watchers were not intended to have wives, He says to Chanok:
"And go, say to the Watchers of heaven who sent you to petition on their behalf, 'You ought to petition on behalf of men, not men on behalf of you. Why have you left the high and set-apart and eternal heaven, and lain with women . . . , and taken wives for yourselves, and done as the sons of the Earth and begotten giant sons . . . And for this reason I gave them (mankind) *wives, namely that . . . Children might be born by them, that thus deeds might be done on the Earth. But you formerly were spiritual, living an eternal, immortal life for all the generations of the world. For this reason I did not arrange wives for you because the dwelling of the*

116

spiritual ones is in heaven.'"

There is much more recorded in the book of Enoch on the subject of the sin of the Watchers, and Nephilim, including some interesting things regarding the source of evil spirits ~ but we will leave that for another time!
~ *John Steed*

"As the twig is bent, so grows the tree"
~ Alexander Pope

"I took a piece of plastic clay,
and idly fashioned it one day ~
"And as my fingers pressed it still,
It moved and yielded to my will ~
"I came again when days were past,
The bit of clay was hard at last ~
"The form I gave it still it bore,
And I could fashion it no more.

"I took the piece of living clay,
And gently pressed it day-by-day ~
"And molded with my power and art,
A young child's soft and yielding heart ~
"I came again when years had gone,
It was a man I looked upon ~
"He still that early impression bore,
And I could fashion him no more!
Author unknown

THE SEEDS OF THE KINGDOM

The Latin word "doctrine" means teaching, and the "teachings" are seeds. They are either sown by the Father, ᴀYᴀⱲ, or an enemy. The evidence of what was sown is revealed by what grows. The true seed sown by the Father is His Commandments. This is illustrated by the parable of the Sower, at Mt. 13. Veiled hearts cannot understand the parables, as you will notice the footnotes in your Scriptures struggle to deal with the true meanings of texts that require spiritual discernment. (As most of them do!).

"The knowledge of the secrets of the Kingdom of heaven has been given to you, but not to them." Mt. 13:11.

Rabbi OWYᴀⱲ explained the meaning of the Sower, but even so, His explanation is not understandable to those whose hearts are veiled.

"Listen then, to what the parable of the Sower means: When anyone hears the message about the kingdom and does not understand it, the evil one comes and snatches away what was sown in his heart." The "birds" came and ate it up. This is Shatan saying, *"this Commandment was done away with",* or *"that Commandment is only for Jews to obey".* Thus, by trickery, the evil one explains we don't need a particular "seed".

"The one who received the seed that fell on rocky places is the man who hears the Word, and at once receives it with joy. But since he has no root, he lasts only a short time. When trouble or persecution comes because of the Word, he quickly falls away." This is like one of us who understands, but then his family, peers or preacher criticize him saying things like *"you've come in contact with some kind of cult"* or *"how can the whole world be wrong?".* Then, they turn away from Truth.

"The one who received the seed that fell among the thorns is the man who hears the Word, but the worries of this life and the deceitfulness of wealth choke it, making it unfruitful." This is like one who works on the 7th day, and is intimidated by bosses or co-workers when he wishes to rest. They say, *"All it means is that we should take off one day in every 7"* or *"I can't afford to eat kosher, the meat is too expensive".* But, you'll find that taking it day-by-day, week-by-week, it's easy to obey. The "Decalogue" (deca, *ten* ~ logue, *words*) will be around *forever.* They will cry *"legalism!!"* ~ and that's the persecution. We must listen to the guiding principles for Gentile beginners from the letter from the Yerushaliyim Council at Acts 15. Leviticus 11, 19, and 23 are still binding upon all believers, and easy to obey; but the enemy has stolen the true seed from most, and replaced it with the tares, or teachings of error. The teachings we live in are either our Father's Words, or they are the "tares" of the enemy, the one who changes the laws. The wife of Adam was deceived in this same way.

When you sincerely pray for Truth, you will receive it. When you cry for help, the eyes of Him who seeks to-and-fro for any who understand will immediately send you the Truth.

"How gracious He will be when you cry for help! As soon as He hears, He will answer you . . . Your teachers will be hidden no more; with your own eyes you will see them. Whether you turn to the right or to the left, your ears will hear a voice behind you, saying 'This is the way, walk in it.' Then you will defile your idols overlaid with silver and your images covered with gold; you will throw them away like a menstrual cloth and say to them 'Away with you!'". ~ Yesha Yahu 30:19-22. No matter how "precious" the Pagan observances were to you, you will become sickened by the whole calendar that spews out their Babylonian vomit. The cakes baked for the Queen of Heaven (birthday cakes), Christmas trees, Easter baskets, jack-o-lanterns, and the broad road of "Sun-day" will be like a men-

strual cloth to you. People will ask you, *"Are you a 'Jew'?"* You should reply "YES"! "Jew" means *Yahudi,* a worshipper of YAH. You are engrafted into the tribe of Yahudah, in Mashiach. You are an "Israelite", of the sect of Messianic Nazarenes! We are ALL priests, of the order of Melchizedek (King of Righteousness). You need not Earthly man's approval, or acceptance; rather, seek the approval of ᴀYᴀZ, through His Son, OWYᴀZ.

"Do not learn the ways of the nations, and do not be alarmed by the signs (Zodiac (ZOO, beasts) constellations, Pagan calendar observances) *of shamayim* (of the heavens), *although the nations are alarmed by them. For the CUSTOMS of these peoples are worthless; for one cuts a TREE from the forest . . . They adorn it with silver and gold, they fasten it with nails and hammers so that it does not topple."* ~ Yerme Yahu 10:3,4.

Again, remember there is no covenant with "Christians", but only with Yisrael. Psalm 147:19,20 says:

"He has revealed His Word to Ya'aqob, His Laws and Decrees to YISRAEL. He has done this for no other nation; They do not know His Laws."

The Torah is for all men to submit to. Wisdom cries out from the Scriptures. Our duty is to obey:

"Of the making of many scrolls there is no end, and much study wearies the body. Now, ALL has been heard;
HERE IS THE CONCLUSION OF THE MATTER: Fear Elohim, and keep His Commandments, for THIS is the DUTY of ALL MEN. For Elohim will bring every deed into judgment, including every hidden thing, whether it is good or evil." ~ Ecclesiastes 12:12-14.

BEWARE THE DOCTRINES OF DEMONS

Following the Pagan calendar's prescribed events, people are unknowingly worshipping demons. Read all of 1 Timothy the first chance you get!

"The Spirit clearly says that in later times some will abandon the faith and follow deceiving spirits and things taught by demons." 4:1.

In this section, Paul explains men will forbid marriage, as was done by Catholicism. The food we eat that has been "consecrated" (meaning approved) by the Word (at Lev. 11) is all good to eat. This text is used to teach that lobsters, shrimp, crab, oysters, clams, swine, rabbit, etc., is now "clean" ~ but this is not what Paul is saying.

"All Scripture is Elohim-breathed and is useful for teaching, rebuking, correcting, and training in righteousness, so that the man of Elohim may be thoroughly equipped for every good work." 2 Tim. 3:16,17.

"Do not merely listen to the Word, and so deceive yourselves. Do what it says. Anyone who listens to the Word but does not do what it says is like a man who looks at his face in a mirror and, after looking at himself, goes away and immediately forgets what he looks like. But the man who looks intently into the PERFECT LAW that gives freedom (from sin), *not forgetting what he has heard, but doing it ~ he will be blessed in what he does."* Ya'aqob (James) 1:22-25.

DING ! ! !
Oh-oh. . . . . .
There's that "eagle" again. And LOOK! He seems to have a dragon along for a friend. Does any of this "ring a bell"? The adversary leaves his signature, if you have the eyes to see it.

BUDDHIST BELL

Bronze Bell from a Buddhist temple in Japan, used in religious rites.

NOTE PALAEO HEBREW

SCROLL FOUND IN SHECHEM

118

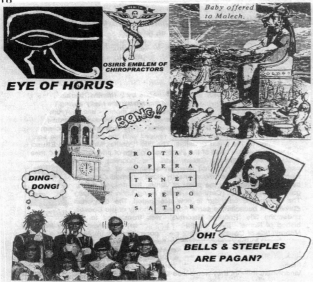

EYE OF HORUS

OSIRIS EMBLEM OF CHIROPRACTORS

Baby offered to Malech.

Bong!!

R O T A S
O P E R A
T E N E T
A R E P O
S A T O R

DING-DONG!

OH! BELLS & STEEPLES ARE PAGAN?

"There is no <u>rest</u> day or night for those who worship the beast and his image, or for anyone who receives the mark of his name." - Rev. 14:11. They will have NO Sabbath, which is the Covenant-sign of <u>Creation</u>, not the resurrection.

When Galileo had refined his optics to the extent that he could see spots on the sun, orbiting moons circling the 5th planet, and had irrefutable proof of the Copernican Theory (sun-centered system), the RCC rewarded his efforts by arresting him. The Inquisitor Cardinal Bellarmine, who arrested Galileo, has a university named after him in Louisville, KY, USA. They almost burned Galileo at the stake, but he agreed to recant, and died under permanent house arrest. In CE 1989 they "re-instated" Galileo back into the Roman Mother Church. The search for truth is often met with violent opposition, and the Inquisition used violence to stamp out truth. They were not interested in truth, otherwise they would have pursued it, and used it to prove whatever it was they were promoting. Inquisitor Bellarmine might not have granted this book a "Nihil Obstat/Imprimatur" either. I'd be killed, and so would anyone else who had ever been in contact with this book.

SUNS, EAGLES, CROSSES, BALLS, STEEPLES, AND BELLS. JUST WHAT WE NEED.
COULD IT BE THAT THE <u>IMAGE OF THE BEAST</u>, THE EAGLE, IS WHAT CROSSES REALLY REPRESENT? THE "GREAT PROSTITUTE", OR FALSE RELIGION, HOLDS IT VERY DEAR. THE INHABITANTS OF EARTH WILL BE ASTONISHED! READ REVELATION, CHAPTERS 13 THROUGH 18.

TOWER OF BABEL

ISIS

OSIRIS

CROSS OF LIFE

SYMBOL OF THE SUN, GOTT!

BEAST IMAGE

SUMMARY

Way back on page 11, you'll notice this tower image, with the "all-seeing-eye" of Nimrod. This same shining "Eye-in-the-Sky" held the people of Egypt in its spell as Horus. Be-

THE GREAT SEAL

cause of Nimrod's idolatry, his uncle Shem killed him. Some have hypothesized that Melchizedek was Shem. Nimrod's wife/mother, Semiramis, was perhaps the first noteworthy woman to be possessed by the adversary. She "deified" her dead husband Nimrod, and led the Babylonians to worship him as Baal, the Sun. She became the Earth Mother, and was also known as the "goddess of the dawn". Towers or turrets were part of her crown all through the ages, based on the Babylonian "ziggurat", the tower of Babel. Diana of Ephesus had a tower headpiece. The Statue of Liberty has both a tower headpiece, and rays. The more one studies history and Pagan-ism, it becomes increasingly apparent that "Satan" has concealed himself as *female* just as often as male. The rising popularity of the "Mother God-dess" is simply another masquerade by which ha shatan diverts worship toward "himself" — a sexless fallen cherub without a name.

The power *behind* powerful men all through history has been this nameless being we refer to as ha shatan, or Lucifer. Most all the popular customs over the Earth point back to ancient Babylon, and it's founder, Nimrod, the builder of towers. Masons celebrate Nimrod as their foun-der. Shem, the preserver of the Torah, points the way for the "children of light". Nimrod, the tyrant who rebelled against ایهاز, has established a pattern of folly, and leads the world to continue the production of ignorant "children of darkness". The "sign" of this Nimrod / Sun God is "Sun-day", and this action is set against the recognition of the true Creator, Who set-apart the seventh day to com-memorate His work (not Sun-day).

The "position" or "office" of the deceiver of men has moved across the Earth over time. It began in Babylon, eventually found the throne of the king of Tyre (Ezek. 28:12-16), Pergamum (Rev. 2:13), Rome, Germany, and now resides in Washington mainly (although he can move about quite quickly around the entire Earth). He has always used the emblem of the eagle as his principal image. His rulership is not only over nations, but all religious government as well. The Papacy has been one of his most deadly instruments. The "anti-Messiah" is one who stands "in place of" the Faithful and True Anointed One, and the title "Vicar of Christ" bestowed on the Pope has the meaning "in-place-

of" Messiah. Daniel 11:37 describes this "office", which will endure until the time of the end, and this man of "celibacy" *"will show no regard for the elohim of his fathers or for the DESIRE OF WOMEN".* Looking at the towers and turrets around the Earth, it is apparent they are of some ancient significance. Could it be that the *"elohim of fortresses"* referred to in Daniel 11:38,39 is Nimrod, and these fortresses are the steeples, towers, turrets, and high places which our Father ایهاز calls pillars of jealousy? Is Nimrod truly "the Great Architect" the Masons worship in their Masonic Temples? Behind Nimrod is ha Shatan, who is also Semiramis, Tammuz, Ashtarte, Asteroth, Ge, Gaia, Molech, Baal, Venus, Woden, Aphrodite, Cupid, Pluto, Jupiter, Mars, Mercury, Orion, Ninus, Zeus, Apollo, and Beelzebub. The names he/she goes by are without end. His/her image is on our currency, so no man may buy or sell without his image, seal, and value given in his name. "In GOD We Trust" is not exactly specific, is it? The GOD of this world exacts worship, honor, and obedience — and he is opposed to the Covenant, and hates those who live by it.

The United Nations' banner displays the whole Earth encircled by the ancient wreath/crown of Caesar. The General Assembly is eventually to be the legislative branch of the New World Order; the Security Council will act as the Judicial branch; NATO will be the execu-tive branch. This beast's false prophet will be the papacy, who will use smooth words to con-vince the world to follow the leader of NATO, which will be a great peacemaker, but also the end-time anti-Messiah. He will anoint himself the leader and sovereign ruler of the Earth. From this position, he will move against those who do not conform to his proclaimed moons and "holy days". This is why we must be as "wise as serpents, but harmless as doves." The "peacemakers" are already fighting under the banner of the UN, and will ultimately move against the wife of ایهاز — Tsion (Zion). Israel has a different calendar than Babylon. She is the bearer of the Covenant (marriage vows / Commandments), and is the wife of the Maker of the universe. The two witnesses will prophesy the end-time message of repentance to the whole Earth, and soon after that planet-wide destruction will threaten all life on Earth.

Nationalism began in ancient Babylon — the people sought to "make a name for them-selves", so others would fear them. Control mechanisms began, national "laws" were insti-tuted, and land was placed under dominion and ownership of powerful rulers. The nations themselves became more than just their populations; they took on a type of incorporeal persona, or life of their own. While individual men would live and die, the nation would go on. The men who were most corrupt, driven by greed, power, and lust, were usually the ones who rose to the top. So, today, and next year, where do our leaders come from? They are all struggling and fighting their way to the top of a pyramid of power, established by Nimrod back in Babylon. Babylon is the "head" of the kingdoms of the Earth. Men's kingdoms are really ruled by Shatan, who was once "the anointed cherub who covers" (Ezek. 28:14), the "star of the morning, son of the dawn" (Yesha Yahu 14:12).

So, mankind's horrific history is not all his own doing, but rather his choices. Mankind has been led by a powerful entity that is filled with intense hatred. Fallen from the highest place of all, our nameless adversary once enjoyed being in the presence of the Throne of ⟨YHWH⟩. He was the most beautiful and powerful creature — above all the Watchers; and was loved dearly by ⟨YHWH⟩. When pride swelled inside him, it corrupted his judgment; he sought equality with ⟨YHWH⟩. This grew into a murderous rage, and there was WAR between the Sons of ⟨YHWH⟩ who followed him, and those who did not. This cherub set up a system of control on this planet, and each person born here unwittingly comes under his sovereignty.

Throughout time, a few of us have been chosen, and trained by the Spirit of Truth (⟨YHWH⟩) to leave a witness to the facts preserved in the writings of the prophets. We do not enter the pages of history, except in the instances that we become a threat, are discovered, and expunged. Of the increase of Yahushua's government there will be no end. This is not to say it will grow larger and larger visibly on the Earth, but that there will always be people awakened as others die — thus it still grows larger. As the time of the Gentiles grows shorter, so does the time for the fallen cherub.

THE SPIRIT WAS MOVING ON THE FACE OF THE WATERS

The "Spirit" is ⟨YHWH⟩ (YHWH). YHWH is Spirit, and cannot be seen. He put His "Spirit" on Mosheh, El Yahu (Elijah), El Yesha (Elisha); and Dawid pleaded "Do not take your Ruach ha Qodesh from me". Some perceive this "Spirit" is the personality of YHWH; others claim it is his "power". Being Spirit, what does YHWH want? He wants to look out through our eyes, completely possessing us. This involves a union that is analogous to a marriage. This is the purpose of all Creation, that YHWH may be "all in all", and the Body of Yahushua is the pre-eminent focus of all

Creation, with Yahushua as the Head. The Spirit of YHWH made "covenants" with Abraham, Yitshaq, and Ya'akob, and the descendants of the 12 tribes / families of Yisrael, at Sinai -- the marriage of YHWH to His Bride, Yisrael. YHWH is ONE, He is not schizophrenic, nor multiple persons. He becomes the fulfillment of our needs, and takes on specific roles, as I can be a managing boss to my employees, a husband to my wife, a father to my sons, a friend to a neighbor, a brother to my brothers -- yet I'm just one man. YHWH can manifest (show) Himself in diverse ways. Mosheh certainly didn't think He was a bush. The Shekinah Kabod was YHWH, and He goes wherever His Name is honored. His "eyes" search back and forth across the Earth to find any who understand. The plural "Elohim" means "mighty-one of oaths". YHWH is the El who swore oaths to Abraham, Yitshaq, and Ya'akob. The oaths are plural, not YHWH. The titles YHWH Rapha, YHWH Yireh, YHWH Nissi, etc., are "roles", they are not different names. Churchianity has come to accept the name "Jesus Christ" as if "Christ" were a last name. The Hebrew original was not "Christ", but Mashiach. This is a title also, meaning He is our "anointed" RULER. In Hebrew, it would be "Yahushua ha Mashiach". In this role, YHWH is our salvation, and "Yahushua" means "YHWH is our salvation".

The New Covenant (Brit Chadasha) sealed in Yahushua's blood is the culmination of YHWH's objective to redeem His chosen bride, the remnant. This New Covenant is: Yahushua WRITING His Torah on our hearts and minds, circumcising our hearts with His Commandments. This is referred to at Hebrews 8:8-12, Yerme Yahu 31:31-34, and Ezekiel 36:26,27. You will note that this Covenant is to be with the "House of Israel" and the "House of Yahudah" -- these are the two houses of the Northern and Southern Kingdoms. The 10 tribes of the House of Israel were scattered by the Assyrians into the nations.

Yahushua's mission, both 2000 years ago, and NOW, is to regather the "lost sheep of the *tribes* of Israel". He is doing this through His Natsarim, because many who thought they were "goyim" and following Nimrod's fossilized customs are returning to their Husband, and turning their backs on tradition. We announce the same "message" of the Kingdom, "Repent, for the Reign of YHWH draws near." Repenting means to return, turn around. Yahushua came to restore the Torah to its fullness so that truth and justice could be restored. He told us to not even think He had come to destroy the Torah.

This verifies that the "APOSTASY" (falling away) spoken of in 2 thess. 2 has happened. It involves some definite "religious lawlessness" -- a delusion -- because those in the apostasy believe the LIE, and delight themselves with lawlessness. This "lawlessness" means they have not received the Spirit of Yahushua, Who circumcises our hearts with His Torah (Commandments) -- and they are not in the "New Covenant", but rather are deluded. Human customs ensnare millions of people, benefiting swindlers who "peddle" the Word of YHWH for profit -- the rich merchants of Revelation 18.

Most perceive that the Scriptures teach we will "see" (GOD) and "Jesus" seated at His "right hand". Two seats? The first problem here is understanding the Hebraism "right hand". It means simply "authority", not literally on the right side of someone. These kind of issues really don't matter salvationally. Remember, the thief on the stake who died next to Yahushua didn't have all his "dogma" worked out in every detail -- but he had enough LOVE, kindness, and sought justice; and excepted his penalty -- while the other thief was making a joke, and inviting Yahushua to do something to rescue them all. In fact, Yahushua WAS DOING something to rescue ALL OF MANKIND. So, in all our struggles attempting to understand these things, we must keep focused on love, joy, peace, patience, kindness, goodness, gentleness, and self control. We must have love for each other, and the Truth; even love our enemies.

Scripture also states that the Father is greater than the Son. Well, when we see Yahushua, we are seeing the Father; this is what Yahushua told brother Philip. Actually, Yahushua is all of the Father we will ever see, and He will be seated on the Throne Himself. YHWH became a man. He took the form of sinful flesh, and died to atone once-and-for-all His bride. The Husband had to die, ending the Old Covenant / Marriage, so the Bride could re-marry; a bride is bound to her husband until he dies, and so, HE DID. The Old Covenant was imperfect, because it was written in stone, not the heart; it was also sealed in animal blood, and atonement required yearly offerings. Obedience was rewarded with blessing, disobedience with curses and death. The New Covenant involves the Torah circumcised on our hearts, so we walk in the Spirit, not the mind of the flesh -- which cannot and will not obey. Our immersion pictures this circumcision, the death of the mind of the flesh, and the resurrection to life of the mind of the Spirit. The Torah thus becomes our way of life, and wells up into unending rivers of LIVING WATER (the eternal Commandments of Life). If we have this seed (the Commandments) within us, we have the Truth, Life, and are children of YHWH; children of LIGHT.

Constantine I decreed that the Venerable "Day of the Sun" was to be the empire's day of complete rest in 321 CE, thus fulfilling Dan. 7:25. This Universal (Catholic) Edict was imposed under penalty of death; and Shabbat (the 7th day, commemorating CREATION (Gen. 2:2, Ex. 20:8-11, Ex. 31:13-17, Ezek. 20:12, 44:24, Yesha Yahu 66:23, Hebrews 4:1-12) and it's observance were abandoned for the ways of Balaam, Nimrod, Shatan, etc.,. The ONE Who covenanted with Abraham, Yitshaq, Ya'akob and spoke with Mosheh in the burning shrub, was the same ONE Who became "the Son": YHWH.

The Father is "greater" because He is infinite in size, time, and power; looking at the majesty of Yahushua is but a small glimpse, and for this reason Yahushua said "Abba is greater than I". Every knee will bow, and every tongue will confess that Yahushua is YHWH, to the esteem of Elohim the Father". Didymus / Thomas fell down and confessed "my Adonai and my Elohim" to Yahushua. The "Captain of the Armies of Yisrael" allowed the man Yahushua / called Joshua to KNEEL before Him.

"And I will pour out on the House of Dawid and on the inhabitants of Yerushaliyim the Spirit of unmerited lovingkindness and supplication, so that they will LOOK ON ME -- WHOM THEY HAVE PIERCED; and they will mourn for Him, as one mourns for an only son, and they will weep bitterly over Him, like the bitter weeping over a first-born." -- Zech. 12:10

This will reflect back to the execution of Yahushua, the Passover Lamb's purpose, and the covering of Adam and Chuwah in the bloody sheepskins put on them. It will also bring to mind the moment Yosef revealed himself to his brothers who sold him into slavery and He became the ruler of all Egypt. Those who looked on Yosef saw the authority of the Pharaoh, but yet it wasn't Pharaoh. Many of these things will become clearer through study, and this is why it is good that we are being forced to go to the Words of YHWH. We must try hard to not go in with the intention of finding the passages that agree with our traditional mindset, but rather let the Truth come through to replace the errors we've been taught. There are not many who know Yahushua is YHWH, but the overcomers are finding out. AT THE EASTERN GATE, WHEN YAHUSHUA RETURNS, Scripture states: "And behold, the esteem of the Elohim of Israel was coming from the way of the east; and His voice was like the sound of many waters; and the earth shone with His esteem." -- Ezek. 43:2.

JUST BEFORE YAHUCHANON (John) TURNED TO SEE THE VOICE SPEAKING, HE HEARD:

"Behold, He is coming with the clouds, and every eye will see Him, even those who pierced Him; and all the tribes of the earth will mourn over Him. Even so, Amein. 'I AM THE ALEF AND THE TAU' says Adonai Elohim, 'WHO IS AND WHO WAS AND WHO IS TO COME, THE ALMIGHTY'". -- Rev. 1:7,8.

Then Yahuchanon turned, to see Yahushua speaking, amid a menorah (seven lampstands), His sign. The menorah represents the Torah, the Tree of Life, the oil of which gives LIGHT to the world (by metaphor, the Commandments). He is the Living Word, the Torah made flesh. The Hebrew word for the personal NAME of YHWH literally means "I was, I am, I will be" ("I will be there" as translated by some). Look closely at the phrase in Rev. 1:8 above *"Who is and Who was and Who is to come"*. Yahushua is describing the meaning of His Name. Those "sealed" with the Name of the Father (see Rev. 7, and 14:1) will *know* His Name; these living saints will number 144,000, and no lie will be found in their mouths.

"You will not see Me again, until you say: 'Baruch haba baShem YHWH'" (Blessed is the One Who comes in the Name of YHWH)

Note that Yahushua is **not** saying we will not see Him again until we say "GOD", or Theos, or Lord. Alexander Hislop's work *The Two Babylons* mentions that Nimrod was widely known by many different names and titles. He traces all fire-worship back to him, and the custom of "purifying" oneself by offering one's children in fire. One of Nimrod's titles was "ADON", meaning LORD. This is simply the root of the Hebrew word *adonai*, which means "my lord". This eventually became *Aden, and "ODIN"* (Woden) in Norse mythology. So, we can see this is but one example of dozens that can show that Nimrod is very much still with us — he's hidden in the name for the 4th day of every week (Woden's Day). People who rationalize that the true Creator "knows our hearts," so we can continue in our Nimrod customs, are playing with not only their own welfare, but any others who may find comfort in large numbers. Remember, Yahushua told us that many would be taken by surprise, and His return would be just like the days of Noah. The majority were swept away, and only eight souls were preserved — because they had the courage to stand apart from the crowd.

A WINNOWING FORK IS SEPARATING US

Here in the US, as well as the UK, witchcraft and the occult have become the counter-culture of the young. The Pagan movements are seeking equal use of public facilities, especially those used by popular Christian sects. The gap between the worldly and spiritual is becoming well defined!

ALL-SEEING-EYE, AND EYE-IN-THE-SKY

The symbolism used on the US Dollar Bill is over 4.000 years old. The eye is seen in the meditation room at the United Nations. The new meanings we read into these symbols represent "revisionism". Those initiated in the occult understand the secret interpretation of the pyramid and eye point back to Nimrod of Babylon. The glowing eye is indeed a symbol of "deity", but a gross Pagan one; the "All-Seeing-Eye" is the same as the Egyptian's symbol of Horus, which was called the "Eye-In-The-Sky", referring to the Sun. Nimrod again. Nimrod was the first king on Earth, establishing Babylon and Nineveh. He was a "tower builder", and most believe his secular title was Sargon I, where "Sargon" means supreme ruler. Nimrod, the name, means "tyrant", equivalent to our idea of a dictator. (The word "deity" means "to shine", and is related to our words day, divine, and diva). Nimrod established human sacrifice, immolating children through "purifying fire", the meaning of the name "Tammuz"!

The Masons were originally stone-masons. During the late Middle Ages, they organized into guilds, the proto-types of today's unions. By 1776, Adam Weisaupt of the Illuminati in Bavaria successfully melded his organization with the Masonic Lodges, which had evolved into a fraternal sect worshipping a mystic "Great Architect". This "architect" turns out to be Nimrod again, who was worshipped by the Babylonians as Baal (LORD), Moloch (KING), and Adon (LORD, SOVEREIGN) -- Adon later turned into the proper name "ODIN", also spelled "Woden", giving us the common name for the 4th day of the week, "Woden's Day". Hislop's own words best describe this fire-worship started by Nimrod, for which Shem slew him:

"The name Moloch originally suggested nothing of cruelty or terror; but now the well-known rites associated with that name have made it for ages a synonym for all that is most revolting to the heart of humanity, and amply justify the description of Milton:

'First Moloch, horrid king,
Besmeared with blood of human sacrifice,
And parents' tears, though,
For the noise of drums and timbrels loud,
Their children's cries unheard, that
Passed through fire
To this grim idol.'

"In almost every land the bloody worship prevailed; 'horrid cruelty', hand in hand with abject superstition, filled not only the 'dark places of the Earth', but also regions that boasted of their enlightenment. Greece, Rome, Egypt, Phoenicia, Assyria, and our own land under the savage

Druids, at one period or other in their history, worshipped the same god and in the same way." (Quoted from *The Two Babylons*, page 151).

The pyramid was sacred to many Pagan civilizations of history, being the top of an obelisk -- called a "pillar of jealousy" in Scripture, which the Israelites would not bow to. It was interpreted as a sun ray, but also as a male fertility symbol. It evolved into various religious towers, or "high places", such as steeples or turrets. They all trace back to the ziggurat of Babel. Poles and high structures were always a part of any Pagan temple, which Scripture refers to as an "image" in places. At Nimrod's death, the Babylonians worshipped him as the Sun -- which later was represented by the eagle, seen carrying the golden orb of the sun across the sky (hence our flag-pole ornaments). The eagle seen on the right side of the back of our dollar bill was first adopted by the Babylonians, and this very same pose can be seen by investigating "Ahura Mazda" (Persian/ Assyrian for "wise lord"). This was only a title, but it was still Nimrod -- they adopted the name "Mithras" for the Sun, and used the eagle as his symbol. The Zoroastrians (also fire-worshippers) had priests called "Magi" (magicians) which bore the emblem of their deity on their chests. They wore black garments, because they were constantly working with the ashes of the "sacred fire". Hence, religious garments of Pagans are black (Israel was told to wear only white linen by YHWH). These Pagan priests made "holy water" by putting a lit torch of "sacred fire" into water. So, it will be found that every detail seen in Catholicism can be traced back to Chaldaen Paganism -- and much came into the daughters of this Mother of Harlots, most especially her CALENDAR.

So, on the US Dollar Bill, the eagle and the "eye" atop the pyramid are both really Nimrod, who was worshipped as the Sun. The Latin words ANNUIT COEPTIS NOVUS ORDO SECLORUM mean "announcing the birth of a new world order". The goal of the Babylonians was also to "make a name for themselves" (become feared as a nation, identified by their unity and power together to conquer). Nationalism was made with bricks, and the pyramid of power has had men in its grip ever since. They scramble to get to the top of it. The reason for all these cryptic symbols used by Franklin, Jefferson, and the other founding fathers is because these men were mostly Masons. The Masons revere Nimrod as their FOUNDER.

The number 13 is "unlucky" because of a Medieval superstition; the Catholics had interpreted that the "last supper" (a Passover Seder) was on an evening just before a "Fri-Day", and there were 13 men at this seder; actually the "preparation day" for the "Sabbath" was not for the "weekly" Sabbath, but rather the preparation day for the annual Sabbath of the 1st day of Matsah, called "Unleavened Bread". Six of the seven annual Sabbaths may fall on any day of the week, thus the "3 days AND 3 nights" works out as long as one doesn't try to interpret it the Catholic way, Fri-Day to Sun-Day. (The seventh-day Sabbath, now called "Satyr-DAy", is a commemoration of CREATION, see Hebrews 4).

We've investigated why "Sun-Day" (the "Day of the Sun" to the sun / fire-worshippers) became the Christian Sabbath in the year 321 CE. Today, a Nazarene (sect of the Natsarim), or what might be called a "Messianic" movement has begun across planet Earth, restoring all things. The Inquisition murdered all of us they could find over the ages, but now we're on the internet. Nimrod, the "lawless one", is the antithesis of the Mashiach. Without the name, or the number of the name of the beast, no man can buy or sell. The real power given to this beast comes from a fallen cherub, called ha shatan; also known by the Latin word, "Lucifer", meaning "light bearer". He is nameless, yet goes by many names. Whose image and inscription is on our currency of exchange? Well, "IN GOD WE TRUST" takes on a strange meaning when you look up the origin of the word "GOD":

"GOD (god) Common Teutonic word for personal object of religious worship, FORMERLY APPLICABLE TO SUPER-HUMAN BEINGS OF HEATHEN MYTH; on conversion of Teutonic races to Christianity, TERM WAS APPLIED TO SUPREME BEING." (Encyclopedia Americana, 1945).

All of this points to the desperate struggle of a creature who is deceiving the whole world, and has successfully hood-winked the nations to conform to a pattern he instituted long ago in Babylon under Nimrod. Alexander Hislop put it into words over 100 years ago, that the papacy was disguised Nimrod worship. His book, *The Two Babylons*, you can order from Loizeaux Brothers, POB 277 Neptune, New Jersey 07754 (ISBN unknown). Phone: 1-800-526-2796

The "New Covenant" promised at Yerme Yahu 31 has nothing to do with "sacraments" or dispensational "grace" — but rather is the Spirit of the Living Yahushua writing His Commandments on our hearts. Instead of beginning by debating whether or not we must obey a given Commandment, we must first ask "why" we are separated from our Creator. The answer is, our sin separates us from Him. We can only define what "sin" is by knowing the Commandments. In fact, sin is defined as the transgression of the Commandments. Without the Commandments to identify sin, there would be no sin. Having established the basic fact that the Commandments define sin, and that our ignoring these same teachings separated us from our Maker, and continue to do so, the next step is to accept the fact that we are, in fact, all sinners — we must be "convicted" of our sinfulness. Instead of just "believing" that all we must do is accept Yahushua's death as our justification for all past and FUTURE transgressions, we must **REPENT**, or turn away from sin. We cannot obey in our "mind of the flesh", but we need help; this is how the New Covenant brings us its most powerful promise: Mashiach IN US. Yahushua literally comes into us, and ENABLES us to actually **LOVE** His Torah, and SAVES us from sin. We can repent of the Paganism, the Popery, the Babylonian fire-worship customs of Nimrod, but without repenting of all the things the Commandments call sin, we will not receive the Spirit of Yahushua (Acts 5:32). Like I've always told my sons, *"You've got to really **want** it!"* (This applies to achieving something they want to accomplish; from getting a higher grade, to playing a sport and scoring — Paul spoke of it using the example of a race — by running in such a way so as to WIN). Without the motivation, a person will just sit back and be an observer. Time is long passed for that, it's now time for the harvest workers to appear. Arise! Shine! For your LIGHT has come! The ideas we've summed up in this book can be further condensed into the following words of any unknown author (please take it as humor, yet truth): "The **Crispians** have the "can opener" (the Mashiach), and the **Frozen Chosen** have the can of beans (the Torah) -- all we need to do as Natsarim is show these 2 groups the New Covenant -- the Torah written on our hearts!" (Heb. 10, Yerme Yahu 31).

DEATH ROW　　Each one of us — no matter how healthy, free, or young — is on death row. None of us knows the day or hour of our death, yet it hangs invisibly right before us all. Those who searched the occult for answers only met failure. Walt Disney had an obsession with the occult, and at the moment of his death, he arranged to be cryogenically frozen at that point — in the hope that one day medical science could revive him and extend his life. We live in bodies of DEATH. mal's natural lifespan. Humans, when compared with the rest of the respirating animals, live longer than expected. We've learned how to extend our lives just a bit. If humans were to live lifespans predicted from the pattern of weight, heart and breath cycles for the rest of the animals, they would only live from 30 to 35 years. But, each of us only has so many breaths and heartbeats, then it's over. We must use our time here wisely.

Christianity, as we know it, is what Paul prophesied would happen after he was gone. Men would rise up and plunder the flock, and lead the Body into apostasy, and follow after myths. Worse still, they have become lawless, replacing the Commandments of YHWH with traditions of men. Having said this, it may sound like I am condemning Christians -- but nothing could be further from the truth. Out of them, YHWH is calling forth a remnant, that will lead the world as Israel was intended to originally, because they are finding out they ARE Israel. YHWH has stated there is to be one "law" for the native born, and foreigner. His Torah is the wedding covenant, and the New Covenant in Yahushua's blood is written on our hearts, not like the old one in stone. Pagans did not know they were only worshipping "idols", the names they used meant just as much to them as they do to most Christians. So, if a Christian learns the true non-Pagan words, and certainly the personal Name of the one they claim to worship, how could it be they would still cling to the uncleanness and errors more so than the Truth? The answer is just as I stated: it's **programming**. Repenting is certainly difficult unless it has been given as a free gift (faithfulness). **Being "faithful" to the programming is not repenting** -- being faithful to the Truth requires real sacrifice. Friends, family, and other brothers and sisters in the old way can be powerful glue to keep change from occurring. This is what the parable of the Sower is all about. Rather than excusing and defending the long history of an apostate religion, we must plow ahead without looking back. It would be far more comfortable to remain within the structure of Christmas, Easter, and Sunday, but we must decide whom we will serve -- witchcraft and Satan, or the Creator YHWH. That's why Satan is called a "deceiver"; he has people thinking they are serving YHWH, but they are really obeying him. Looking at what YHWH says He likes, then turning away and following the Pagan format is truly a strange way of showing it. Satan is masquerading. You can't peel away YHWH's ways and find dirty Paganism underneath them, because He is not wearing a costume like Satan is.

YOUR FIRST STRUGGLE: OBEDIENCE

OBED — Hebrew for "servant". Who is a servant of ㄹㆸㄹㄥ? The one who obeys. Like the rainbow He has set in the clouds as a "sign" of His Covenant with all living creatures to never destroy the Earth by water again, He has established a "sign" between Him and His bride, those who have chosen to obey His Voice, His Word.

Starting in Genesis, the 7th day was established as a sign which shows to YHWH who we worship as CREATOR, since this 4th Commandment was given to commemorate creation. The Great Prostitute hates the "mark" of ㄹㆸㄹㄥ, which is the "sign" of His Covenant. The Sabbath has nothing to do with the Resurrection, but people have been hypnotized to believe otherwise. The texts we usually hear used to "prove" the disciples changed the Sabbath to "Sun-day" to celebrate the Resurrection of Yahushua are examined here, because you will find great resistance to obeying the true Shabbat. Concerning the "Day of ㄹㆸㄹㄥ" (translated "day of the LORD") at Rev. 1:10, many have been taught that this was "Sunday", yet it is really the future time of testing which Yahuchanon was writing about, as he said he was "in the spirit", a vision of the time of wrath was being shown to him. If he wanted us know what day of the week it was, he would have said so, by saying "on the first day of the week" like other passages did.

Let's look at the texts about "SUN-DAY", which people seem to "see" in Acts 20, and 1 Corinthians. I can understand how strong the pressure is to not rock the boat, but it is only Tradition that has "interpreted" selected texts in order to attempt some Scriptural basis for a "Sun-day" observance. You will notice that the "Sabbath" is referred to in Hebrews 4, and it remains for the people of YHWH. Paul never stated that it was any other day, nor did Luke in his mentioning it in Acts. Acts 1:12 even mentions the "Sabbath's distance" of about 3/4 mile, and the NIV footnotes verify this. This was not a "Sun-day". The best way to prove to yourself that Shabbath is the same day as it has always been is to just go through the entire book of Acts, and circle the word "Sabbath" every time it appears. Acts was written many years after the Resurrection. It was Constantine who instituted the "Sun-day Sabbath" change.

At Acts 20:7, Paul was preparing to leave the next morning, and the Sabbath had ended at sunset, and he and Luke (the writer) came together with a small group in a house, "on the first day of the week". Luke records "there were many lamps" in this upstairs room, because it was after dark, the beginning of the 1st day of the week -- and Paul went on speaking until midnight. Little Eutychus fell asleep and dropped out the window!

It says they "broke bread", meaning they had a meal, like the meal Yahushua had with the two men on the road to Emmaus. (Yahushua was invited in, and "When He was at the table with them, He took bread, gave thanks, BROKE it, and began to give it to them" - Luke 24:30). "Breaking bread" is just eating.

At 1 Cor. 16:2, Paul was writing to the Corinthians to prepare for their gift to YHWH's PEOPLE (the poor in Yerushaliyim), since he would be soon passing through on his way to Yerushaliyim. This was not a collection for YHWH's "work", but rather it was for the poor, and it was only for that specific occasion! The "first day of the week" was (and still is) the first **work** day of every week, and so the people were to make this collection then, so everyone would do it in an orderly way - there is no "Scriptural" law of any kind to have this done at all times everywhere. The Corinthians may have met together at their synagogue on the 7th-day Sabbath (those who wished to), and then the funds for the poor were collected the following day, from the previous week's proceeds. This is not a big mystery, but it has been turned into a business by the ravenous wolves who plunder the flocks, and has been the tradition for well over 1,000 years under the authority of the Great Prostitute. Pesach (Passover) is the remembrance of our Passover Lamb, and Yahushua is metaphorically called the "Bread" of life, which came down from Shamayim. It is apparent that the wolves want to take 10% from their followers, and yet Paul wept for years over this, if you check what he told the elders at Acts 20:13-38. We take the emblems of bread & wine only ONCE every year, at Pesach, which is twilight as the 14th of the first moon begins Scripturally. Our "Roman" calendar is the "beast's", the golden cup filled with abominations in the prostitute's hand (man-made festivals, not YHWH's).

At 1 Cor. 5:7-10, Paul says "For Mashiach, our **Passover Lamb**, has been slain. Therefore LET US KEEP THE FESTIVAL, not with the old yeast . . . but with bread made without yeast, the bread of sincerity and truth." Christendom has consistently framed Sabbaths and the festivals like Passover as "legalistic", and a "yoke" of bondage -- missing the meaning. It has turned previously Pagan observances into its own "legalism", and made man-made traditions replace the Torah observances, lived by and taught by the first Nazarenes. Christianity as it developed from Catholicism, later giving birth to her daughters the Reformers, HAS NEVER HAD a Passover, but instead invented their own "method", bent on plunder and deception, re-inventing previously Pagan observances (mixing the clean with the unclean, and darkness with light). If the blind lead the blind, BOTH will fall into a pit. If you are asking men who are blind to show you the way, what will be the end of it? Please just start by circling every occurrence in Acts where the word "Sabbath" occurs, and you will begin to see the **Truth**, and it will set you free. How "evil" would it have been if we had simply inherited the "tradition" of obeying the 4th Commandment as it is written? Even "Pentecost", called "Shabuoth", is one of the commanded festivals in Lev. 23, and commemorates the giving of the Torah at Sinai. The Nazarenes had the Torah written on their hearts, fulfilling the prophesied "New Covenant" described in Jer. 31:33, Ez. 36:26,27, Heb. 10:16. Satan has led away and deceived the whole world, and we have inherited the echoes of his sun-worship pattern, and not our Father's pattern. We are labeled "Judaizers" for obeying the Commandments, and rejecting human traditions.

Some of us are even now feeling the "chiseling" and refining of our hearts as we are being "hewn" by the Spirit of Yahushua. We are being ripped away from the common bedrock of tradition, and are encountering persecution. The "darkness" will not approach the "Light" for fear of exposure, and the enemies of the Torah flee from those who are likely to follow the example of Yahushua, by saying "IT IS WRITTEN . . . " If I may, I'd like to point out that it is really not the remnant which you have been seeking; you are the called-out remnant! We are the "Living Stones", and the Temple of ᚨᛃᚨᛋ. Wherever two or more of us are gathered, He is in our midst—no building can ever be as set-apart as ourselves.

When I stopped searching for the "place", the "people", and the "organization", I turned to Him ~ and begged for the Truth. I found Him, and now work for Him. He is Wisdom, and by Wisdom all things were created! Daniel 11:33-35 describes the struggle with the Great Prostitute, but Daniel 12:10 is being fulfilled today. The Hebrew word for "wisdom" is CHOKMAH. In Him resides all the depths of knowledge, and He will equip us for every work we are to accomplish while in our flesh. The Keys to the Kingdom of YHWH have been given to us, and in our obedience to His Torah, we show our love for Him. With the wisdom of Torah, we can "bind & loose" (forbid & permit), so others can be guided by Truth. There will be many times your steadfastness will be tested, but remember to keep your eyes on Him, not the "winds" of human logic and tradition. Some will pull on you to believe diverse things regarding when an appointed day begins, or certain "rules" regarding Shabbaths, and Kabalistic

"leavening" (puffed up knowledge), but remember all you need is written down in the inspired Word, which is useful for all teaching, rebuking, and correcting in righteousness. Practicing what it says will strengthen you like exercise strengthens muscles, and deeper understanding comes from observing the appointed times (Shabbath, Pesach, Shabuoth, Yom Teruah, Yom Kippur, and Sukkot). The adversary HATES the Covenant, and attacks Yahushua's bride. His servants you should avoid, because we have been warned to not cast our pearls before swine, or they will attack us! In all things, be filled with love, joy, peace, patience, kindness, goodness, faithfulness, gentleness, and self-control. If you treat others as you would have them treat you, you will achieve desirable results. One thing I've learned is, that when you are "debating" with someone who seeks to "prove" that staying where they are is the right thing to do, and they argue over the Name or Shabbaths, THEY ARE AT A CRITICAL POINT, and their "passion" reveals the struggle within them ~ they really WANT to be shown the Truth! Be patient and loving, and ask them if they love the Commandments . . . this will give them a perspective, and all the Scripture stored in their hearts will convict them of sin. This is the beginning! They must be convicted of their sinfulness - but all their lives they have been "programmed" to believe their sins are "covered", and never started in the right place. They started off out-of-step. Their sins are only "covered" when they "repent", and turn from sin! Yahushua enables them in their spirit to agree with the Torah, and they will pass from their mind-of-the-flesh into our realm, the mind-of-the-Spirit. They will never be able to go back, thinking that the Commandments are "done away". The Torah is Spiritual, and the mind-of-the-flesh cannot obey. Be patient with everyone who wants to learn the evidence and foundation of your faith. They are where we all were once; and as it happened for us, they can be used to carry the true message to many others.

No one is hopeless, if they are praying for the Truth. When it is shown that human traditions have become "religion", and partial truths have been **mixed** with lies and doctrines of demons, a rebellion will occur like no other has before, all over the Earth ~ and then Yahushua will return to rule over us. We are part of the restoration, the re-building of the Temple of YHWH made without hands. This is the "Temple" that will come from the skies ~ it will be us. You have found the true Nazarenes. We are hated without a cause, like Yahushua; and we are in a war of Truth against lies, Light against Darkness.

✡ THE STAR OF DAVID

Many will indicate that this symbol was used by Pagans, but there is an origin to it that is overlooked. It isn't a "religious" symbol, yet is a Scriptural fulfillment. (The symbol of the Torah, Yahushua, is the menorah — a representation of the Tree of Life).

Yesha Yahu (Isaiah) 11:10-13 describes a "banner", which is a flag. "Ephraim", one of the 10 "lost" families of Israel, is mentioned, along with Yahudah, and Adonai YHWH is said to reach out His hand A SECOND TIME to reclaim the remnant of His people who were "lost", dispersed over the Earth. On this "banner" is the "root of Yesse", and this word "root" means descendant, and this is none other than Dawid! It's a king's SEAL, the literal name of Dawid.

The "star" is really Dawid's NAME, written in two palaeo-Hebrew letters, as a dalet and another dalet -- the beginning and ending of Dawid's name. It stands as a banner, the flag of Israel, and is the symbol for ALL Israel, including the lost 10 families. Over time, Satanists began to use it, but only with a circle around it, since in conjuring up demons they believe they must stand in a circle of protection when doing so. (It's really nonsense, since candles and circles with symbols in them cannot protect anyone from demons). Many Christian teachers are actively promoting the notion that this "star" is demonic, and even elude to Acts 7:43, but they are mistaken. The "shrine of Molech and the star of your god Rephan" is the symbol used by Islam today, which is a moon and star, symbolizing child sacrifice to Molech. The moon symbol represents Semiramis / Diana / Artemis / Asherah / Ishtar / Easter; and the star is Tammuz, her child.

Some will try to convince you that it is an evil talisman, able to be inhabited by demons. Try to educate them, but at all costs avoid being offensive. 1 Pet. 3:8-12 is a text that should guide us in love, and applies to many areas. But, if you have made up your mind already, try to except those who don't agree with you on every point. There are so many things addressed in this book, it's most likely there will be differences of opinion — we don't all have the same knowledge; but we should be of the same MIND.

PAUL AND CIRCUMCISION

One of Paul's biggest challenges came from those Nazarenes who insisted on circumcising Gentiles. Those who reject or misunderstand Paul sometimes force ritual circumcision on new converts. When Nazarenes discuss these kinds of issues, I like to bear in mind that while there is an ideal and goal in all of YHWH's wonderful teachings, our LOVE has to remain the foremost goal.

Achieving absolute perfection halachally speaking, and not having love, we are doomed. Our love is the real test, and by the measure we judge, we will be judged -- if I am even 25% correct, it will be a miracle! The thief who died next to Yahushua certainly didn't have every detail of understanding we all strive for. But, specifically, circumcision is an eternal covenant. It is a covenant of land inheritance, but not eternal life. Our immersion (in the Name of Yahushua who we covenant with) has become our circumcision, as Paul states it very clearly: "In Him you were also circumcised, in the putting off of the sinful nature, not with a circumcision done by the hands of men, but with the circumcision done by Mashiach, having been buried with Him in (baptism) and raised with Him through your faith in the power of YHWH Who raised Him from the dead." Col. 2:11,12. Immersion represents our "circumcision" by the Sword of the Spirit, the Torah. The whole issue of the "council" recorded at Acts 15 regarding "Gentiles" turning to YHWH involved the controversy of fleshly circumcision, and the decision reached remains unclear even to many Nazarenes today. Those who believe and are immersed will be saved -- Yahushua didn't include fleshly circumcision here, but can a Gentile become a "Yahudi" without a fleshly circumcision? Is the "sign" (oth) of the Eternal Covenant circumcision, or the Sabbath? The "sword" of the Spirit actually circumcises our hearts, so we can walk in the Spirit, obeying the Torah willingly, as an obedient bride. Eph. 2:11 onward discusses how a Gentile's citizenship in Israel is accomplished by Yahushua's blood, and the dividing wall is abolished between believing Gentiles and the "circumcised". Romans 3:28,29 states: "A man is NOT a Yahudi (Jew) if he is only one OUTWARDLY (circumcision), nor is circumcision merely outward and physical. No, a man is a Yahudi if he is one INWARDLY; and circumcision is circumcision of the heart, by the Spirit, not by the written code. Such a man's praise is not from men, but from Elohim." Romans 3:30 states that YHWH "will justify the circumcised by faith and the uncircumcised through that same faith." But, Romans 4 goes into answering your question better than I or anyone ever could. I know this is and always has been an issue of controversy among Nazarenes, but I am not contentious over it -- but accept all who love Yahushua, and seek to follow Him, trusting in His salvation. This faith makes us children of Abraham, who was justified even before he was circumcised. All believers who have been circumcised by the sword of the Spirit in their hearts are children of

YHWH. I don't wish to be rebuked like Peter was, who would not sit with "Gentile" Nazarenes.

MANIFESTATION OF YHWH: YAHUSHUA

"They will look upon ME, the one they have pierced, and they will mourn for Him as one mourns for an ONLY CHILD, and GRIEVE BITTERLY for Him as one grieves for a first-born Son." -- Zech. 12:10.

"The Son is the radiance of Elohim's esteem and the **exact representation** of His Being, sustaining all things by His powerful Word." -- Heb. 1:3.

Many words can be written to counter the above, but they will never change their meaning. The SECRET is withheld, being veiled to those who cannot accept that the HUSBAND had to die to end the Covenant. (Rom. 7:2, Heb. 9:15-17). If Yahushua were not Who He is, He could not possibly alter or amend any former covenant made by YHWH.

"Even to this day when Mosheh is read, a veil covers their hearts. But whenever anyone turns to YHWH, the veil is taken away. Now YHWH is the Spirit, and where the Spirit of YHWH is, there is freedom." -- Rom. 3:15,16.

"Who, being in very nature Elohim, did not consider equality with Elohim something to be grasped, but made Himself nothing, taking the very nature of a servant, being made in human likeness. And being found in appearance as a man, He humbled Himself and became obedient to death -- even death on a nas (pole, stake)!" -- Phil. 2:6-8.

"He is the image of the invisible Elohim, the firstborn over all creation." -- Col. 1:15.

~ Now, which creature would be able to take this attribute upon itself? Michael the Archangel perhaps? The veil has been removed for some of us, but remember that the thief who died next to Yahushua didn't have to know a great deal. Our defining attribute must be LOVE. Where there is contention and strife over what we believe, we don't exhibit love. If we who believe Yahushua is YHWH are to be cast out as "idolaters", then we were misled by many, many Scriptures. He is Wonderful, Counselor, Everlasting Father, Mighty El, Sar Shalom, El Elyon, El Shaddai, YHWH Tzedekenu, and Maker of all things seen and unseen. He appeared to Abraham. He walked with Enoch, Adam, spoke face-to-face with Mosheh, and wrestled with Ya'akob. And, He died for me, His pitiful servant. He did this for each of us, and wants to save each of us who will accept Him, by writing His Torah on our hearts. His resurrection is the central focus of all history, when death was swallowed up — and by faith in this, we all can have His life. He is the resurrection and the life.

DAWID IS NOT IN "HEAVEN"

Paul says to be absent from the body is to be present with YHWH; after death, the very next thing you will know will be awakening and being with Yahushua. I may only differ with some on the passage of time, but we can easily see that Acts 2:34 clearly says: "For Dawid did not ascend into the heavens . . . " and we also read that NO ONE ascended into the heavens -- EXCEPT the One Who descended. So, Dawid is not yet with Yahushua, but sleeps in the grave, awaiting his resurrection. Daniel was told "many of those who sleep in the dust of the Earth will wake up . . ." (12:2). He was also told to "go his way to the end, and rest", and he would rise to "his lot" at the end of days.

I know that tradition interprets things in easily understandable ways, but really such unprovable details like this are not salvational issues. The thief who died next to Yahushua didn't have every single detail worked out, but Rabbi Yahushua assured him "I tell you TODAY, you will be with Me in paradise". See the comma? I'm not the only one who sees it this way, but Yahushua was simply emphasizing His decision when He said, "I tell you today, . . ." We have to be careful, and not snatch one sentence out of Scripture and build a case on it. Wisdom is to be found where there are many counselors, and two or more witnesses are necessary to provide evidence of truth.

Now that you have come to the end of this little book, you might ask yourself if there were enough "witnesses" brought forth to prove that human traditions have intentionally masked and altered the Truth. Many will not be convinced no matter how much evidence is presented, and to a large degree it is simply because they don't wish to repent — sin is fun for a season, but it will reap only death. The same amount of energy can be expended for doing what is right. We're all gambling with our own lives, and we must also realize that we are responsible for our children, and others who make contact with us. Your mission is to GO, make disciples, and immerse them in Yahushua's Name — this is not just for "leaders", but all of us. He will ask to see what you did with the 'talents' He left you with. When you have studied Scripture thoroughly, you will find that the CONGREGATION participates in every facet of getting people converted; we are all involved in teaching, immersing, correcting, and so on.

Dealing With Those Who Don't Understand

Please don't get **discouraged** by the enormous lack of love in many people's responses. Whether they are brash, new believers who have not yet "mellowed" and come into fuller knowledge, or they are deceived deceivers like anti-missionaries or Jesuits, it's hard to keep pace, or have peace in your heart, when all you get are arguments and debates constantly. Here I will briefly touch on the fact that there are 10 "lost tribes", and the anti-missionaries may be under the impression that there are only 2 or 3 tribes, now visibly called "Jews". Reading Ezekiel 36:17-38, and 37:1-28 (noting especially 36:27), they will find that the TWO HOUSES of ISRAEL (Yahudah, the southern kingdom, and Ephraim / Israel, the northern kingdom) will be UNITED as "one stick" in YHWH's hand. We are about to witness the return of the **10 lost tribes**, now embedded in the Gentiles; and see the return of Yahushua of Natsarit. When He reveals Himself to His brothers, it will be a day of great mourning, as it is described in Zech. 12, and one will be reminded of how it was when Yosef revealed himself to his brothers in Egypt, after being sold into slavery, imprisoned innocently by Potiphar, and rising to the highest position of the kingdom.

Not long ago, someone wrote to me from prison saying they were about to be released, but didn't think they could return to their wife and child because they were "Christian". Since learning the Truth, this individual was only interested in being with others like himself. So, I realized that to some degree, many others have these same tendencies -- so I've put a few paragraphs together to help straighten this confusion out.

Accepting Those Who Are Different

1 Cor. 9:19-23, (pilot text): Paul can be easily misunderstood, can't he? In this whole area of his letter, my "take" is that Paul is on a tangent, or line of thought, which pertains generally to his "right" to be called an emissary. He was under great stress, because other Nazarenes were questioning him constantly -- they didn't trust him completely. He seemed to be associating with people others turned their noses up at. Some even thought he 'believed' differently. He wanted only to say that he was under compulsion to spread the message of the Reign of YHWH to all mankind, not for any boasting or reward. He tries to explain why it is that he speaks to anyone who will listen. He doesn't seem to see anyone as a lost cause, but all have the potential to win. He calls his journey a race -- and he encounters all types of people along the way. Some are beginning. Others are farther along in knowledge.

Even though Paul understood many things more deeply than other Nazarenes, like the meaning of the New Covenant (the Torah written on our hearts and minds), he knew we needed **other** basic advice; like how to get along with each other, and others who were not yet "all there".

Many nations are the seed of the Abrahamic Promise -- and the Spirit of Yahushua within us has a **goal** which many of us push into the background. He wants to *use us to reach the lost sheep of the tribes of Israel* -- the 10 lost tribes -- with the message of the Kingdom of YHWH. How committed to this are we? Many place their highest goal on **finding** and **meeting** with others who believe like they do. Seeking others who use the same words, observe the same appointments, and a similar knowledge-level make the Kingdom of YHWH more like an **"Us versus Them"** meeting. We can "see" the Kingdom of YHWH, because we are of it; but ALL of us are sent to gather more to the wedding supper. We must have more workers for the harvest!

A prisoner wrote to me, and shared that he could not stay with his wife and child any longer, because they were "Christians". In 1 Cor. 9, Paul is telling us we must become "like" the people around us -- that is, "infiltrate" them. This prisoner was dedicated to the Name, the appointed times, and so on; but he could not accept others who were different, even his own wife and child. I wrote to him about this. Even if it takes a lifetime, our place on this Earth is to help those who need us the most. It is NOT our mission to group together **only** with others who already follow and understand; we are **SENT** to help those being called-out.

I am sometimes criticized for the type of people I attract as my clientele -- the customers who come into my store are often adulterers, drug-addicts, alcoholics, thieves, liars, -- you know; REGULAR PEOPLE. But, I have been **sent** to them. From this number of sinful people, Yahushua is calling forth Children of YHWH. I understand Paul, because I am sent to the same kind of people -- all kinds. I talk to observant Yahudim who don't know that Mashiach has come. They are "under the law", which according to Deut. 28-30 only promises blessings for obedience, and curses for disobedience. Paul sees this as very narrow with his eternal perpectives, given to him by the New Covenant. Paul has much to teach us all, but sadly few seem to understand him -- that's why Peter warned us in his letter about misinterpreting Paul "lawlessly". While we put forth our greatest efforts to *meet with the saved*, perhaps we should put forth as much effort to *reach the lost*. As seen today, the "2-tiered system" of pastor/flock is a remnant of centuries of human control. Often only one or two are ever heard speaking in assemblies. We must not remain stagnant, frozen pew-sitters. Most of us must become teachers ourselves, and become like our teacher. We need pastors, but this is not to say a pastor will rule over us for all our lives. Some of us must become pastors, evangelists, teachers, healers, givers, etc.,. these are "gifts" for the Body, and to the Body, which is served by all of us. This "Body" is Yahushua's Bride -- and many of them are waiting to hear from us. (The "givers" should carefully read 2 Cor. 8:3,4: *"For I testify that according to their ability, and beyond their ability they gave of their own accord, begging us with much entreaty for the favor OF PARTICIPATING IN THE SUPPORT OF THE SAINTS."* The idea continues in v. 14, *"At this present time your abundance being a SUPPLY FOR THEIR WANT, that their abundance* (one day) *also may become a supply for your want, that there may be equality."* This "support" was for those saints in dire NEED.)

At our meetings, we should let the Spirit of Yahushua speak to the group through *whoever can give a teaching.* You can plan a lecture topic, then the BODY of believers should ALL have the opportunity to speak, as Paul directed us. Note: 1 Cor. 14:26 states, *"When you assemble, EACH ONE has a psalm, HAS A TEACHING, HAS A REVELATION, has a TONGUE, has an INTERPRETATION."* This does not sound like one man dominating the group — the Spirit of Yahushua uses each one to speak to the Body!

I've found that the smaller the study group is, *the better.* Some things may come up that everyone needs to hear, but no one saw coming. The Spirit uses His Body to speak to us, so we should not imitate the Nicolaitans by just having one person's voice still everyone else's. It seems that many Natsarim *focus* on finding others to meet with, which is of course great; however our MAIN objective is to carry the message to the lost. Our meetings should encourage us, and we should gain instruction in how to accomplish our real goal -- *teaching others, and immersing them.* Remember, this is for ALL of us to do, not just a "leader".

The students of Yahushua took 3 1/2 years to get the basics. He left us so that He could live in all of us -- and we should listen to Him, and let Him use us to reach those who would otherwise never hear the Truth. We are sent to the lost -- so let's not turn our backs on those we were sent to. Let him use you to perfect and call-out His Bride. Take Paul's advice, and become "as" an unbeliever, in order to save some of them. As you get nearer to the "finish-line", you should be less critical of those you see just starting out across

from you on the path.

"Be wise as serpents, but harmless as doves".

"If you abide in My Word, then you are truly disciples of Mine; and you shall know the Truth, and the Truth shall make you free." -- Yahuchanon 8:31,32.

The reason I did this research was to find out why there were so many hidden, mysterious things about religion, and to learn why Christian "faith" and Paganism were so closely aligned. It all seemed like such a paradox! My hope is you won't do as so many have, but stay where you were planted. Most who learn the Truth flee their surrounding friends, loved ones, and congregants, because they can't "relate" anymore. Some even wish to leave their spouse. But it is to these very people we are sent. The Truth will drive away the darkness, but if you shine it so as to blind them, they will have no part of you. You must just let an illuminating glow emanate, and then only when someone is interested in learning more. They only learn when they want to. It may take a lifetime for some, while others soak up the Truth like a sponge. Some will base what they choose to believe on a previous paradox they couldn't find any way of resolving, like where Cain could find a wife, or how the Great Deluge could have been global in scope. Within my own family, one of the dearest people to me was told that Constantine wrote the Scriptures, and this has caused a great barrier for any Truth to get through. I wonder how Constantine managed to stash those old scrolls in the hills of the Dead Sea, don't you? It was probably not an easy trick to get them into synagogues all over the world either. The point is, we all have to face people who need us, but we must be discerning, patient, and not judgmental. Believe it or not, you can live in the same house with someone who celebrates Halloween, Easter, and Christmas. It's your endurance that is put to the test, not theirs. Benjamin Franklin wrote, "you can catch more flies with honey than with vinegar."

Leaving Babylon is a spiritual journey, not a physical one. Behind Nimrod is Shatan, and all his lying wonders are deceiving the whole world. You may have a bath towel with a sun on it. If it has a face, it's Nimrod. The Orientals who honor the Dalai Lama or the "child of the sun" are also trapped in worshipping Nimrod. Nimrod is represented in many ways — eagles, gold balls, obelisks, steeples, cruxes, the Christmas Tree, Santa, the eye on the pyramid; and together with his mother, Semiramis, the whole world is caught up in witchcraft.

Resources and Materials

The Truth is the Torah, the Word of ∃Y∃z. Torah means "teaching". Everything needed is there. To show yourself approved, study it. It's your sword, and your dedication to it will shield you. *"To the Torah and the Testimony! If they do not speak according to this Word, they have no light of dawn."*~ Yesha Yahu (Isaiah) 8:20. *"If you continue in My Word, then are you My disciples indeed; and you shall know the Truth, and the Truth shall make you free."* Yn.8:32. Truth has stumbled in the street (Commandments).

NOTE: This author recommends the following for further study, however there may be *certain* teachings you would not agree with; prove all things.

Interlinear NIV Hebrew-English Old Testament

This inter-linear can show you the word-for-word Hebrew-to-English if you order this item (about $64.95): it's called the Kohlenberger 4-volumes-in-1, available as stock # 6297 from Christian Book Distributors, POB 7000, Peabody, MA, 01961, USA. Phone 1-978-977-5000. CBD's web site: http://www.christianbook.com

This Hebrew-to-English Interlinear will show you the Hebrew Text letter-by-letter, **as inspired**; it is written in 'modern' Hebrew letters. The English words are below each Hebrew word! CBD also has *Exhaustive Concordances*, and these have wonderful Hebrew and Greek dictionaries to reference each word in English by number.

CBD carries Philo (#75931) and Josephus (#73868), as well as the *Jewish New Testament*, Greek Interlinears, and the *"Pseudepigrapha"*, containing the books of Enoch, Jubilees, etc.,. In my research, I used **Hendrickson's Interlinear Hebrew-Aramaic-Greek-English B-ble**, as well as all these resources mentioned.

You can order the books of Enoch (mentioned at Gen. 4:17, 5:18, Heb. 11:5, Jude 14) as well as the books of Jubilees and Yasher from **American Archives**, POB 21, Dept. G-3, Keene, TX 76059.

OTHER RESOURCES USED FOR RESEARCH:
The Two Babylons, by Alexander Hislop.
Oxford Dictionary of English Etymology.
American Heritage Illustrated Encyclopedic Dictionary.
Babylon Mystery Religion, by Ralph Woodrow.
Dictionary of Symbols, by J. E. Cirlot.
The Final Reformation (now titled *Come Out Of Her My People*, by Chris J. Koster). This is highly recommended. Available in the US from Lew White, $9.95 + $3.00 S&H.

The Scriptures (which restores the Name in Hebrew) can be ordered in the US from Lew White ($20 soft cover, $30 hard cover, + $3 S&H each: or internationally from:
ISR (Institute for Scripture Research USA-Africa)
Director: Wilhelm Wolfaardt,
POB 1830, Northriding 2162, South Africa

Web site: http://www.isr-messianic.org
Wilhelm's e-mail: isr@messianic.co.za
General E-mail: isr@messianic.co.za
Search The Scriptures Elder: Frank Brown
POB 32, Clarksville, AR 72830-0032 USA
Web site: http://www2.arkansas.net/~efbrown
YNCA *Light Magazine:*
Yahweh's New Covenant Assembly
POB 50, Kingdom City, MO 65262 USA
Web site: http://www.ynca.com
Jacob O. Meyer: (order his books) Elder of
Assemblies of Yahweh
POB C, Bethel, PA 19507 USA
Web site: http://www.assembliesofyahweh.com
Petah Tikvah bi-monthly zine and new book (*A Messianic Jewish Commentary on Matthew*) by **Rick Chaimberlin!**
165 Doncaster Road, Rochester,NY 14623 USA
Web site: http://www.etz-chayim.org/petah1.htm
Other Natsarene websites:
www.yourarmstoisrael.org (Israel: 12 tribes!)
www.eliyah.com
www.qumran.com
www.nazarene.net
The Shofar Elder: **John Steed**
Http://geocities.com/athens/acropolis/8142
Http://membersaol.com/user723492/helps.html
fossilizedcustoms.com (Web site)
E-mail: strawberryislands@worldnet.att.net
Lew White (Scriptures, COOHMP, FC)
Gates of Eden (Daniel Botkin)
POB 2257, East Peoria, IL 61611-0257 USA
B'Nai Avraham Messianic Congregation
102 S. Webster, Ottumwa, IA 52501
E-mail: bnaiavraham19@hotmail.com
Elder: Edward Nydle
BET SHAVEI-TZION INT'L
120 Mt. Zion Road, RR#7,
Tunkhannock, PA 18657 USA
PLEASE PRAY ALWAYS FOR THE TRUTH, THE ELDERS, AND THE PEACE OF YERUSHALIYIM. MAY RABBI YAHUSHUA BLESS YOU AND YOURS. SHALOM!
"Future generations will be told about ∃Y∃z *~ they will proclaim His righteousness* (Torah) *to a PEOPLE YET UNBORN — for He has done it."* Ps. 22:30,31.

MODERN IDOLATRY

"EGAD" A FORM OF SAYING "OH-GOD"

JUST LIKE DRESSING UP THE ORIGINAL JUPITER IMAGE IN "NEW CLOTHES" AS SHOWN ON PAGE 45, OUR HABITS AND CUSTOMS HAVE BEEN "DRESSED UP" IN NEW MEANINGS TO CONCEAL THEIR PAGAN ORIGINS.

VOODOO: FIDDLING WITH CROSSES, TREES, ASHES, ALTARS, WATER, ROSARIES, STATUES, CANDLES, WAVING IN THE AIR, KISSING RELICS, WEARING MEDALIONS, AND TALKING TO BREAD WHILE KNEELING BEFORE IT DOES NOT HONOR THE LIVING ELOHIM.

"Blessed rather are those who hear the Word of ⳊᎽⳊᒪ and OBEY IT." - Luke 11:28

"He has also set eternity in the hearts of men, yet they cannot fathom what Elohim has done from beginning to end." - Ec. 3:11

Wreaths, branches, boughs, and trees were originally used to worship the sun at the winter solstice, known as the *"re-birth"* of the unconquered sun. Nimrod of Babylon, slain by Shem, began to be worshipped as the sun, and branches of trees represented him as the reborn Tammuz ~ that's why wreaths are round. They were absorbed or "inculturated" by Christendom. Tammuz' mother (Semiramis) was later worshipped as *Mother Nature,* under various names like Ishtar, Easter, Ashtar, Astoreth, Asherah, Astarte, Artemis, Eastre, Nana, Nut, Frigga, Gaia, Maia, and many others. The hearth was the Pagan Roman family's place of worship, because fire was associated with the Sun, and thought to be sacred. In this book, you will find out who Santa Claus is too.

Most people don't think for themselves. They don't ask for evidence, look too closely, or ask questions. They just "believe" everything. *"The simple inherit folly, but the prudent are crowned with knowledge."* ~ Prov. 14:18. 14:15 says, *A simple man believes anything; but a prudent man gives thought to his steps."*

DANGER!

READING THIS BOOK COULD ALTER YOUR BELIEFS ABOUT THE CREATOR AND HIS PLAN FOR YOUR LIFE.

The fake name of the Mashiach, "JESUS", is a Greco-Romanism, and means absolutely nothing in Hebrew. If it were a "translation", then it could be "re-translated" back to Hebrew. When taken back to the Greek, it means *"hey-Zeus"*, or *"hail Zeus"*. Since the closest word to "sus" in Hebrew is *"soos"*, it means *"horse"*. Zeus is depicted as a Centaur, and this half-man, half-horse is found in Babylonian Astrology in the constellation **Sagittarius**. In this book, you will discover the true Name by which we must be saved, which is Yahushua, meaning "YAH is our

INQUISITION TORTURE ROOM
BY PICART (1673-1733)

salvation". Many things have been concealed from us. In order to control people, those in authority tortured and executed millions of innocent people over many centuries. Now, in the fullness of time, all that was concealed and done in secret is laid bare in a logical framework. The motive:

TO MISDIRECT WORSHIP TO: THE ADVERSARY, by way of Fossilized Customs!

CARRYING MONEY ON SHABBAT?

Let's put on our thinking caps. Many of us have been taught conflicting things over the years, and **steered** into outcomes that benefited those who were doing the teaching. We know that the average Torah-observant person over the centuries would not carry something on Shabbat that required both hands, and walk around the town with it. Neither would they have a money bag hanging from their cloak-belt, jangling all over the place on Shabbat -- this would give the "appearance" of having just sold something, or the intention of going out to buy something. Even the giving of alms would cease on Shabbat. The beggars would have to take the day off from begging, no one would be carrying money anyway.

So, how is it that there are "collections" taken in to support the teachers (and calling them "tithes") on Shabbat? Going into an orthodox synagogue on a Shabbat might underscore my point here. If you asked the people there, "When's the collection to be taken?", you'd get some funny looks. It is not a custom, nor has it ever been, for observant Yahudim to carry even one coin with them on Shabbat. This illuminates the passage of 1 Cor. 16:1-5, where Paul writes concerning the "collections" for the set-apart ones (the saints — the poor Yahudim in Yerushaliyim like widows, and fatherless children):

(v. 2): "On the first day of the week, let each one of you set aside, storing up whatever he is prospered, SO THAT THERE ARE NO COLLECTIONS WHEN I COME."

Contrary to popular interpretation, this "first day of the week" collection was not a permanent policy, but was just to be done up until Paul passed through on his way to Yerushaliyim. Nor was it because "Sun-day" was a "meeting day", or the "new Sabbath" of believers. It was an organized way to prepare for Paul's arrival, that's all, and was for THE POOR. It was done on the "first day of the week" because Paul knew they wouldn't be carrying money with them on Shabbat. Christians (led in the ways of the Chaldeans) have had the basket-passing method conducted in their assemblies for centuries, done on the man-made "Sabbath" called Sun-day, and everyone who drops something into the basket is basically shamed into it -- everyone is watching around them. Many "Messianic" groups do this also, or provide a box for it. This is not intended to judge individuals who have been doing this to the flock, but rather to point it out, de-program our habits,

and restore a more scriptural method. It should be apparent that our "assembling together" shouldn't cost us anything. Teaching the Torah for pay is also not to be done. Teach harp, harmonica, architecture, geometry, or square-dancing if you want to support your family; not Torah.

You may have heard the excuses about the "Sabbath distance" (Acts 1:12), insisting that we MUST assemble even if the distance is greater than 1000 cubits. The saying is, "it is more important that we assemble, so we over-rule the Sabbath-distance to keep the Command to assemble." What Command? Lev. 23 declares convocations "in all our dwellings", not "drive hundreds of miles", or "go find an elder setting up a meeting". We should assemble whenever and wherever we can, sure; especially the 3 appointed times in a year (but a convocation can be just 2 people). Is it possible that the over-ruling of the Sabbath distance principle is taught so that those who have been gathering wealth from the flock can continue to do so? I'm not criticizing, I'm just asking.

If Exodus 35:3 says "You shall not kindle a fire in any of your dwellings on the Sabbath day", do we just go outside and do it? Of course not. We just obey the Commandment -- and this is decried as "Pharisaical". If we feel "others" are not observing the annual feast correctly, do we run to Yerushaliyim and cut the wave sheaf ourselves, wave it, and do what only the High Priest is to do? Of course not. If Exodus 16:29 says, "Let each one stay in his place, do not let anyone go out of his place on the seventh day", do we ignore this teaching and travel 60 miles? Of course "place" means immediate area, or village. But, if your "village" grows to the size of Los Angeles, can we rely on common sense?

The Body of Yahushua must endorse the decisions reached by the elders, and search out and prove all things. If we cease from carrying money on Shabbat, do you imagine this may be disagreeable to any of the pastors? A pastor who serves without pay is a true pastor, one who cannot be bought. Remember Balaam, the prophet for hire! Reading Acts 20:28-35 carefully may shed a great light on this plundering that has gone on unchecked for centuries. Speaking to the ELDERS of Ephesus (Acts 20:17), Paul says:

(v.20:28-35): *"Therefore take heed to your-*

selves and to all the flock, among which the Set-apart Spirit has made you overseers (elders), *to shepherd the assembly of Elohim which He has purchased with His own blood. For I know this, that after my departure SAVAGE WOLVES shall come in among you, not sparing the flock. Also from among yourselves men shall arise, speaking distorted teachings, to draw away the taught ones after themselves.*

"Therefore watch, remembering that for three years, night and day, I did not cease to warn each one with tears. And now, brothers, I commit you to Elohim and to the Word of His favor, which is able to build you up and give you an inheritance among all those having been set apart. I HAVE COVETED NO ONE'S SILVER OR GOLD OR GARMENTS. And you yourselves know that these hands supplied my needs, and for those who were with me. All this I did show you, by laboring like this, that YOU OUGHT TO HELP THE WEAK. And remember the words of the Master Yahushua, that He said, 'It is more blessed to give than to receive.'" Have we ever heard these words used to make you feel we should give more to your pastor?

It may not be a very popular message with those making a bundle of easy money from the Body, but the Body needs to know they can now help support the poor in their own families, and it will be a true "tithe". (For further study, see Acts 4:32-35, Romans 15:27, 1 Tim. 5:3-16, James 1:27, 2 Peter 2:3.)

We do many things because it became customary to do them, never knowing about the "law of first discovery". If something is done a certain way, and amended or changed later because there is a better way, fine. But, the original way shouldn't be hidden or covered up. The origin of the word "cop" is an innocent example of doing something, yet very few knowing why. In Chicago, Illinois during the early part of the 20th century, policemen wore uniforms with very large, prominent COPPER buttons. The slang term "coppers" developed from this uniform, and the word was shortened to "cops". When we go back to Scripture and explain the TRUE reasons for things, and not the "invented" interpretations, the messenger of the Truth is often labeled "heretic". Study on your own, and expose the insidious lies to everyone around you, but do it with LOVE. All knowledge without love is worthless.   A pastor who works "full-time" traveling and teaching the poor

wanted to know how he is to receive support. Well, we all aren't called to travel full-time, but brother Paul did it extensively for a while. He claimed he supported himself and those with him at Acts chapter 20, and was not a burden in the least on anyone else -- and speaking to these elders, he told them to imitate his example. So, how do we manage it?

The tithe, or ma'aser, was for the support of the Lewite priests. If we were to continue in that pattern, we'd be amiss in our duty if we couldn't prove we were descendants of the tribe of Lewi, and even more so if we didn't continue in all the duties they were obliged to perform. But, in the Brit Chadasha, we are all priests, under our Kohen Gadol, Yahushua. It is not the PERSONAL responsibility of just one individual to go, teach, and immerse others into the Name Yahushua, but **each one of us**. Our "assembling" is for one reason: "let all things (done in the assembly) be for edification." 1 Cor. 14:26. This means we are to have the ultimate goal of getting "built up" in knowledge, meaning educated. This costs nothing. If we choose to *create circumstances* that require a huge crowd of us to congregate into a hall and listen to ONE PERSON PREACH, this is man-made situation. Mortgages, rents, utilities, and insurance costs are the result of circumstances we have control over, and we can make them disappear. 1 Cor. 14:26 also says that when we assemble, **EACH ONE** has a teaching, a prophecy, a message, a tongue, etc., -- and this is evidence that Yahushua has been GAGGED, because traditionally only one man gets to address His assembled Body. Try standing up in one of the Christian meetings, and telling everyone it's your turn to speak, and watch what happens to you. We've been led by the pattern of the Nicolaitans, which goes all the way back to the Chaldean priests.

How each of us gets out there and spreads the message of the Reign of YHWH, immersing others into the Name of Yahushua, should be facilitated by the specific GIFT we have been given by Yahushua's Spirit, not molded after a man-made technique, or one we've just cooked up by ourselves. The poor who receive sustenance through the social security and welfare programs in place will hear the message, because it will be carried to them for free as we learn to get out of Yahushua's way and let Him do His wonderful work. He is working in many others besides ourselves.

It isn't my personal responsibility to abandon

earning a living so I can specialize in going into poor neighborhoods and little rural pockets of the world. I have to rely on the ability of the Message reaching them through the power of Yahushua's Spirit, by teaching the pure truth of the message, so it will be able to be CONVEYED THROUGH MANY OTHERS. Just because *I know the message* doesn't entitle me to a permanent "donation" from all the other believers *who also know the message*. We share a **common responsibility**, and the "pastors" who from time-to-time travel and visit distant places should be housed and fed by the brothers *at their destination*, but they must not be an undue burden, or over-stay their welcome. I know well the costs involved in printing, and I also buy gasoline. But, I also know I must work to earn the money to pay for these things, and not be a burden on those who would otherwise be led to give me 10% of their hard-earned incomes, for the rest of their natural lives.

My advice is, get a paying job; and discern how to teach and immerse others with the special gift you have received from the Spirit, and serve the Body of Yahushua properly. In the final outcome, much more can be accomplished. If we don't know what the "New Covenant" is, then we should learn what it is, and then go and teach it to those around us. It will spread on its own; like fire in dry grass, *if we only teach it*. People will believe it much more readily when its free, as it should be. We labor in the harvest not with our money, but with our personal efforts to reach those lost around us. We don't have to travel to find them, but the message itself will. Stand still, and watch YHWH win the battle. *"Not by power -- not by might -- but by My Spirit"* - declares YHWH. We don't know where the wind comes from, nor where it will go, and the Spirit is like that -- and the Message will go wherever the Spirit goes.

From: *Sunday Law Countdown*: South Dakota Latest State To Endorse Ten Commandments Version Change" (quoted text follows):
["   During the legislative process the South Dakota Senate has followed the state house's lead and approved a bill that would permit the commandments to be posted in public schools...The bill says the words of the Ten Commandments may be displayed along with other objects and documents of cultural, legal or historical significance...No word on whether South Dakota Governor Bill Janklow intends to sign it." Now, a very interesting happened with this bill during the legislative process. In the South Dakota bill HB 1261 introduced to the House 01.21.2000, **"the version of the Ten Commandments to be displayed was recorded in the Old Testament of the Bible"** (cited from the bill) - which would be the correct version, having both the Second Com-

mandment intact and the Fourth Commandment about the Seventh-Day Sabbath with full text. BUT THEN SOMETHING HAPPENED. When the bill came to the State Affairs Committee, the bill text was totally changed and the reference to the Old Testament was deleted! Now why would such a thing happen? To permit display of the changed version of the Ten Commandment law of (God)? To avoid using the correct version which mentions the Seventh-Day Sabbath, thus giving honor to the Sabbath? (Added 02.25.2000) [CBN Now HB 1261 bill status HB 1261 bill text introduced HB 1261 bill text] enrolled Changed Ten Commandments now considered by Colorado legislature: From the bill SB114: **"Each school district shall post in every public school classroom and in the main entryway in every public school a durable and permanent copy of the Ten Commandments as specified in paragraph (b) of this subsection....The text here used is a compromise version developed by interfaith scholars..."** - and then follows a version of the Ten Commandments where the Second Commandment about the worshipping of images is left out, and the Fourth Commandment about the Sabbath day (now third) is heavily changed - **the portion of the Sabbath day being the seventh day is totally left out.** Thus the change made to this sacred Law of (God) by the Catholic Church's is honored and support is given to the false Sabbath day, the heathen day of worship and feasting and celebration, SUNDAY - and the posting of this CATHOLIC INSPIRED DOCUMENT is now even in the process of becoming LAW, backed by RAW STATE POWER, in several states nationwide. Its time to Wake Up America! This has been prophesied! (Added 02.16.2000) "] -- (quoted as sent by e-mail.)

If you read the full text of the 4th Commandment from Exodus 20, it becomes apparent that this "Sabbath" of rest doesn't honor the day, but rather the Creator, YHWH. By entering into His rest, we show Him that we honor Him as our Creator, and so this weekly commemoration of the Creation sets us apart from all other people. We are Israel, and all those who join to us by engrafting will inherit great reward -- but we will suffer incredible hardships from the attacks of the evil one who hates us, and leads the whole world astray. A big clue is given to us:

"And the woman whom you saw is the great city, which reigns over the kings of the Earth." -- Rev. 17:18. Can you figure it out?

The very CENTER of The Scriptures is the verse at Psalm 118:8: *"It is better to take refuge in YHWH than to trust in man."* And yet trusting in man's religious designs is what is most commonly done. Psalm 118 contains this phrase 3 times: *"In the Name of ᴚYᴚⱬ   I will surely cut them off."* And, it contains the phrase Yahushua told us we would say before we would see Him again: *"Baruch haba bashem YHWH"* The " LIE " has become the thing that is believed by most in today's Christian denominations. It is taught that a person will still enter the Kingdom, and have a close relationship with ᴚYᴚⱬ, without having to obey His Covenant marriage vows, because "they believe" that Yahushua's death paid for all their sins; past, present, and future! We're talking about DELIBERATE sins. Their *consciences* have become "seared", because even though they may be confronted with a specific marriage vow / Commandment, they will tell you it was "nailed to the cross". Once in the re-newed Covenant, a believing follower has no interest in sin, because they now walk in the mind of the Spirit. They have received a *love for the Torah*. A repentant person turns away from what is offensive to their Maker, which includes Pagan customs; they don't return to their sin as a washed pig returns to a mud puddle.

"Do we then nullify the Law through faith? May it never be! On the contrary, we establish the Law." — Romans 3:31

What shall we say then? Are we to continue in sin that grace might increase? May it never be! How shall we who died to sin still live in it?" — Romans 6:1,2.

So, you stop celebrating birthdays, Christmas, Easter, and stay home and rest on Shabbat, teaching your children the WAY (Torah). Then, a close relative wants to bring a cake to your house for one of your children's birthdays, and celebrate with them (gross idolatry). This is where the rubber meets the road; do you love ᴚYᴚⱬ more than your parents, brothers, and sisters? They may remain unconverted in their hearts, and don't even begin to understand why you've changed so. They may blame this book; or claim you have become involved in a cult. Don't expect them to understand, because the unconverted human is hostile toward ᴚYᴚⱬ —

"For those who are according to the flesh set their mind on the things of the flesh, but those who are according to the Spirit, the things of the Spirit. (The Commandments are spiritual). *For the mind set on the flesh is death, but the mind set on the Spirit is life and peace, BECAUSE THE MIND SET ON THE FLESH IS HOSTILE TOWARD ELOHIM; for it does not SUBJECT ITSELF TO THE LAW OF ELOHIM, for it is not even able to do so; And those who are in the flesh cannot please Elohim.*

"However, you are NOT IN THE FLESH, but IN THE SPIRIT, if indeed the Spirit of Elohim dwells in you. But if anyone does not have the Spirit of Mashiach, he does not belong to Him.
(Note here, that the "Spirit of Elohim" is synonymous with the "Spirit of Mashiach" — so Yahushua IS ELOHIM, and He is the "Spirit"— and YHWH is ONE YHWH. There is no other elohim with Him).

And if Mashiach is IN YOU, though the body is dead because of sin, yet the spirit (of the individual) is alive because of righteousness. But if the Spirit of Him who raised Yahushua from the dead DWELLS IN YOU, He who raised Mashiach Yahushua from the dead will also give life to your mortal bodies through His Spirit who indwells you."
Romans 8:5-11 (read context, because Paul is explaining how the New Covenant actually works in chapters 6, 7, and 8 of Romans).

Look at it like this; if I am trying to trick you, and I am really doing the bidding of the adversary, would I be trying to point you in the direction of obedience so that you will be condemned? Or, maybe it can be said that now obeying the Commandments will get us into trouble with He who gave these Commandments! I will tell you this: even if a servant obeys out of fear, not love, his master will not punish him. But, we have received love, not fear! Now, we can obey in the renewed Covenant, having Yahushua's Spirit within us, having His Torah written on our HEARTS. The same vows (Commandments) will stand forever and ever, because they reflect the personality of ᴚYᴚⱬ. It is WE who have changed.

It is not widely known, but only Yahushua's BRIDE will be raised and live during the 1000 years after His return to rule Earth: *"The rest of the dead did not come to life until the thousand years were completed. This is the first resurrection."* (read Rev. 20:4-6). This will possibly occur at "midnight", due to the passages of the parables referring to "watching", a thief in the night, the returning master, two lying in a bed, and the Bridegroom coming at the midnight cry. Some believe it will be on the first day of Sukkot, or Yom Kippur (the Fast, Acts 27:9); making it obvious who those are who are "watching" (or observing) His appointments carefully. When He has finished sealing His 144,000 Natsarim with His Name, **watch out** — and this sealing is going on right now. Repent, or perish. Inventing new reasons for Pagan customs and observances may conceal their character to most of mankind, but this is a wake-up call to those lost sheep who hear their

Shepherd's voice beckoning them to return to His flock. His Voice sounds different than human tradition's teachings. If you are being called, your heart recognizes His voice, and you will follow it, and obey it. He told us at Hosea 2:16, 17 . . . *That you will call Me Ishi* (my Husband) *and will no longer call Me Baali* (my LORD), *for I will remove the names of the Baals from her mouth, so that they will be mentioned by their names NO MORE."* Many will someday know His Name, take His Name, and realize we're His WIFE; and stop the "my LORD" nonsense. How did He know? He dwells in infinity, and the future and the past are all before His eyes. The knowledge of the Truth has been kept from us, because the adversary has kept us from learning anything from his masquerading messengers of light. *"My people are destroyed for LACK OF KNOWLEDGE. Because you have rejected knowledge* (of His Torah, Word, Will), *I also will reject you from being My priest. Since you have forgotten the Torah of your Elohim, I also will forget your children."* Hos.4:6.

Ephraim, tribes of Yisrael, RETURN!! *You are the prodigal son.* You have left your Father's House (the Torah), and gone to distant lands, and worshipped according to the Gentiles / Goyim. Now you are aware that you are sitting in a pig pen, eating (worshipping) with pigs; you yearn for the food (Torah) of your Father's House, don't you? RETURN!! Rise up, start on your journey home, to your Father. He will see you coming from afar off, and run to you. He will tell your older brother (Yahudah, the "Jews") who never left Him why He drew you home, and why He celebrated because of your return:

"But he answered and said to his Father, 'Look! For so many years I have been serving you, and I have never neglected a Command of yours; and yet you have never given me a kid, that I might be merry with my friends; but when this son of yours came (Ephraim, the lost tribes who return), *who has devoured Your wealth with HARLOTS* (false idols, Pagan customs), *You killed the fattened calf for him.'*

"And He said to him, 'My child, you have always been with Me, and all that is Mine is yours. But we had to be merry and rejoice, for this brother of yours was DEAD, and is now ALIVE; and was LOST, and has been FOUND.'" — Luke 15:29-32. And you didn't suspect you'd ever see yourself written about in Scripture, did you?

Paul was overwhelmed with grief after his conversion, and lived with a pain he called a "thorn". Most likely this thorn was the daily knowledge that he had hunted down Natsarim and caused them to be put to death because they

pronounced the Name. What else could be worse, bad eyesight? He then spent the rest of his life in the flesh spreading the Name and the message of the Reign of ⴰⵢⴰⵣ.

SABBATH'S DISTANCE — is there one?

First, let me say that meeting together with other saints is very important, for edification; this little study brings up points on how we have been used in a power-play by ravenous wolves who have enslaved our minds with deceptions.

There is not a specific Shabbat "distance" in Torah as a Commandment to keep, however we are specifically told to "stay *in our place*" on Shabbat (Ex. 16:29). This means your "vicinity". Consider that we're not to ride on our animal, because the Commandment says to not make our animals work in any way. The providing of the manna in the wilderness was used to teach Israel how to observe Shabbat, which they had not done during their 430-year captivity in Egypt / Mitzraim. Manna is Hebrew, meaning "what is it?"

Concerning the gathering of **manna**, the camps of Israel had to walk some distance away to find enough to eat for the day; it wasn't just lying around a few feet from their tents / sukkot. Look closely at this passage:

"See, ⴰⵢⴰⵣ has given you the Sabbath; therefore He gives you bread for two days on the sixth day. REMAIN EVERY MAN IN HIS PLACE; LET NO MAN GO OUT OF HIS PLACE ON THE SEVENTH DAY." Ex. 16:29.

This text spells out the fact that there is no reason for us to have to GO anywhere on Shabbat. Neither is there any Command for everyone "gathering to hear the Torah" every week. Although the English word "convocation" is used in reference to weekly and certain annual Sabbaths, the *Hebrew* word is "MIQRA" (#4744, from #7121) and comes from the root word "QARA" (#7121), to call, ANNOUNCE, or **proclaim**. This root word has no use or meaning of "gathering together" whatsoever. It can mean cry, shout, dictate, or call. (I'm sorry if this sounds like "pontificating"). A "gathering" or "council" is the Hebrew word "SOD" (#5475). To assemble is the Hebrew word QABATS (#6908). The Hebrew word "YAAD" (#3259) is used at Numbers 10:3, and is specifically a summoned gathering -- a meeting together -- and this was for the leaders of the congregation to come together to prepare to set out. None of these words meaning "to meet together" are used in association with how to observe Shabbat. I thought this was odd, considering how we're programmed; but it started to make sense.

Of course Shabbat is a day to read Torah,

WAIT TILL YOU GET A LOAD OF THIS . . . . .

but even this is not a *commanded* activity. However, common sense should prevail so that if we find ourselves needing to go on a long journey to be "with others", we've missed the point -- the command is to have a MIQRA QODESH, a set-apart proclaiming (to 'rest' is what is to be proclaimed). It was Rabbi Yahushua's custom to go to the synagogue on Shabbat, or even go to the Temple on a daily basis. Within the walls of Yerushaliyim, the largest community in the land, one could easily go from one end of it to the other in hardly any time; certainly within a distance not considered to be a journey. His hometown was considerably smaller. YHWH's Temple is to be a "house of prayer" -- and we are told to *"pray without ceasing"*; this is because WE ARE THE TEMPLE OF YHWH, Yahushua's Body. The physical Temple is symbolic for Yahushua, which makes His "play-on-words" even more interesting: *"Destroy this Temple, and in 3 days I will raise it up."* -- Yn. 2:19. We really don't have to go very far to be in His presence at all. Pastors call the buildings they have "services" in *the LORD's house*. A "church" is thought of as a building; see the programming?

We may be missing more than we know here, because if we go back and look at the Hebrew passages, the word "MIQRA", based on the word "QARA", may refer only to the DAY being *"proclaimed"* as set-apart, as a day of rest. So, a "set-apart convocation" might simply mean "QODESH PROCLAMATION", not "assembly" at all. We've forced the word "MIQRA" to mean only "assembly" -- but the Hebrew words for "assembly" are QAHAL, EDAH, KNESSET, SOD, or the summoned gathering, "YAAD". *MOED* is the Hebrew word for appointment, or set time. It can also mean a set-apart place. It is translated "assembly" twice out of over 200 uses. Translators bend words this way all the time. We never find the literal Hebrew words for "assembly" (QAHAL, KNESSET, EDAH, YAAD, or SOD) used in conjunction with the proper way to observe Shabbat. Maybe there is some reason. "Sabbath gathering" is actually not a *commanded* practice, but we've been programmed to think so by the translators who saw fit to tint certain passages. This was so they could make us drink their poisoned waters, and plunder us.

Concerning the fact that Luke wrote the words *"Then they returned to Jerusalem from the mount called Olivet, which is near Jerusalem, A SABBATH DAY'S JOURNEY AWAY"* (Acts 1:12), it could be based simply upon the "man-made" custom to only travel a maximum of 1000 cubits (roughly 500 yards). If a person *didn't* travel more than this distance on a Shabbat, no big deal. He's resting, so why not concede that 1000 cubits is reasonable and prudent to not exceed if possible? This distance is coincidentally the distance of the encampments of Israel from the tent of meeting in the wilderness (by traditional reckoning). It really was their "place", or "vicinity". Since we cannot build a solid SECOND witness from Scripture that would restrict our general movements on our day of rest, there is the possibility that one would not be in error for exceeding 1000 cubits, except that Luke did mention a "Sabbath's distance". But, consider that *3 TIMES* in Lev. 23 the phrase *"in all your dwellings"* is used in reference to how to observe various Sabbaths. It doesn't say "in all your gatherings". I've walked 1000 cubits on certain Sabbaths to attend baseball games my younger son played one summer. Getting there and back was a chore, especially in the hot sun! I know people today who drive 60 miles one-way each Shabbat to get to the assembly of their choice. This is almost like driving from Nazareth to Jerusalem in Israel. (OK, that may be 83 miles). Not to judge anyone, we're just discussing all this. Conservatively, I would rather teach someone to focus on RESTING primarily each Shabbat; and if I am wrong, I will be corrected in the resurrection of the saints. If, on the other hand, I teach everyone to travel to get to an assembly each Shabbat, I feel I will receive greater correction if I am wrong about that. I would rather see a person sleep all day on Shabbat, and get some serious rest! After all, the reason there was a double-portion of manna provided on the sixth day was to eliminate the gathering, *and the need to go anywhere* -- "Let no man go out of his place on the seventh day." If you have a small group that can get together each Shabbat where each of the people reside within a reasonably close proximity, that's marvelous! Like Yahushua said, two or more gathered together in His Name is all it takes to listen to Him speak through us; and *each one should be able to speak* (1 Cor. 14:26). Then there are the 3 annual "pilgrimage" festivals. Yahushua told the woman of Shomeron at the well, *"Woman, believe Me, the hour is coming when you shall neither on this mountain, nor in Yerushaliyim, worship the Father."* Yn. 4:21. We are commanded to *come up* to only Yerushaliyim for the place of worship in Scripture; but the day has come that all we can do is observe the TIME where we are; and these times are *shadows of things coming*. Today, believers pass each other on interstates going in opposite directions, to get to the assembly "sites" of their choice, and sincerely believe this is obeying the Commandment. Then they pour out their cash as an offering to those throwing the bash. Please don't read into this any condemnation; but if I report this in a neutral way, it just comes out sounding like a set-up every time. We all desire to get to the root of things, and want the Truth — even if it hurts.

The bottom line is, we have been led to believe that we must "assemble" each and every Shabbat, simply based on the word *MIQRA* -- and then we have been taught to "tithe" *to the men who have taught us to come to these assemblies*. It feels like a set-up to me, since there is **no example** in Scripture of an assembly on a Shabbat where *money was poured into baskets that were raked over the crowds*. I think the thrust of the Commandment is to rest, and to stay in our immediate vicinity. One could just as easily say that Hebrews 10:25 is only "**one witness**" in Scripture speaking of the "assembling together" of ourselves; and I'm **certainly** encouraging such assembling, although I'm simply pointing out that it is not commanded to do so *as we have inherited the pattern*.

I'd love to hear anyone's ideas on this topic, because I can't imagine anything in the Commandment that supercedes the Command to rest. Falling short of the Command would have more to do with NOT RESTING, than NOT ASSEMBLING, it would seem. Oops — I think my eyes rolled a little there. Hebrews 4:11 tells us to be diligent to enter His REST, not **diligent to scurry down the road to meet anyone**. (Now, smile sideways like this: :-)) The Command to "assemble" may be only an interpretation, but even if it is *accurate*, it's hard to picture the effort to assemble could negate the importance of resting. This will not be very popular with those engaged in looting the flock, will it? When Yahushua stood up to read in the synagogue, there were no collections made. People today who sell books and videos on Shabbat need to look at what they are really doing: buying and selling. No donations were ever made on Shabbat in Scripture, and they certainly aren't today in orthodox synagogues. If what I am teaching on this is true, and I believe it is, then the plundered should feel that the Truth has set them free; but the plunderers will be greatly disturbed. All the "good works" like "tithing" on Sun-day will be stubble, burned-up like hay; *it will do no good to pay a pastor to do what you were supposed to be doing, at no cost. Why waste your money on what is not bread?* (See Yesha Yahu 55, Micah 3:11; also, read Acts 20:17-38 carefully, where Paul met with the elders at Ephesus).

Think of how Yahushua drove out the men who had turned His Temple into a *house of merchandise*, and then picture in your mind **the baskets of cash passing around in the assemblies.** ᴢYᴢ⅄ owns *quasars, galaxies, and can create*

universes out of nothing — *does He really need our cash?* The offering to Him was to be received by the poor, Lewite, widow, and fatherless; and this should not be *intercepted* by anyone posturing themselves to receive it instead. If you give your money to me, an elder called to serve and teach, are you giving it to ᴢY ᴢ⅄? *"He who shows favour to the poor lends to ᴢY ᴢ⅄"* — Pr. 19:17.   So, if I am poor, unable to work, then YES you can give to Him by giving to me. Objectively, it would seem we have reconstructed some new form of artificially created house of merchandise all over again. This situation is the sustaining economic power-plant that gives life to the beast system in place; The great prostitute **lives luxuriously**, while spewing poisonous lies across the whole Earth. *Come out of her, My people*; the great prostitute must pay for her sins -- drinking from her poisoned cup (false teachings) has made most of the world drunk (numb to Truth). *Please* wake up.   Wormwood represents "poisoned water", which you will soon see. The Living Water, the Torah (and by association, the Spirit of Mashiach), has been tainted with deadly teachings mixed into it by *human traditions* and *interpretations* for centuries.   By all means MEET TOGETHER when you can do so -- but watch out for the ravenous wolves who try to control the gatherings.   They are the source of the poisoned waters, the wormwood, the lies.

Take away the money, and the pastors who remain are not masquerading — they seek a reward that thieves cannot steal.   Think about it — have you helped your pastor build bigger barns to store up his wealth?   Are you such a pastor?   Micah 3:11 is clear.   When Rabbi Yahushua exposed the corruption of His day, the corrupt men plotted to kill Him.   Today, it is a printing press they will have to stop, or they must somehow manage to outlaw Truth.

ONLY A PROPHET?

"Take courage, My son, your sins are forgiven." — Mt. 9:2.   Yahushua spoke these words to a paralyzed young man.   What prophet was given the authority to forgive sins?   Can Michael or Gabriel do this?   Azazel?

To *cover* sins, the blood of animals was used as atonement (*kaphar*).   This blood is *life*, given on the altar, and it was offered *in place of* the life of the person who sinned.   Who was it that decided when sins were covered?   Only YHWH can forgive sins, and He gave this authority to His Son, Who came and spoke to us in the authority of YHWH, not the authority of a prophet.   Many don't yet know Who Yahushua really is.   *All the Scriptures* are about Him.   He is the Living Waters. The following is a very special article written by a sister in Arizona, named **Mary Lou Frommert**, and she points out many Scriptures that show that Yahushua is the Living Waters that came down to us. She also explains "wormwood" using Scripture:

LIVING WATERS

Our Messiah Yahushua said He is the Living Waters springing up into everlasting life at Yn. 4:10-14. Yirme Yahu 17:13 states: *"Those who depart from Me shall be written in the Earth, because they have forsaken Yahuah, the fountain of living waters."* Yirme Yahu 2:13: *"For My people have done two evils; they have forsaken Me, the fountain of living waters, to hew out for themselves cisterns; cracked cisterns, which do not hold water."* Yn. 3:5: *"Yahushua said, 'Truly, truly, I say to you, unless one is born of water and the Spirit, he is unable to enter into the reign of Elohim."*

We must be born of the Spirit and of His Water, His *Living Waters* — look at Ps. / Tehillim 1, and 36:8,9. It speaks of being filled with His Word. His Word is His *Water*, and we are washed clean by His Word. 1Cor. 10:4: *"All drank the same spiritual drink. For they all drank of that spiritual Rock that followed, and the Rock was Messiah."* Ibrim / Hebrews 10:22: *"Let us draw near with a true heart in completeness of belief, having our hearts sprinkled from a wicked conscience and our bodies washed with clean water."* We must let Him wash us with the water of His Word. Ephesians 5:26: *"Husbands love your wives, as Messiah also did love the assembly and gave Himself for it, in order to set it apart and cleanse it with the washing of water by the Word."* There it is; this is what our Messiah does for us His bride — Yn. 1:1,2: *"In the beginning was the Word, and the Word was with Elohim, and the Word was Elohim. He was in the beginning with Elohim."*

Now I will show you what Yahuah has given me about His **Word** becoming **Wormwood**. Wormwood is already here, and it has been here poisoning our spiritual waters from Yahushua. Yirme Yahu 9:12b-15: *"Why has the land perished, has it been burned up like a wilderness, with none passing through? And Yahuah says, 'Because they have forsaken My Torah which I set before them, and have not obeyed My voice, nor walked according to it, but they have walked according to the stubbornness of their own heart and after the Ba'als, which their fathers had taught them.' Therefore thus says Yahuah of hosts, the Elohim of Yisrael, 'See, I am making this people eat wormwood, and I shall make them drink poisoned water.'"*

Yirme Yahu 23:11 *"'For both prophet and priest have become defiled. Even in My House I have found their evil', declares Yahuah. Therefore thus said Yahuah of hosts concerning the prophets, 'See, I am making them eat wormwood, and shall make them drink poisoned water.'"* Amos 5:7: *"O you who are turning right – ruling to wormwood, and have cast down righteousness to the Earth!"* Rev. 8:10,11: *"And the third messenger sounded, and a great star fell from the heaven, burning like a torch, and it fell on a third of the rivers and on the fountains of water, and the name of the star is called Wormwood. And a third of the waters became wormwood, and many men died from the waters, because they were made bitter."* Daniel 8:9-12: *"And from one of them came a little horn which became exceedingly great toward the south, and toward the east, and toward the Splendid Land. And it became great up to the host of the heavens. And it caused some of the host and some of the stars to fall to the Earth, and trampled them down. It even exalted itself as high as the Prince of the host. And it took that which is continual away from Him, and threw down the foundation of His set-apart place. And because of transgression, an army was given over to the horn to oppose that which is continual. And it threw the Truth down to the ground, and it acted and prospered."*

Now please look with your eyes open and see that Wormwood has been with us since the Truth of Yahuah (and Yahushua's) true Name was cast down. When the Law — the Torah — was cast down, these were some of the stars that fell and were trampled down; *and we have drank the poisoned waters of lies of Wormwood.* Many men have died drinking from the wrong spiritual waters. Everyone is waiting for our natural water to turn poisoned, and I'm sure they will soon; but let us also see that Wormwood is *already here*, and has been here for many, many years. Let each of us turn, repent, and seek Yahuah to show us His pure Waters; His Word, His Truth. Let us drink only pure Truth in these days of darkness all around us.

Here is a Truth Yahuah has shown me about our Messiah and His birth.

Yesha Yahu 7:14: *"Therefore Yahuah Himself gives you a sign; Look, a virgin shall conceive and bear a Son and shall call His Name Immanuel."* Luke 1:30-35: *"The messenger said to her, 'Do not be afraid Miryam, for you have found favour with Elohim. And see, you shall con-*

ceive in your womb, and shall give birth to a Son, and call His Name Yahushua. He shall be great and shall be called the Son of the Most High. And Yahuah Elohim shall give Him the throne of His father Dawid. And He shall reign over the house of Ya'aqob forever and there shall be no end to His reign.' And Miryam said to the messenger, 'How shall this be, since I do not know a man?' And the messenger answering, said to her 'The The Set-apart Spirit shall come upon you and the power of the Most High shall overshadow you. And for that reason, the Set-Apart One Born of you shall be called: Son of Elohim.'"

(A child in a woman's womb carries the father's blood.)

Matt 1:25: "Yoseph knew Miryam not until she gave birth to her Son, the first born."

1 Yohanan 5:6-8: "This is the one that came by water and blood. Yahushua Messiah, not only by water, but by water and blood. And it is the Spirit who bears witness because the Spirit is the Truth. Because there are three who bear witness: the Spirit and the water, and the blood. And the three are in agreement."

Gen. 4:10: "The voice of your brother's blood cries out to Me from the ground."

Gen. 2:24: "Husband and wife became one flesh."

1 Cor. 6:15-20 talks about our bodies belonging to our Messiah and to flee fornication because it defiles our bodies. Remember in marriage a pure wife will bleed when they become one flesh, and this is why Miryam had to stay pure for the birth of her Son. This beautiful Messiah of ours had to come down out of His mother's pure womb through a pure passage untouched by a man. The first thing that happened was her water broke, and that had a voice; and then her blood flowed, which was pure and that had a voice; the Spirit bears witness of this in Luke 1:30-35 and Yohanan 5:6-8.

Yohanan 19:30: "So when Yahushua took the sour wine, He said, 'It has been accomplished!' And bowing His head, He gave up His spirit."

V. 34: "But one of the soldiers pierced His side with a spear, and instantly blood and water came out."

Our precious Messiah came into this world with the Spirit making Him in a pure womb, and with water and blood; the last thing He did was to leave this world giving us His Spirit, His Water, and His Blood. Let us walk in His Word; the pure water of His Word. Hungry and thirsty for His righteousness and truth, keeping our bodies and minds clean for Him as we are His Dwelling Place. I encourage you to walk pure and clean for your first love, Yahuah. Let us not be cracked cisterns

that we have made, let us hold His sweet waters. Remember Yaaqob 3:11, "Does the fountain send forth the sweet and the bitter from the same opening?" Let us speak the truth, and live the truth Yahushua has called us to. His Spirit lives in us; His Blood washes away our sins. His Water is His Word we wash ourselves with each and every day. Let us not forsake our Living Waters — ayaz. The Spirit, the Water, and the Blood bear witness, and we hear the Truth, and we are free. I leave you with these 3 Scriptures to wash with: Yesha Yahu 3: 20, 21; 1 Yn. 2:12-17; Rev. 21:27. We are not written in the Earth as in Yirme Yahu 17:3, but we are written in the Lamb's Scroll of Life! Praise you, Father ayaz, we hear Your Voice! May the favour of our Master Yahushua Messiah be with you.

Shalom — **Mary Lou Frommert**

Stunning prophetic Truth, I say. She mentioned that "stars" in Revelation represent certain Commandments, caused to fall by a "great horn" (power). Well, Rev. 8:10,11 quoted in her essay mentions a "great star" falling. This is indeed most likely the "Key of Knowledge", His personal Name! His Name was used in Scripture at least 7,000 times, but taken out completely for some reason. Which Commandment in the "big ten" has the most words? Which Commandment is mentioned throughout Scripture with the most fervor? Which Commandment is mentioned the most times? Overwhelmingly, it is the Sabbath. This single observance will announce to anyone in this world Who you serve. It will "mark" you in their eyes. Most will even say, "are you Jewish?" This "star" is indeed also great, and the "great horn" must be the BEAST. Yes, the beast is here, and will remain until the return of Yahushua.

Often, we can't see what we're involved in because we are so close to it all. You'd admit that there is a great deal in human customs that a person could simply not ever be involved in, and still be included in the assembly of the saints, or even the Bride itself, which is a much smaller number.

We have to start at the foundation. We believe in a Creator Being, Who is eternal, and exists outside of time: in infinity. He made all we see and perceive. He told us He is the LIVING WATERS, which metaphorically is His Spirit, but it is also what the Spirit brings to us: His Personality, or teachings, called Torah. All through time, sages have known that the Torah is the Living Waters, the Word of YHWH. Yahushua is called the Living Waters, and the Word, made flesh.

Why don't we all see things the same?

Because something polluted these Living Waters: WORMWOOD. Wormwood is "poisoned waters", and this is what has been taught, causing men to die (spiritually). The falling star called "Wormwood" took away the Name from us. I've been calling wormwood "Fossilized Customs". We don't have to debate about how many personalities YHWH has, or how many heads, manifestations, and so on; we have to *begin* by teaching the message (gospel) of the coming kingdom, *"Repent, for the reign of YHWH draws near."* (See Mt. 4:17, Mk. 1:14, and other references).

This involves the fundamental process that involves the Torah, which CONVICTS EVERY MAN TO BE A SINNER. This will cause wise men to repent. The next step is to teach them how to covenant with their Maker, which is their *circumcision,* called "baptism". The NEW COVENANT cut in Yahushua's blood involves *His* "circumcising" their hearts with His Torah. There is no other New Covenant, but this one. Romans chapters 6 through 8 explain this. YHWH is much more than a Trinity. Trinities are the pattern or paradigm embraced by every Pagan religion on Earth, from Babylonian times forward. YHWH has manifested as a ROCK, a burning BUSH, a MESSENGER (to "Joshua" and Abram). He wrestled with Ya'aqob. He was in the Shekinah above the Ark of the Covenant (the box which held the marriage covenant with Israel). He spoke as a friend to both Abram and Mosheh at various times, and walked in the garden with Adam and his wife --- and yet each of these manifestations were about Yahushua. There is only one Elohim, and His last manifestation was the son, Yahushua ha Mashiach of Natsareth (being the product of YHWH's Spirit and the virginal human woman He chose).

The celebration of birthdays is strictly Pagan, and is only a custom that is preserved carefully because our flesh enjoys it so. Find the birthday celebrations in Scripture, and you will notice calamity surrounds each one. Iyyob (Job) lost all his children while they celebrated "each one on his day". Surely you can see that the candles, the making of a wish, and the cake (baked for the queen of heaven) is idolatry -- the Spirit will reveal this to you. The mark of the beast is very insidious. It is a mark, name, or number. It can be received by being led astray by the "first beast", which Scripture defines as Babylon. Revelation 13 through 18 will back this up, and as you know, Daniel prophesied FOUR beasts, each one based on the idolatry of the first. The last one will endure until the end (ROME). The highest sin, the grossest offense to 𝙰𝚈𝙰𝚉, is idolatry. Whose "mark" we bear identifies us as to whose servant we are. The MARK is not shown to those who lack wisdom -- ("My people are destroyed for a lack of knowledge"). The sign of the Everlasting Covenant (remember the marriage vows, the Ten Commandments) is the sign of the 7th day Sabbath of rest. This goes back to Creation, and shows YHWH we are His people. It is our "mark", showing YHWH we honor Him alone as Creator, by *commemorating* His work of creating, each 7th day. If we are His, Yahushua's Spirit is in us, and we show our love for our Husband by our obedience. And this is love: "THAT WE OBEY HIS COMMANDS".

Israel is more than just the "Jews" -- they are but one tribe of 12. 10 of the tribes are in the nations, and Yahushua was, and IS being sent to the "lost sheep of the TRIBES of Israel" — through us, today. The manna for 6 days was to RE-TRAIN Israel in the observance of Shabbat. Those being called from the nations are called "Ephraim" at Ez. 37, but are really 10 tribes. The parable of the "prodigal son" is about Ephraim, who is today mostly the Christians. The younger son (the lost 10 tribes) left the Father's House (His Torah). Upon drifting through the world of darkness, he came to his senses and realized he was living and eating (worshipping) among PIGS (Gentiles). He returned to his Father, and the OLDER brother (the tribe of Yahudah, the Jews) told the Father he had never left, and that he had always obeyed each Command of the Father. The Father explained that "this son of Mine" (the lost 10 tribes) was DEAD, and is now ALIVE". He was LOST, but is now FOUND.

Israelite, if you return to YHWH, embrace the New Covenant as it is written (not as it is poisoned - the wormwood), you too will see the mark of the beast. It is the mark of the dogs, sorcerers, and all who practice a lie: the SOLAR mark of Babylon: SUN-DAY, established under the penalty of death by Constantine, and enforced by the Inquisition for centuries. They proclaimed Death to back-sliding "Judaizers" -- this is the martyring of the saints, which reaches all the way back to Babylon, the great prostitute who has made the whole world drink from the cup of her fornication (false teachings, wormwood, poisoned waters). It's <u>Sun</u>-day Israelite. I'm so glad you're interested in the Truth; I hope Yahushua writes His Torah on your heart, and you become a worker. We are labeled a cult because the world is so dark, and getting darker; but we are not. In the past, it was the term "heretic" that enabled Christians to justify burning most of us. The harvest is ripe, but you must first stop fighting against the Torah, and admit you love it. I love it, and so can you if you will ask for a love for it. <u>Show</u> Him you love Him.

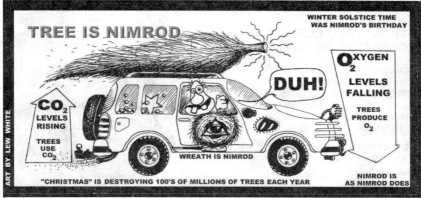

CANCER EPIDEMIC — Nobel Prize-winning German biochemist Dr. Otto Warburg, in researching into the cause of our world-wide cancer epidemic, has proof that it is largely caused by our increasingly oxygen deficient atmosphere. **Evergreens** produce *oxygen* and consume *carbon dioxide* all-year-round. High CO2 levels cause the green-house effect. If you **wanted** to cause the most damage possible, you couldn't improve on the course of action chosen: destroying evergreens by the 100's of millions each year. And, we are doing it *religiously* [pun intended]. There is no doubt that the adversary is using his scheme to destroy trees in order to cause the maximum damage, and human suffering as well. Imagine how he laughs at our stupidity as he watches the anguish he's caused; the loss of mothers, fathers, and children to the slow agonizing death of cancer. We're helping him to destroy the world, and ourselves along with it. With all our pompous sophistication and higher learning, we're *fabulously stupid* socially.

"Do not learn the customs of the Gentiles, and do not be awed by the signs of the heavens, for the Gentiles are awed by them. For the prescribed customs of these peoples are worthless, for one cuts a tree from the forest, work for the hands of a craftsman with a cutting tool. They adorn it with silver and gold, they fasten it with hammers so that it does not topple." — Yerme Yahu 10:2-4.

The customs of the decorated tree in the home originated with Tammuz, led into the groves by his mother Semiramis, to place a gift on or beneath a tree of the forest. This custom was at the time of the sun's "birth" — the winter solstice, which in the ancient world was our December 25th. The tree was decorated with gifts by the rest of the Pagans, and it represented NIMROD. The custom echoed through the cultures, until at last it found its way to the Celtic DRUIDS, who also worshipped the sun as Baal, among other names. Boniface influenced them to change from the oak tree to the evergreen tree during the 8th century. (See tree, page 3).

We need much more oxygen. Air bubbles preserved in amber (ancient tree sap) contain a 38% oxygen content, indicating that oxygen levels in the ancient world were much, much higher. 50 years ago, our air contained 21% oxygen. In many urban areas now, it is as low as 12%. If it gets near 7%, we all die. No wonder we can't think — and our school children can't read. Our gas furnaces use the oxygen from inside our homes to combust the gas, *drastically reducing the precious-little oxygen inside.* We're literally causing our own cancers. Get a furnace that uses outside air for combustion, quickly; *and take vitamins each day.* We have to wise-up to what's going on. The way we live is harmful to life in many ways, but the decision to change is within the grasp of each of us. Read Yerme Yahu chap. 11, and you will see that we are all the victims of a **conspiracy**. The conspiracy involves not obeying the Creator, and instead obeying the Pagan customs. I sincerely hope this book has been enriching to your knowledge, and lifted you up to a higher level so that you can see history with more clarity and truth. I'll see you in the world-to-come!

IT HAD TO BE DARKENING AS HE DIED

Many of you have wondered why it was required that the Passover Lamb be slain at twilight, "between the evenings". And, if Yahushua is our Lamb, His death at 3 p.m. seems to be at a strange time of day (only to some), because it was not twilight. But it was. Even though it was a full moon and an eclipse would be impossible, *darkness* hung over the land for 3 hours — much longer than any eclipse could ever be. YHWH *made* it happen correctly. It's wonderful to watch how He works.

COST FOR ONE COPY:

THE SCRIPTURES
FOSSILIZED CUSTOMS
COME OUT OF HER MY PEOPLE

$33.00 These costs include
$ 5.00 packing and postage.
$12.95 Add 30% outside US

Strawberry Islands produces and distributes this book, **Fossilized Customs** by Lew White. **The Scriptures** and **Come Out Of Her My People** are also available, in association with Institute for Scripture Research.
 Order in North America from:

Strawberry Islands
2303 Watterson Trail PMB #26
Louisville, KY 40299

THE SCRIPTURES   ISBN: 0-620-22490-8
HARD COVER, *RESTORES THE NAME OF OUR CREATOR TO THE TEXT IN EACH PLACE IT OCCURS IN THE INSPIRED HEBREW.* THIS NEW VERSION IN ENGLISH IS A LITERAL TRANSLATION OF GENESIS THROUGH REVELATION, AND USES THE "MODERN" HEBREW LETTERS FOR THE NAME: [YHWH: יהוה   YAHUSHUA: יהושע]   1 COPY: $33.00; CASE OF 10 COPIES: $220.00

FOSSILIZED CUSTOMS (ILLUSTRATED) ISBN: 0-9584353-6-7
(144 PAGES) BY LEW WHITE; A MESSIANIC ISRAELITE BOOK EXPLAINING THE PAGAN ORIGINS OF CHRISTMAS, EASTER, SUN-DAY, THE CALENDAR, AND MUCH MORE. A UNIQUE OUTREACH TOOL THAT WILL ANSWER QUESTIONS YOU HAVEN'T EVEN THOUGHT TO ASK! IF YOU'D LIKE TO HAND SOMEONE SOMETHING (IN ADDITION TO THE SCRIPTURES) THAT CONTAINS EVERY-THING YOU'D LIKE TO TELL THEM, THIS WOULD BE THE BOOK. 1 COPY: $5.00;
 5 COPIES: $15.00 — 10 COPIES: $25.00 — 20 COPIES: $2.00 EACH
 (PRINTER'S CASE OF 90 BOOKS IS $180.00 — BECOME A DISTRIBUTOR OF FC)

COME OUT OF HER MY PEOPLE   ISBN: 0-620-20144-4
(160 PAGES) BY CHRIS KOSTER; A COMPANION BOOK WITH FOSSILIZED CUSTOMS. WELL DOCUMENTED, IT PROVIDES THE READER WITH DETAILED ETYMOLOGY, AND SHOWS HOW CHRISTIANITY BECAME PAGANIZED, EMBRACING THE GENTILE CUSTOMS OF SUN WORSHIP FROM BABYLON. 1 COPY: $12.95; 10 COPIES: $80.00

HEALTH PRODUCTS AVAILABLE FROM STRAWBERRY ISLANDS
(PRICES INCLUDE PACKING AND POSTAGE)

VIRUS FIGHTER: SAMBUCOL LOZENGES (30) $11.00
FIGHTS FLU, COLD, HERPES; MADE KOSHER IN JERUSALEM, ISRAEL, FROM BLACK ELDERBERRY

CANCER FIGHTER: FLOR-ESSENCE (DRY, MAKES 3 QTS) $25.00
8-HERB "TEA", ATTACKS ONLY THE CANCER

VITAMINS: NATURE'S PLUS (90 TABLETS) WORLD'S BEST! $25.00
MULTI-VITAMIN & MINERAL SUPPLEMENT (HELP CELLS NOT MAKE "COPY ERRORS")

SHIRTS: L, XL WITH NAME " ayaz " IN WHITE LETTERING $15.00
"POLO-STYLE" SHIRT, AQUA BLUE, WITH 1" LETTERS IMPRINTED ON LEFT FRONT BREAST

INCLUDE YOUR COMPLETE ADDRESS WITH ZIP, CLEARLY ITEMIZE YOUR ORDER, AND MAKE CHECKS OR MONEY ORDERS PAYABLE TO " STRAWBERRY ISLANDS ". NORMAL DELIVERY SHOULD TAKE 2 TO 3 WEEKS.

ayazy wg4 gayyag